MW01226400

# AUTOCOURSE

## CHAMP CAR™

### OFFICIAL CHAMP CAR® YEARBOOK
# 2003 2004

BRIDGESTONE
PRESENTS
CHAMP CAR WORLD SERIES
POWERED BY
Ford

# CONTENTS

AUTOCOURSE
OFFICIAL
CHAMP CAR®
YEARBOOK
2003-2004

is published by:
Hazleton Publishing Ltd,
5th Floor, Mermaid House,
2 Puddle Dock, London,
EC4V 3DS.

Colour reproduction by
Radstock Repro,
Midsomer Norton, Somerset

Printed in England by
Butler and Tanner Ltd,
Frome, Somerset

Hazleton Publishing Ltd is a member of
Profile Media Group Plc.

ISBN: 1 903135 33 8

DISTRIBUTORS

UNITED KINGDOM
Haynes Publishing Plc
Sparkford
Near Yeovil
Somerset BA22 7JJ
Telephone: 01963 442030
Fax: 01963 440001

NORTH AMERICA
Motorbooks International
PO Box 1
729 Prospect Avenue
Osceola
Wisconsin 54020, USA
Telephone: (1) 715 294 3345
Fax: (1) 715 294 4448

REST OF THE WORLD
Menoshire Ltd
Unit 13
21 Wadsworth Road
Perivale
Middlesex UB6 7LQ
Telephone: 020 8566 7344
Fax: 020 8991 2439

Dust-jacket photographs: 2003
Champ Car Champion Paul Tracy.
Front: Gavin Lawrence/LAT
Back: Phil Abbott/LAT

Title page photograph: Rookie of the
Year, Sébastien Bourdais.
Mike Weston/LAT

director
EDDIE TAYLOR

editor
JEREMY SHAW

managing editor
IAN PENBERTHY

art editor
STEVE SMALL

business development manager
PETER MERCER

publishing assistant
LAURA FELL

photography
LAT PHOTOGRAPHIC

## Acknowledgments

The Editor and Publishers wish to thank the following for their assistance in compiling the Autocourse Official Champ Car
Yearbook 2003–2004:

Chris Pook; John Anderson, Justin Anderson, Tom Blattler, Katie Brannan, Merrill Cain, Pat Caporali, Francois Cartier,
David Clare, Wally Dallenbach, Kevin Diamond, Robert Dole, Lee Dykstra, Darla Elkins, Steve Fusek, Wendy Gabers,
Kika Garcia-Concheso, Billy Kamphausen, Chris Kneifel, Kelby Krauss, Kathi Lauterbach, John Lopes, Cathie Lyon, Eric
Mauk, Brent Maurer, Max d'Orsonnens, Paige Pell, Nadia Petrossi, David Phillips, Andrew Punzal, Tara Ragan, Rick
Ratajczak, Kathi Reichert, Rick Roso, Anne Roy, Adam Saal, Alex Sabine, Nate Siebens, Jeff Swartwout, Melissa
Kliethermes; and Tamy Valkosky.

This book is dedicated to all the fans and friends of Champ Car racing.

## Photographs

Photographs published in the Autocourse Official Champ Car Yearbook 2003–2004 have been contributed by:

LAT Photographic: Mike Levitt, Gavin Lawrence, Phil Abbott, Brad Bernstein, Dan Boyd, P. Cocciadeferro, Rick Dole, Mark
Elias, Gregg Feistmann, Maria Grady, Malcolm Griffiths, Leland Hill, Mark Horsburgh, Michael Kim, Lesley Ann Miller, Paul
Mounce, Guenter Reinhold, Dan Streck, Steven Tee, Mike Weston and Kevin Wood.

AUTOCOURSE
www.autocourse.com

# FOREWORD

## by PAUL TRACY
### 2003 Champ Car World Series Champion

IT'S been a hell of a journey from being just a kid from Scarborough to becoming known as the "Thrill from West Hill." The full impact of that finally hit me as I was handed the Vanderbilt Cup in Australia.

I've won a lot of races in the past and I'm not one who typically gets over-emotional, but winning the 2003 Champ Car World Series drivers championship was just such a release. It was the fulfillment of a goal that I had been striving to reach for 13 years. I had been in contention a few times previously, but somehow the championship had always eluded me. To finally get there was kind of overwhelming.

I now have the incredible honor of having my name among the list of champions who were my mentors. They instilled and fostered my passion to drive. Guys like Mario Andretti and Emerson Fittipaldi and Rick Mears and the Zanardis, Montoyas, all the great champions I've raced against really hard. I've looked up to these people because they've been great champions and have their own different types of personality.

There have been so many highlights through the years, but this past season has produced more than its fair share. Each race had its memorable moment. Battles on and off track may be nothing new for me but this season's have been some of the most fun. Fans have always seemed to appreciate that about me, but it was the fans who left me speechless — possibly for the first time ever! — as the entire crowd sang the Canadian national anthem after my win in Toronto.

The 2003 season was particularly special for me because of the opportunity to race for Player's/Forsythe. Player's and Jerry Forsythe share my passion for Champ Car racing, and the fact it was going to be the farewell year for Player's after 40 years of involvement in motorsport added extra incentive to reward Bob Bexon and Jerry for the confidence they expressed in me as a driver.

Champ Car racing is all about teamwork, and I can't say enough about the craftsmanship and dedication to duty that were exhibited by the crew at Team Player's, from the engineers and technical personnel, to the mechanics and the guys in the pits. I owe special thanks, as well, to my teammate Patrick Carpentier, who shared information with me and pushed me to excel.

Now that everything is rolling forward for the 2004 season, I want to thank all the supporters of Champ Car racing and say that I will be back to defend my championship, and hopefully try to win another one in the new era of Champ Car racing.

# GOOD NEWS AND BAD NEWS

**Above: Bridgestone/Firestone and Ford Motor Company placed their faith and resources behind the Champ Car series.**
Gavin Lawrence/LAT

IT was entirely appropriate not only that Paul Tracy should clinch the 2003 Champ Car World Series crown, but that he should do so in dramatic style. The enigmatic Canadian had emerged as one of the staunchest supporters of Champ Car competition, and he became embroiled in a tantalizing to-and-fro contest with preseason favorite Bruno Junqueira before lifting the coveted Vanderbilt Cup at Surfers Paradise, Australia. Tracy's roller-coaster ride was an effective metaphor for the beleaguered Championship Auto Racing Teams, Inc. (CART) sanctioning body, which continued to experience a variety of pitfalls and setbacks as the year unfolded.

There had been an altogether different feel about the Champ Car scene when the teams assembled for the first race of the new season. And not just because the campaign kicked off at a brand-new venue in St. Petersburg, Florida. There was a new series title, a host of rookie teams and drivers, a reconceived engine formula, some subtle tweaks to the rules and a fresh sense of camaraderie as the entire genre of Champ Car racing fought, quite literally, for its survival.

At times, it seemed like an impossible mountain to climb. The departure to the all-oval Indy Racing League of Target/Chip Ganassi Racing, Team Green and Mo Nunn Racing, all of which chose to follow the gravy train provided by Honda and Toyota, left a void that had to be filled if CART was to meet the contractual obligations to its race promoters and television partners. CART was forced to invest heavily in its teams simply to ensure that the newly monikered 2003 Bridgestone Presents the Champ Car World Series Powered by Ford could proceed as planned. Hence the introduction of an Entrant Support Program that ensured a guaranteed income for new and old teams alike to augment their individual sponsorships.

The "ESP" made it possible for several new teams to join the fray: American Spirit Team Johansson, Fittipaldi-Dingman Racing and Mi-Jack/Conquest Racing. In addition, former BAR Formula 1 team principal Craig Pollock and businessman/racing enthusiast Kevin Kalkhoven combined forces to form PK Racing, which took over the assets of the former PacWest/PWR organization, and vastly accomplished Trans-Am owner/driver Paul Gentilozzi also committed to entering the Champ Car ranks with his Rocketsports team. All of the new outfits benefited, too, from several cost-cutting measures that had been introduced under the direction of CART President and CEO Christopher R. Pook.

The most high-profile of these changes was the wholesale adoption of a new engine package developed by stalwart Champ Car supporter Ford Cosworth. Once again, the withdrawal of Honda and Toyota had necessitated desperate measures, but the re-engineered XFE power plant proved to be a resounding success. A lower rev limit was offset by more boost from the turbocharger to ensure a very similar level of horsepower to that seen in 2002. The combination ensured that rebuilds were required only every 1,200 miles, rather than the previous norm of around 350 miles. A mandatory and simplified electronic control unit also contributed to a level playing field for the teams while permitting the blight of traction control to be removed. The engines proved to be slightly "peakier" than before, but that was of no concern to the experienced Champ Car hands, who agreed that the revised motors put a renewed accent on driver skill.

"I was really surprised with the power," said Tracy after gaining

**Left: A freeze on chassis development and a reduced-cost engine package helped to attract new teams, such as Rocketsports.** Mike Levitt/LAT

**Below: Champ Car racing discovered a fresh vitality by running under the lights; the Cleveland event was a huge success.** Michael Kim/LAT

**Bottom: Paul Tracy joined Team Player's and claimed his first title, but had to work hard to beat Newman/Haas Racing's Sébastien Bourdais and Bruno Junqueira.** Gavin Lawrence/LAT

his first taste of the Ford Cosworth XFE engine in January. "It comes off the corners hard and it's different from a Honda [which he ran in '02] because it goes from no boost to, all of the sudden, wham! I had a couple of spins because it caught me out. There is no traction control and it's not an easy engine to drive because of that swing in boost, but it's the same for all of us and that's good."

In short, Tracy was impressed. "The engine is revving lower, but you can't tell because the gears are realigned and you're still shifting at the same places," he said. "The cars won't be any slower and the engine reliability should be excellent."

He was right on all counts. Indeed, there was just one engine failure during the 18-race season, which encompassed more than 56,000 racing miles. The impressive reliability was supported by economies of scale that ensured substantially lower costs than before, so it was truly a win-win situation.

The commitment from both Ford and Bridgestone, which continued to supply its top-quality Potenza radial racing tires to every Champ Car team, provided a new impetus for the championship. Chris Pook readily acknowledged this when the new series logo – and a fresh CART corporate identity – was unveiled on January 15.

"Today's announcement is a major step toward taking this series not only where we want it to be, but to a position befitting the heritage, status and challenge of the Champ Car World Series," declared Pook. "The new look of the series will provide a solid platform for Champ Car, Bridgestone and the Ford Motor Company to move into what will be a very successful future."

More exciting news came with confirmation that for the first time in CART Champ Car history, two races would be held under lights – at Milwaukee and Cleveland. The experiment proved to be

Above: **For the second year in a row, Mexico City provided one of the season's highlights.**
Gavin Lawrence/LAT

## FONTANA FINALE FOILED BY FIRE

THE original schedule called for 19 races to comprise the 2003 Bridgestone Presents the Champ Car World Series Powered by Ford. Indeed, that was the plan until just a few days prior to what should have been the final race of the season, the King Taco 500 at California Speedway. By the time the teams had disembarked at Los Angeles International Airport, however, returning from the previous weekend's race on the Gold Coast of Queensland, Australia, it was apparent that the finale was in serious jeopardy due to a series of massive wildfires that had hit Southern California. One of the blazes even reached within a few miles of the racetrack in suburban Fontana, about an hour's drive east of Los Angeles.

California Speedway management elected to call off the event on the Tuesday evening prior to the race weekend. CART Champ Car officials made several attempts to reschedule the race, including even investigating the possibility of a change in venue, but eventually that was deemed impossible. Therefore, the season was concluded with 18 races in the books.

The championship, of course, already had been decided in favor of Paul Tracy. Rookie of the Year honors also had been firmly grasped by Frenchman Sébastien Bourdais. But the cancellation brought a premature end to several other significant battles, including that for second place between Bruno Junqueira and Michel Jourdain Jr., who were separated by a mere four points following the race at Surfers Paradise.

extraordinarily popular with the fans, despite the fact that qualifying at Milwaukee was rained out and the race itself, which marked the track's centennial anniversary, was held in bitterly cold conditions. Musco Lighting did an excellent job of providing the illumination for both venues, while the firework displays that concluded the activities in Cleveland after both qualifying (on July Fourth) and the race added an extra dimension to the entertainment.

But it wasn't all plain sailing. Far from it. In March and April, CART and Road America became embroiled in an unseemly squabble over sanctioning fees. Lawsuits were filed by both parties, although, thankfully, honor was saved by the intervention of one of Champ Car racing's most loyal advocates, Mario Andretti, who stepped into the breach and quickly found some common ground. On April 23, confirmation came that the event had been saved – and would be renamed the Mario Andretti Grand Prix of Road America. Disappointingly, appalling weather conditions turned the race itself, held August 3, into something of a farce; but let there be no doubt that the inclusion on the Champ Car calendar of the famed road course in rural Elkhart Lake, Wisconsin, was thoroughly appreciated – by fans and drivers alike.

On a far more positive note, Alex Zanardi's sensational return to the cockpit in May provided one of the highlights of the entire sporting year, and not just in the Champ Car realm. The charismatic Italian's visit to EuroSpeedway Lausitz, the scene of an accident that took away his legs but miraculously not his life in September 2001, was truly inspirational. Cheered to the rafters by a massively enthusiastic European crowd, he climbed aboard a current Reynard Champ Car and turned laps fast enough to have earned him a top-five qualifying position on the grid. It was an incredibly indomitable display.

Several other feel-good stories emanated from the Champ Car World Series during 2003 too. The new season-opening event in St. Petersburg, Florida, proved very successful, while the return to

EuroSpeedway showed once again that the German oval is an excellent venue for the Champ Cars. The European foray also included a visit to the storied Brands Hatch road course in England, and despite overtaking opportunities being at a premium on the short "Indy" circuit, a large and enthusiastic crowd thoroughly appreciated the Champ Car experience.

Indeed, crowd figures remained strong throughout the season, ending on a magnificent note as the final two events at Mexico City and Surfers Paradise attracted respective weekend attendances of 402,413 (an all-time record for a Champ Car race, excluding the Indianapolis 500) and 306,184 (an event record for the Australian Gold Coast). A total of 2,397,435 spectators came to watch the Champ Cars during the 18-race season, marking the 18th consecutive year that the series had drawn in excess of 2.1 million fans. Domestic television ratings remained depressingly low, however, in common with several other sports, although the global broadcast reach of the series ensured impressive per-event numbers of between eight and nine million.

But there had been a high cost to pay. CART's Entrant Support Program, as well as other sums paid to the teams, plus the high cost of its domestic television package and its reluctant role as an event promoter had combined to deplete its previously plentiful financial resources at an extravagant rate. By midseason, it had become apparent that CART's future was in serious jeopardy. The investment banking firm Bear, Stearns & Co., Inc. was retained in June to explore any potential revenue-raising strategies. The writing was on the wall.

Curiously, Formula 1 boss Bernie Ecclestone had been mooted as a potential savior at one point, and his longtime friendship with Pook and CART COO David Clare tended to add credence to the rumors. Ecclestone did, indeed, express an interest, but soon backed out to concentrate on his own extensive business affairs.

Instead Champ Car needed to look no farther than within its own ranks for salvation. Longtime team owner Gerald R. "Jerry" Forsythe, PK Racing co-principal Kevin Kalkhoven and Rocketsports owner Paul Gentilozzi stepped up to the plate in August to form a new entity, Open Wheel Racing Series, LLC, which offered to take over the troubled sanctioning body, lock, stock and barrel. Negotiations were arduous and drawn out, due primarily to stringent laws protecting the shareholders of publicly held companies. But finally, at the end of January, a U.S. bankruptcy court in Indianapolis threw out an opposing bid from Tony George, president of the Indianapolis Motor Speedway and founder of the rival Indy Racing League, and sided with OWRS.

After an especially turbulent few months, the future of the Champ Car World Series was conclusively assured. And an exciting new chapter in Champ Car history had begun.

Jeremy Shaw
Rancho Santa Margarita, California
February 2004

## PERFORMANCE CHART

| Driver | Wins | Poles | Fastest laps | Most laps led |
|---|---|---|---|---|
| **Paul Tracy** | 7 | 6 | 1 | 8 |
| **Sébastien Bourdais** | 3 | 5 | 4 | 2 |
| **Bruno Junqueira** | 2 | 2 | 2 | 3 |
| **Michel Jourdain Jr.** | 2 | 1 | 2 | 2 |
| **Patrick Carpentier** | 1 | 1 | 2 | 1 |
| **Adrian Fernandez** | 1 | 1 | 2 | 1 |
| **Ryan Hunter-Reay** | 1 | – | 1 | – |
| **Mario Dominguez** | 1 | – | – | – |
| **Alex Tagliani** | – | 2 | 1 | 1 |
| **Jimmy Vasser** | – | – | 1 | – |
| **Mario Haberfeld** | – | – | 1 | – |
| **Roberto Moreno** | – | – | 1 | – |

## CHRONOLOGY OF THE OWRS TAKEOVER

**JUNE 16** – CART officials admit that financial troubles are looming and that the investment banking firm Bear, Stearns & Co., Inc. has been retained to "assist us in exploring the availability of needed financing and other strategic alternatives that may be available to CART."

**AUGUST 11** – CART's second-quarter financial results reveal an operating loss of $43 million, and management reiterates the expectation that it would "need to raise additional capital for the 2004 season."

**AUGUST 18** – CART confirms it has received a proposal from Open Wheel Racing Series, LLC (investors in which include Gerald R. Forsythe, Kevin Kalkhoven, Paul Gentilozzi, Carl Russo and MotoRock, LLC) to acquire all outstanding CART shares for $0.50 per share.

**SEPTEMBER 10** – A definitive agreement is announced whereby OWRS (now comprising only Messrs. Forsythe, Kalkhoven and Gentilozzi) would acquire CART for $0.56 per share.

**OCTOBER 30** – CART's third-quarter financial results show a loss of $34.4 million, and a loss of $77.9 million on the year to date.

**NOVEMBER 10** – CART announces that a shareholder vote on the bid from OWRS "could take place as early as December 18."

**NOVEMBER 19** – CART reveals that a meeting of its stockholders, seeking approval of the "merger agreement" with OWRS, has been convened for December 19.

**DECEMBER 2** – CART announces that OWRS believes that "a number of conditions of the impending merger" likely would not be satisfied prior to the December 19 stockholders' meeting, and OWRS has "indicated it will not waive any condition of the closing." The CART board of directors says it is "evaluating alternatives to the merger, including the possibility of ceasing operations, winding up the Company's affairs and liquidating its remaining assets." OWRS also makes a "preliminary proposal contemplating an alternative transaction" under which CART would "commence reorganization under Chapter 11 of the Bankruptcy Code."

**DECEMBER 15** – OWRS makes a firm bid for "specific assets, including contracts with promoters, sponsors and teams" through the planned Chapter 11 bankruptcy process.

**DECEMBER 16** – CART confirms it has entered into an Asset Purchase Agreement with OWRS, whereby OWRS would continue to operate the Champ Car World Series and the Toyota Atlantic Championship in 2004.

**DECEMBER 30** – U.S. Bankruptcy Judge Frank J. Otte accepts the OWRS offer as a "qualified bid" and states that any other offers for the CART assets must be made before January 23. Judge Otte says he will make a final decision on January 28.

**JANUARY 14** – OWRS claims it is "not concerned" by information that Tony George's Indy Racing League has "expressed an interest" in acquiring some CART assets.

**JANUARY 21** – OWRS reaffirms its intention to conduct a full 2004 Champ Car World Series season, commencing with the 30th annual Toyota Grand Prix of Long Beach on April 18.

**JANUARY 23** – The IRL confirms it has made a "substantial bid" for certain CART assets prior to the court's deadline.

**JANUARY 28** – At the Bankruptcy Court hearing held in Indianapolis, the IRL increases its bid from $3.26 million to $13.5 million, but Judge Otte still approves the transfer of CART assets to OWRS "with no stipulations attached." Says Otte: "It's [about] the survival of an entity versus the end of it. That's the issue. Based on the information I've heard and knowing full well we have another side in this matter, I feel like the best business judgment is to approve the sale and asset transfer to OWRS."

# IN MEMORIAM

**LES GRIEBLING,** founder of the Mid-Ohio Sports Car Course, died February 6, aged 78. A garage owner and sports car enthusiast from Mansfield, Ohio, Griebling designed and built the now famed parkland road course, which opened in 1962, and operated the facility until he sold out in 1981 to Jim Trueman.

**CLARENCE CAGLE,** who died July 5, aged 88, was track superintendent of the Indianapolis Motor Speedway for 30 years and oversaw renovation of the famed Brickyard after it was purchased, in a dilapidated state, by Tony Hulman in 1945. Cagle's services were recognized when he was inducted into the Indianapolis 500 Auto Racing Hall of Fame in 2000.

**JOE GRANATELLI,** who helped younger brother Andy build the revolutionary turbine-engined car with which Parnelli Jones came agonizingly close to winning the 1967 Indianapolis 500, died September 13, at age 84. The Granatelli family first entered a car at Indy in 1946 and became a fixture at the Brickyard over several decades.

**BOB SPROW,** who died September 19, aged 50, graduated from the Ford Motor Company Technical School in 1972 and went on to forge a successful career that included working with many of the top teams in Champ Car racing. He also took part in championship-winning efforts in IMSA sports car and Mickey Thompson Entertainment Group off-road competition.

**LOU MORALES,** a member of a renowned Southern California racing family, died December 11, aged 93. Older brother Alex began building a sprint car in 1945, and Lou worked as a mechanic with the family team until well into his 70s. The Morales Brothers' "Tamale Wagon" cars, named after the family food business, achieved national success, including a third-place finish in the 1982 Indianapolis 500 with Pancho Carter.

**JIM PHILLIPPE** was a member of the Indianapolis Motor Speedway's public-address team from 1950 until his death, aged 84, on December 15. Phillippe also announced races at Michigan International Speedway, Cleveland's Burke Lakefront Airport and Nazareth Speedway.

**CHUCK MATTHEWS** (above right), one of the most passionate of race engineers, passed away March 18, 2002. A lifelong racing enthusiast, Matthews, 66, enjoyed a successful career with General Motors, but was also a fixture on the Champ Car

scene for almost 20 years and worked with a variety of top teams. He walked only with the aid of braces, due to a medical condition called neuropathy, but was never without a smile.

**CARROLL SMITH,** race car driver, mechanic, team manager, engineer, author and so much more, died May 16, aged 71. Smith, one of the sport's arch-enthusiasts, played a central role, along with Carroll Shelby, in the success of the Ford GT program at Le Mans in the 1960s. The first in his highly acclaimed series of "To Win" books, Prepare to Win, was published in 1975.

**JOHNNY BOYD,** a well-known California midget car racer who also made a dozen Indianapolis 500 starts, died October 26, at age 78. The highlight of his career at Indy came in 1958, when he led 18 laps in one of the Bowes Seal Fast Specials and went on to finish third.

**TONY RENNA** (below), one of North America's brightest young stars, was tragically killed in a crash while testing an IRL car at Indianapolis on October 22. Renna, 26, from DeLand, Florida, worked his way through the ranks of quarter-midgets and karts before honing his road racing skills with the Skip Barber Racing School. He won a Team USA Scholarship in 1996 and joined Jerry Nadeau in earning a silver medal at the Formula Opel Nations Cup at Donington Park, England. Renna claimed Barber Dodge Pro Series Rookie of the Year honors in 1996 and was a winner in Indy Lights, but he never was given an opportunity to break into the Champ Car ranks. Instead he made an impressive IRL debut with Kelley Racing in 2002 and seemed to be on the verge of major success after being snapped up by Target/Chip Ganassi Racing for the 2004 campaign.

# TOP TEN DRIVERS

In accordance with the AUTOCOURSE tradition, Editor Jeremy Shaw offers his personal ranking of the best of the best in the 2003 Bridgestone Presents the Champ Car World Series Powered by Ford, taking into account their individual performances, their level of experience and the resources at their disposal.

# 1 PAUL TRACY

**N**OT many drivers have been more deserving of a major championship than Paul Tracy. The Jekyll and Hyde personality that had threatened regularly to derail his career in the past once again rose to the surface on occasion, but by and large he maintained a much better overall focus than in years past.

He needed it. "PT" and Bruno Junqueira – or "Junky" as he was quickly dubbed by the Canadian – became involved in an epic contest. And a roller-coaster ride.

Tracy gained the upper hand early, riding some good fortune and an impressive turn of pace to win the first three races for Player's/Forsythe Racing. But he mustered a mere two points from the next three – forced out by a gearbox meltdown in England, followed by a dismal time in Germany and a pit-lane miscue in Milwaukee – which allowed Junqueira and Michel Jourdain Jr. to vault ahead. In previous years, Tracy might have buckled. Not this time. He bounced back to regain the advantage on the strength of five consecutive podium finishes, including a pair of magnificent victories on home soil. Then came a crass error at Road America, where he crashed in the wet, which again allowed Junqueira into the frame.

The season continued in a similar vein. For both men. Tracy won handsomely at Mid-Ohio and Mexico. Junqueira did likewise at Road America and Denver. In between, both made silly mistakes in Miami. And at Surfers Paradise, after being spun out by Bourdais at the start, Tracy's natural aggression once more got him into trouble. But just as Junqueira seemed poised to take the championship battle to the scheduled finale at Fontana, the Brazilian erred again, which secured the crown for Tracy.

The tears that uncharacteristically rolled down Tracy's cheeks told how much the title meant to him. He had stood by his ideals, become an avid disciple for the Champ Car cause, and worked assiduously on his mental and physical fitness. And he proved the naysayers wrong. He was undoubtedly the class of the field.

**Date of birth:** December 17, 1968

**Residence:** Las Vegas, Nevada

**Team:** Player's/Forsythe Racing

**Equipment:** Ford Cosworth/Lola/Bridgestone

**Champ Car starts in 2003:** 18

**Points ranking:** 1st

**Wins:** 7; **Poles:** 6; **Points:** 226

Photograph: Mike Levitt/LAT

N O one should have been surprised that Sébastien Bourdais made his mark on the Champ Car World Series. After all, he had won the previous year's FIA Formula 3000 Championship against some tough opposition, following in the footsteps of the likes of Juan Pablo Montoya and Bruno Junqueira.

The bespectacled Frenchman looked more like a student than a racing driver, yet his calm demeanor and scholarly approach quickly endeared him to his Newman/Haas crew. Bourdais largely eclipsed teammate Junqueira in winter testing and continued to do so once the season began in earnest. He even merited comparison with Nigel Mansell (no mean feat in itself) by snatching the pole on his debut at St. Petersburg. Then he went one better than the Briton by taking the lead at the start. (Mansell had been ousted by Emerson Fittipaldi on the first lap at Surfers Paradise in 1993.) Unlike Mansell, however, Bourdais didn't emerge victorious; instead he fell victim to a strategic miscue and then glanced the wall while trying to make up lost ground. The error was a sobering reminder of his rookie status.

Amazingly, Bourdais also took the pole in the next race at Monterrey, and again made a mistake following a poorly timed pit stop. Still, he had made his mark. It was only a matter of time before his pace translated into tangible results. The breakthrough came, appropriately, in Europe. Paul Tracy took the pole at Brands Hatch and led early; but Bourdais emerged in front following the pit stops. He never looked back. Win number two came merely a week later in Germany, following a thrilling duel with Mario Dominguez. Thereafter, Bourdais seemed to be the recipient of any bad luck in the Newman/Haas camp. (He also suffered the only race engine failure to occur all year, at Long Beach.) He won only once more, at Cleveland, but whenever he finished he was among the top five, and ended up a worthy fourth in the points table. He also accrued the best overall qualifying average to cap a memorable rookie campaign.

**Date of birth: February 28, 1979**

**Residence: Miami, Florida**

**Team: Newman/Haas Racing**

**Equipment: Ford Cosworth/Lola/Bridgestone**

**Champ Car starts in 2003: 18**

**Points ranking: 4th**

**Wins: 3; Poles: 5; Points: 159**

2

SÉBASTIEN
BOURDAIS

Photograph: Gavin Lawrence/LAT

# 3 MICHEL JOURDAIN JR.

Date of birth: **September 2, 1976**

Residence: **Mexico City, Mexico**

Team: **Team Rahal**

Equipment: **Ford Cosworth/Lola/Bridgestone**

Champ Car starts in 2003: **18**

Points ranking: **3rd**

Wins: **2**; Poles: **1**; Points: **195**

**T**HE easygoing Mexican had been Mr. Consistency in 2002. He completed more laps and miles than anyone else, and scored points in every race except the last one, almost doubling his tally from the previous six years combined. Problem was, he generally qualified near the back so left himself a lot of work to do in the races. Still, he learned an awful lot during his first year with Team Rahal, including the fact that he could run with the leaders.

In 2003, Jourdain took full advantage of that experience and new-found confidence. He retained that knack for consistency, too, and once again led the charts in laps and miles completed. Incredibly, he finished all but 32 of the year's total of 1,922 laps (98.3 percent) and failed to see the checkered flag only twice – at Long Beach, where he was cruelly denied a maiden victory by a gearbox problem, and at Road America, where he made a rare mistake in the wet.

More importantly, Jourdain was fast. He qualified among the top ten in 17 of the 18 races. (The only exception was at Laguna Seca, where, ironically, his car narrowly and mysteriously failed a post-qualifying weight check after he had posted the fastest time.) His average grid position (5.83) was bettered only by Bourdais, Tracy and Junqueira. No one improved upon his average finishing position of 5.56.

This was certainly a breakthrough year for Jourdain. He finished second to Tracy in each of the first two races, then took his first-ever pole at Long Beach. Victory eluded him on that occasion, but after a strong run in Germany, he traveled to the Milwaukee Mile brimming with confidence, then swept past Tracy at the start and dominated Champ Car racing's first ever nighttime race. It was an extremely popular victory, and one that took him briefly into the championship lead. Oddly, he struggled for speed in a few late-season events – notably Denver and Miami – which ultimately cost him a legitimate chance of winning the championship; even so, it was an impressive campaign.

# BRUNO JUNQUEIRA

**A**FTER finishing the 2002 season ranked second in points to Cristiano da Matta, then grasping an opportunity to fill the void left at Newman/Haas Racing by his Brazilian countryman's decision to graduate into Formula 1 with Toyota, Bruno Junqueira began the new year as a firm championship favorite. But frankly, he never really lived up to expectations. Sure, he remained in the hunt until the last race, but he was frequently eclipsed by rookie teammate Sébastien Bourdais and made far too many mistakes for his level of experience.

Curiously, Junqueira's 2003 season was virtually a mirror image of his sophomore campaign with Chip Ganassi's team in '02, when he began with a whimper, netting just two points from the first two races, and ended with a relative flourish. This time it was the other way around. He started out with five consecutive top-five finishes (before crashing out on the first lap in Milwaukee) and recorded only one top-five in the final six races.

It wasn't until Round 12 at Road America that Junqueira finally claimed his first pole. (Bourdais already had four to his credit by then.) He made light of treacherous conditions to score an emphatic victory (albeit with Bourdais hot on his heels), and seemed set to offer a serious challenge to Paul Tracy's title hopes. Then it all fell apart. Junqueira was unfortunate at Mid-Ohio, where he was punted off by Oriol Servia; at Montreal, he spun not once but twice and finished out of the points in 13th. He rebounded to earn a dominant victory in Denver, for the second straight year; then, in Miami, after Tracy had taken himself out of contention, Junqueira threw away a certain podium when he allowed himself to be distracted while lapping Tiago Monteiro. He chased a dominant Tracy gamely in Mexico, despite severe stomach cramps, but lost heart, and valuable position, in the late stages. Finally, in Australia, after Tracy once again had left the door open, Junqueira was disadvantaged by a curious decision in Race Control and then crashed while trying to make up lost ground. Game over.

Date of birth: **November 4, 1976**

Residence: **Miami, Florida**

Team: **Newman/Haas Racing**

Equipment: **Ford Cosworth/Lola/Bridgestone**

Champ Car starts in 2003: **18**

Points ranking: **2nd**

Wins: **2**; Poles: **2**; Points: **199**

# 5

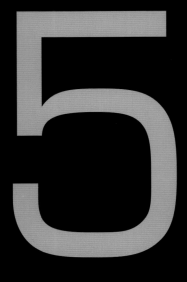

**MARIO DOMINGUEZ**

**T**HE end-of-season banquet saw Mario Dominguez an excited recipient of the Bosch Most Improved Driver Award, as determined by his peers. It was an appropriate reward for a year in which he had worked hard to apply the experience gained during a tough rookie campaign with the Herdez Competition team. Yes, he had secured Jim Trueman Rookie of the Year honors in 2002 (against a weak field). He also had won a race (in the streaming wet at Surfers Paradise), although even he will concede that the victory was a function of luck rather than speed. Dominguez, indeed, had regularly languished toward the back of the pack in '02 and only rarely had showed glimpses of his true ability. Such was emphatically not the case one year on.

His new-found confidence came as a result of a productive winter testing program, and he benefited enormously from the addition of a teammate in the shape of veteran Roberto Moreno. Qualifying remained his weakest link – Dominguez started among the top five only once – although he was regularly to be found among the top ten. The highlight of his year came at Miami, where, admittedly, he was helped by the fact that several other front-runners made silly mistakes. Still, Dominguez didn't, and no one could say his victory wasn't well deserved. He also claimed back-to-back podium finishes in England and Germany.

Dominguez, arguably, passed more cars than anyone else during the 18-race season. Certainly he displayed a fighting spirit that was the envy of many, and was often one of very few drivers attempting to move forward in the races. On occasion, however, his exuberance went too far. At Vancouver, after being involved in a first-lap fracas and losing several laps, he should not have allowed himself to be in a position to collide with Patrick Carpentier, who was running in second place at the time. Dominguez was rightly admonished by race officials. Later, in Denver, he punted off Mario Haberfeld and was involved in various other lesser scrapes. Still, while he certainly made some mistakes, at least he deserved credit for trying.

**Date of birth: December 1, 1975**

**Residence: Mexico City, Mexico**

**Team: Herdez Competition**

**Equipment: Ford Cosworth/Lola/Bridgestone**

**Champ Car starts in 2003: 18**

**Points ranking: 6th**

**Wins: 1; Poles: 0; Points: 118**

# 6

## DARREN MANNING

**D**ARREN Manning finished a distant second to Sébastien Bourdais in the Rookie of the Year contest, but still created an excellent impression and was the only Reynard driver to break into the top ten in points. After a strong Champ Car debut in '02 at Rockingham, the plucky Englishman concluded a deal to join Derrick Walker's newly expanded two-car team. That was the good news. The bad news was that teammate Rodolfo Lavin wasn't able to offer much in terms of setup assistance; and funding was extremely tight, so Manning never had the luxury of a backup car at his disposal.

But that didn't faze him one iota. Manning had faced much stiffer handicaps during his climb up the auto racing ladder. He was bound and determined to make the most of his hard-earned opportunity. He ran well from the get-go, overcoming an early problem during the opening race at St. Petersburg to climb into the top six before being forced out by a broken clutch. A run of five top-ten finishes was ended by an oil-pump problem at Laguna Seca, but Manning bounced back to create a new rookie record by placing among the top ten in each of the next eight races. Once again the sequence was halted by a mechanical failure (gearbox), in Miami, but the rate of attrition was such that he was still classified 11th, which meant he was able to extend his point-scoring streak to 11 races by the end of the year.

Mistakes were few and far between, but one came at Milwaukee, where the combination of cool evening conditions and fresh tires almost caught him out following an early pit stop. Manning did a fabulous job to regain control after all but collecting the inside wall on the back straightaway. At the time, he was running ahead of Oriol Servia, who went on to finish a close second. Manning had to be content with a still excellent fourth. He added a fifth in Vancouver, but kept the best for last when he finished second at Surfers Paradise.

**Date of birth: April 30, 1975**

**Residence: Indianapolis, Indiana**

**Team: Walker Racing**

**Equipment: Ford Cosworth/Reynard/Bridgestone**

**Champ Car starts in 2003: 18**

**Points ranking: 9th**

**Wins: 0; Poles: 0; Points: 103**

# 7

## ADRIAN FERNANDEZ

**Date of birth:** April 20, 1963

**Residence:** Paradise Valley, Arizona

**Team:** Fernandez Racing

**Equipment:** Ford Cosworth/Lola/Bridgestone

**Champ Car starts in 2003:** 18

**Points ranking:** 8th

**Wins:** 1; **Poles:** 1; **Points:** 105

THE highlight of Adrian Fernandez's tenth full season of Champ Car racing was a magnificent victory at Portland in June. It was the eighth win of his career, but the first since the formation of his own team, in partnership with Tom Anderson, prior to the 2001 season. The triumph also marked the first time a Champ Car owner/driver had taken the checkered flag since Bobby Rahal achieved the feat at Nazareth in 1992.

Fernandez had to work hard for his laurels. He had qualified third, but moved up to second after Mexican countryman Michel Jourdain Jr. was involved in a controversial collision with polesitter Paul Tracy. Fernandez kept the pressure on the Canadian before pouncing with 15 laps remaining and pulling off a classic last-of-the-late-brakers move into the Festival Curves. It was perhaps the pass of the season. He should have won at Miami, too. Once again he pulled off a breathtaking pass, this time on Bruno Junqueira, who had stolen the advantage at the start, and was controlling the pace from the front until Junqueira made an error of judgment and took them both out of contention.

Fernandez also was very competitive in several other races. He qualified third at St. Petersburg and ran well in the early stages before suddenly falling off the pace and then receiving an inadvertent punt from Mario Dominguez; he set fastest lap at Brands Hatch after being nerfed off by Ryan Hunter-Reay; and he qualified on the second row in Denver. The one aspect that was missing was consistency. All too often his Tecate/Quaker State/Telmex Lola was to be found languishing far down the order. And no one seemed to be really sure why. Take the race in Mexico City, for example. He qualified a dismal 15th – emphatically not what he wanted in front of his adoring home crowd – and ran erratically for most of the race before suddenly coming alive in the closing stages. What a shame he didn't display that flair all weekend long. Or all season.

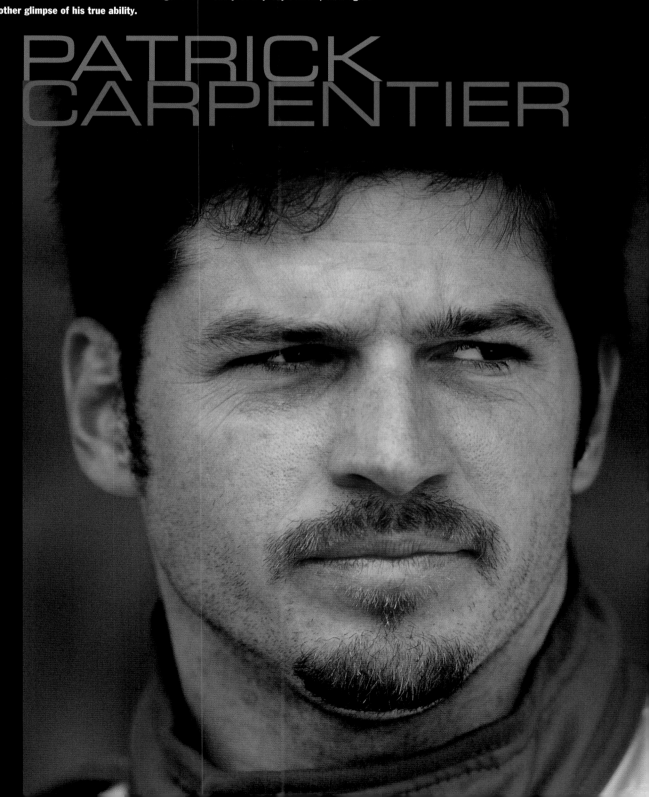

Much was expected of Patrick Carpentier in 2003. He was coming off his most successful year to date in the Champ Car World Series, having won twice for Team Player's, and seemed set to build on that success, especially following the team's switch to proven Lola chassis in place of the supposedly inferior Reynards.

His season had a promising beginning. Winter testing went well; he was generally quicker than new teammate Paul Tracy. But for one reason or another, it didn't last, and the commensurate results didn't follow. And as in past years, Lady Luck rarely seemed to look his way.

Carpentier qualified fourth at St. Petersburg and moved up to second before making a mistake soon after a pit stop as he attempted to put pressure on Tracy. In Monterrey, he was laid low by a stomach virus that, at one point, seemed likely to cause him to miss the race. He elected, bravely, to make the start and drove superbly to climb as high as fifth before an over-ambitious move on Bruno Junqueira went awry and cost him a few places. Still, nothing ventured, nothing gained. He made the best of his team's poor interpretation of the aerodynamic regulations in the German 500, rising from 17th to seventh, and set the fastest lap at Milwaukee en route to a third-place finish, hot on the heels of Michel Jourdain Jr. and Oriol Servia. Then came the highlight of his season, at Mazda Raceway Laguna Seca, where he claimed the pole and was never headed during the 87-lap race.

The omens looked good at that stage. Carpentier lay fourth in the championship table, a mere 19 points behind the leader, and clearly had momentum on his side. But then things began to slide. He was fortunate to emerge relatively unscathed from a bicycling accident near his home and seemed to become increasingly frustrated by Tracy's success. A surprising lack of self-belief — and an inordinate number of errors — blighted his championship aspirations, although a strong second at Mid-Ohio gave another glimpse of his true ability.

# PATRICK CARPENTIER

Date of birth: August 13, 1971

Residence: Las Vegas, Nevada

Team: Player's/Forsythe Racing

Equipment: Ford Cosworth/Lola/Bridgestone

Champ Car starts in 2003: 18

Points ranking: 5th

Wins: 1; Poles: 1; Points: 146

**Date of birth:** October 18, 1972

**Residence:** Las Vegas, Nevada

**Team:** Rocketsports Racing

**Equipment:** Ford Cosworth/Lola/Bridgestone

**Champ Car starts in 2003:** 18

**Points ranking:** 10th

**Wins:** 0; **Poles:** 2; **Points:** 97

N common with Patrick Carpentier, his former teammate at Player's, many of us were unsure what to make of Alex Tagliani's Champ Car season. On his day, he could be brilliant; on others, he looked decidedly mediocre.

Of course, it was never going to be easy with a brand-new team, even one owned by hugely accomplished businessman/racer Paul Gentilozzi. Tagliani, who had been dropped after the 2002 season by Player's/Forsythe in favor of Paul Tracy (despite the fact that he had an ongoing contract), resolved to make the best of his new circumstances at Rocketsports Racing. A fresh, calmer demeanor – fostered largely by his delightful new wife, Bronte (the pair had tied the knot during the off-season) – helped with the transition, and he quickly found a rapport with team manager Phil Howard and race engineer Andy Borme. Tagliani had never driven a Lola before, but was quick from the outset, despite a late start to his testing program. He was fast in practice at St. Petersburg, too, then crashed in qualifying and again in the early stages of the race. A month later, he qualified and finished an excellent third in Monterrey. He was third on the grid also at Long Beach, despite the fact that Borme had baled out on the team and Tagliani instead was working with an entirely new engineering staff.

He was undone by excessive fuel consumption in California, slipping to tenth at the finish, and similar profligacy cost him an almost certain victory in Montreal. That was cruel. Tagliani had been the class of the field all weekend. Even though he had made pit stops earlier than his rivals, he would have held on for a long overdue maiden Champ Car victory if not for a pair of inopportune caution periods.

Consistency remained similarly elusive. He finished third and set fastest lap at Portland, yet a week earlier at Laguna Seca he had been all but invisible. Still, he did earn a third podium finish, at Road America, and was unfortunate to have a couple more strong runs ended by inattentive backmarkers.

ALEX TAGLIANI

9

ORIOL SERVIA

10

**O**NE of the most popular men in the Champ Car paddock, Oriol Servia might have considered trading in his Mr. Nice Guy image for a race win. Nah, probably not a good idea. Still, the happy-go-lucky Spaniard – sorry, Catalan – mirrored Tagliani in coming agonizingly close to victory for the first time. In fact, he finished second on two occasions – at Milwaukee and Montreal. Ironically, each time he was beaten to the line by close buddy Michel Jourdain Jr.

Servia joined Pat Patrick's Visteon-backed team midway through the 2002 season, after rookie Townsend Bell had been shown the door following a series of incidents. Paradoxically, 12 months later, Servia reportedly came close to suffering the same ignominy for the opposite reason – a lack of aggression!

Servia was usually fast – witness his record in accumulating the fifth-best average qualifying position. Only once, in Mexico City, did he fail to start among the top ten. But the chips rarely seemed to fall his way. In St. Petersburg, for example, after moving from ninth to fourth, he was felled by an ignition problem. He started fourth in Monterrey, but his hopes were dashed by a radio miscue prior to the first round of pit stops; then he spun off. He ran out of gas in Long Beach with three laps remaining. Three championship points from the first three races was not what the team was looking for. Nor he, come to that. Fortunately, the situation soon turned around. He finished a strong fourth at Brands Hatch, commencing an impressive run of seven top-six finishes that catapulted him to sixth in the points chart. But then came three non-finishes in succession, all due to accidents (at Vancouver, Road America and Mid-Ohio), during which time he completed a grim tally of just nine green-flag laps.

Servia bounced back to claim second in Montreal – although he could have won if he hadn't allowed Jourdain to make a pass when he was still on cold tires immediately following his first pit stop. That rather summed up his year – so near and yet so far.

Date of birth: **July 13, 1974**

Residence: **Miami, Florida**

Team: **Patrick Racing**

Equipment: **Ford Cosworth/Lola/Bridgestone**

Champ Car starts in 2003: **18**

Points ranking: **7th**

Wins: **0**; Poles: **0**; Points: **108**

PAUL TRACY
WORTH
THE WAIT

by David Phillips

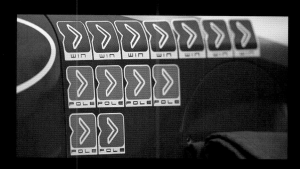

**A**FTER 13 seasons, 209 races, 19 pole positions, 3,386 laps led and 26 victories, Paul Tracy finally added a Champ Car title to his resume in 2003. It's a title some thought he would never win. Nobody, not even his detractors, doubted that Tracy possessed the speed and the desire to win the Champ Car World Series. But there was no shortage of people who believed he lacked the patience and the maturity to mount a championship-winning effort, one where points counted more than race wins, pole positions and laps led.

Tracy, though, had a different take. Win enough races, capture enough poles, lead enough laps, and the points take care of themselves. That's not to say the points for seconds and thirds or, for that matter, sixths and 12ths, aren't important. But great race drivers, or at least those cut from the same cloth as Tracy, attack every weekend, every session, every lap of every race, instead of calculating points.

To be sure, they don't win every time. In fact, they fail to finish more than their fair share. Win, lose or DNF, however, they rest easy, secure in the knowledge that they held nothing back, made their own luck and drove like racers, not actuaries.

"I have always given 110 percent effort all the time into my driving, and every time it is time to go racing and qualify, I put it all out on the line," said Tracy. "I don't think anybody can take that away from me. But there come times in your career when you think, 'Man, I won all these races, but am I going to win a championship? How do I do it?'

"Finally, now it's come. I am just relieved that it's come. It's taken a long time, but you know, it is worth the wait."

The first of those 209 races occurred in the spring of 1991, a short off-season after Tracy had dominated the American Racing Series (later to become Indy Lights) to earn his first professional driving title. Such was the spirit of the times – and the myopia of most Champ Car team owners – that he was not courted by the major CART teams. Instead he made his first Champ Car start for Dale Coyne Racing at Long Beach and more than held his own,

qualifying 14th out of 26 and moving up a few places in the race before suffering a blown engine.

That was just the prelude to an odyssey that saw Tracy pinball between some of the most illustrious teams in the sport, from Team Penske to Newman/Haas Racing and back to Penske before landing at Team KOOL Green for a five-year stint. Along the way, he delighted and infuriated his bosses, battling wheel to wheel with World Champion Nigel Mansell at the tender age of 24, logging thousands of test miles while some of his more established teammates pursued other interests, and finishing third in the championship on three occasions. But his candor and unconventional nature made Tracy the proverbial square peg in Roger Penske's world of politically-correct round holes; and for all the success he enjoyed at TKG, Tracy clashed with Barry Green on occasion and saw his relationship with the team end on a sour note in the wake of Green's decision to sell the organization to a group headed by Michael Andretti.

In hindsight, Tracy seemed destined to enjoy his greatest success with a team that not only wanted him, but also coveted him just the way he is.

That would be Player's/Forsythe Racing, a team owned jointly by Gerald Forsythe and Player's Ltd., a subsidiary of the Imperial Tobacco Company of Canada. Forsythe and Player's had been hot on Tracy's trail for years, but the modern trend of three-year driver contracts always seemed to put him just out of reach. When he was unceremoniously dumped by Penske late in '97, Player's/Forsythe already had the late Greg Moore and Patrick Carpentier under contract and was in no position to add a third car; when Moore was poised to move to Penske at the end of '99, Tracy had just finished third in the championship with TKG and was loathe to change teams.

But the '02 meltdown at TKG/Andretti Green Racing enabled Tracy to go "home" to a place he'd never been before. Of course, given the fact that Player's and KOOL were both arms of the British American Tobacco empire, and that Player's boss Bob

Above: The message on the nose of Tracy's Lola succinctly captures his my-way-or-the-highway credo, but his new team made him feel more at home than any of his previous employers. It showed.

Bexon had been the catalyst in the formation of Team KOOL Green during his time at KOOL, Tracy found some familiar faces awaiting him at Player's/Forsythe.

What's more, he encountered a team willing to leave no stone unturned in its efforts to make him feel at home and to follow his lead rather than treating him like a recalcitrant adolescent.

"The people behind the team, Bob Bexon and Jerry Forsythe, they believed in me for a long time as a driver," said Tracy. "I worked with Bob, who was in charge of KOOL, when I joined Team KOOL Green. Then he moved back over to Player's after about a year-and-a-half. From that point in time, he was a big believer in me and wanted me to come to Player's. We tried a couple of times, but it just wouldn't come together.

"Once I came to the team, they basically told me, 'Whatever you need, or you feel you need, to win the championship, just tell us what you need.' I have never been in a situation with any team where they basically said to me, 'Who are the people you want? What are the cars you want? Who are the guys you want to work with?' It's always been, 'Come and we will tell you what you are going to do.'"

A key player already in place was Tony Cicale, who had infused Tracy with some of his Zen-like focus during their time at TKG before leaving for Player's/Forsythe. Tracy quickly struck up good working relationships with his easygoing but fiercely competitive partner, Patrick Carpentier, as well as Team Vice President Neil Micklewright, Team Manager Phil LePan and engineer Mike Pawlowski. Then, when Tracy's assigned race engineer Kelly Loewen unexpectedly quit the team days before the season-opener, Player's/Forsythe, at Tracy's request, recruited another former TKG colleague – Todd Malloy – to fill his place.

Talk about feeling wanted...

"All of us just clicked and really that was the difference," said Tracy. "They just put a whole package around me of what I thought that I needed, and it all worked out."

Case in point: After investing millions of dollars and several years to develop the Reynard into a championship proposition, Player's switched to Lola for 2003 at Tracy's urging. He had driven the Reynard for years at TKG before the team changed to Lolas in mid-'02, and was convinced that the Lola was the better car.

The switch was costly. Not only did the team turn its back on years of Reynard experience, but also the move meant the end of technical director Bruce Ashmore's time with the organization, to say nothing of hundreds of thousands of dollars in spare parts that would no longer be needed. In addition, the team was forced to learn a new car, with Carpentier on a particularly steep learning curve, never having sat in a Lola Champ Car previously.

Thus, while Tracy romped to three straight wins to open the season, he was by no means a dominant force. Rookie Sébastien Bourdais, in fact, had the legs on everyone at St. Petersburg and Monterrey before mistakes intervened, while Michel Jourdain Jr. snatched defeat from the jaws of victory at Long Beach when his transmission failed.

There followed a disastrous tour of Europe, where Tracy earned just two points thanks to a broken gearbox at Brands Hatch and a costly aerodynamic miscalculation that rendered his car woefully uncompetitive at EuroSpeedway. His team let him down again at Milwaukee, where a wheel fell off his car after the final pit stop, costing him a likely podium; but one and all rebounded with solid performances at Laguna Seca, which saw Carpentier emerge victorious while Tracy was a useful third.

Tracy was forced to concede Portland and Cleveland to Adrian Fernandez and Bourdais respectively, but he destroyed all comers on home ground in Toronto and Vancouver to regain momentum.

Just as quickly, he threw it away with a first-lap "off" at Road

Some were quick to note that Tracy's championship capped a topsy-turvy Champ Car season, one that saw established stars like Andretti, Dario Franchitti, Tony Kanaan, Kenny Bräck and Scott Dixon migrate to the rival Indy Racing League, to be replaced by relative unknowns with varying levels of skill and experience.

At the same time, of course, the introduction of the spec Ford Cosworth XFE engine and strict limitations on testing and aerodynamic development meant that no driver enjoyed a significant technical advantage, apart from the obvious chasm separating the performance of the Lola and Reynard chassis.

To Tracy's way of thinking, the technical equality made winning the 2003 season's championship all the more fulfilling.

"The series has somewhat become mostly a spec series," he said. "Everybody has the same engine. Everybody has the same tires. There's nobody with a horsepower advantage or a fuel-mileage advantage, or a different turbo that's better, or whatever.

"So it's put a lot more into the driver's hands and the team's hands. The team that does the best job will ultimately end up winning races, and [so will] the driver that does the best job. So that gives me a lot of satisfaction. I can't say, 'Our engine wasn't as good as so-and-so's engines,' or, 'He had better this or better that.' Everybody pretty much has the same stuff. I can say that myself and our team, we just did a better job than everybody."

And in the case of Tracy, it's really the same job he's been doing since he first drove Dale Coyne's Champ Car at Long Beach in '91, indeed the same job he's been doing since he first raced a go-kart as a kid in suburban Toronto.

"I went out there and won the championship the way that I drive," he said. "That's racing to the maximum every weekend. You can say I did it my way because I didn't go out there and race for points, or cruise around to collect points. I went out and gave it everything I had every weekend, and sometimes I won and sometimes I failed.

"The way I have driven my whole life, is to go out there and try to win and try to...put it all out on the line every time. A leopard can't change its spots, I guess. This is the way I am.

"As much as people told me throughout the year, 'You have got to do this,' and, 'You have got to do that,' I can't change what my natural instincts are. Some people are guys that will not take risks and go out there and finish in the points every weekend. Some guys are natural risk-takers. I guess that's the category that I am in. I go out and I give it everything I have. I take chances. Sometimes they pay off and sometimes they don't."

After 13 seasons and 20,818 laps racing Champ Cars, Tracy's instincts paid off big-time in 2003.

**Above left:** Tracy with Bob Bexon of Player's Ltd. after his win in Toronto.
Gavin Lawrence/LAT

**Above:** The tobacco company had coveted the Canadian for several years, and the partnership reaped immediate rewards.
Phil Abbott/LAT

**Below:** Tracy had a harmonious relationship with easygoing teammate Patrick Carpentier despite enjoying far more success.
Gavin Lawrence/LAT

America, regained it by leading Carpentier home to a Player's/Forsythe 1-2 at Mid-Ohio, then lost it again when he ran out of fuel on the final lap at Montreal and was soundly beaten by Bruno Junqueira at Denver.

In Miami, both Tracy and Junqueira threw away golden opportunities to put a lock on the title race, but it was PT who scored a critical win at Mexico City, while the Brazilian trailed home a food-poisoned seventh. That set the stage for the climactic race at Surfers Paradise, a battle of changing fortunes that began with Tracy being nudged into a spin to the bottom of the charts. He recovered to seventh, only to be body-slammed in a four-car shunt and fall back down the order while effecting repairs. Finally, he had the title handed to him on a platter when Junqueira crashed under pressure from, of all people, Carpentier.

It was a tumultuous conclusion to a tumultuous season in a tumultuous career. As Tracy is the first to admit: "Looking at how the season went...basically my career has always been hot/cold, hot/cold. It's never been kind of lukewarm the whole time. We started off the year with three wins, and we went to Europe and had basically three bad races. We scored three points. We had a mechanical failure, gearbox failure, in England; went to Germany and we were uncompetitive. We chose the wrong aero package to go there. And then came back to Milwaukee, and we were running up front and we had a wheel fall off after the last pit stop. That's kind of how the season went. We would go hot and cold; then hot and cold. There were a few races, the middle there, where we scored some third and fourths, but it wasn't just on an even keel the whole time."

Indeed, even Tracy's championship celebration proved unconventional, as the wildfires that swept Southern California in late October forced the cancellation of his Victory Tour in the season finale at California Speedway.

# BOWING OUT ON TOP by Alex Sabine

I T'S a safe bet that the Molson Indy Toronto ranked as the busiest and most emotionally charged race meeting of the 2003 season for Player's/Forsythe Racing. For starters, there was the deluge of PR and promotional work that the team routinely discharges in the run-up to each of the three Canadian events – a telling index of the stature of the Champ Car World Series (and open-wheel racing generally) north of the border.

A more obvious reason why the Toronto weekend will not soon be forgotten by anyone at Team Player's is that it was capped by a crushing victory by Paul Tracy in front of 73,000 of his countrymen – almost literally in his own back yard, for Tracy hails from the nearby suburb of West Hill. The supposedly thick-skinned 34-year-old was moved to tears by the rousing reception he was given during the post-race rendition of the Canadian national anthem.

And yet the heady atmosphere was tinged with poignancy, due to an announcement on the Thursday before the event that would have far-reaching implications not only for the Player's/Forsythe team, but also for the larger canvas of Canadian motorsport. Not unexpectedly, Player's Ltd., the team's longtime sponsor and co-owner, officially served notice that it would have to bow out of the sport at season's end owing to the Canadian federal government's impending ban on tobacco-company sponsorship of sporting events, which was to take effect on October 1.

"The Tobacco Act is currently under appeal by the three major Canadian tobacco manufacturers, but [until the case is heard] we have no choice but to comply and withdraw from motorsport sponsorship," stated Bob Bexon, president and CEO of Imperial Tobacco Canada, which markets the flagship Player's brand. "We are taking our leave with a great deal of reluctance and sadness, but we do so with considerable pride in what has been accomplished in the last 42 years."

Player's had been a mainstay of Canadian motorsport since it promoted the country's first international fixture way back in 1961 – the Player's 200 at Mosport Park, Ontario. The new track's first professional race attracted a sizeable crowd (estimated at 40,000), which witnessed a masterclass given by Stirling Moss aboard a lime-green Lotus 19 sports/racer.

That initial foray into motorsport sponsorship heralded the arrival of big-time racing not just at Mosport, but in Canada as a whole. In 1966, Player's staged the first ever Can-Am sports car race at Mont Tremblant-St. Jovite, another new circuit in the picturesque Laurentian mountains north of Montreal. It thereby rescued the event from the brink of cancellation and ensured that the Can-Am series duly got off the ground, ushering in a spectacular nine-year epoch of free-formula sports car racing in North America, the like of which hadn't been seen before or since.

The tobacco giant's next pioneering venture was to sponsor the inaugural Canadian Formula 1 Grand Prix, at Mosport in 1967. When the race switched to St. Jovite the following season, Player's once again signed the check. By the late 1970s, Canada's two premier venues had fallen into disrepair, and F1 found a new home at Circuit Gilles-Villeneuve a stone's throw from downtown Montreal. The cosmopolitan city quickly developed into one of the most popular stops on the F1 calendar, and the annual jamboree now draws crowds of over 300,000. Player's continued to be involved as title or associate sponsor of the GP until Y2K. It also provided stalwart support to primary sponsor Molson at CART's thriving street races in Toronto and Vancouver.

In the meantime, the company had played a pivotal role in launching the Formula Atlantic championship as Canada's top single-seater category in 1974, replacing the amateurish Formula B and substituting more powerful cars that offered aspiring young drivers a better opportunity to showcase their abilities. Player's served as the series' presenting sponsor (it was then known as the Player's Challenge) and worked energetically to attract both paying spectators and the interest of a wide cross-section of media, securing nationwide TV coverage on the CTV network's weekly Wide World of Sports program.

The Player's Challenge quickly became one of the best-packaged championships in the Americas, boasting good prize money, full grids and ever closer and more professional competition. The phenomenon of 30-car fields blanketed by only a couple of seconds was totally new in North American road racing, which for the first time had a class worthy of direct comparison with European Formula 2.

"Player's was the first [sponsor] to put a racing series on television in Canada,"

remembers Bill Brack, who claimed successive Atlantic titles in 1974 and '75. "That brought many good drivers from all around the world, which was a first. Future world champions like Keke Rosberg, as well as CART champions like Bobby Rahal, cut their teeth in Atlantic. The competition was extremely tough."

The event that really thrust Formula Atlantic onto the global stage was the annual thrash around the streets of the St. Lawrence river town of Trois-Rivières – still the jewel in the series' crown today. By the mid-1970s, it was attracting an international entry, with a number of the top Grand Prix drivers of the day making cameo appearances. In 1976, a jockey-sized young French-Canadian hotshoe by the name of Gilles Villeneuve decimated the opposition, upstaging a bevy of F1 regulars in the process – including soon-to-be World Champion James Hunt. The Englishman was so impressed that he recommended to his McLaren bosses that they keep a close eye on this fellow Villeneuve, with a view to procuring his services in the near future...

The rest, as they say, is history. Villeneuve went on to assure himself a very special place in the pantheon of world motorsport thanks to his spectacular exploits at the wheel of recalcitrant Ferraris. However, the Player's Challenge (and its blue-riband event at Trois-Rivières) not only catapulted Villeneuve to international stardom, but also laid the foundations for the future of the Atlantic series through to its present incarnation as the CART Toyota Atlantic Championship, the lynchpin and final rung of CART's Ladder System.

Nor has Player's Ltd's involvement been confined to the fields of event and series sponsorship. In the early 1990s, the company set up a generous and effective Driver Development Program, providing financial backing for Canadian rising stars coming through the ranks of Formula Ford, Toyota Atlantic and Indy Lights. The scheme spawned a whole new generation of homegrown talent, including 1995 CART title holder and '97 World Champion Jacques Villeneuve, the late, lamented Greg Moore, and current Champ Car front-runners Patrick Carpentier and Alex Tagliani. Carpentier has no doubts as to the value of the program in plucking him from obscurity, facilitating his progress through the sport's junior categories and grooming him for the top echelon.

"I think back to my karting days and my early years in racing, and I realize that my career path would very likely have run into a big detour, if not for the Player's racing program," he remarked. "For me, it came along at just the right time. And I was lucky enough that the people running the program saw the potential in me to invest the time and money so that I could refine my skills."

Player's patronage of up-and-coming Canadian talent soon paid handsome dividends,

as the second-generation Villeneuve rose to prominence driving for Forsythe-Green Racing under the Player's banner, scooping CART Rookie of the Year honors in 1994. The following season, Jerry Forsythe and Barry Green went their separate ways, but Player's struck gold with Villeneuve, who won both the Indianapolis 500 and the Champ Car crown for Team Green, becoming the first Canadian to accomplish either feat.

In 1996, Player's forged a new alliance with Forsythe, entering into co-ownership with the American business tycoon and fielding a single-car effort for the precociously talented Indy Lights champion Moore. Sensationally, the Vancouver native came within an ace of victory on each of his first two outings, and later etched his name in the history books as the youngest ever winner of a CART-sanctioned race by triumphing at Milwaukee during his sophomore campaign (a record subsequently eclipsed by Scott Dixon). Ultimately, however, Moore's boundless potential went largely unfulfilled, as a niggling succession of incidents and mechanical woes militated against a concerted championship challenge in each of his four years in the sport. His tragic death in the 1999 season finale at California Speedway sent shock waves reverberating through the entire Champ Car community, but its effect on the Player's/Forsythe squad was especially devastating.

The battered outfit (which had expanded to a two-car operation with the addition of Carpentier in 1998) gamely regrouped and by 2002 finally had developed into a consistent force to be reckoned with, paving the way for a triumphant '03 season. The marriage of Player's and Paul Tracy after a lengthy courtship proved to be something close to the proverbial match made in heaven; with the benefit of hindsight, no doubt both parties rue the fact that they only tied the knot in the sponsor's final year. Tracy's long-awaited maiden Champ Car title – the first also for the Player's/Forsythe partnership – ensured a fitting send-off for one of Canadian racing's most productive, resourceful and loyal benefactors.

"The events that were presented, the teams that were sponsored, the drivers who were funded – our aim has always been to provide Canadians with access to top-caliber motorsport and nurture the development of homegrown drivers in their career pursuits," concluded Bob Bexon. "Through the years, the drivers and teams affiliated with Player's have been outstanding ambassadors for Canada."

Happy to report, Champ Car racing and motorsport in general continue to enjoy a solid profile across Canada – thanks in no small measure to the outstanding contribution made by Player's over 42 years. The void left by the company's enforced departure will be mighty hard to fill.

# IN WITH THE NEW

by Alex Sabine

I N his famous movie "Butch Cassidy and the Sundance Kid," Paul Newman (playing Butch) incredulously mutters about the phantom-like posse that is hot on the trail of the two legendary outlaws, "Who are those guys?" Many veterans of the Champ Car World Series could be found scratching their heads in similar bewilderment when the largest rookie contingent in memory showed up at St. Petersburg in February, at the dawn of one of the most open and unpredictable seasons in the championship's history.

As a tumultuous 2002 wore on, a variety of factors, but principally the defection of a number of established teams and drivers to the IRL – part of the ongoing toll of American open-wheel racing's ruinous fissure – appeared to strike a body blow to CART's prospects for 2003. Happily, however, fears of the series' imminent demise proved to be greatly exaggerated, thanks in large measure to the sanctioning body's seminal decision to adopt a chassis freeze and a spec Cosworth engine formula, and the associated drastic reduction in team operating costs. That, combined with an innovative Entrant Support Program worth the better part of $1 million per car, was enough to entice a host of new teams into the fold to replace the outgoing behemoths. Against all the odds, a respectable field of 19 cars materialized when the season kicked off in Florida.

There was a parallel changing of the guard among the ranks of the drivers. In place of departing stars such as Michael Andretti, Dario Franchitti and Formula 1-bound 2002 champion Cristiano da Matta came an influx of fresh blood, with as much as half the starting entry being made up of rookies. Over the course of the season, some 14 newcomers, representing nine countries and four continents, made at least one Champ Car start. With the single exception of 1993 (something of an aberration due to the rash of one-off or irregular entries), you had to go back to CART's formative years of 1979–83 to find such an abundance of neophytes.

Viewed from a broad-brush historical perspective, both the quantity of rookies per season and the impact they have made have fluctuated in a cyclical manner in response to specific stimuli. The first infusion of new talent came in the early 1980s, when CART's diversification into road racing attracted the likes of Bobby Rahal, Teo Fabi, Danny Sullivan and Roberto Guerrero, as well as second-generation starlets Al Unser Jr. and Michael Andretti, from backgrounds in Formula 1, Formula Atlantic and sports car racing.

By contrast, the latter half of the decade failed conspicuously to turn up any diamonds in the rough – partly because of the absence of a well-defined grass-roots/ladder system, no doubt, but also because the finds of the early 1980s had morphed into the new establishment. Rahal, Sullivan and the junior members of the Unser and Andretti clans quickly rose to prominence, joining Rick Mears, Mario Andretti and company as the sport's leading lights, who exercised a vice-like grip on the most sought-after seats. Their reign was to last until a sweeping internationalization of the series transformed the complexion – and with it the intensity and quality – of Champ Car competition during the 1990s.

The seeds of this second phase of regeneration had been sown in the mid-1980s, when Brazilian double World Champion Emerson Fittipaldi, disillusioned after several fruitless years running his own Grand Prix team, rejuvenated his driving career in the friendlier waters of Champ Car racing. Fittipaldi's success ensured that CART at last began to register on the international motorsport radar screen, and sparked an upsurge of interest in his homeland. The next generation of Brazilian hopefuls started to look seriously at what the series had to offer – so much so that they began to outnumber their American counterparts by the mid-1990s.

Meanwhile, the arrival of reigning World Champion Nigel Mansell in 1993 had generated an unprecedented level of worldwide exposure, as well as boosting CART's credibility at a stroke. While Mansell flounced away from the North American scene at the end of 1994, his spectacular two-year stint was the catalyst for an exponential growth in the series' international profile. A steady stream of up-and-coming chargers from the European junior formulae crossed the "Pond" from 1995 onward, supplemented by a handful of F1 refugees.

Main photograph: After falling at the last hurdle in his attempt to secure a Formula 1 testing berth for 2003, Sébastien Bourdais switched his focus to Champ Cars and was a runaway Rookie of the Year.
Phil Abbott/LAT

Insets, far left and center left: Ryan Hunter-Reay faced a steep learning curve driving for Stefan Johansson's startup team, but conjured a surprise victory in Australia; Bourdais took five poles and three wins.
Photographs: Mike Levitt/LAT

Insets, center right and right: Tiago Monteiro and Mario Haberfeld joined the stampede of Formula 3000 refugees.
Photographs: Gavin Lawrence/LAT

Above: Darren Manning's yeoman efforts for the underfinanced Walker Racing outfit impressed everyone, as did his uncomplaining, no-nonsense attitude.

Above right: The Brit rounded out his season with a splendid second place in fickle conditions at Surfers Paradise.

Photographs: Gavin Lawrence/LAT

Some domestic critics complained that these overseas arrivals had a tendency to treat CART as a finishing school for what they believed to be their ultimate destiny in F1; but such misgivings missed the point. Who would deny, for example, the pizzazz injected into the series by Juan Pablo Montoya in 1999–2000 after the Colombian was "loaned" to Chip Ganassi by Frank Williams? Or that he upped the ante and compelled would-be rivals to raise their game? Moreover, the (albeit sometimes temporary) participation of much of the cream of European driving talent created a virtuous circle whereby departing aces like Alex Zanardi found worthy successors such as Montoya and Bruno Junqueira, with the result that the talent pool was constantly being replenished.

In reality, the cozy certainties that had prevailed on the driver front in the 1980s had simply given way to a more dynamic, international and competitive culture – a shift that was reflected less in an increase in the annual complement of rookies than in their presence at the business end of the grid.

The winds of change blowing through the Champ Car paddock made for a more turbulent backdrop going into 2003, and the plethora of first-year teams and drivers inevitably faced an uphill struggle to fill the void left by household names like Andretti and Target/Chip Ganassi Racing. Encouragingly, however, many of them proved equal to the task, and the overall depth of the field comfortably exceeded preseason expectations.

The brightest new star in CART's firmament was reigning FIA Formula 3000 champion Sébastien Bourdais. Landing the coveted berth with defending title holder Newman/Haas Racing was a priceless advantage, and the quiet, cerebral Frenchman took to his new environment like the proverbial duck to water. He paced much of preseason testing and unceremoniously qualified on pole for the first two races. Between them, Bourdais and the team contrived to let victory slip through their fingers on each occasion, but the 24-year-old soon made amends by winning both legs of the European tour – notwithstanding the fact that the German 500 at EuroSpeedway Lausitz was his first acquaintance with an oval under racing conditions! If the second half of his season was less spectacular, Bourdais nonetheless remained a force to be reckoned with everywhere. He won the Jim Trueman Rookie of the Year award at a canter, and served ample notice that he will be gunning for overall honors in 2004.

Most of Bourdais' fellow rookies had to fight with one hand tied behind their respective backs, embarking on their maiden

Champ Car campaigns with new teams and/or aging Reynard chassis. Darren Manning performed wonders on a shoestring budget with Derrick Walker's RAC-sponsored Reynard, barely putting a scratch on the car all season and ending up as the Brackley marque's top representative in the point standings (two places ahead of 1996 CART Champion Jimmy Vasser). The chirpy Englishman reinvigorated Walker's engineering department, and only a niggling series of gearbox woes prevented him from making an even bigger impact.

While Bourdais and Manning were classic products of the traditional European proving grounds of Formula Vauxhall/Renault, F3 and F3000, young American Ryan Hunter-Reay was the poster boy for CART's Ladder System, having graduated through a karting scholarship into the Barber Dodge Pro Series and thence to Toyota Atlantic. RH-R overcame some initial teething problems to show his true colors in the latter part of the year. His unexpected win in Australia may have required a slice of good fortune, but he kept his wits about him while a roll-call of more seasoned rivals lost theirs. He was similarly flawless at Mid-Ohio en route to a breakthrough third-place finish, while at Mexico City he wrung more pace out of the Reynard than anyone else managed all year.

Another pair of F3000 recruits, Brazilian Mario Haberfeld and Portugal's Tiago Monteiro, also made a generally favorable impression. The enigmatic Haberfeld struggled to build any real momentum from one race to the next, but there were enough flashes of promise to suggest that he could develop into a bona fide contender with a little more experience. Monteiro, meanwhile, raised the hackles of several of his peers with a couple of ill-judged passing attempts, but improved immeasurably as the season progressed once he settled down under the tutelage of Emerson Fittipaldi.

Nine other rookies took part in the 2003 campaign at one stage or another, although the ebb and flow of personal sponsorship backing meant that many of them contested only a handful of races. The most significant addition was F1 alumnus Mika Salo, who took over the reins at PK Racing from Denver and quickly provided the sort of concise feedback – and results – that the startup outfit had hitherto been lacking.

As the sun set on the 2003 season, it was clearer than ever that a talented crop of rookies, emanating from the full gamut of feeder categories the world over, remains at the heart of the continued vitality and quality of Champ Car racing's on-track product – long the series' proudest boast.

Above: Rodolfo Lavin rode the wave of Mexican interest in the Champ Car World Series to procure backing from Corona beer, but struggled to match teammate Manning's pace.

Right: Haberfeld shone on occasion in Eric Bachelart's Reynard (as here at Denver), but consistent speed eluded him.

Photographs: Gavin Lawrence/LAT

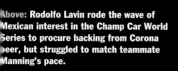

**Far left:** Toyota Atlantic ace Luis Diaz acquitted himself well in a one-off Champ Car outing in his native Mexico.

**Left:** The arrival of F1 veteran Mika Salo heralded an upturn in fortunes for PK Racing in the twilight of the season.
Photographs: Gavin Lawrence/LAT

Main photograph: **Hunter-Reay** came on in leaps and bounds toward the end of the year, converting potential into hard results.
Mike Weston/LAT

# ALEX ZANARDI
# SIMPLY AMAZING
by David Phillips

**T**HE man never ceases to amaze. Airlifted from EuroSpeedway in the wake of a crash that severed his legs 13 laps from the finish of the inaugural German 500 in 2001, Alex Zanardi was not expected to survive, let alone recover to lead a relatively normal life. And yet, eight months later there he was, kicking out the first ball in a charity soccer match a few days before the Grand Prix of Monaco.

Two months after that, Zanardi made an emotional return to the Champ Car scene in Toronto, where he received the Greg Moore Award and served as chief starter of the Molson Indy. Little could we have known – although we should have expected – the best was yet to come. The first inkling that something special was in the works for CART's return to EuroSpeedway came during a teleconference naming Zanardi Grand Marshall of the 2003 German 500. At the time, he hinted that he might have a surprise up his sleeve come race weekend, but apart from a handful of officials, mechanics, technicians and two team owners, few knew what was planned.

What was in the works was Zanardi's stunning return to the cockpit of a Champ Car, a Ford Cosworth-powered Reynard owned by Walker Racing and outfitted by Mi-Jack/Conquest Racing's crew with hand controls for the throttle, clutch and brakes. The finishing touch came in the paint job: burgundy, black and white, just like the one Zanardi had campaigned for Mo Nunn Racing in 2001.

Mi-Jack/Conquest owner and former Indy Lights champion Eric Bachelart gave the car a shakedown test before it was shipped to Europe. Friday evening of race weekend, Zanardi ran about 40 laps in the car, working out a few minor bugs in order to be fully ready for the big event on raceday: completing the "missing" 13 laps from that fateful 2001 race.

As Zanardi rolled down the pit lane in front of 68,000 standing, clapping, cheering, flag-waving, airhorn-blaring fans, the atmosphere was not electric –

it was atomic. And if anyone thought he was out for a Sunday-afternoon cruise, they were disabused of the notion in the 40.546 seconds it took him to complete his first flying lap, less than two seconds slower than Adrian Fernandez's qualifying run the previous afternoon.

But Zanardi was just getting started. His second lap took 38.918s, lap three 38.381s, lap four 38.096s, and on lap five he was down to 37.661s. The crowd reacted with a roar as each lap's time and speed were announced, and began following Zanardi around the two-mile speedway with "the wave," German-style. Zanardi saved the best for last, tripping the timing lights in 37.487s on his 13th and final lap, good enough to have qualified fifth on the grid.

"It was just fantastic," he said later. "Obviously, this is something that I've been doing all my racing career. In the past year-and-a-half, I never even got close to driving a proper racing car. So just for this reason it was great again to feel the speed, to feel the downforce. Most of all, what made it particularly enjoyable was the love of all the people in the Champ Car community, in particular the drivers, and certainly the fans. It was just awesome."

But what about the speed? Surely even he was a little surprised at how fast he had gone after just 40 laps in the car the previous evening, and after being out of a race car for 20 months, not to mention the matter of driving at 200+ mph with prosthetic legs.

"It was flat out," he said. "Wide open. I can't say pedal-to-the-metal, because I didn't have a pedal. I just had a little knob, but that was all I had in the car.

"I was really surprised how rapidly it came back to me. You know, I can only say that. It felt like I was doing the same thing the day before and the day before. I didn't feel like I was out of the car for one-and-a-half years. Especially if you consider that in this one-and-a-half years, all I've been doing, I've been adjusting prosthetical legs, spending time with my son, and the fastest

**Left: Do you believe in miracles?** Alex Zanardi in a Champ Car again, moments before venturing out onto the Lausitz oval to complete a remarkable return.

**Main photograph:** Astonishingly, Zanardi's lap times stood comparison with those of the leading contenders for the German 500.
Photographs: Phil Abbott/LAT

**Top:** Signing autographs for the fans on his return to competition at Monza.

**Above center:** Zanardi puts his Ravaglia Motorsport BMW throught its paces.

**Above:** Jimmy Vasser and Tony Kanaan made a surprise visit to Italy to support their friend and former teammate.
Photographs: LAT

thing I've driven is my road car. So it was nice. It was a very pleasant surprise for me too."

A man of deep passion and emotion, Zanardi is also a pragmatist. As such, he admitted to experiencing conflicting feelings when his run came to an end.

"I was kind of disappointed that it was over," he said. "But nevertheless, I have great memories from racing. I've enjoyed beautiful satisfactions. And certainly from a sporting point of view, this was not the highlight of my life. I had races that for me personally were by far more important than these 13 laps.

"This was something that was very symbolic, if you like, very emotional for the people that saw me taken away [from EuroSpeedway in 2001] from the helicopter, leaving a big trace of blood, and then when I come back here and I drive the same speed I was driving last time I was here. So certainly this is surprising. It looks like a miracle. But for me, that I've lived through day to day, it's not a miracle."

Inevitably, Zanardi's remarkable performance prompted some to ask if he might be tempted to consider additional forays into motorsports, perhaps even a return to actual competition.

"God knows what's next," he said. "But for sure this is my answer also to the fans that wanted to know why I haven't come back to racing. Is it because it's impossible or is it because I don't want to come back, or is it probably simply because I'm really scared about what happened in my accident?

"Well, the answer is simply because life goes on, and I'm just in the process of moving on to other things. But at least I think now they know that if I really want it, I could do it again. Maybe not at this level, but at other levels. I think eventually I will be driving again, maybe in a race but always [to] be for my own, just for fun, never just a profession any more."

In truth, the wheels were already spinning in Zanardi's head – and in those of some old friends and new associates back in Italy – about a possible return to competition. Earlier in the spring, a casual trip to a local karting track near Zanardi's home in Padua got the competitive juices flowing again.

"I was there with my brother-in-law and the kids, and just out of a bet I jumped on a go-kart and I made a guy tie my feet with plastic tie-wraps on the pedals, just to do a lap," he said. "I realized when I went out that I could drive and I had a lot of sensitivity on my feet, so that was a sort of inspiration. I realized I could possibly drive also a racing car that way."

Next came a casual conversation with longtime friend and Ravaglia Motorsport Technical Director Roberto Trevisan, and team principals Roberto Ravaglia, Aldo Preo and Umberto Grano.

"They took me to the local circuit," related Zanardi. "We saw that I could run pretty competitively, and then we just came naturally to saying, 'The last race of the European Touring Car Championship is in Monza. Why don't we organize a car for it?'

"And I said, 'OK let's go for it.'"

However, there were formidable technical obstacles to Zanardi's return to competition: hand-operated throttle controls to be installed in the steering wheel; an electric potentiometer on the shift lever to operate the clutch. Then came the brakes.

"Initially, we installed about 120 pounds of equipment in terms of servicommands and pumps...to be operated just with my hands," said Zanardi. "And then we weren't going anywhere. The brakes were like a switch. I couldn't brake at all, or else slam my face on the front screen. There was nothing in between.

"So it was actually my idea, once again, to say, 'Let me try to brake with my foot.'

"And they said, 'No. It's really difficult. You can't do it.'

"I said, 'Listen, let me try.'

"And then we went and I would say it was a good 75 percent of what it is today, right from the word go. So then we worked a little bit with seat position, with the shape of the pedal itself. Basically, my brake pedal is like a second shoe on which I put my foot. So it's held in that position and then [using] the mechanical knee as a simple joint and pressing down with the upper part of my leg, I transfer the pressure on the brake.

"The surprising thing is that I don't feel pressure on my leg, but I feel pressure on my foot. This tells you once again that the brain is an incredible machine. I was talking to some doctor about this and he said it's absolutely normal; that the brain will develop itself and adapt to the needs required.

"And really, when I have my prosthetical legs on, I know exactly where my feet are and I really feel the pressure on the foot. Recently, I've been able to tune that even better as I drove the car in some testing and I can really use the brakes pretty efficiently...I mean, it'll never be like having my own legs, but pretty close."

Ultimately, Zanardi's BMW carried 15–18 pounds of excess weight; far less than the roughly 90 pounds of ballast the ETCC rules dictate for "one-off" entries. Given Zanardi's other challenges, however, officials decided to cut him some slack.

Despite moral support from ex-Champ Car teammates Jimmy Vasser and Tony Kanaan, who made a surprise visit to Monza, Zanardi did not enjoy a trouble-free run. Clutch problems sidelined him in one of the two practice sessions, while a slight handling imbalance – coupled with a missed shift on his best qualifying lap – relegated him to 11th on the grid. Next a multi-car pileup at Monza's infamous tight first chicane sidelined him in the heat race.

Happily, the team repaired Zanardi's mount for the final and, after starting 17th out of 18, he came through to a remarkable seventh place.

"I started very cautiously because, obviously, I did not have the experience, I did not have the feeling that other drivers had," he said. "I lost a little bit of time in the first part of the race. Then I got in [harmony] with the car. I start to feel better and toward the end I was running competitive lap times in comparison with the guys that were leading the event. But it was obviously too late to try to recover something because I was really too far behind, bearing in mind I started next to last.

"But anyway I'm happy. I passed some guys, I was able to draft and outbrake them in the corners, which is remarkable in a way considering my own problems...

"I had fun. I would have had more fun if I would have ended up winning the event, but that was clearly impossible."

As was the case following his run in the Champ Car at EuroSpeedway, the question had to be asked whether Zanardi was contemplating racing in the future. His response was typical: "Frankly, I don't know because, normally, the decision is related to money, to the competitiveness of the car, to sponsors, to this and that. For me, the decision is only related to the fact that I love to go to school and pick my son up in the afternoon. And I want to find out exactly how many times I won't be able to do this if I am to race here next year. Because too much is too much. First is my family and then is my passions. This is one of my passions...but I've got others."

Further indication of the way Zanardi was leaning came in November, when he teamed with Vasser, Oriol Servia and Michel Jourdain Jr. in a 500-km go-kart race in São Paulo against an all-star lineup featuring the likes of Rubens Barrichello, Juan Pablo Montoya, Christian Fittipaldi and Mario Haberfeld. Zanardi & Co. gave a pretty fair account of themselves, too, coming home fourth in what was the first time any of them had competed in the event.

Then in December came news that, in fact, Zanardi had accepted an offer from Ravaglia Motorsport/BMW Team Italy-Spain to contest the 2004 European Touring Car Championship.

"I'm happy to take part in the ETCC with a BMW Team Italy-Spain car, and I wish to thank BMW Italy and the team for trusting in this project since the beginning," said Zanardi. "Racing in Monza was great, and made me feel again strong sensations and a lot of fun. The car was very competitive, especially in the engine, and this is a great motivation to keep on with its development. Our competition are valiant and they won't give us presents, but we are facing the 2004 season with the goal to be competitive from the first race."

It is an understatement to say that Zanardi and his teammates will face extraordinary challenges in 2004. But he has never been one to shy away from challenges. As he said in an interview with the British magazine Motorsport News, "I want to challenge myself to the limit. That's not to prove anything to anyone or myself – only because it's fun. You can only do some things in the time you're given on this planet, but the future is unknown. That's why it's interesting to be alive."

Kevin Kalkhoven (right), Paul Gentilozzi (far right) and Jerry Forsythe (below) never lost faith in the product and emerged as saviors of the Champ Car World Series.
Photographs: Mike Levitt/LAT

# A NEW BEGINNING

## Paul Gentilozzi and Kevin Kalkhoven outline the future of Champ Car racing

THERE was a collective sigh of relief within the Champ Car community at around 5 p.m. on January 28, 2004, when Judge Frank J. Otte declared at a U.S. Bankruptcy Court in Indianapolis that Open Wheel Racing Series, LLC (OWRS) had been given the green light to take over operations of the Champ Car World Series. The decision, which came in the face of a rival bid from Indy Racing League/Indianapolis Motor Speedway proprietor Tony George, finally brought to an end months of uncertainty over the troubled series, especially following the announcement on December 16 that its previous administrator, Championship Auto Racing Teams, Inc. (CART), had made a filing under Chapter 11 of the U.S. Bankruptcy Code.

One day after the ruling, two of the three OWRS principals, Paul Gentilozzi and Kevin Kalkhoven, laid out their plans and answered some pertinent questions regarding the future.

**Kevin Kalkhoven:** "Obviously, it was a very important day for open-wheel racing – not as a company but as an entity that will be providing racing throughout the world. We want to thank our supporters, and there were millions of them, literally, who filled the seats last year, and we want to thank our sponsors and our teams for their invaluable support during this period."

*What are your next few steps?*

**Paul Gentilozzi:** "Well, we never really stopped getting ready for [the 2004] season, but this morning at 8 o'clock there was a new pulse of life threading throughout the Champ Car office, and I think throughout teams all over Indianapolis and the Midwest. As everybody is now convinced that there will be a season and that we're all gonna be racing in less than 90 days, that specific work in getting ready for the first event of the season has swung into high gear. We've lost a little bit of time, but everyone feels that urgency and has gone to work to make up that time."

*You've said repeatedly that you're convinced you can attract at least 18 cars to the first race of the 2004 season in Long Beach. Where do you stand on that today?*

**PG:** "We've stuck our neck way out and I think we're gonna have the race cars we need to satisfy our promoters. It isn't something that we have doubt about, and we've talked to our teams on a daily basis and they're ready now to go to work. Most of them were in the courtroom yesterday and we've visited their shops, so we know where they are and we also know where the variables were: which drivers were waiting with their sponsors for confirmation of our success. Now that that's done, today they've all been unified and energized and are moving forward to make their decisions."

*There's a lot of excitement about the judge's ruling. On the other hand, some longtime CART supporters have mixed feelings, because there is a strong body of opinion that open-wheel racing would benefit dramatically if there was only one series.*

**PG:** "Well, we have a five-year plan. And our five-year plan was about building the Champ Car World Series. It was *never* based on anything else. And we're moving forward with that. We're not besieged but [we're] busy with calls about the future and we know where we're going. The three partners have worked hard to make sure we have a vision and a business plan, and it's based on the growth of the Champ Car World Series, nothing else."

*Kevin, any thoughts on that?*

**KK:** "Very much as Paul says. As a businessman, I would not have been involved in this transaction out of pure emotion. This is a logical set of decisions we made. I've done so many business plans in my life I can't even begin to count 'em. This is amongst the best that we've done; we're very confident about this and we're very confident about the business aspect of being able to put this series together and grow it as a Champ Car World Series, and the plan calls for some very detailed activity over the next five years."

*Is the acronym "CART" being dropped and, if so, what is the new official name?*

**PG:** "It is our intention to be known as the Champ Car World Series. Champ Car is a name that has a great deal of history, it means a lot, and we intend to amplify on that name."

*What is Open Wheel Racing Series going to do differently (to CART) to make sure it doesn't lose $80 million?*

**PG (chuckling):** "You know, that was a topic that certainly was discussed and analyzed in great detail. Kevin was able to bring in experts from his field that told us exactly why they lost it, how they lost it. I mean, they didn't lose it; somebody found it! And spent it. And we know now how that happened and we know from having the advantage of seeing that lesson, in black and white, how not to let it happen again."

**KK:** "We believe that we will be able to operate within the budgets that we have got in our plans, including the television, including the 'support payments' – not the team assistance, support payments for the teams. We believe that the revenues that we will be getting are pretty much nailed down and we've gone a long way toward reducing a lot of the other expenses.

"Let me just emphasize, I'm doing this as a business venture; this is not something that I set about doing lightly, nor did Paul, nor did [third OWRS principal] Jerry [Forsythe]. This is a business venture. We have analyzed this thing for several months now and we have had the ability to do so and the insight to do so in great detail. We are not exactly business fools and we intend to make sure that the series can operate – and grow – with the budgets that we have given it."

*Mr. Forsythe has been notable for his absence from many of these events – he was absent from the court and the teleconferences. Is there more to that than him trying to be the only guy with a full head of hair left at the end of the day?*

**KK:** "Jerry prefers to keep a low key when it comes to the public side of things, but be assured that he is absolutely present at all our planning meetings and has been an integral part of the

**Above:** A hugely successful Trans-Am driver and team owner, Gentilozzi has a firm vision for Champ Car racing's future.
Mike Levitt/LAT

**Below right:** Kalkhoven (right) soaks up some of the knowledge that former CART CEO Chris Pook has accumulated.

**Top right:** Bobby Rahal and Adrian Fernandez – the two most recent race winners from the ranks of owner/drivers.
Photographs: Dan Boyd/LAT

**Main photograph:** Street races, such as the Molson Indy Toronto, which draw massive crowds, are widely acknowledged as the series' strength.
Mike Levitt/LAT

whole planning process. He's left it to the bald-headed guys to go out and speak to the world!"

*How do you plan on selling this series differently on TV, as opposed to, say, your predecessors?*

**PG:** "As we've approached the topic of television, we analyzed the costs and the results of the 2003 season and we saw significant deficits in several areas. The first issue is to develop where the audience is and why they're not watching – not only Champ Car but all kinds of sports car racing and open-wheel racing around the world. There isn't the audience that there used to be. Which means they've either gone somewhere else or they've been distracted by other forms of programming. It is our firm belief that we need to be on a consistent network and we need to be on at a consistent time.

"The next thing we need to do is to focus our marketing efforts on letting fans who don't traditionally watch motorsports, or who don't traditionally watch open-wheel racing…we need to market to them what the excitement is of the program we present. And then we get to the third element, which is the program, and quite honestly, the conventional format of green-to-checker motorsports broadcasting hasn't been real interesting for people to watch, so we've looked at creative production methods, we've looked at creative production companies, and we're asking them what we can do. Let's go to successful people who make other good kinds of programming, that people are watching, and try to bring them into our genre."

*Television ratings in the U.S. are a fraction of where they were, say, ten years ago. Is there a market for this type of racing?*

**PG:** "I really think you have to take a macro view of where the television audience has been and gone over the last ten years, and what's successful and what's not. There are lots of conventional programming that have lost market share; as we've seen reality television become more of an issue, audiences have gone to that, because there is an attraction to an unrehearsed drama. Well, motorsports contains that, but very few people have been able to portray it, so we need to make partners with people who can help us portray that. I mean, what's more ultimate than a live motorsports contest at high speeds, with great danger, with conflicts between people?"

**KK:** "I think there's another point we ought to make, which is

that the audiences around the world for our racing are very, very significant and continue to grow. The surprising thing is that while we sort of think that audiences are declining, this will be the 11th year where we've got over 2 million spectators, and in many, many areas of the proposed schedule, you'll see the crowds will actually grow."

**PG:** "That's a real important point, Kevin, and we talk of just the domestic rating – we might do a 1.7 or a 1.5 or a 1.3 [million] on any given Sunday – but when we add the rest of the world in, our numbers are frequently over 7 or 8 million people that have watched an event. Now, we don't get credit for that, and when we compare it to other forms of competition, our numbers are right there, but we need to understand that we are a world event; we are more international than people give us credit for."

*Are you going to learn from the way in which NASCAR has marketed its personalities?*

**PG:** "Champ Car has not done a good job in the past about making stars of its drivers, and the way you do that is to expose them to the public.

"You know, you're gonna have guys with white hats and guys with black hats, and sometimes the villain is gonna be popular and sometimes the hero isn't gonna be as popular; but people need to know them and they need to understand their personalities, what drives them, what's interesting about them – all of the things that attract us to people. I mean, you've got great-looking young men who are out there risking their lives every week in competition, and for too long we've emphasized just what the car is and what it can do. We wanna tell you what these young men and women can do and how difficult it is to be a race driver and how difficult it is to have a career as a race driver, so we're gonna talk about all those things as you get to know them throughout the year."

**KK:** "I think, to reemphasize that point, every race is a story, and a story needs characters. A story without characters is completely irrelevant, and that's the one thing that we've got to emphasize, the story and the characters, because that's what goes to make great drama and that's what makes people want to watch the race."

*In 2003, several teams existed only as a result of handouts from CART. How are you going to get away from sponsoring teams and sponsoring events?*

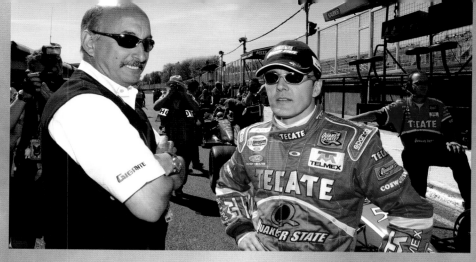

**PG:** "First of all, we made a concerted effort to reduce the costs of operating a car in the series. Agreements like we had with Cosworth and Ford. That brings the teams' engine budgets to a fixed number, approximately 20 or 25 percent of their gross operating budget – a number that is well within the norm of operations. Then we fixed the tire program. We know that the tires will cost approximately $200,000 a year. Let's assume an average budget is around $5 million, or $5.5 million. We're convinced that there are an adequate number of teams that can raise an adequate amount of financing as long as we do two things – give them proper venues to market in and control costs to operate in."

*So you don't think you're going to have to support teams this year, which was a huge chunk out of the CART budget last year?*

**PG:** "Breaking the rules of a private company, we've been honest [enough] to talk about our entrant-support prize money package – and essentially there will be a guaranteed prize money; there will not be direct team support, there will be a guaranteed prize money for participation in the entire season."

**KK:** "I also think you ought to be aware that as the economy is improving, there are new sponsors coming on board, and I think you'll see a number of new sponsors on the cars this year. So it's not all doom and gloom. You know, the economy has been through a bad cycle, it is improving, new sponsors are there, and once yesterday was out of the way, I can genuinely say that the discussions have been hot and heavy with sponsors all day long, including new ones."

*What is the status on possible European races?*

**PG:** "It's very unlikely for 2004, but for the future, we're gonna keep an eye on it. They sell a lot of cars there and a lot of our sponsors do business there."

*How are you going to look at the month of May? Are you going to try to keep things open and allow or even encourage your teams to try to participate in the Indianapolis 500?*

**PG:** "Not even a topic for us. You know, it rains in April and in May the flowers grow, so we're gonna look at each individual promoter event and take them as they come. We're not at all involved in conflicts or issues with the [Indianapolis Motor] Speedway. We're gonna race on weekends [when] it's proper for us to race."

## TIME TO MOVE ON

**V**IRTUALLY everyone within the close-knit Champ Car community had an opinion on the decision that was handed down from the court in Indianapolis on January 28. Here are a few of them:

**PAUL TRACY** (2003 Champ Car World Series Champion, Forsythe Racing): "I was very, very happy to hear the news that OWRS won the Champ Car bid. The waiting game with all the questions and speculation is finally over. I am glad to say I'll be defending my Champ Car championship and trying for another for Forsythe Racing in 2004! I am relieved to know where my future is, and that's in Champ Car!"

**BOBBY RAHAL** (Team Rahal co-owner and three-time series champion): "Over the course of my life, I have poured a lot of sweat, a lot of my soul and a great deal of my personal finances into CART. I understand, maybe better than many, due to my time as interim president and CEO of CART [in 2000], the great challenges that face OWRS and the new CART. Champ Car has had a rocky few years, but I am extremely optimistic after my discussions with OWRS that their dedication and the business plan will mean better days are ahead. The last few months have been focused on courtrooms and legal jargon and not on the beauty of our sport. I hope that this decision allows us to move beyond jockeying for position on court dockets and allows us to begin to focus on fighting for position on track."

**EMERSON FITTIPALDI** (1989 Champ Car World Series Champion): "I think it's a historical day for racing, internationally. I think it was a great win for CART, for open-wheel racing. We have one of the best products in the world – for the sponsors, for the racing fans, for the drivers, for the teams. I think we are going to give a great future to young talent, to new sponsors, and to the racing fans worldwide."

**JORGE QUINTANILLA** (director, Gigante Racing): "Grupo Gigante is very pleased with Judge Otte's resolution, as it gives Champ Car another chance to showcase the demands of this premier open-wheel racing series. We are big supporters of the versatility of the Champ Car World Series, from the unique mixture of road and street-course races and ovals to the venues in Mexico, the United States and Canada. The ruling also assures the continuation of both Mexican Grand Prix races, which allows Grupo Gigante to share with our clients and vendors two of the premier sporting events in our country."

**ADRIAN FERNANDEZ** (owner/driver, Fernandez Racing): "It's great news for Champ Car. There's a lot of people who put a lot of effort behind it, and they're being rewarded by it. It's good for a lot of people, and a lot of teams are going to be able to race, and that's important. It's been difficult for everybody just not knowing what you're going to do. That's always a difficult situation, with the sponsors, with everything. It's something that, now that it's over, it's a great relief."

# from the other side of the pond...

With new horizons, new goals and ever increasing demands on global sponsorship, the necessity is even greater to gain additional seconds of media exposure.
The machine must become a moving billboard which must sell an instant message to the consumer.

To stand still is to move backwards.
To move forward, you must recall the past building on knowledge and experience.

Hutchinson Design International Limited, recognised as the leading motor sport livery design agency has both the knowledge and experience...

For further information and CD pack, please contact Nicola Curtis:

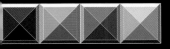

# Hutchinson
## design international limited

Telephone: +00 44(0)1634 730305
Facsimile: +00 44(0)1634 730306
ISDN: +00 44(0)1634 721544
E-mail: nicolacurtis@ianhutchinson.com

## www.ianhutchinson.com

TEAM St. GEORGE

CART: Total team image and production by Hutchinson

# TEAM-BY-TEAM REVIEW

A total of 13 different teams and 27 drivers contested the 2003 Bridgestone Presents the Champ Car World Series Powered by Ford. In the following pages, Editor Jeremy Shaw analyzes what went right – and wrong – for each organization.

# PLAYER'S/FORSYTHE RACING

**Base:** Indianapolis, Indiana

**Drivers:** Paul Tracy, Patrick Carpentier

**Sponsors:** Player's Ltd., Indeck

**Engines:** Ford Cosworth XFE

**Chassis:** Lola

**Tires:** Bridgestone Potenza

**Wins:** 8 (Tracy 7, Carpentier 1)

**Poles:** 7 (Tracy 6, Carpentier 1)

**Total points:** 372
**Tracy 226 (1st)**
**Carpentier 146 (5th)**

PAUL TRACY

PATRICK CARPENTIER

JERRY Forsythe made some fundamental changes to his team prior to the 2003 season, replacing Alex Tagliani with Paul Tracy and trading in his Reynard chassis for Lolas. The substitutions soon paid off as Tracy won the first three races in a row. Then he parried midseason challenges from Bruno Junqueira and Michel Jourdain Jr. to claim a long-overdue first Champ Car title for both driver and team owner.

Tracy himself was instrumental in the chassis switch, having benefited from a similar move in 2002 while driving for Team KOOL Green. To its credit, the Player's team quickly came to grips with the Lola package, despite having worked exclusively with Reynards for nine years. Even more impressively, Patrick Carpentier, who had never driven anything other than a Reynard in his Champ Car career, initially proved to be faster, on a fairly consistent basis, than his new teammate.

That trend continued through the first day of practice and qualifying in St. Petersburg, where Tracy was faced with the distinct handicap of losing his assigned race engineer, longtime crew member Kelly Loewen, quite literally on the eve of the race weekend. Technical Advisor Tony Cicale, who had worked previously with Tracy at TKG, stepped into the breach. The veteran's input, along with the cooperation of Carpentier and his race engineer, Michael Cannon, brought about an overnight transformation. After struggling on Friday, Tracy was right on the pace on Saturday morning. Then he qualified second and went on to win the race.

Todd Malloy, who also had worked with PT at TKG, joined the squad for the next race (after baling out on the Mi-Jack Conquest team) and immediately built an excellent rapport with Tracy and Cicale. Several times in subsequent races they adopted Carpentier's setup, and almost invariably Tracy used it to greater effect, much to Carpentier's chagrin.

This aspect of "teamwork" paid big benefits for the Neil Micklewright-headed, Phil LePan-managed operation, which enjoyed a banner year. Dave Brzozowski led the crew with his usual aplomb, and newly-promoted chief mechanics Steve Moore (Tracy) and Jason Weatherford (Carpentier) performed sterling duty on the wrenches. The result was a well-deserved maiden championship title for Player's/Forsythe Racing.

**Left: Tracy in full flight at Mid-Ohio.**
Mike Levitt/LAT

**Above: Tracy's relationship with Tony Cicale was a major key to his success.**

**Above center: The mercurial Tracy exhibited a much better focus in 2003.**
Photographs: Mike Levitt/LAT

**Right: Carpentier won at Laguna Seca while Tracy was third – the first time two Player's drivers had ever shared the podium.**
Gavin Lawrence/LAT

**Left:** Carpentier remained cool under pressure from Tracy at Laguna Seca.
Phil Abbott/LAT

**Right:** The popular Greg Moore will live forever in the Player's team's memory.

**Below left:** A proud moment – Bob Bexon and Jerry Forsythe with the magnificent Vanderbilt Cup at the awards banquet.
Photographs: Mike Levitt/LAT

## GLORY AT LAST

ALL good things come to those who wait. The old adage certainly applied to Gerald "Jerry" Forsythe, who had waited a long time for his first Champ Car title. Twenty years in fact. It was in 1983 that Forsythe first formed his own team, initially in partnership with his brother, John. The pair hired Barry Green to manage the effort, and ex-Formula 1 driver Teo Fabi caused something of a sensation as he sped to six poles and four race wins in his rookie campaign. Indeed, the diminutive Italian missed out on the overall championship by only five points to Penske Racing's Al Unser.

The Forsythes bowed out of racing at the end of a disappointing '84 season to concentrate on their business interests. Ten years later, Jerry was back in the Champ Car ranks, this time having entered into a partnership with Green and attracted major sponsorship from Player's Ltd. Actually the pair had rekindled their association in '93 in Toyota Atlantic, before graduating into the top realm of American open-wheel racing one year later with emerging star Jacques Villeneuve as their driver. Unfortunately, the marriage soon broke up. Green, Villeneuve and Player's went their own way, winning the championship in '95 and giving Villeneuve the launchpad he was looking for to move into Formula 1. Meanwhile, Forsythe had reinvented Forsythe Racing for the '95 season and once again hired Fabi, who took one pole and some respectable results en route to ninth in the championship table.

But that was merely a stopgap, since part of the separation agreement between Green and Forsythe called for the Player's sponsorship in Champ Car racing to revert to Forsythe's control in '96. And so Player's/Forsythe Racing was born as a Champ Car entity – after having dominated the previous year's PPG-Firestone Indy Lights Championship with another up-and-coming Canadian star, Greg Moore.

The youngster's precocious talent quickly came to the fore. Moore won a pair of races in his sophomore season, '97, and added two more victories in '98, by which time the team had doubled in size to accommodate the arrival of '96 Toyota Atlantic Champion Patrick Carpentier. The outlook was extremely promising; it seemed to be only a matter of time before Player's/Forsythe Racing would be celebrating title glory. But then things began to unravel. The team's Mercedes-Benz/Ilmor engines were no match for the emerging Hondas, nor the Ford Cosworths, and Moore announced halfway through the '99 season that he would be switching to Marlboro Team Penske, which had secured a supply of Honda motors, for the Y2K campaign. Tragically, of course, he lost his life in a freak crash at California Speedway in what should have been his final race in Player's colors, ensuring the bleakest day in the team's history.

Player's/Forsythe Racing regrouped over the winter, forged a new partnership with Ford Cosworth and signed up Alex Tagliani – like Carpentier, a graduate of Toyota Atlantic – to maintain its two-car quest for the title. In three seasons, Carpentier notched up three wins, and in 2002, enjoyed his best season to date in Champ Cars, finishing third in the final standings to produce Forsythe's strongest result since his rookie season as a team owner in 1983.

Then came the changes that ultimately would lead to title glory for Player's and Forsythe.

# NEWMAN/HAAS RACING

**Base: Lincolnshire, Illinois**

**Drivers: Bruno Junqueira,
Sébastien Bourdais (R)**

**Sponsors: PacifiCare, Eli Lilly,
McDonald's**

**Engines: Ford Cosworth XFE**

**Chassis: Lola**

**Tires: Bridgestone Potenza**

**Wins: 5 (Bourdais 3, Junqueira 2)**

**Poles: 7 (Bourdais 5, Junqueira 2)**

**Total points: 358
Junqueira 199 (2nd)
Bourdais 159 (4th)**

BRUNO JUNQUEIRA

SÉBASTIEN BOURDAIS

WHEN the 2003 season began in St. Petersburg, Newman/Haas Racing was hotly favored to scoop its fifth Champ Car title, and second in succession. Cristiano da Matta had elected not to defend his crown, opting instead for a golden opportunity to join the burgeoning Toyota Formula 1 operation, and as his replacement Paul Newman and Carl Haas had signed up Bruno Junqueira who, driving for Chip Ganassi, had finished as runner-up to da Matta in 2002. Christian Fittipaldi also having departed, Formula 3000 champion Sébastien Bourdais was snapped up to ensure the team's usual solid pairing. Winter testing went very well indeed. The team already had an excellent handle on its Lola chassis, and the transition to Ford Cosworth motors proved straightforward. The only surprise was that rookie Bourdais generally proved slightly quicker than Junqueira. All the signs were good.

While both drivers were new, the remainder of the team was virtually unchanged. General Manager Brian Lisles, Senior Engineer Peter Gibbons and Team Manager John "TZ" Tzouanakis had over 45 years of service with the Chicago-area team between them and knew exactly what was required to win. Kevin Chambers had been promoted to overall crew chief in the off-season, leaving Don Hoevel to oversee Junqueira's PacifiCare Lola, while Pedro Campuzano was elevated to chief mechanic status for Bourdais. "Rocky" Rocquelin, whose relationship with da Matta had played a major role in their success, settled in as Junqueira's race engineer, and Craig Hampson was quickly excited by the prospect of working with the talented Bourdais. Everything was in place.

What could go wrong? Well, not a lot, actually. At least one of the Newman/Haas drivers qualified on the front row for 13 of the 18 races – and within the top four positions on all but one occasion; the exception was at Milwaukee. They amassed seven poles and a handful of wins, taking the team's overall tallies to 77 and 74 respectively, both tops among active teams. The only issues that precluded another championship success were a propensity for driver mistakes – and the brilliance of Paul Tracy.

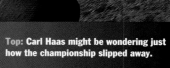

**Top:** Carl Haas might be wondering just how the championship slipped away.

**Above center:** Paul Newman remained as fervent a Champ Car supporter as ever.

**Above:** Sébastien Bourdais displayed immense promise in his rookie campaign.

**Left:** Bruno Junqueira was a hot title favorite, but didn't quite deliver the goods.
**Photographs: Gavin Lawrence/LAT**

# TEAM RAHAL

**Base:** Hilliard, Ohio

**Driver:** Michel Jourdain Jr.

**Sponsors:** Gigante, Office Depot

**Engines:** Ford Cosworth XFE

**Chassis:** Lola

**Tires:** Bridgestone Potenza

**Wins:** 2

**Poles:** 1

**Total points:** 195 (3rd)

MICHEL JOURDAIN Jr.

**A** SPONSORSHIP shortfall led Bobby Rahal to downsize his Champ Car operation to a singleton entry, but that certainly had no adverse effect on Michel Jourdain Jr. The affable Mexican had learned a massive amount while working alongside Jimmy Vasser in 2002, including the fact that he could mix it with the front-runners. He did precisely that in '03, albeit on a more regular basis, and emerged as a legitimate championship contender.

Stability within the Ohio organization undoubtedly helped his cause. Chief Operating Officer Scott Roembke continued to run a tight ship on Rahal's behalf, while longtime employee Ray Leto was entrusted with overall responsibility for the Champ Car program. Todd Bowland, who had worked with Vasser in '02, took charge of race engineering duties, with Tim Reiter overseeing all technical matters. Bharat Naran started the year as chief mechanic, before electing to remain in Southern California following the Long Beach race, whereupon Greg Cates stepped neatly into the breach.

Preparation was exemplary. Jourdain completed more laps and miles than anyone else (for the second straight year) and failed to see the checkered flag only twice – at Long Beach, where his gearbox broke during his final pit stop, and at Road America, where he spun off in the rain. Aside from that, he completed all except one lap in the remaining 16 races – a remarkable achievement.

Many tears were shed following the late failure at Long Beach, where Jourdain was in control of the race and seemed set to score his very first win. To everyone's credit, he was able to bounce back quickly from that bitter disappointment. He ran strongly in Germany, despite an early penalty for a pit-lane infraction, then dominated the proceedings in Milwaukee. Victory at last! He won only once more, in Montreal, but would have been in a position to do so at Laguna Seca, had not his car been found to be marginally under the weight limit after he had posted the fastest time in qualifying. It was a rare blemish on an otherwise excellent campaign, which saw Jourdain finish a strong third in the championship. Indeed, he was looking at a real chance of besting Bruno Junqueira for second before the anticipated California Speedway finale was canceled as a result of nearby massive wildfires.

**Top:** Bobby Rahal was very impressed by Michel Jourdain Jr.'s progress in 2003.
Mike Levitt/LAT

**Above:** The Gigante Lola was a bona fide championship challenger for the first time.
Phil Abbott/LAT

**Left:** Team Rahal's pit work was top notch.

**Below:** Jourdain established an excellent rapport with race engineer Todd Bowland.
Photographs: Gavin Lawrence/LAT

# HERDEZ COMPETITION

**Base:** Indianapolis, Indiana

**Drivers:** Mario Dominguez, Roberto Moreno, Roberto Gonzalez (R)

**Sponsor:** Grupo Herdez

**Engines:** Ford Cosworth XFE

**Chassis:** Lola

**Tires:** Bridgestone Potenza

**Wins:** 1 (Dominguez)

**Poles:** 0

**Total points:** 188
Dominguez 118 (6th)
Moreno 67 (13th)
Gonzalez 3 (24th)

ROBERTO MORENO

ROBERTO GONZALEZ

MARIO DOMINGUEZ

IN most respects, 2003 was a breakthrough year for the Mexican-financed Herdez Competition team. True, it had claimed a maiden victory in 2002, when Mario Dominguez scored in a chaotic, rain-marred event in Surfers Paradise, but that result was due to good fortune and timing rather than pace.

Managing Director Keith Wiggins, acting on behalf of enthusiastic owners Enrique and Hector Hernandez-Pons Torres, expended a great deal of time and energy during the off-season in extending his squad to field a second full-time entry – for indefatigable veteran Roberto Moreno. Appropriately, Wiggins was able to keep his core nucleus of people intact. Many of them, including Chief Engineer Tom Brown and Team Manager Vince Kremer, had been with the organization since the Bettenhausen days. New Zealander Daryl Fox remained in charge of Dominguez's #55 car, while English-born Mark Mason looked after the #4 Lola of Moreno. Race engineering duties were shared by Brian Ma, who quickly developed an excellent rapport with Dominguez, and Englishman Chris Gorne (Moreno).

Surprisingly, there were very few hiccups associated with the expansion. Quite the contrary. Moreno's vast experience proved beneficial in several key areas, most notably in evaluating different technical configurations, be they aerodynamic or mechanical, and assisting in Dominguez's development as a driver. Certainly, Moreno's influence and attention to detail rubbed off on the youngster, whose confidence was boosted enormously as he learned that his technical feedback mirrored the feelings experienced by his new mentor. The result was the emergence of Dominguez as a bona fide challenger.

Moreno's contribution to the team, therefore, was immense, although sadly he didn't produce the expected results. He outqualified Dominguez only seven times in 17 races (Moreno was replaced by rookie Roberto Gonzalez for a one-off appearance in Mexico City) and secured just two top-five finishes. Happily, he was able to share in the team's glory at Miami, where he shadowed Dominguez to the checkered flag in a glorious 1-2 punch.

**Above:** Moreno played a prominent role in the team's rise to prominence in 2003.
Phil Abbott/LAT

**Left:** Keith Wiggins used his wealth of experience in the sport to excellent effec
Gavin Lawrence/LAT

**Below:** Enrique Hernandez-Pons Torres stepped up to support a two-car challenge
Dan Boyd/LAT

**Far left:** Dominguez improved immensely..
Gavin Lawrence/LAT

**Below:** ...in part due to the relationship h established with race engineer Brian Ma.
Mike Levitt/LAT

# AMERICAN SPIRIT TEAM JOHANSSON

**Base:** Indianapolis, Indiana

**Drivers:** Jimmy Vasser, Ryan Hunter-Reay (R)

**Sponsor:** Merlins Energy Source

**Engines:** Ford Cosworth XFE

**Chassis:** Reynard

**Tires:** Bridgestone Potenza

**Wins:** 1 (Hunter-Reay)

**Poles:** 0

**Total points:** 136
**Vasser 72 (11th)**
**Hunter-Reay 64 (14th)**

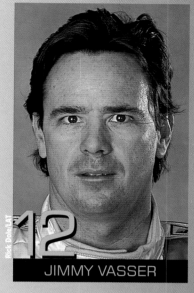

JIMMY VASSER

RYAN HUNTER-REAY

**A**MERICAN Spirit Team Johansson officially came into being on January 2, so had a mere seven weeks to get ready for the first race. Everyone realized it was a monumental task. Yet not only was ASTJ present and correct with two cars in St. Petersburg, it had even managed to attend the traditional Spring Training test session, which had taken place at Sebring a couple of weeks earlier.

"When you consider where we were even one week ago, it's an incredible effort for the entire team," said team principal Stefan Johansson at the time. "It embodies the meaning of the term 'team effort.'"

Not surprisingly, there were a few glitches as the year progressed, and various shufflings among team personnel. Rob Hill, who had enjoyed much success with Target/Chip Ganassi Racing, including four consecutive Champ Car titles (1996–99), played an important role in getting the ball rolling. Eventually, he ceded the team manager's position to ex-Arrows Formula 1 Chief Engineer Graham Taylor, who had started out as race engineer on Ryan Hunter-Reay's car, leaving Hill to concentrate on his specialty – overseeing the crew. A variety of chief mechanics and race engineers came and went, but Ed Nathman was a constant on the technical team, and his wealth of experience, most recently with Patrick Racing (where he had worked with Jimmy Vasser in 2001), certainly paid dividends. Later, he was joined by another ex-F1 man, David Brown, who made rapid progress in what, for him, was a totally new environment.

The pairing of Hunter-Reay and Vasser, the 1996 CART champion, represented a smart choice. The latter's experience and the former's youthful exuberance proved a fruitful combination. The late start meant that Reynard chassis provided the only real option, and perhaps this handicapped the team's progress. Then again, both drivers shone from time to time, and the season culminated in a sensational, if somewhat fortunate, victory for Hunter-Reay at Surfers Paradise. It was no more than he or the team deserved.

**Top:** Stefan Johansson faced a tough task after his plans reached fruition so late in the day.
Mike Levitt/LAT

**Top center right:** Graham Taylor, Ryan Hunter-Reay and David Brown confer.
Gavin Lawrence/LAT

**Center right:** Vasser's best result, a third, came in the final race at Surfers Paradise.
Phil Abbott/LAT

**Above:** Vasser and race engineer Nathman.

**Left:** An impressive rookie year for RH-R.
Photographs: Gavin Lawrence/LAT

# WALKER RACING

**Base: Indianapolis, Indiana**

**Drivers: Darren Manning (R), Rodolfo Lavin (R), Luis Diaz (R)**

**Sponsors: RAC/Autowindscreens, Sportsbook.com, Corona**

**Engines: Ford Cosworth XFE**

**Chassis: Reynard**

**Tires: Bridgestone Potenza**

**Wins: 0**

**Poles: 0**

**Total points: 120**
**Manning 103 (9th)**
**Lavin 17 (18th)**

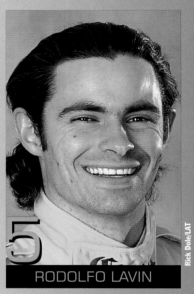
5 RODOLFO LAVIN
Rick Dole/LAT

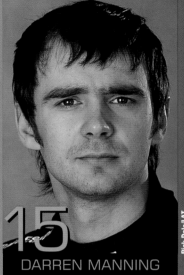
15 DARREN MANNING
Rick Dole/LAT

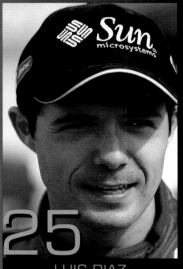
25 LUIS DIAZ
Gavin Lawrence/LAT

AFTER three years of being obliged by his Honda and Toyota paymasters to run Japanese drivers, Derrick Walker relished the opportunity of working with at least one native English speaker. Briton Darren Manning fit the bill. Walker also secured a deal to run Mexico's Rodolfo Lavin, who had spent seven years in the CART Ladder System, competing in Indy Lights and Toyota Atlantic.

Team Manager (and accomplished engineer) Rob Edwards remained the lynchpin of Walker's efforts, and while the organization had lost some longtime staff members over the winter, before Manning's program was finalized, there were plenty of talented individuals on hand to fill their shoes. Mike Wright, who had spent much of 2002 developing the Reynard chassis (for which Walker had acquired the rights), was assigned as Manning's race engineer, while fellow veteran Al Bodey worked with Lavin. Larry Ellert, ex-Team Rahal, was due to be chief mechanic for the Englishman, but quit just before the first race. Quietly spoken Neil Brown, who had been expecting to remain at the shop, was persuaded to take over the traveling duties, while veteran Les Channen looked after Lavin's Corona-liveried car.

The team did an excellent job, the talented Manning predictably scoring the lion's share of the results. The frailty of the Reynard gearbox came to the fore a few times, but generally the cars ran extremely well, as evidenced by Manning's feat of scoring points in every race bar two.

Lavin, frankly, was always likely to struggle at this level, although he did enjoy a few moments in the sun. He was impressive at EuroSpeedway, running in tandem with Manning until losing ground when he was clobbered by Michel Jourdain Jr. during an early pit stop. He also lost time later with a refueling glitch. Even so, he bounced back to score his first championship points by placing ninth. Subsequently, he took advantage of high attrition to finish eighth in both Vancouver and Surfers Paradise.

**Left:** Derrick Walker enjoyed his best year since running Gil de Ferran in the late-'90s.

**Below:** Manning was a force on several occasions, including the German 500.

**Below left:** Two Englishmen together – Manning and race engineer Mike Wright.
Photographs: Gavin Lawrence/LAT

**Left:** Diaz impressed again in Mexico, but for the second straight year hit misfortune.

**Far left:** Rodolfo Lavin always gave his best in the distinctive Corona-liveried car.
Photographs: Gavin Lawrence/LAT

# PATRICK RACING

**Base:** Indianapolis, Indiana

**Driver:** Oriol Servia

**Sponsors:** Visteon, Infineon Technologies

**Engines:** Ford Cosworth XFE

**Chassis:** Lola

**Tires:** Bridgestone Potenza

**Wins:** 0

**Poles:** 0

**Total points:** 108 (7th)

ORIOL SERVIA

WITH just a modicum of good fortune, Champ Car racing's oldest-established team would have made a welcome return to Victory Circle in 2003. As it was, veteran owner U.E. "Pat" Patrick and his equally accomplished general manager, Jim McGee, had to be content with several near misses and a brace of second-place finishes.

The team remained largely unchanged following a disappointing '02 campaign. Steve Krisiloff stayed on as operations manager and Oriol Servia retained his job as driver of the #20 Visteon car, while Don Oldenburg stepped up to the chief-mechanic role following the departure of Mark Shambarger.

New for '03, however, were a pair of Lolas in place of the unloved Reynards, and Director of Engineering Steve Challis. They came from Team KOOL Green and proved to be valuable additions. Challis, who had played an important role in developing Greg Moore's talents in the early stages of the sadly missed Canadian's career, had worked on the same cars in '02, when they were driven by Paul Tracy. Therefore he had an excellent grasp of what was required to ensure their competitiveness. He was pivotal in effecting a smooth transition for the team, and Servia responded by posting some good times in preseason testing and carrying forward that promise into the early races.

Servia was one of the more consistent performers, especially in qualifying. Only once, in Mexico City, was he not a force to be reckoned with. Furthermore, the team was as well-prepared as usual, and its pit stops were always among the best. The only thing missing was the odd slice of good fortune. Servia came in for some internal criticism for a lack of aggression, but perhaps that was understandable after he garnered a mere two points from the opening three races. It was typical of his luck when he found himself in the wrong place at the wrong time at Surfers Paradise and was inadvertently punted into the wall at the first corner by Adrian Fernandez, who had been distracted by an incident just ahead between Paul Tracy and Bruno Junqueira.

**Top left:** One of CART's founding fathers, Pat Patrick emerged winless from '03.
Mike Levitt/LAT

**Above:** Oriol Servia came close to victory on several occasions, but just missed out.
Gavin Lawrence/LAT

**Left:** Jim McGee has seen it all, done it all during 40 years in Champ Car racing.
Phil Abbott/LAT

**Below:** A quick tweak to the suspension settings on Servia's Lola at Brands Hatch.
Mike Levitt/LAT

# FERNANDEZ RACING

**Base:** Indianapolis, Indiana

**Driver:** Adrian Fernandez

**Sponsors:** Tecate, Quaker State, Telmex

**Engines:** Ford Cosworth XFE

**Chassis:** Lola

**Tires:** Bridgestone Potenza

**Wins:** 1

**Poles:** 1

**Total points:** 105 (8th)

ADRIAN FERNANDEZ

Mike Levitt/LAT

I T is often said in auto racing circles that it takes three years to build a successful team. Well, in 2003, three years after its formation, Fernandez Racing finally achieved its first victory when owner/driver Adrian Fernandez triumphed at Portland in memorable style. It was a proud moment for Fernandez and his partner, Tom Anderson, who previously had guided Target/Chip Ganassi Racing to a record four consecutive Champ Car titles in the 1990s.

"The emotion is extremely high as everyone would expect," said Anderson, who concentrated his efforts in '03 on the team's parallel Indy Racing League program and, coincidentally, was making a rare appearance at a Champ Car race. "We delivered what we promised [sponsors Tecate, Quaker State and Telmex] at our first meeting back in Mexico City in November of 2000. We talked about winning then and we finally backed it up."

In the past, several organizations have foundered in attempting to contest more than one top-level series, but Fernandez Racing didn't seem to have any real difficulty. While Anderson led the fledgling IRL operation, Gustavo del Campo took charge of the Champ Car effort and headed a tight ship. Veteran Mike Sales, unflappable as ever, took charge of the crew and once again was content to leave the pit-stop duties to his younger teammates.

Ever since the team's formation, however, engineering has been perceived, rightly or wrongly, as the weakest link. There was more shuffling in '03. David Watson started out in charge and seemed to be doing just fine, as Fernandez qualified among the top seven in seven of the first eight races. The lone exception was EuroSpeedway Lausitz, where a high-downforce setup proved embarrassing, and Fernandez languished at the back of the pack all weekend. He was not happy. Watson eventually parted company with the team in August, whereupon Chris Finch, who had been with Fernandez since the outset as a junior engineer, was promoted to the lead role. The switch didn't seem to have much effect, as Fernandez still struggled to find consistency. He looked especially strong at the street races, however, and was unfortunate not to win again at Miami.

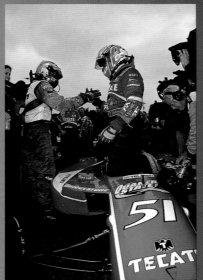

**Above:** Fernandez Racing is one of the best-organized crews in the business.
Dan Boyd/LAT

**Left:** Tracy is the first to congratulate Fernandez on his memorable Portland win.

**Below left:** Tom Anderson has come a long way since starting as a mechanic.
Photographs: Mike Levitt/LAT

**Below:** Fernandez pushes his Lola to the limit during the Molson Indy Montreal.
Gavin Lawrence/LAT

# ROCKETSPORTS RACING

**Base: East Lansing, Michigan**

**Driver: Alex Tagliani**

**Sponsor: Johnson Controls, Microchip, Futaba, Saputo**

**Engines: Ford Cosworth XFE**

**Chassis: Lola**

**Tires: Bridgestone Potenza**

**Wins: 0**

**Poles: 2**

**Total points: 97 (10th)**

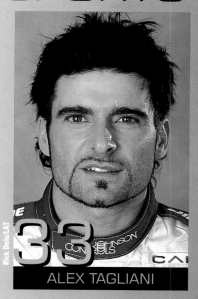

ALEX TAGLIANI

**T**HREE-TIME Trans-Am champion Paul Gentilozzi examined a variety of options while seeking to expand the horizons of his successful Rocketsports Racing team. He announced plans to enter the Champ Car ranks at the Mexico City race in 2002, and three months later was on the grid at St. Petersburg for the '03 season-opener. Six months later again, Gentilozzi had emerged not only as a serious player in the Champ Car ranks, but also as one of the series' potential saviors (along with PK Racing principal Kevin Kalkhoven).

Needless to say, Gentilozzi, who also had taken over promotion of the venerable Trans-Am brand, had plenty on his plate. That didn't have any adverse effect on his newest challenge, however, since he had hired experienced team manager Phil Howard to get the ball rolling and take on the day-to-day responsibilities. Howard, who had performed a similar task with the short-lived Sigma Autosport team in 2001–02, used his practical skills to good effect. He encountered all the usual headaches associated with a startup operation – like attracting a well-qualified crew (especially to a location away from Indianapolis), then finding all the necessary equipment and achieving everything in the proper time frame. But Rocketsports made it to the first major preseason test at Laguna Seca, just, and Alex Tagliani was very soon posting competitive times.

Another no-nonsense veteran, Tom Howatt, was a good choice as chief mechanic, while race engineer Andy Borme, who had left Marlboro Team Penske after a fruitful relationship with two-time Indy 500 winner Helio Castroneves, settled in right away and established a rapport with Tagliani. The combination was strong enough to secure a podium finish at Monterrey in only their second race. Impressive. Unfortunately, Borme decided he wanted to be based closer to his family in Indianapolis, so quit abruptly. Howard brought in two more experienced engineers to fill the gap, and the combined qualities of Will Phillips and Adam Schaechter ensured there was barely any disruption. The team had good days and bad days, which was no surprise for a rookie organization, but generally created a very good impression and will be expected to build on its successes in '04.

**Above: Tagliani has a distinctive helmet.**
Gavin Lawrence/LAT

**Top right: Paul Gentilozzi and Phil Howard (right) on the "war wagon."**
Mike Levitt/LAT

**Center right: Tags in action at Monterrey.**
Gavin Lawrence/LAT

**Right: The Ford Cosworth XFE engine is fired up, ready for practice at Mid-Ohio.**
Mike Levitt/LAT

# MI-JACK CONQUEST RACING

**Base:** Indianapolis, Indiana

**Driver:** Mario Haberfeld (R)

**Sponsors:** Mi-Jack

**Engines:** Ford Cosworth XFE

**Chassis:** Reynard

**Tires:** Bridgestone Potenza

**Wins:** 0

**Poles:** 0

**Total points:** 71 (12th)

MARIO HABERFELD

A ROAD racer at heart (and an accomplished one at that, having won the 1991 Firestone Indy Lights Championship), Eric Bachelart faced a dilemma at the end of the 2002 season. His Mi-Jack Conquest Racing team had just clinched Rookie of the Year honors in the Indy Racing League, but spiraling costs and the lack of vital manufacturer support left him little chance to progress in the all-oval series. So after exploring various possibilities, Bachelart and enthusiastic team co-owner (and Mi-Jack principal) Mike Lanigan realized their best option lay in Champ Cars.

The procurement of four Reynard chassis (two each from Team KOOL Green and Player's) provided the basis for the switch, along with support from Brazilian ex-Formula 3000 contender Mario Haberfeld and, later, an agreement to oversee an additional entry for Fittipaldi-Dingman Racing. Englishman Chris Mower joined the operation as team manager after selling his interest in the former Formula 3000 championship-winning Nordic Racing team, while equally highly respected Crew Chief Tim Broyles moved over from Walker Racing.

The only problem area, at least to begin with, was the engineering department. Another Briton, Andy Miller, who had developed a good rapport with Haberfeld in winning the 1998 British Formula 3 Championship with Paul Stewart Racing, initially took the role of race engineer, but was replaced before the first race by Todd Malloy, formerly with Team KOOL Green. Malloy, though, baled out when the Player's team came knocking, whereupon veteran John Ward filled in for a while before Andy Borme (ex-Penske Racing) jumped ship from Rocketsports as he sought employment closer to his Indianapolis home. Haberfeld and Borme formed a fruitful relationship, which, allied to excellent reliability (only twice in 18 races did Haberfeld not reach the finish line), resulted in a tally of 11 top-ten finishes. Ironically, the rookie's best result came in the very first race, when he attracted the ire of Bruno Junqueira with a very bold early move, but he showed well on several other occasions too, most notably at Denver, where he posted the fastest time in both practice and the race.

**Top: Eric Bachelart built a strong team.**
Mike Levitt/LAT

**Above: Bachelart and crew chief Tim Broyles listen in as Haberfeld explains a problem to race engineer Andy Borme.**
Dan Boyd/LAT

**Left: The Mi-Jack car receives attention in the narrow pit lane at Long Beach.**
Lesley Ann Miller/LAT

**Below: Cresting the rise at Laguna Seca.**
Gavin Lawrence/LAT

# PK RACING

**Base:** Indianapolis, Indiana

**Drivers:** Patrick Lemarie (R), Bryan Herta, Max Papis, Mika Salo (R)

**Sponsors:** Scientific Atlanta, Optium

**Engines:** Ford Cosworth XFE

**Chassis:** Lola

**Tires:** Bridgestone Potenza

**Wins:** 0

**Poles:** 0

**Total points: 61**
**Salo 26 (16th)**
**Papis 25 (17th)**
**Lemarie 8 (21st)**
**Herta 2 (25th)**

PATRICK LEMARIE

MAX PAPIS

BRYAN HERTA

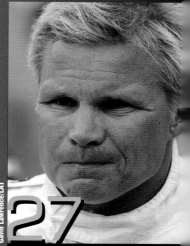

MIKA SALO

IF anyone needed confirmation that there is no guaranteed success in auto racing, PKR provided a perfect illustration. On paper, the team seemed to have everything. Physical education teacher-turned-racing manager Craig Pollock and massively accomplished businessman Kevin Kalkhoven combined forces with Russell Cameron, who had held on to many of the assets of the former PacWest/PWR organization, to create what was effectively a turnkey operation. The team had a solid budget – not extravagant, but certainly enough to do the job – and proven '02 Lola chassis, which had been raced only three times (before Bruce McCaw pulled the plug on PWR). In addition to Cameron, who remained as team manager, most of the crew were Champ Car veterans, including Chief Mechanic Chris Schofield, formerly with Team Player's.

The only surprises were the choice of rookie driver Patrick Lemarie and race engineer James Robinson, who had a wealth of Formula 1 experience, but none whatsoever in Champ Cars. Neither lasted long. Lemarie (who had spent several years as a test driver for the BAR F1 team and got the PKR ride on the basis of his longtime friendship with BAR founder Pollock and Jacques Villeneuve) struggled through the first few races, and then, just as there were signs of improvement – he ran well at EuroSpeedway before being eliminated in a pit-lane accident, then was taken out on the first lap at Milwaukee – he was given the boot. Deserving American Bryan Herta was invited to fill in for merely one race at Laguna Seca before Max Papis was installed in the #27 Lola. The Italian posted a few respectable results, including a fourth at Elkhart Lake, but never qualified better than 15th and he, too, was released from his contract in favor of another F1 veteran, Mika Salo.

Not surprisingly, perhaps, the Finn fared little better than his predecessors, although he did begin to build a rapport with the team in the final few races, which yielded a couple of top-five finishes. Tellingly, PKR's best grid position all year was a measly tenth, achieved on only two occasions – by Lemarie at Lausitz and Salo at Surfers. Verdict: Could do better.

**Top left:** Craig Pollock split his time between Formula 1 and Champ Car.
Gavin Lawrence/LAT

**Above center left:** Kevin Kalkhoven certainly made his mark during 2003.

**Above:** Veteran engineer John Ward brought a wealth of knowledge to PKR.
Photographs: Mike Levitt/LAT

**Left:** Ex-F1 racer Mika Salo soon made his presence felt in the Champ Car ranks.
Gavin Lawrence/LAT

# FITTIPALDI-DINGMAN RACING

**Base:** Indianapolis, Indiana

**Driver:** Tiago Monteiro (R)

**Sponsors:** O₂ Diesel

**Engines:** Ford Cosworth XFE

**Chassis:** Reynard

**Tires:** Bridgestone Potenza

**Wins:** 0

**Poles:** 0

**Total points:** 29 (15th)

Mike Levitt/LAT

TIAGO MONTEIRO

**E**MERSON Fittipaldi has been involved in a variety of business ventures during his long and illustrious career, but since his enforced retirement from the cockpit following an accident at Michigan in 1996, he has never strayed far from Champ Car racing. The charismatic Brazilian frequently intimated there was a possibility that he might return as a team owner, and in 2003 he did just that. Fittipaldi joined forces with a young New York-based businessman, James Dingman, and concluded an arrangement to run alongside Eric Bachelart's Mi-Jack Conquest Racing team.

The alliance made sense. For starters, the Fittipaldi-Dingman partnership was finalized extremely late in the off-season. Bachelart, meanwhile, already had ample shop space, several Reynard chassis and most of the personnel in place to run a second car alongside Mario Haberfeld.

Chris Mower, who had run the Formula 3000 championship-winning Nordic team prior to joining Bachelart, did an excellent job of managing both Conquest and FDR teams. Rich Howard, formerly with Walker Racing, was installed as crew chief, while Don Bricker, who had cut his teeth with Tasman Motorsports/Forsythe Championship Racing in Indy Lights, was given the opportunity to become a fully fledged race engineer for the first time. The new team's driver, Tiago Monteiro, joined so late that there was time only for a brief shakedown test at Road Atlanta en route to the first race in St. Petersburg, so it was to everyone's enormous credit that the amiable Portuguese did a very respectable job to lead a few laps and finish seventh on his debut.

Sadly, that was to remain Monteiro's best result until the penultimate race in Mexico City, where he stunned everyone by starting on the front row after posting the fastest time in Saturday qualifying. Eventually, he slipped to sixth, but it was still a fine effort for a man who had been involved in far too many incidents in the middle of what turned out to be a character-building first season for both driver and team.

**Top:** Tiago Monteiro's crew goes to work under the lights in Milwaukee.
Dan Boyd/LAT

**Above center:** Monteiro and race engineer Don Bricker confer at Long Beach.
Lesley Ann Miller/LAT

**Above:** Emerson Fittipaldi remained as enthusiastic about the series as ever.
Gavin Lawrence/LAT

**Left:** Monteiro struggled for consistency, but showed occasional flashes of form.
Phil Abbott/LAT

# DALE COYNE RACING

JOEL CAMATHIAS

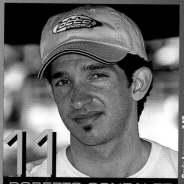
ROBERTO GONZALEZ

ALEX YOONG

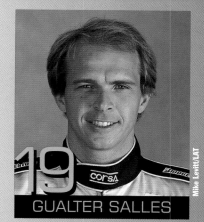
GUALTER SALLES

GEOFF BOSS

ALEX SPERAFICO

**Base:** Plainfield, Illinois

**Drivers:** Joel Camathias (R), Roberto Gonzalez (R), Alex Yoong (R), Gualter Salles, Geoff Boss (R), Alex Sperafico (R)

**Sponsors:** Alpina, Golden Cross, Cross Pens, Lacoste

**Engines:** Ford Cosworth XFE

**Chassis:** Lola

**Tires:** Bridgestone Potenza

**Wins:** 0

**Poles:** 0

**Total points: 29**
Salles 11 (19th)
Boss 8 (20th)
Camathias 6 (22nd)
Yoong 4 (23rd)

C HAMP Car stalwart Dale Coyne made a welcome return to the ranks on a full-time basis after sitting out most of the 2002 season due to a lack of funding. Once again, it remained very much a hand-to-mouth operation, although there were some promising signs early on when well-respected team manager/crew chief/engineer/former F3000 and sports car team owner John Bright joined the team to help with management duties, and experienced Chief Mechanic Eric Haverson was also enlisted. Sadly, neither stayed long.

The team's finances, as ever, remained extremely tight. Mexican Roberto Gonzalez concluded a late deal and contested the first race in Monterrey, but was quickly ousted when the promised sponsorship failed to materialize. Ex-Minardi Formula 1 driver Alex Yoong took over the ride for the next four races and showed some real glimpses of promise before the Malaysian's money also evaporated. Hugely tall and personable Swiss Joel Camathias lasted through six races before meeting the same fate. He, too, showed more speed than had been expected, most notably in Milwaukee, where he ran ahead of the likes of Sébastien Bourdais early on, and in his final outing at Mazda Raceway Laguna Seca, where he posted a very respectable seventh-fastest lap.

The balance of the season at least brought a degree of stability, as veteran Gualter Salles found some support from Brazil to rejoin the series after a two-year absence, and experienced Barber Dodge and Indy Lights racer Geoff Boss stepped up into the Champ Cars after a similarly lengthy hiatus. Results were still hard to come by, although Salles drove well at Surfers Paradise in treacherous conditions and was rewarded with a career-best sixth-place finish (the best for Coyne since Roberto Moreno took a fine third at Michigan in 1996).

Boss, who had last raced regularly in 2000, claimed a pair of top-tens – his reward for persistency rather than pace. Barber Dodge grad Alex Sperafico also ran a couple of races when Salles was absent due to prior commitments with his own stock car team in Brazil.

**Top left:** Dale Coyne made a welcome return to the Champ Car World Series.

**Left:** Rookie Geoff Boss discusses fine details with engineer David Morgan.
Photographs: Mike Levitt/LAT

**Above:** Gualter Salles split his time between the U.S. and Brazil in 2003.

**Left:** Geoff Boss struggled to rebuild his confidence after a lengthy hiatus.
Photographs: Mike Levitt/LAT

# FACTS & FIGURES

| Position | Driver | Car | Tires | St. Petersburg | Monterrey | Long Beach | Brands Hatch | Lausitz | Milwaukee | Laguna Seca | Portland | Cleveland | Toronto | Vancouver | Road America | Mid-Ohio | Montreal | Denver | Miami | Mexico City | Surfers Paradise | Points total |
|---|---|---|---|---|---|---|---|---|---|---|---|---|---|---|---|---|---|---|---|---|---|---|
| 1 | Paul Tracy (CDN) | Forsythe Racing Player's/Indeck Ford Cosworth/Lola B02/00 | BS | 1† | 1† | 1 | 17p | 12 | 12 | 3 | 2p† | 2† | 1p† | 1p† | 15 | 1p† | 6 | 4 | 16 | – | – | 226 |
| | | Forsythe Racing Indeck Ford Cosworth/Lola B02/00 | BS | – | – | – | – | – | – | – | – | – | – | – | – | – | – | – | – | 1p† | 13 | |
| 2 | Bruno Junqueira (BR) | Newman/Haas Racing PacifiCare Ford Cosworth/Lola B02/00 | BS | 3 | 5 | 3 | 2 | 4 | 17 | 2 | 4 | 3 | 3 | 2 | 1p† | 13 | 13 | 1p† | 9 | 7 | 15† | 199 |
| 3 | Michel Jourdain Jr. (MEX) | Team Rahal Gigante Ford Cosworth/Lola B01/00 | BS | 2 | 15p† | 6 | 3 | 1† | 4 | 12† | 7 | 2 | 4 | 16 | 4 | 1 | 6 | 7 | 4 | 4 | 4 | 195 |
| 4 | *Sébastien Bourdais (F) | Newman/Haas Racing Lilly Ford Cosworth/Lola B02/00 | BS | 11p | – | – | – | 1p† | – | – | – | – | – | – | – | – | – | – | – | – | – | 159 |
| | | Newman/Haas Racing Lilly Ford Cosworth/Lola B01/00 | BS | – | 17p | 16 | 1† | – | 9 | – | – | – | – | – | – | 5 | 19 | – | – | – | – | |
| | | Newman/Haas Racing Lilly Ford Cosworth/Lola B2K/00 | BS | – | – | – | – | – | – | 17 | 14 | – | 3 | 2 | – | – | – | 2 | – | – | – | |
| | | Newman/Haas Racing McDonald's/Lilly Ford Cosworth/Lola B01/00 | BS | – | – | – | – | – | – | – | – | 1p | 4 | – | – | – | – | – | – | – | – | |
| | | Newman/Haas Racing McDonald's/Lilly Ford Cosworth/Lola B2K/00 | BS | – | – | – | – | – | – | – | – | – | – | – | – | – | – | – | 17 | – | – | |
| | | Newman/Haas Racing Cialis/Lilly Ford Cosworth/Lola B2K/00 | BS | – | – | – | – | – | – | – | – | – | – | – | – | – | – | – | – | 2 | 17p | |
| 5 | Patrick Carpentier (CDN) | Forsythe Racing Player's/Indeck Ford Cosworth/Lola B02/00 | BS | 8 | 8 | 6 | 5 | 7 | – | – | 16 | – | – | 5 | – | 3 | 17 | – | – | – | – | 146 |
| | | Forsythe Racing Player's/Indeck Ford Cosworth/Lola B03/00 | BS | – | – | – | – | – | 3 | 1p† | – | 4 | 7 | 13 | – | 2 | – | – | 6 | – | – | |
| | | Forsythe Racing Indeck Ford Cosworth/Lola B03/00 | BS | – | – | – | – | – | – | – | – | – | – | – | – | – | – | – | – | 14 | – | |
| | | Forsythe Racing Indeck Ford Cosworth/Lola B02/00 | BS | – | – | – | – | – | – | – | – | – | – | – | – | – | – | – | – | – | 5 | |
| 6 | Mario Dominguez (MEX) | Herdez Competition Ford Cosworth/Lola B02/00 | BS | 14 | – | – | – | – | – | – | – | – | – | – | – | – | – | – | – | – | – | 118 |
| | | Herdez Competition Ford Cosworth/Lola B03/00 | BS | – | 13 | 5 | 3 | 2 | 8 | 10 | 10 | 5 | 12 | 10 | 14 | 16 | 5 | 7 | 1 | 3 | 10 | |
| 7 | Oriol Servia (E) | Patrick Racing Visteon Ford Cosworth/Lola B02/00 | BS | 12 | 18 | 12 | 4 | 5 | 2 | 6 | 5 | 6 | 5 | 16 | 18 | 18 | 2 | 3 | 19 | 13 | 19 | 108 |
| 8 | Adrian Fernandez (MEX) | Fernandez Tecate/Quaker State/Telmex Ford Cosworth/Lola B02/00 | BS | 15 | 4 | 2 | 12 | 15 | 6 | 7 | 1 | 11 | 9 | 12 | 12 | 7 | 8 | 5 | 8p† | 8 | 12 | 105 |
| 9 | *Darren Manning (GB) | Walker Racing RAC/Autowindscreens Ford Cosworth/Reynard 02I | BS | 13 | 7 | 8 | 10 | 6 | 4 | 18 | 6 | 10 | 8 | 5 | 6 | 8 | 10 | 8 | – | – | – | 103 |
| | | Walker Racing RAC/Sportsbook.com Ford Cosworth/Reynard 02I | BS | – | – | – | – | – | – | – | – | – | – | – | – | – | – | – | 11 | 9 | 2 | |
| 10 | Alex Tagliani (CDN) | Rocketsports Racing Johnson Controls Ford Cosworth/Lola B01/00 | BS | 19 | 3 | 10 | – | – | – | – | – | – | – | – | – | – | – | – | – | – | – | 97 |
| | | Rocketsports Racing Johnson Controls Ford Cosworth/Lola B02/00 | BS | – | – | – | 8 | 18 | 5p | 14 | 3 | 8 | 17 | 14 | 3 | 6 | 4p† | 9 | 13 | 16 | 7 | |
| 11 | Jimmy Vasser (USA) | American Spirit Team Johansson Ford Cosworth/Reynard 01I | BS | 6 | 14 | – | – | – | – | – | – | – | – | – | – | – | 16 | 11 | 4 | 17 | 3 | 72 |
| | | American Spirit Team Johansson Ford Cosworth/Reynard 2KI | BS | – | – | 4 | 19 | 8 | 11 | 8 | 7 | – | 13 | 11 | 9 | 15 | – | – | – | – | – | |
| | | American Spirit Team Johansson Ford Cosworth/Reynard 02I | BS | – | – | – | – | – | – | 13 | – | – | – | – | – | – | – | – | – | – | – | |
| 12 | *Mario Haberfeld (BR) | Mi-Jack Conquest Racing Ford Cosworth/Reynard 02I | BS | 4 | 16 | 9 | 9 | – | – | 5 | 8 | 15 | 19 | 7 | 8 | 10 | 11 | 10 | 5 | 12 | 14 | 71 |
| | | Mi-Jack Conquest Racing Ford Cosworth/Reynard 2KI | BS | – | – | – | – | 14 | 7 | – | – | – | – | – | – | – | – | – | – | – | – | |
| 13 | Roberto Moreno (BR) | Herdez Competition Ford Cosworth/Lola B01/00 | BS | 5 | 6 | 17 | – | – | 19 | – | – | 18 | 6 | 17 | – | – | – | – | 2 | – | – | 67 |
| | | Herdez Competition Ford Cosworth/Lola B03/00 | BS | – | – | – | 7 | 10 | – | 15 | 9 | – | – | – | 7 | 19 | – | – | – | – | 16 | |
| | | Herdez Competition Ford Cosworth/Lola B2K/00 | BS | – | – | – | – | – | – | – | – | – | – | – | 7 | 16 | – | – | – | – | – | |
| 14 | *Ryan Hunter-Reay (USA) | American Spirit Team Johansson Ford Cosworth/Reynard 02I | BS | 16 | 12 | 7 | 16 | 11 | 16 | – | – | – | – | – | – | – | 17 | 15 | 12 | 11 | 1 | 64 |
| | | American Spirit Team Johansson Ford Cosworth/Reynard 01I | BS | – | – | – | – | – | – | 12 | 17 | 9 | 11 | 6 | 10 | 3 | – | – | – | – | – | |
| 15 | *Tiago Monteiro (P) | Fittipaldi-Dingman Racing Ford Cosworth/Reynard 02I | BS | 7 | 19 | 11 | 14 | 13 | 10 | 9 | 19 | NS | 10 | 15 | 17 | 11 | 18 | 13 | 15 | 6 | 18 | 29 |
| 16 | *Mika Salo (SF) | PK Racing Ford Cosworth/Lola B02/00 | BS | – | – | – | – | – | – | – | – | – | – | – | – | – | 14 | 3 | 5 | 11 | – | 26 |
| 17 | Max Papis (I) | PK Racing Ford Cosworth/Lola B02/00 | BS | – | – | – | – | – | 15 | 12 | 16 | 9 | 4 | 9 | 9 | – | – | – | – | – | – | 25 |
| 18 | *Rodolfo Lavin (MEX) | Walker Racing Corona Competition Ford Cosworth/Reynard 02I | BS | 18 | 15 | – | 15 | 9 | 14 | – | 11 | 14 | 15 | 8 | 19 | 12 | 15 | 19 | 18 | 18 | 8 | 17 |
| | | Walker Racing Corona Competition Ford Cosworth/Reynard 01I | BS | – | – | 18 | – | – | – | 19 | – | – | – | – | – | – | – | – | – | – | – | |
| 19 | Gualter Salles (BR) | Dale Coyne Racing Alpina/Golden Cross Ford Cosworth/Lola B2K/00 | BS | – | – | – | – | – | 13 | – | 18 | 17 | – | NS | 11 | 17 | 12 | 18 | – | 15 | 6 | 11 |
| 20 | *Geoff Boss (USA) | Dale Coyne Racing Cross Pens Ford Cosworth/Lola B01/00 | BS | – | – | – | – | – | – | 16 | 13 | 16 | 14 | NS | 13 | 14 | 14 | 12 | 10 | 20 | 9 | 8 |
| 21 | *Patrick Lemarie (F) | PK Racing Ford Cosworth/Lola B02/00 | BS | 10 | 10 | 13 | 11 | 19 | 18 | – | – | – | – | – | – | – | – | – | – | – | – | 8 |
| 22 | *Joel Camathias (CH) | Dale Coyne Racing Ford Cosworth/Lola B01/00 | BS | 9 | 11 | 14 | 13 | 16 | 15 | – | – | – | – | – | – | – | – | – | – | – | – | 6 |
| | | Dale Coyne Racing Ford Cosworth/Lola B2K/00 | BS | – | – | – | – | – | – | 13 | – | – | – | – | – | – | – | – | – | – | – | |
| 23 | *Alex Yoong (MAL) | Dale Coyne Racing Ford Cosworth/Lola B2K/00 | BS | – | 9 | 19 | 18 | 17 | – | – | – | – | – | – | – | – | – | – | – | – | – | 4 |
| 24 | *Roberto Gonzalez (MEX) | Dale Coyne Racing Ford Cosworth/Lola B2K/00 | BS | 17 | – | – | – | – | – | – | – | – | – | – | – | – | – | – | – | – | – | 3 |
| | | Herdez Competition Ford Cosworth/Lola B01/00 | BS | – | – | – | – | – | – | – | – | – | – | – | – | – | – | – | – | 10 | – | |
| 25 | Bryan Herta (USA) | PK Racing Ford Cosworth/Lola B02/00 | BS | – | – | – | – | – | – | – | 11 | – | – | – | – | – | – | – | – | – | – | 2 |
| | *Alex Sperafico (BR) | Dale Coyne Racing Alpina/Golden Cross Ford Cosworth/Lola B2K/00 | BS | – | – | – | – | – | – | – | – | – | – | – | 18 | – | – | – | – | 14 | – | |
| | *Luis Diaz (MEX) | Walker Racing Sun/Telcel/Motorola Ford Cosworth/Reynard 01I | BS | – | – | – | – | – | – | – | – | – | – | – | – | – | – | – | – | 19 | – | |

**Black type indicates car still running at finish**     * rookie     p pole position     † led most laps     NS did not start

## Pole positions

| | | |
|---|---|---|
| 1 | Paul Tracy | 6 |
| 2 | Sébastien Bourdais | 5 |
| 3 = | Bruno Junqueira | 2 |
| 3 = | Alex Tagliani | 2 |
| 5 = | Patrick Carpentier | 1 |
| 5 = | Adrian Fernandez | 1 |
| 5 = | Michel Jourdain Jr. | 1 |

## Nation's Cup

| | | |
|---|---|---|
| 1 | Canada | 298 |
| 2 | Mexico | 262 |
| 3 | Brazil | 228 |
| 4 | France | 161 |
| 5 | United States | 107 |
| 6 | Catalonia | 106 |
| 7 | England | 103 |
| 8 | Portugal | 28 |
| 9 | Finland | 26 |
| 10 | Italy | 25 |
| 11 | Switzerland | 6 |
| 12 | Malaysia | 4 |

## Manufacturer's Championship

| | | |
|---|---|---|
| 1 | Ford Cosworth | 395 |

## Constructor's Championship

| | | |
|---|---|---|
| 1 | Lola | 387 |
| 2 | Reynard | 161 |

## Jim Trueman Rookie of the Year

| | | |
|---|---|---|
| 1 | Sébastien Bourdais | 159 |
| 2 | Darren Manning | 103 |
| 3 | Mario Haberfeld | 71 |
| 4 | Ryan Hunter-Reay | 64 |
| 5 | Tiago Monteiro | 29 |
| 6 | Mika Salo | 26 |
| 7 | Rodolfo Lavin | 17 |
| 8 | Geoff Boss | 8 |
| 9 | Patrick Lemarie | 8 |
| 10 | Joel Camathias | 6 |
| 11 | Alex Yoong | 4 |
| 12 | Roberto Gonzalez | 3 |

# ENGINES

## FORD COSWORTH

THE decision by Honda and Toyota to withdraw from Champ Car competition following the 2002 season certainly left a void, especially for those teams that had previously enjoyed factory support. By the same token, it paved the way for perhaps the most level playing field, technically, since the middle 1980s, before the advent of serious competition for the hitherto ubiquitous Ford Cosworth DFX engines. Coincidentally, Ford Cosworth once again provided the series' lifeblood in 2003.

An arrangement was concluded prior to the completion of the 2002 campaign whereby Ford Cosworth would produce a modified version of its XF motor, the XFE, for the exclusive use of all Champ Car teams. The XF originally had been introduced for the 2000 season and proved immediately successful. Lighter, significantly smaller and more powerful than the superseded XD, it won the coveted CART Manufacturer's Championship at its first attempt and went on to accumulate 13 poles and 18 race wins during a three-year span.

The XFE represented a radical departure from the accepted Champ Car norm in that the design engineers were not so much concerned about seeking ultimate performance, as had been required in the face of stiff opposition from Honda and Toyota; instead they concentrated on longevity and cost-effectiveness. They did so to startling effect. Whereas the previous breed of engines needed to be rebuilt every 350 miles or so, the XFE required an overhaul only after 1,200 miles. Equally impressive was the fact that absolute horsepower was close to that attained by the XF, around 750 hp in road-course trim and a little over 700 hp for the ovals. To achieve this, the engineers adopted a substantial decrease in the rev limit – from over 16,000 rpm to 12,000 rpm – and to compensate increased the turbocharger boost pressure from 34 inches to 41.5 inches.

A standardized electronic control unit was supplied to all the teams, and was distributed by CART on a random basis, à la pop-off valves. Furthermore, since all the engines were maintained by Ford Cosworth, there were no concerns about cheating. Thus traction control was banished to the history books. Good riddance!

"I think for sure it's going to produce much, much better races, because it's going to be easy to make a mistake," declared Bruno Junqueira upon gaining his first experience of the XFE. "Sure, the engine is a little less powerful [than in '02], but because of the extra boost, it's almost as fast as last year, so it's good!"

Junqueira's opinion was shared up and down the pit lane. Spectators, too, quickly became enamored of the XFE, since its characteristics ensured the return of full-blooded power slides as drivers struggled to transfer 750 hp onto the road without the benefit of traction control.

The other major effect of the XFE was a dramatic reduction in costs for the teams – at least for those that previously had not been "sponsored" by the engine manufacturers. In 2002, the cost of a Ford Cosworth engine lease had stretched to well over $4 million. One year on, every team was required to pay around $1.25 million for the package. Sure, that's not exactly cheap, but given the levels of performance, reliability and consistency, it certainly represented excellent value.

A great deal of time and effort was expended on making sure the product lived up to expectations. The XFE was developed at Cosworth Racing's base in Northampton, England, then track tested for the first time just a few days after the 2002 season finale in Mexico City, when a handful of young Americans – and veteran Roberto Moreno – were invited to turn some laps at Firebird Raceway, Arizona, in one of Dale Coyne Racing's Lolas. Although the car suffered a few gearbox problems, the engine ran virtually flawlessly.

"We were there a week putting in a couple hundred miles a day and we finally got that engine to 1,200 miles," recalled CART Program Director, Cosworth Racing, Bruce Wood. "I think that surprised quite a lot of people, and I think that it was definitely sort of a feather in the cap. It was nice to get that under our belt. Really, from there we never looked back."

Prior to the start of the season, eight examples of the XFE had completed 1,200 miles apiece on the dynamometers. A further 13,500 miles had been logged in total during a pair of major preseason tests at Laguna Seca and Sebring. All told, after almost 25,000 miles of development, the engineers had encountered just two breakages – one on the dyno and one in Paul Tracy's car at Sebring. Both failures occurred at right around 1,000 miles and were traced to the same source (piston), which was addressed before the opening race in St. Petersburg.

"Two failures out of 25,000-odd miles we don't think is too bad," reckoned Wood, "and hopefully, we've now nipped that particular mechanism in the bud so it won't happen on the track this weekend."

Wood's confidence was not misplaced. Indeed, there was only one XFE meltdown in a race all year long – experienced by Sébastien Bourdais at Long Beach. A remarkable record. No doubt about it, the 2003 engine package more than lived up to expectations.

**Production base:**
Northampton, England; Torrance, California

**Wins: 18**
(Tracy 7, Bourdais 3, Jourdain 2, Junqueira 2, Carpentier 1, Fernandez 1, Dominguez 1, Hunter-Reay 1)

**Poles: 18**
(Tracy 6, Bourdais 5, Tagliani 2, Junqueira 2, Jourdain 1, Carpentier 1, Fernandez 1)

**Top:** Fernandez Racing's Mike Guger "dresses" an engine prior to installation.

**Above:** The '03 XFE motors displayed an impressive blend of power and reliability.
Photographs: Dan Boyd/LAT

CHASSIS

# LOLA

**T**HE emergence of Lola Cars International from the depths of despair in the late 1990s to a position of dominance represents one of the most remarkable turnarounds in auto racing history. Even so, the transformation has been more steady than spectacular. After failing to win at all in 1997, '98 and '99, the British manufacturer garnered seven victories in Y2K, then ten in '01 and an impressive 16 out of 19 races en route to its first CART Constructor's Championship in '02.

It came agonizingly close to a clean sweep in 2003 – agonizing, that is, for its only rival, Reynard. In fact, only a bizarre twist of events in what turned out to be the final race of the season at Surfers Paradise, Australia, prevented Lola from completing the whitewash.

A "chassis freeze" introduced by CART in 2002 meant that no major (i.e. expensive) development could be carried out on the existing B02/00 chassis. However, there were a number of subtle tweaks, notably to the "flugelhorns" on the

sidepods in front of the rear wheels and the nose, which provided some aerodynamic gains. More importantly, virtually all of the most established and well-funded teams were equipped with the Huntingdon cars, so the odds were stacked heavily in their favor. They also had numerical superiority: 13 of the 19 cars on the grid at St. Petersburg were Lolas.

Four new chassis were built over the winter – three were sold to Herdez Competition and one to Player's/Forsythe Racing (Patrick Carpentier) – but the vast majority of Lolas were updated cars, some of them dating back to the 2000 season. Many had previously been fitted with Honda or Toyota power plants and had been converted to accept the newly mandated Ford Cosworth XFE engines (at a cost of around $110,000 apiece, which included a revised fuel cell, oil tank, rear bulkhead and a new bellhousing to mate with the gearbox). They were all equally competitive, and Lola duly wrapped up its second successive Constructor's Championship with ease.

**Production base: Huntingdon, England**

**U.S. base: Indianapolis, Indiana**

Number of cars built in 2003: 4
(plus 18 conversion kits)

**Wins: 17**
(Tracy 7, Bourdais 3, Jourdain 2, Junqueira 2, Carpentier 1, Fernandez 1, Dominguez 1)

**Poles: 18**
(Tracy 6, Bourdais 5, Tagliani 2, Junqueira 2, Jourdain 1, Carpentier 1, Fernandez 1)

Laps led: 1,871
(97.35 percent)

# REYNARD

**R**EYNARD was faced with two major problems prior to the season. First of all, rightly or wrongly, its car was perceived as being inferior to the Lola, and the introduction of the "chassis freeze" in 2002 meant that only detail modifications were permitted, so there was little hope of relative improvement. Also, the top Reynard exponent from 2002, Player's/Forsythe Racing, switched allegiance to Lola over the winter – largely at the behest of new recruit Paul Tracy.

Consequently, only six of the 19 drivers on the grid for the opening race at St. Petersburg were equipped with Reynards, and all but one were rookies. The lone exception was 1996 CART Champion Jimmy Vasser, but the benefit of the California native's vast experience was negated somewhat by the fact that the organization for which he drove, American Spirit Team Johansson, had been put together very much at the last minute.

It was no surprise that the Reynards generally struggled. Still, there were flashes of real speed. For example, Vasser posted

the fastest lap at Mid-Ohio and rookie teammate Ryan Hunter-Reay did the same in Mexico City; Mario Haberfeld displayed stunning speed in practice at Denver; Tiago Monteiro was quickest of all in final qualifying in Mexico; and Darren Manning looked superb on the Milwaukee Mile oval and set the fastest lap of the entire weekend in Mexico. The Englishman, indeed, was Reynard's most consistent performer, regularly snapping at the heels of the front-running Lolas.

It was generally accepted that the Reynard was not a bad car, but as Walker Racing Team Manager Rob Edwards pointed out, "It lacked a little downforce compared to the Lola, and the Lola was more consistent – it was less susceptible to variations in track temperature or ride-height.

"The Reynards were often quick in the first session of a race weekend, but as more rubber was laid down on the track, the Reynard proportionally lost more downforce on the front end, so tended to understeer more. And it tended to lose downforce as the ambient temperature increased."

**Production base: Brackley, England**

**U.S. base: Indianapolis, Indiana**

Number of cars built in 2003: 0
(plus 10 conversion kits)

**Wins: 1**
(Hunter-Reay)

Poles: 0

Laps led: 51
(2.65 percent)

**Above: Well-heeled teams like Player's/ Forsythe (left) ran Lola chassis, leaving the minnows to uphold Reynard honor.**
Gavin Lawrence/LAT

# BRIDGESTONE

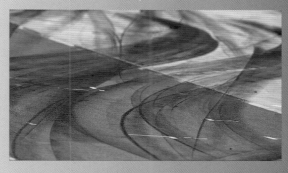

A MONOPOLY situation in any auto racing series generally means both good news and bad news for a tire manufacturer. The good news is that it can gain valuable exposure in the media – as long as things go well. The bad news is that more often than not, when a tire company is mentioned, it's because something bad has happened. Not so with Bridgestone/Firestone's involvement in the 2003 Bridgestone Presents The Champ Car World Series Powered by Ford.

"Everyone within the company was extremely happy with the exposure we got out of the Champ Car series," said Al Speyer, executive director of Bridgestone Motorsport. "The [full] series title was quite awkward and not often used by the media in general, but the logos and the branding we received really helped us gain the exposure we were looking for this season, which was a plus for us."

Furthermore, the range of Bridgestone Potenza tires used during the 2003 season performed virtually flawlessly.

"I think they do a great job," declared newly crowned series champion Paul Tracy, "not only in our series but also in Formula 1. They were pushed to the limit this year in Formula 1 and still managed to win the world championship – and they gave us in Champ Car a superb tire which made the competition very equal for everybody, which was great. It's something you don't have to worry about with Bridgestone; they always bring a quality tire."

A total of seven different dry-weather tires were used at Champ Car racing's trademark wide variety of racing venues. There were specific "soft" and "hard" compounds for both street courses and road courses, plus three different oval tires – one each for the entirely

different characteristics of EuroSpeedway Lausitz, Milwaukee and Fontana (although the latter were unused due to the cancellation of the originally scheduled King Taco 500 finale). Impressively, through all 18 races, there was nary a hint of a problem.

"The tires were pretty much problem-free," agreed Speyer. "Of course, it helps that we're well established now; we know what to expect and we're getting used to what is required.

"There were a few times, a few tracks, where some of the drivers might have liked to have a softer compound, and we've told them to tell us what they want. They told us [originally] they wanted a durable tire, one that wouldn't leave a lot of marbles on the racetrack, and that's what we produced. In some places perhaps we did go a little too conservative – which is a luxury we couldn't afford if we had competition from another tire maker – and we're quite willing to listen to the drivers, so if they would prefer a softer tire, we'll try to provide one for them. But the difficulty for us is that it's been very hard to get any kind of consensus."

Speyer did not discuss specifics, but it's well known that some drivers tended to work their tires harder than others. That discrepancy was more evident than usual in 2003, given the absence of traction control following the adoption of a common engine control system provided by Ford Cosworth.

"That did, in some cases, give a little more rear tire wear," acknowledged Speyer, "but nothing of real significance. Some drivers seemed to have more of a problem than others, which is what we expected, but in the big picture it was a minor issue."

**Production base: Akron, Ohio, and Tokyo, Japan**

**Wins: 18**
(Tracy 7, Bourdais 3, Jourdain 2, Junqueira 2, Carpentier 1, Fernandez 1, Dominguez 1, Hunter-Reay 1)

**Poles: 18**
(Tracy 6, Bourdais 5, Tagliani 2, Junqueira 2, Jourdain 1, Carpentier 1, Fernandez 1)

**Above left: Making tracks.** Bridgestone gained much positive exposure from its strengthened association with the Champ Car World Series in 2003.

**Below:** The lastest range of Potenzas exhibited the usual high standards of durability and consistency.
Photographs: Gavin Lawrence/LAT

# TIRES

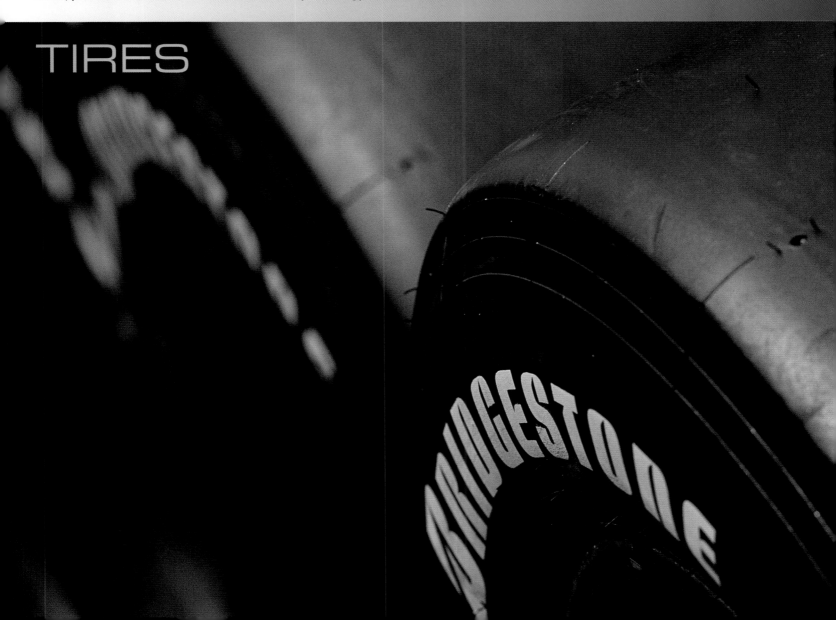

# 2003

## BRIDGESTONE PRESENTS
## THE CHAMP CAR WORLD SERIES POWERED BY FORD

Gavin Lawrence/LAT

# ST. PETERSBURG

**Right:** A leaner and more focused Paul Tracy laid down an early marker as the man to beat in 2003.

**Far right:** Sunset over St. Pete – a popular addition to the Champ Car calendar.

**Below right:** Sébastien Bourdais made a stunning impression on his debut, but came away with crumbs after glancing the wall following a pit-stop miscue.

Photographs: Phil Abbott/LAT

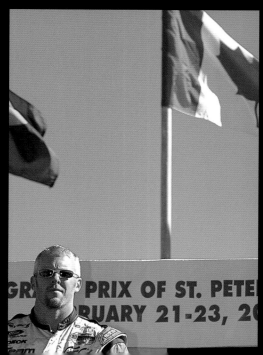

THE opening round of a brand-new season of Champ Car competition – on a challenging new street circuit in St. Petersburg, Florida – witnessed a fascinating confrontation between youth and experience. On the one hand was French rookie sensation Sébastien Bourdais, who caused quite a stir by qualifying his Newman/Haas Racing Ford Cosworth/Lola on the pole. Lined up against him was veteran Paul Tracy, who was intent on laying down an early marker after joining Team Player's during the off-season.

Bourdais led the way in the early stages, until his rhythm was interrupted by a strategic miscue. Later he clipped a wall as he tried to make up time, costing him several laps in the pits while his team effected repairs. This left the door open for Tracy to romp away and secure the 20th victory of his career – the perfect way to begin his 13th campaign.

"I can't be any happier than I am right now," said Tracy. "The car has been fast all weekend and that was the case again today. This is how I wanted to start the season."

Bourdais had become the first rookie driver since Nigel Mansell to claim the pole for his first ever Champ Car race. Unlike the Englishman, however, who had been beaten into the first corner on his debut at Surfers Paradise in 1993 (by fellow ex-Formula 1 World Champion Emerson Fittipaldi), Bourdais held on to his advantage at the start and became the first man ever to lead his first competitive lap. Impressive. Bourdais didn't flinch in the face of Tracy's challenge, and even began to edge away a little from the Canadian, who continued to be chased by second-row qualifiers Adrian Fernandez and Patrick Carpentier.

Michel Jourdain Jr. maintained fifth at the start in Team Rahal's Gigante Lola, chased by Brazilian rookie Mario Haberfeld's Mi-Jack/Conquest Racing Reynard. Next initially was pre-season championship favorite Bruno Junqueira, who had stepped into the #1 Newman/Haas Racing Lola after 2002 champion Cristiano da Matta had departed for Formula 1. Junqueira, having started a disappointing seventh on the grid, made a bid for the inside line on the front straightaway at the end of the first lap, only to be squeezed unceremoniously against the pit wall by Haberfeld. The pair braked impossibly late for Turn One, and while Junqueira held the inside line, he was carrying too much speed and

only just managed to avoid slamming into the side of an unsuspecting Jourdain.

Oriol Servia was the big winner, jumping two places in Pat Patrick's Visteon Lola and moving into sixth ahead of Junqueira, while Haberfeld lost another couple of positions to Mario Dominguez (Herdez Lola) and British rookie Darren Manning (RAC/Autowindscreens Reynard).

The multitude of inexperienced drivers among the 19-car field suggested a high likelihood for mistakes. Instead it was one of the veterans, Alex Tagliani, who ensured the first full-course caution of the season when he nosed Champ Car newcomer Paul Gentilozzi's Johnson Controls Lola into the tire wall at Turn Ten.

Bourdais displayed his preparedness once more by withstanding Tracy's challenge at the restart and inching clear of his primary pursuer. Tracy quickly pulled away from Fernandez's Tecate/Quaker State/Telmex Lola, which in turn began to come under pressure from Carpentier in the second Team Player's Lola.

Again the action was short-lived, this time due to an incident involving Rodolfo Lavin's Corona/Walker Racing Reynard. Immediately after the restart came yet another interruption when Patrick Lemarie (PK Racing Lola) performed a quick spin.

Now the focus shifted to the pit lane. It was decision time for the teams. Sixteen laps were in the books – one more than the minimum for cars to reach the finish with just three pit stops and a maximum of 30 laps between pit visits. The Newman/Haas team chose not to call its man, Bourdais, into the pits. Team Player's, however, adopted the opposite approach for Tracy. Everyone else followed suit except Fernandez and Tiago Monteiro, who already had made a couple of trips into the pits as his brand-new Fittipaldi-Dingman team attempted to pick up valuable experience.

Bourdais, Fernandez and Monteiro duly led away at the restart, after 18 laps, and the Frenchman immediately used the clear track to his benefit. Within five circuits, Fernandez was more than five seconds in arrears. By lap 29, the gap had swollen to 12.8 seconds. Bourdais was charging. Tracy, meanwhile, had been unable to find a way past Monteiro and was almost 24 seconds adrift of the race leader when "Kermit," as Bourdais had been dubbed by his crew, brought the #2 car into the pit lane for its first service, right on schedule, after 30 laps.

**Right:** After a year on the sidelines, ever-popular veteran Roberto Moreno was back in the saddle at the ripe old age of 44, and marked the occasion with a fifth place for Herdez Competition.

**Below right:** Swiss rookie Joel Camathias kept his nose clean to take ninth for Dale Coyne Racing.

**Below:** Bourdais receives the plaudits of the Newman/Haas Racing crew after claiming pole position by more than 0.5s.
Photographs: Gavin Lawrence/LAT

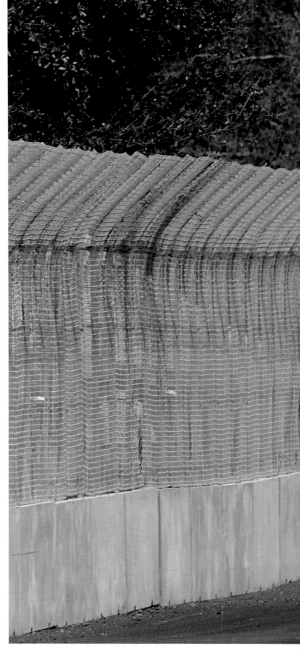

## QUALIFYING

Rookie Sébastien Bourdais lost no time in making his presence felt in the 2003 Bridgestone Presents the Champ Car World Series Powered by Ford. He posted the fastest time in practice on Friday morning (1m 02.426s, an average speed of 104.149 mph), then turned an even faster lap (1m 01.847s/105.124 mph) a mere four minutes into the opening qualifying period. No one else could match that time during the 40-minute session, which included several red-flag stoppages due to a variety of incidents, although that didn't prevent the Frenchman from clipping another 0.2s from his earlier standard. Thus he was assured of both the very first championship point of the season and a guaranteed front-row starting position for the Grand Prix of St. Petersburg.

"To be on the first row in my first event in Champ Cars is as good as it can get today," he enthused. "I think I was not expecting such a good result. The Lilly car was perfect."

Lap times continued to tumble on Saturday, and when the forecast rain failed to materialize, the grid order wasn't settled until the closing moments of final qualifying. Once again many drivers found it difficult to find a rhythm during the oft-interrupted session. Bourdais, though, rose to the occasion.

"It was difficult to manage the red flags," he admitted, "but it was probably harder for the others because, for sure, we were going to start no lower than second place. The pressure was on the other drivers. It was a perfect situation for us."

The two closest challengers to Bourdais on Friday, Oriol Servia (Patrick Racing) and his own teammate, Bruno Junqueira, both were obliged to forfeit their fastest laps after causing red-flag stoppages. Paul Tracy was the only man to knock Bourdais off his perch briefly, but eventually even he was forced to settle for second best. Adrian Fernandez posted a strong third-fastest time, narrowly ahead of the second Player's Lola of Patrick Carpentier and Michel Jourdain Jr.'s Gigante/Team Rahal car. Fastest of the Reynard contingent was Brazilian rookie Mario Haberfeld, who drove impressively for the brand-new Champ Car team owned by former Indy Lights champion Eric Bachelart.

The stop was good. With a full tank of methanol fuel and four fresh Bridgestone Potenza tires, Bourdais accelerated out of the pits just as the leaders were passing by. Crucially, however, he was on cold tires; not so the leaders. By the time he was completely up to speed, Bourdais had slipped to seventh behind Monteiro, Tracy, Carpentier, Jourdain, Servia and Dominguez, who had passed Haberfeld on lap 31.

Bourdais needed to stay calm. Sure, he was in seventh rather than the lead, but clearly he had a very fast car – already he had set what would stand as the fastest lap of the race – and there were still over 70 laps to run. Furthermore everyone would have to make two more pit stops.

But the pressure proved too much. On lap 34, Bourdais overstepped the boundary, clipped a wall and broke his Newman/Haas Lola's left rear suspension.

"I was upset and tried to push to stay in a good position," he related. "I did a small mistake and the consequence was big."

Pedro Campuzano's boys made repairs, which, thanks to a high rate of attrition, enabled Bourdais to secure a couple more championship points when he was classified 11th.

On lap 35, Tracy finally found a way past Monteiro for the lead. Teammate Carpentier also snuck past the Portuguese rookie. Then Tracy put his head down, turning laps appreciably faster than when he had been bottled up behind Monteiro. By the time he made his second visit to the pit lane, after 46 laps, the gap between the two Player's cars had grown to around five seconds. Sadly for team owner Jerry Forsythe, however, hopes of a resounding 1-2 result were dashed when Carpentier, like Bourdais, found the wall.

"I came out [of the pits] on cold tires and wanted to close the gap [to Tracy]," he said. "I hit a bump coming into Corner Seven and the rear end snapped [sideways]. I then slowly hit the tire wall, damaging only the front wing."

Unfortunately Carpentier also stalled the engine, and he lost a couple of laps before being restarted by the Simple Green Safety Team. "I'm thinking [about the] championship and this is not the way to win it," he reflected morosely.

The French-Canadian's slip boosted a steady Jourdain into second place ahead of Junqueira, who had fallen to 14th after a poor first pit stop, but who had driven well to work his way back into contention.

The second half of the 105-lap race wasn't nearly as eventful as the first. Tracy was firmly in control. An advantage of around six seconds was wiped out by a final caution period on lap 63, after rookie Ryan Hunter-Reay went off at Turn Ten, but there was never any cause for concern. Tracy reestablished his margin at the restart, enjoyed another flawless pit stop by his Steve Moore-led crew on lap 76, then reeled off the laps to claim a popular victory.

"It's a great start to the season," said Tracy. "We had to work extremely hard this week. [Technical Advisor] Tony Cicale and the whole Team Player's crew deserve a lot of thanks. Tony's a great influence on me. We think alike and we get along really well. It was a tremendous team effort. I'm proud to be on Team Player's, an all-Canadian effort, and it's a great feeling to be in the winner's circle in my first race with them."

Jourdain, the revelation of 2002, was equally delighted to begin the new season with a career-best second.

"It was a very long race and the track changed a lot during the race to the point where it got extremely slippery," said the Mexican. "It was easy to make a mistake and therefore there were a lot of yellows today."

Junqueira applied some pressure on Jourdain after the final pit stops, whereupon a couple of big slides on the treacherous surface led him to settle for third. Haberfeld also drove well to become the first rookie finisher, while Roberto Moreno, making his return to the series after a one-year hiatus, was elated to finish fifth in his first drive with the Herdez Competition team.

*Jeremy Shaw*

**Above: A poor qualifying effort left Junqueira with much to do on raceday, but the Brazilian recovered from an early pit-stop delay to claim third.**
Gavin Lawrence/LAT

**Left: Haberfeld earned the rookie bragging rights, placing fourth for Eric Bachelart's Mi-Jack/Conquest Racing Team (and displaying some adventurous racecraft while defending his position from countryman Junqueira).**
Phil Abbott/LAT

# BOURDAIS MAKES HIS MARK

**S**ÉBASTIEN who? That was the oft-asked question when Newman/Haas Racing announced the identity of the man who would partner Bruno Junqueira on the defending champion team for the 2003 Bridgestone Presents the Champ Car World Series Powered by Ford. But it was not long before the wisdom behind the decision made by the most successful active team in Champ Car racing became apparent.

Bourdais displayed explosive pace in both major preseason tests, at Sebring and Mazda Raceway Laguna Seca, each time eclipsing his more fancied teammate, who had finished as runner-up in the 2002 title chase, driving for Target/Chip Ganassi Racing. The amiable, studious-looking Frenchman continued that form at St. Petersburg.

Of course, serious race aficionados were not surprised by Bourdais' pace. His only prior experience in North America had been a drive in the 2001 Sebring 12 Hours sports-car race, but he had carved impressive credentials during his climb up the open-wheel racing ladder in Europe. Bourdais, from Le Mans, France, had taken the traditional route from karting into Elf-Campus and Formula Renault, then clinched the French Formula 3 championship in 1999. Three years in Formula 3000 (which has produced a series of Champ Car winners over the past few years, including Alex Zanardi, Christian Fittipaldi, Juan Pablo Montoya and Cristiano da Matta) culminated in the 2002 championship crown, which in turn led to an invitation to test for Newman/Haas Racing in the fall of 2002. Bourdais was immediately impressive.

Less than a week shy of his 24th birthday, Bourdais displayed prodigious pace on his race debut (right, leading Tracy) in St. Petersburg. "Kermit" also exhibited the same blend of confidence, measured with a degree of humility, that had endeared him to the Newman/Haas crew members.

Clearly he had no problems whatsoever in coming to terms with his new surroundings.

"I would say it's like a big F3000 car – not the one from the last year, but the one between 1999 and 2001," he said of his transition to the Champ Car ranks. "It's just, like, more downforce and twice the power. Power is not always an issue. Power is something you get used to pretty easily. For the first time I jumped into the Champ Car, I was just getting back from Europe, after testing the F1 [Renault], so it was not a big deal."

# EQUALITY MOTORING

**O**F all the changes that had taken place within the Champ Car ranks during the three-and-a-half months between the final race of the 2002 season in Mexico City and the opening round of the 2003 campaign in St. Petersburg, none was more far-reaching than the decision to adopt a standardized motor package. Of course, CART didn't have many options following the withdrawal of both Honda and Toyota at the conclusion of the 2002 campaign. Still the feedback from drivers, teams – and fans – following winter testing and the first race was entirely positive.

The latest turbocharged Ford Cosworth XFE engine, a derivative of the XF motor that had won seven races en route to the CART Manufacturers Championship in 2000 (and accumulated 11 more race victories in 2001 and '02), represented a massive step forward in terms of cost-effectiveness. In recent seasons, engine lease packages had been costing teams as much as $5 million per annum. For 2003, that figure had been slashed to around $1.25 million. How? Well, with no need to be concerned about competition, the Ford Cosworth engineers were able to dramatically lengthen the time required between rebuilds. Historically Champ Car motors had needed major service every 300–400 miles (with the obvious exception of 500-mile races, when the engines were detuned slightly to ensure reliability). The XFE required service after 1,200 miles.

The rev limit also was changed significantly – down to 12,000 rpm from over 16,000 – which further improved reliability. In addition, the manifold boost pressure was increased, from 34 inches to 41 inches, which ensured a minimal power loss compared to 2002 (down from 780 hp to around 755 hp). This change had the added effect of raising torque by almost 30 percent, which, coupled with the banishment of computerized traction control, served to place a far greater emphasis on driver skill. At last, full-blooded power slides were back for all to see!

"I think, for sure, it's going to provide much better racing," declared Bruno Junqueira prior to the season-opener, "because it's going to be easy to make a mistake. Sure, the engine is a little less powerful, but it's almost as fast as last year, so it's good."

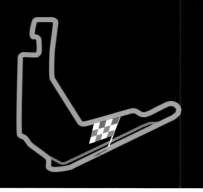

# GRAND PRIX OF ST. PETERSBURG

**ROUND 1**

## ST. PETERSBURG STREET CIRCUIT, FLORIDA

**FEBRUARY 23, 105 laps of 1.806 miles – 189.630 miles**

| Pl. | Driver (Nat.) | No. | Team Sponsors Engine/Car | Tires | Q Speed | Q Time | Q Pos. | Laps | Time/Status | Ave. (mph) | Pts. |
|---|---|---|---|---|---|---|---|---|---|---|---|
| 1 | Paul Tracy (CDN) | 3 | Forsythe Racing Player's/Indeck Ford Cosworth/Lola B02/00 | BS | 105.758 | 1m 01.476s | 2 | 105 | 2h 04m 28.904s | 91.401 | 21 |
| 2 | Michel Jourdain Jr. (MEX) | 9 | Team Rahal Gigante Ford Cosworth/Lola B01/00 | BS | 105.183 | 1m 01.812s | 5 | 105 | 2h 04m 41.040s | 91.253 | 16 |
| 3 | Bruno Junqueira (BR) | 1 | Newman/Haas Racing PacifiCare Ford Cosworth/Lola B02/00 | BS | 105.003 | 1m 01.918s | 7 | 105 | 2h 04m 45.474s | 91.199 | 14 |
| 4 | *Mario Haberfeld (BR) | 34 | Mi-Jack Conquest Racing Ford Cosworth/Reynard 02I | BS | 105.093 | 1m 01.865s | 6 | 105 | 2h 05m 10.264s | 90.898 | 12 |
| 5 | Roberto Moreno (BR) | 4 | Herdez Competition Ford Cosworth/Lola B01/00 | BS | 103.118 | 1m 03.050s | 15 | 105 | 2h 05m 25.689s | 90.712 | 10 |
| 6 | Jimmy Vasser (USA) | 12 | American Spirit Team Johansson Ford Cosworth/Reynard 01I | BS | 104.875 | 1m 01.994s | 8 | 104 | Running | | 8 |
| 7 | *Tiago Monteiro (P) | 7 | Fittipaldi-Dingman Racing Ford Cosworth/Reynard 02I | BS | 101.608 | 1m 03.987s | 16 | 104 | Running | | 6 |
| 8 | Patrick Carpentier (CDN) | 32 | Forsythe Racing Player's/Indeck Ford Cosworth/Lola B02/00 | BS | 105.274 | 1m 01.759s | 4 | 103 | Running | | 5 |
| 9 | *Joel Camathias (CH) | 19 | Dale Coyne Racing Ford Cosworth/Lola B01/00 | BS | 101.206 | 1m 04.241s | 17 | 103 | Running | | 4 |
| 10 | *Patrick Lemarie (F) | 27 | PK Racing Ford Cosworth/Lola B02/00 | BS | 103.277 | 1m 02.953s | 14 | 102 | Running | | 3 |
| 11 | *Sébastien Bourdais (F) | 2 | Newman/Haas Racing Lilly Ford Cosworth/Lola B02/00 | BS | 106.710 | 1m 00.928s | 1 | 97 | Running | | 4 |
| 12 | Oriol Servia (E) | 20 | Patrick Racing Visteon Ford Cosworth/Lola B02/00 | BS | 104.760 | 1m 02.062s | 9 | 96 | Running | | 1 |
| 13 | *Darren Manning (GB) | 15 | Walker Racing RAC/Autowindscreens Ford Cosworth/Reynard 02I | BS | 104.462 | 1m 02.239s | 11 | 75 | Clutch | | |
| 14 | Mario Dominguez (MEX) | 55 | Herdez Competition Ford Cosworth/Lola B02/00 | BS | 104.694 | 1m 02.101s | 10 | 71 | Accident | | |
| 15 | Adrian Fernandez (MEX) | 51 | Fernandez Tecate/Quaker State/Telmex Ford Cosworth/Lola B02/00 | BS | 105.291 | 1m 01.749s | 3 | 69 | Accident | | |
| 16 | *Ryan Hunter-Reay (USA) | 31 | American Spirit Team Johansson Ford Cosworth/Reynard 02I | BS | 104.350 | 1m 02.306s | 12 | 61 | Accident | | |
| 17 | *Roberto Gonzalez (MEX) | 11 | Dale Coyne Racing Ford Cosworth/Lola B2K/00 | BS | 100.105 | 1m 04.948s | 18 | 21 | Gearbox | | |
| 18 | *Rodolfo Lavin (MEX) | 5 | Walker Racing Corona Competition Ford Cosworth/Reynard 02I | BS | 97.729 | 1m 06.527s | 19 | 12 | Accident | | |
| 19 | Alex Tagliani (CDN) | 33 | Rocketsports Racing Johnson Controls Ford Cosworth/Lola B01/00 | BS | 103.987 | 1m 02.523s | 13 | 3 | Accident | | |

\* denotes rookie driver

**Caution flags: Laps 5–7,** accident/Tagliani; **laps 13–14,** spin/Lavin; **laps 16–17,** spin/Lemarie; **laps 48–50,** accident/Carpentier; **laps 62–67,** accident/Hunter-Reay. **Total: Five for 16 laps.**

**Lap leaders: Sébastien Bourdais,** 1–30 (30 laps); **Tiago Monteiro,** 31–34 (4 laps); **Paul Tracy,** 35–105 (71 laps). **Totals: Tracy,** 71 laps; **Bourdais,** 30 laps; **Monteiro,** 4 laps.

**Fastest race lap: Sébastien Bourdais,** 1m 01.825s, 105.161 mph on lap 29 (establishes record).

**Championship positions: 1** Tracy, **21; 2** Jourdain Jr., **16; 3** Junqueira, **14; 4** Haberfeld, **12; 5** Moreno, **10; 6** Vasser, **8; 7** Monteiro, **6; 8** Carpentier, **5; 9** Camathias & Bourdais, **4; 11** Lemarie, **3; 12** Servia, **1.**

## ST. PETERSBURG SNIPPETS

Phil Abbott/LAT

• Several teams arrived in Florida with precious little TESTING under their belts, but none was as stretched as Fittipaldi-Dingman Racing. Portuguese rookie Tiago Monteiro (above), a graduate of Formula 3 and Formula 3000 in Europe, had time for only a brief shakedown – in bitterly cold conditions – at Road Atlanta en route from the team's base in Indianapolis.

• The Grand Prix of St. Petersburg temporary circuit, comprising a mix of city streets, some of them adjacent to the waterfront, and one of the runways at the Albert Whitted Municipal Airport, was universally WELL RECEIVED by the drivers. "I think, for a street track, it's quite technical, it's quite challenging," said Bruno Junqueira. "Fast corners, slow corners, medium corners – you have everything here." The very fast Turn 11/12 chicane was especially note-

worthy: "It reminds me of La Piscine [the 'swimming-pool' section] at Monaco – only quicker," declared polesitter Sébastien Bourdais. Added new Champ Car team owner Emerson Fittipaldi, grinning broadly, "What a great track! It makes me want to drive again."

• Aside from when Alex Zanardi was invited to perform the duties of Honorary Starter at the Molson Indy Toronto in 2002, only Nick Fornoro and Jim Swintal had served as official STARTERS since CART's inception in 1979. Add Joe "J.D." Wilbur to that exclusive list. Following the decision to move Swintal into a position within Race Control, Wilbur took up his new posting at St. Petersburg. Originally from the Chicago area, he had been a longtime starter for the CART Toyota Atlantic Championship and previously had spent many years in the sprint-car ranks.

• Player's/Forsythe Racing was thrown a CURVE BALL just one day before official practice and qualifying were due to commence when Paul Tracy's race engineer, Kelly Loewen, abruptly quit. "That was a little disappointing," said Tracy, with more than a hint of sarcasm. "We were dropped in a little bit of a hole this week-end. On Thursday afternoon, the crew chief was supposed to receive the starting setup, and there was no engineer around." Technical Advisor Tony Cicale stepped into the breach for the weekend, ably assisted by Michael Cannon, who continued as Patrick Carpentier's race engineer. Tracy struggled to find any speed on Friday, but made a dramatic improvement on Saturday and, of course, went on to win the race.

• Rodolfo Lavin had a ROUGH INITIATION to the Champ Cars – or rather his crew did. The young Mexican, a graduate of Indy Lights and CART Toyota Atlantic, was plagued by minor technical issues

on Friday, forcing him into Walker Racing's backup car. Then he endured a heavy crash on Saturday morning. He also spun off in final qualifying, breaking the car's differential housing. "It's been one of those days my mom told me about," quipped Crew Chief Les Channen.

• PATRICK RACING signed on Infineon Technologies as a major associate sponsor at St. Petersburg. Oriol Servia was very competitive throughout the weekend and was running in fourth until his Visteon Lola was afflicted by an electrical malaise shortly after half-distance.

• American Spirit Team Johansson's Jimmy Vasser hit TROUBLE on the grid when the engine refused to run cleanly. The 1996 CART champion (below) was obliged to start from the back, but worked his way superbly up the order, running as high as fifth until hampered by a major loose condition in the closing stages.

Gavin Lawrence/LAT

P AUL Tracy was the man to beat in Monterrey. He was fastest during each of the two practice sessions on Friday morning and cemented his authority by leading the way in first qualifying. Matters took a turn for the worse, however, on Saturday morning. He lost control in the quick Turn Three/Four chicane, spinning across the abnormally high curb and tearing off his Lola's gearbox oil cooler, before slamming into the wall. The initial impact tore a hole in the underside of the chassis, rendering it hors de combat for the remainder of the weekend.

The Player's/Forsythe Racing team was faced with a dilemma. If Tracy switched to the backup car for final qualifying in an attempt to secure the pole position, he would have to forfeit the time he had already posted in provisional qualifying – which assured him of a front-row starting position. It wasn't worth the gamble. "The only logical choice was to sit out," he explained.

Ultimately Tracy had to settle for second on the grid after final qualifying proved substantially faster. As in St. Petersburg, though, he chased polesitter Sébastien Bourdais in the opening laps, then took control when the rookie fell out of contention.

Looking back after scoring the 21st victory of his Champ Car career, Tracy reckoned the misfortune on Saturday might actually have worked to his benefit: "I guess that was a little bit of a silver lining because I think today the key for the race for me was the tires. We had a brand-new set of tires for every stint because we didn't run yesterday.

"You know, from about midway through every stint, I was saving the tires, then I could really turn it on and pull a gap out. That was beneficial going into the pit stops because the first pit stop, the engine stalled on me just as we dropped the car off the jacks. We had to cycle the ignition and get it started again. But at that time we had about a 20-second lead. If it wasn't for that, we would have probably come out of the pits about seventh or eighth."

Tracy also was quick to praise his Player's team, which, since St. Petersburg, had hired a new race engineer, Todd Malloy, to work alongside the vastly experienced Tony Cicale.

"The team has done a fantastic job all winter, getting prepared, moving guys around, hiring some new people," said Tracy. "Todd I worked with for five years at Team Green, and Tony for a couple years. I kind of feel like I'm at home. It makes the job a lot easier."

**Left:** To the victor, the spoils. Paul Tracy sprays the bubbly on the rostrum, flanked by Alex Tagliani and Michel Jourdain Jr.
Mike Levitt/LAT

**Above:** Once again, polesitter Sébastien Bourdais exposed no chink in his armor away from the start. Tracy, Tagliani, Oriol Servia, Jourdain and the rest of the pack give chase.
Gavin Lawrence/LAT

# MONTERREY

BRIDGESTONE PRESENTS THE CHAMP CAR WORLD SERIES POWERED BY FORD • ROUND 2

Gavin Lawrence/LAT

## QUALIFYING

Gavin Lawrence/LAT

Sébastien Bourdais (above) etched his name in the record books by becoming the first driver in Champ Car history to qualify on the pole in each of his first two events. Statisticians might claim that Nigel Mansell achieved the same feat in 1993, but in fact the Englishman took three races to do so, because he was obliged to sit out the second round at Phoenix after crashing heavily during official practice.

Bourdais was only sixth quickest in Friday qualifying, complaining of a general lack of grip, but on Saturday morning he posted the second-fastest time, a scant 0.008s adrift of Oriol Servia. Then he eclipsed everyone in the final 40-minute session to end up virtually a full half-second clear of the pack.

"After the practice sessions, we were pretty happy this morning, but it's always hard to imagine that you can do such a lap during qualifying," said the personable Frenchman, who had bettered Kenny Bräck's existing track record by 0.306s. "Yesterday it was really difficult to handle the car. The team did a fantastic job. The car today was really good."

Paul Tracy was not a factor on Saturday, having crashed his primary Player's Lola beyond immediate repair during practice (see sidebar), but the Canadian, for the second straight race, was already assured of a front-row starting position after setting the pace on Friday. Fellow Canadian Alex Tagliani was an impressive second quickest in final qualifying with Paul Gentilozzi's Johnson Controls/Rocketsports Racing Lola, while Servia maintained his strong form by completing row two of the grid with Pat Patrick's similar Visteon car.

"Obviously I am glad about our performance today, but at the same time I'm disappointed," said the Spaniard. "I thought we had a shot at the pole, but I got caught behind Alex Tagliani when he was slowing down to get a clear lap and didn't get in my last timed lap."

Row three was an all-Mexican affair. Michel Jourdain Jr. continued his strong start to the campaign with Bobby Rahal's Gigante Lola, just edging out Adrian Fernandez, who qualified his own Fernandez Racing Lola among the top six for the second successive race. Bruno Junqueira, surprisingly, could manage no better than seventh in the second Newman/Haas entry, just ahead of Mario Dominguez (Herdez Lola) and the fastest of the Reynards driven by American rookie Ryan Hunter-Reay.

THE Tecate/Telmex Grand Prix of Monterrey unfolded in almost precisely the same manner as the opening round of the 2003 Bridgestone Presents the Champ Car World Series Powered by Ford. Rookie Sébastien Bourdais qualified Newman/Haas Racing's #2 Lilly Ford Cosworth/Lola on the pole, whereupon an early pit-stop snafu, compounded by a driver error, allowed Paul Tracy to take control with his #3 Player's/Forsythe Racing Ford/Lola. The Canadian duly romped to victory, chased once again by Mexican Michel Jourdain Jr. (Gigante/Team Rahal Lola), while Alex Tagliani bounced back from a disappointing season-opener to claim third for Paul Gentilozzi's fledgling Rocketsports team.

"When [Bourdais] went off sequence and I managed to get the lead, I knew I was in good shape," commented Tracy, who became the first man since Rick Mears in 1982 to win the opening two races of the season. "This is a key win in my quest for the championship."

Perfect weather ensured that once again the Mexican fans arrived in droves at the spectacular Fundidora Park venue. Starting from the outside of the front row, Tracy figured he had a good shot at beating Bourdais when J.D. Wilbur waved the green flag. For the second race running, however, the rookie held firm.

"I was going to try and jump the start," declared Tracy. "I jumped ahead of him, but I was on the other side of the track where it was dusty. I just spun the tires through two gears. He hooked up because he was kind of on the line in the middle of the straightaway."

The leading positions remained unchanged from qualifying, with Tagliani in third ahead of Oriol Servia (Visteon Lola) and Jourdain, although behind them, Bruno Junqueira (PacifiCare Lola) did sneak in front of crowd favorite Adrian Fernandez (Tecate/Quaker State/Telmex Lola) for sixth.

After an early full-course caution, when Tiago Monteiro's Fittipaldi-Dingman Reynard was stranded by a broken gearbox, Bourdais once more took off into the lead. Tracy remained virtually glued to his rear wing for the first few laps, but just as Bourdais began to edge clear after two scorching laps at around 1m 16.7s, the Frenchman's advantage was negated for a second time by the yellow flags. This time his countryman, Patrick Lemarie, had been halted out on track by an electrical gremlin.

The Newman/Haas team radioed its man into the pits for routine service during the full-course caution, but Bourdais failed to hear the call. Almost all the other leaders, save Servia, took the opportunity to make pit stops. Bourdais and Servia therefore led away at the restart, chased by Roberto Moreno – whose Herdez Lola had stopped during the previous caution period – Tracy and Tagliani. Then came yet another interruption, when Mexican

rookie Rodolfo Lavin spun Derrick Walker's Corona Reynard to a halt at Turn Three.

This time Bourdais and Servia elected to cut their losses and make for the pits. They duly resumed at the back of the field. Tracy was out front at the restart, having passed Moreno moments before Lavin went off the road. He used the clear track ahead of him to its fullest advantage when the race resumed, and the gap between first and second ballooned to over 12 seconds before Moreno peeled off into the pits for his second stop after 31 laps.

Tagliani inherited second place, but he was no match for Tracy, who continued to stretch his lead. By lap 39, Tracy led Tagliani by almost 23 seconds. Jourdain, after dropping back for a while, had picked up his pace to home in on Tagliani, with Junqueira, Fernandez and Mario Dominguez (Herdez Lola) in hot pursuit. The biggest mover of all, however, was Bourdais. After resuming in 16th following his first pit stop, during which he stalled the engine briefly, the Frenchman passed Servia, the two Dale Coyne Racing Lolas of Joel Camathias and debutant Alex Yoong, then Ryan Hunter-Reay (American Spirit Team Johansson Reynard), Mario Haberfeld (Mi-Jack/Conquest Reynard) and Darren Manning (RAC/Autowindscreens Reynard) in fairly quick succession. Circulating as much as a second per lap quicker than the race leader, Bourdais had risen all the way to seventh, close behind Dominguez, when, on lap 40, a spin by Servia brought out the double yellow flags once more.

The caution came at the perfect time for the leaders, all of whom pulled immediately into the pit lane. Bourdais, though, undid all his great work when he carried a little too much speed into the pit entrance and slid sideways into the wall. The impact didn't seem too severe, but it was enough to break a toe-link in his Lola's right rear suspension.

"The team figured that it wasn't likely we would get into the points-paying range [after making repairs], so we just stopped our race," related the distraught Bourdais. "It's so frustrating not to get a better result from the potential we had."

An electrical glitch caused Tracy to stall the engine during his pit stop, but his advantage was such that he was able to retain the lead. Tagliani, meanwhile, lost a couple of positions while in the pits, although he recouped one of them soon after the restart, on lap 46, when Junqueira made a mistake in Turn Six.

"I locked the rear tires and went off course," said the Brazilian, who dropped from third to ninth.

Tracy remained untroubled, gradually inching clear of second-placed Jourdain. The gap later stabilized at around four seconds – until lap 58, when Tracy ran off the road at Turn Ten.

"It was really just my mistake," admitted the Canadian. "I braked at the same spot every time, but I rushed the downshift a little bit. It locked up the gearbox and started to chatter the back wheels. The back was locked up, the engine was stalled. You know, I wasn't going to turn in like that and have it go around on me. I just decided to go straight and take the shortest route over the side of the track."

It was a graphic illustration of how the latest breed of Champ Cars, with their spec Ford Cosworth engines, were significantly more tricky to handle than their traction-controlled predecessors.

"Just one of those things," reckoned Tracy. "It's a slippery track. One little mistake on the downshift, you can go right off the track. You know, it's very easy."

Tracy was lucky. The excursion cost him virtually all of the time he had made up over Jourdain, but that was all. He put his head down, cleaned off his tires and began to rebuild his advantage. The gap had grown again to over four seconds by the time he

made his way into the pit lane for the third and final time on lap 66. This time the stop was flawless. Tracy resumed with a clear edge over Jourdain.

The Mexican was thrown a lifeline when Tracy's teammate, Patrick Carpentier, ensured a late caution after spinning while attempting to pass Junqueira for fifth. But the final restart saw Jourdain separated from Tracy by the lapped car of Hunter-Reay. The chase was effectively over.

"Unfortunately Ryan did not move over as quickly as I would have hoped, and I ended up going wide and got some dirt on my tires. Then I could not catch Paul, but he was very fast all day," said Jourdain, who was still delighted to finish second – for the second successive race.

Tagliani couldn't quite match the pace of the two leaders, but also drove an excellent race to claim third.

"It's a very good day for this new team," he said. "We had a decent car – not the fastest, but consistent all race long. It's a very small team at the moment. There's a lot of good things to come in the future."

Tagliani remained just clear of several entertaining battles as the race progressed. In the middle stages he was chased by a pair of Mexicans, Fernandez and Dominguez, until the latter was involved in an incident with Manning right after his final pit stop. Then Fernandez had his work cut out to fend off a charging Junqueira, who had recovered well after his earlier error.

Moreno rewarded his team with another top-six finish, despite running a different pit-stop strategy to the other leaders. He profited from an incident just two laps from the end when Manning's attempt to oust Vasser from sixth place resulted in the American being punted off the road in Turn Five.

*Jeremy Shaw*

**Top: The Champ Cars are dwarfed by the imposing architecture of Fundidora Park.**
Phil Abbott/LAT

**Above, left to right: Jimmy Vasser and Stefan Johansson soak up the atmosphere with buddy Nick Jones; Patrick Lemarie posted a second straight top-ten finish for PK Racing; local color courtesy of Tecate.**
Gavin Lawrence/LAT

**Facing page, above right: The Monterrey fans turned out in force and provided their usual frenzied brand of support to the four-strong contingent of Mexican drivers.**
Mike Levitt/LAT

**Facing page, below right: Jourdain was the toast of the locals after coming home a strong second.**
Gavin Lawrence/LAT

**O**NE of the most noteworthy performances in the Tecate/Telmex Grand Prix of Monterrey was posted by Alex Tagliani, who finished a fine third in only the second Champ Car outing for Paul Gentilozzi's Rocketsports Racing team.

The Rocketsports name, while new to open-wheel racing, already was a fixture in the North American sports-car ranks, Gentilozzi himself having claimed numerous victories, including three Trans-Am Championships. He had been talking about spreading his team's wings for a year or so, and after leaning initially toward entering the Indy Racing League, he changed his mind in the fall of 2002 when he realized the Champ Car World Series offered a broader opportunity.

Gentilozzi confirmed his intentions at the final round of the 2002 season in Mexico City, and hired veteran Champ Car chief mechanic/team manager Phil Howard to turn his dream into reality. The next few months were hectic, to say the least. Howard set about pulling together an entire team of personnel and equipment at the organization's established base in Lansing, Michigan, while Gentilozzi concentrated on the business aspects.

Longtime Rocketsports supporter Johnson Controls, a global market leader in automotive systems and facility management and control, signed on to provide primary sponsorship. In mid-January, Gentilozzi announced he had procured the services of veteran Champ Car driver Tagliani. Experienced chief mechanic Tom Howatt already had joined the fledgling team to oversee preparation, and highly respected race engineer Andy Borme, who had spent the previous four years with Marlboro Team Penske, guiding Helio Castroneves to a pair of Indianapolis 500 victories, also became part of the fold.

The team's debut in St. Petersburg was low-key. Tagliani qualified a disappointing 13th, then found the wall after just three laps. Monterrey, however, saw Rocketsports leap into contention. Tagliani was justifiably proud of his crew after starting third and emerging with the sixth podium finish of his career.

"Those guys had to go through nightmares," said Tagliani. "I mean, I never thought we were going to be ready for the first or the second race. There's so many things to get ready for a team to go racing. I think with all those things, finishing third here, it's a great boost for all the guys that have been working Saturday and Sunday, every day, to get everything ready."

Tagliani steered his Rocketsports Lola to the podium in only the team's second race.
Phil Abbott/LAT

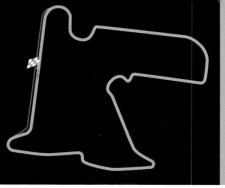

ROUND 2

# TECATE/TELMEX
# GRAND PRIX OF MONTERREY

**PARQUE FUNDIDORA, NUEVO LEON, MEXICO**

**MARCH 23, 85 laps of 2.104 miles – 178.840 miles**

| Pl. | Driver (Nat.) | No. | Team Sponsors Engine/Car | Tires | Q Speed | Q Time | Q Pos. | Laps | Time/Status | Ave. (mph) | Pts. |
|---|---|---|---|---|---|---|---|---|---|---|---|
| 1 | Paul Tracy (CDN) | 3 | Forsythe Racing Player's/Indeck Ford Cosworth/Lola B02/00 | BS | 98.089 | 1m 17.220s | 2 | 85 | 2h 03m 04.677s | 87.184 | 22 |
| 2 | Michel Jourdain Jr. (MEX) | 9 | Team Rahal Gigante Ford Cosworth/Lola B01/00 | BS | 99.835 | 1m 15.869s | 5 | 85 | 2h 03m 06.716s | 87.160 | 16 |
| 3 | Alex Tagliani (CDN) | 33 | Rocketsports Racing Johnson Controls Ford Cosworth/Lola B01/00 | BS | 100.407 | 1m 15.437s | 3 | 85 | 2h 03m 16.707s | 87.042 | 14 |
| 4 | Adrian Fernandez (MEX) | 51 | Fernandez Tecate/Quaker State/Telmex Ford Cosworth/Lola B02/00 | BS | 99.745 | 1m 15.938s | 6 | 85 | 2h 03m 18.916s | 87.016 | 12 |
| 5 | Bruno Junqueira (BR) | 1 | Newman/Haas Racing PacifiCare Ford Cosworth/Lola B02/00 | BS | 99.640 | 1m 16.018s | 7 | 85 | 2h 03m 19.527s | 87.009 | 10 |
| 6 | Roberto Moreno (BR) | 4 | Herdez Competition Ford Cosworth/Lola B01/00 | BS | 98.108 | 1m 17.205s | 14 | 85 | 2h 03m 35.610s | 86.820 | 8 |
| 7 | *Darren Manning (GB) | 15 | Walker Racing RAC/Autowindscreens Ford Cosworth/Reynard 02I | BS | 98.428 | 1m 16.954s | 13 | 85 | 2h 03m 39.860s | 86.770 | 6 |
| 8 | Patrick Carpentier (CDN) | 32 | Forsythe Racing Player's/Indeck Ford Cosworth/Lola B02/00 | BS | 97.872 | 1m 17.391s | 15 | 84 | Running | | 5 |
| 9 | *Alex Yoong (MAL) | 11 | Dale Coyne Racing Ford Cosworth/Lola B2K/00 | BS | 96.674 | 1m 18.350s | 17 | 84 | Running | | 4 |
| 10 | *Patrick Lemarie (F) | 27 | PK Racing Ford Cosworth/Lola B02/00 | BS | 98.457 | 1m 16.931s | 12 | 84 | Running | | 3 |
| 11 | *Joel Camathias (CH) | 19 | Dale Coyne Racing Ford Cosworth/Lola B01/00 | BS | 95.510 | 1m 19.305s | 19 | 84 | Running | | 2 |
| 12 | *Ryan Hunter-Reay (USA) | 31 | American Spirit Team Johansson Ford Cosworth/Reynard 02I | BS | 98.969 | 1m 16.533s | 9 | 83 | Running | | 1 |
| 13 | Mario Dominguez (MEX) | 55 | Herdez Competition Ford Cosworth/Lola B03/00 | BS | 99.506 | 1m 16.120s | 8 | 83 | Running | | |
| 14 | Jimmy Vasser (USA) | 12 | American Spirit Team Johansson Ford Cosworth/Reynard 01I | BS | 97.060 | 1m 18.038s | 16 | 83 | Running | | |
| 15 | *Rodolfo Lavin (MEX) | 5 | Walker Racing Corona Competition Ford Cosworth/Reynard 02I | BS | 96.375 | 1m 18.593s | 18 | 81 | Running | | |
| 16 | *Mario Haberfeld (BR) | 34 | Mi-Jack Conquest Racing Ford Cosworth/Reynard 02I | BS | 98.483 | 1m 16.911s | 11 | 67 | Accident | | |
| 17 | *Sébastien Bourdais (F) | 2 | Newman/Haas Racing Lilly Ford Cosworth/Lola B01/00 | BS | 101.076 | 1m 14.938s | 1 | 40 | Accident | | 1 |
| 18 | Oriol Servia (E) | 20 | Patrick Racing Visteon Ford Cosworth/Lola B02/00 | BS | 100.355 | 1m 15.476s | 4 | 38 | Accident | | |
| 19 | *Tiago Monteiro (P) | 7 | Fittipaldi-Dingman Racing Ford Cosworth/Reynard 02I | BS | 98.942 | 1m 16.554s | 10 | 2 | Electrical | | |

\* denotes rookie driver

**Caution flags:** Laps 4–6, tow/Monteiro; laps 14–15, tow/Lemarie; laps 17–18, spin/Lavin; laps 39–43, tow/Servia; laps 78–80, tow/Carpentier. **Total: Five for 15 laps.**

**Lap leaders:** Sébastien Bourdais, 1–16 (16 laps); Paul Tracy, 17–85 (69 laps). **Totals: Tracy, 69 laps; Bourdais, 16 laps.**

**Fastest race lap:** Bruno Junqueira, 1m 15.700s, 100.058 mph on lap 59.

**Championship positions:** 1 Tracy, 43; 2 Jourdain Jr., 32; 3 Junqueira, 24; 4 Moreno, 18; 5 Tagliani, 14; 6 Haberfeld & Fernandez, 12; 8 Carpentier, 10; 9 Vasser, 8; 10 Monteiro, Manning, Camathias & Lemarie, 6; 14 Bourdais, 5; 15 Yoong, 4; 16 Servia & Hunter-Reay, 1.

# MONTERREY SNIPPETS

• Monterrey's Fundidora Park has become WELL ESTABLISHED on the Champ Car World Series calendar since hosting its first event in 2001. Rookie Sébastien Bourdais was certainly impressed: "It's a beautiful place. I think I have never raced in such a great track. I never took so many pictures [with fans] and signed so many autographs in my entire life. The fans are very enthusiastic."

• Bourdais looked to be on course to maintain Newman/Haas Racing's unbeaten RECORD at the track (Cristiano da Matta won in both 2001 and 2002), until his incident on lap 40. Teammate Bruno Junqueira set the fastest lap of the race in his PacifiCare Lola, but lost any chance of at least a podium finish when he made a mistake. "Maybe between our difficult race in St. Pete and today we have all of the bad luck behind us and we can have a good race in Long Beach," said the Brazilian, who finished fifth.

• Patrick Carpentier endured a ROLLER-COASTER weekend. He was third quickest in Friday's provisional qualifying session, despite feeling decidedly under the weather. The French-Canadian's medical condition worsened overnight, and while he bravely ventured out in first practice on Saturday, he made a mistake on only his fourth lap and – like Player's teammate Paul Tracy – damaged the chassis of his primary car when he bounced heavily over the curbs. Carpentier spent the remainder of the day resting in his hotel room. He made good progress in the race, rising as high as fifth, before spinning out on lap 78 in a vain attempt to pass Bruno Junqueira.

• The usual massive crowd (92,713) on raceday was treated to an exciting race. The LOCAL DRIVERS rose to the occasion, too, with Michel Jourdain Jr. claiming a strong second and Adrian Fernandez fourth. "Two Mexicans in the first four

is really fantastic for our country," said Fernandez, who finally ended a poor stretch of results dating back to the 2002 season. Mario Dominguez also displayed an excellent turn of speed, rising to fifth before being involved in a late incident. He posted the second-fastest lap of the race en route to an unrepresentative 13th.

• DARREN MANNING was very encouraged by his progress going into the final qualifying session with Derrick Walker's RAC/Autowindscreens Reynard. The young Englishman (below) had been among the top ten in every session, but his hopes of a top grid placing were thwarted by a broken third gear. Manning instead qualified a disappointing 13th.

• The entry list showed five Mexican drivers, but when Roberto Gonzalez failed to produce the promised sponsorship, he was replaced in Dale Coyne Racing's #11 Lola by fellow ROOKIE Alex Yoong (above). The 26-year-old Malaysian, who had contested 11 Formula 1 races in 2002 with the Minardi team, made steady progress during the weekend, despite being handicapped by the fact he had not so much as even tested the car prior to first practice. He mimicked polesitter Bourdais by spinning on his way into the pit lane during the race, but survived the incident to finish a respectable ninth.

# LONG BEACH

## SO NEAR, YET SO FAR

**M**ICHEL Jourdain Jr. was the revelation of the 2002 Champ Car season, emerging from mediocrity to become a bona fide challenger after joining forces with Team Rahal. Jourdain actually led the points hunt briefly, following a sequence of strong results in the early races, before fading to an eventual tenth place in the point standings. Later he acknowledged that he needed to improve his performances in qualifying if he was to take the next step forward in his career.

Indeed, in 2002, while Jourdain finished more times among the top ten than anyone else (14), he qualified only four times within the first five rows of the grid, with a high of sixth in the very first race. Jourdain and his team worked hard over the winter to pinpoint their shortcomings, and their diligence obviously paid off. The 26-year-old from Mexico City started fifth in each of the first two races of 2003, then qualified on the pole at Long Beach.

"Last year's qualifying killed me," he admitted. "We were racing very good, we were always very fast in the races, but everything was going wrong in qualifying. Sometimes I made mistakes, sometimes I couldn't get a lap together. Many times our strategy was not very good, you know. Just little things. Something was always happening.

"We knew we had to do better. So far this year it's been good, but there are many races to go. We just have to keep doing the same. Every race is a new race. We can't say because we've qualified better this year, we have the problem solved. We have ovals, permanent road courses. Especially the permanent road courses last year were very bad for us. So we have all that to work on, too."

Jourdain followed up his pole-winning effort by driving a characteristically heads up race. He did not become flustered when he was ambushed – perhaps unfairly – by Paul Tracy at the start. He kept his focus concentrated on keeping the pressure on his rival and conserving fuel, and emerged in the lead after the first pit stops. Then he took control of the race – until his Gigante Lola's gearbox failed during his final stop just seven laps shy of what would have been a thoroughly well-deserved maiden Champ Car win. Jourdain was distraught.

"I don't know if it's the best or the worst day of my life," he said. "It is terrible when everything goes so perfect and you don't win. Days like this don't happen very often. This is the first time it has happened in 123 races for me."

Typically he remained in upbeat mood. "That win is going to come soon, for sure," he promised.

## QUALIFYING

The "usual suspects" – Paul Tracy, Bruno Junqueira and Sébastien Bourdais – topped the timing charts in the provisional qualifying session on Friday afternoon, but when push came to shove 24 hours later, several more contenders emerged from the shadows.

Final qualifying was held in perfect weather conditions, warm and sunny, and after 20 minutes Patrick Carpentier was the first to eclipse the time set one day earlier by Tracy, his Player's teammate. Moments later, after clipping virtually a full half-second from Carpentier's best, Michel Jourdain Jr. bounced to the top aboard Team Rahal's Gigante Lola. Then it was the turn of Alex Tagliani to take the limelight, vaulting ahead with Paul Gentilozzi's Johnson Controls/Rocketsports Racing entry.

But Jourdain was on a tear, putting the pole position beyond the reach of his rivals – for the first time in his career – with just three minutes remaining. The Mexican was justifiably elated.

"Many times I've been so close," he exclaimed. "Yesterday in qualifying we thought we had a very competitive car. We made a [setup] change in the middle, and it didn't work. Today we made a little change in the middle, and it worked pretty good."

Tracy didn't venture out until almost halfway through the final period, whereupon his hopes of holding on to the pole went awry when he clipped one of the omnipresent walls and broke a control arm on his Player's Lola's left rear suspension. The good news was that the incident prevented him from using his second fresh set of Bridgestone Potenza tires, which, ultimately, proved extremely fortuitous for the race.

Tagliani posted the second-fastest lap in qualifying, just as he had done in Monterrey, but once again he was obliged to line up third on the grid behind Tracy, who already had assured himself of a front-row starting position by virtue of leading the way on Friday. Tagliani's effort was especially meritorious given that he was working with two new race engineers (see Snippets), who wisely opted not to stray away from the team's basic setup.

The two Newman/Haas Lolas qualified fourth and fifth, Junqueira ahead of Bourdais for the first time, followed by Carpentier and Adrian Fernandez. Darren Manning's Walker Racing entry was the fastest Reynard in tenth.

**Above right:** Ryan Hunter-Reay recorded the best finish of his young Champ Car career with seventh.
Mike Levitt/LAT

**Right:** American Spirit Team Johansson stablemate Jimmy Vasser used his wealth of experience to good effect to clinch fourth.
P. Cocciadeferro/LAT

MICHEL Jourdain Jr. seemed set to follow his second-place finishes in each of the first two races by claiming a long-overdue maiden victory in the Toyota Grand Prix of Long Beach. After securing his first ever pole, the 26-year-old from Mexico City was beaten away from the start by Champ Car World Series points leader Paul Tracy, then regained the advantage following the first round of pit stops. Jourdain held a small, but apparently secure, lead when he made his final pit stop with just seven laps remaining. Team Rahal completed the service with its usual alacrity, only for the transmission in his Gigante Ford/Lola to fail abruptly. Game over.

Tracy instead went on to take the checkered flag in Jerry Forsythe's Player's/Indeck Ford Cosworth/Lola, at a new event record speed of 91.590 mph. The Canadian's triumph marked the first time in CART history that one driver had won the opening three races of a new season (although Al Unser had achieved the feat under USAC sanction in 1971).

"We needed some luck to keep the winning streak alive, and we had some of that today," acknowledged Tracy. "I was pulling out all the stops, doing everything I could, but it wasn't enough to overtake Michel. He definitely had the measure of me until that last pit stop."

Owner/driver Adrian Fernandez parlayed an inspired pit strategy – and a rapid pace – to finish second in his Tecate/Quaker State/Telmex Lola, while Bruno Junqueira guided Newman/Haas Racing's PacifiCare Lola to the final podium position.

Almost two hours earlier, under generally overcast skies and in front of the usual large, enthusiastic Southern California crowd, there was controversy when Tracy appeared to jump ahead of the polesitter as the green flag waved.

"I was really disappointed in the start," related Jourdain. "I am not sure what [the officials] were thinking because it was like Paul was in the lead when they threw the green flag."

Tracy, meanwhile, proclaimed his innocence.

"The Starter said he wanted to see three to four rows lined up," said the Canadian. "We came out [of the Turn 11 hairpin] together, side by side, and it was a fairly quick roll-up in second gear and we waited, waited, waited. I jumped on the throttle where I thought that we should. We were pretty much simultaneous. I hooked up and got through it without any wheelspin. I think he probably spun the tires just a bit, and that's all it takes."

The officials clearly sided with Tracy, because there was no call from Race Control. The familiar blue-and-white Player's car duly led into Turn One for the first of 90 laps around the challenging street circuit. Junqueira, who had started fourth, tucked in behind Tracy to squeak past third-place qualifier Alex Tagliani's Johnson Controls Lola in Turn One, followed by Sébastien Bourdais and Patrick Carpentier.

The first significant change of position came on lap 20, when Tagliani's pressure on Junqueira finally paid off and he was able to slide through into third place. By then, though, the two leaders were almost ten seconds up the road. Tracy and Jourdain were never separated by more than a few car lengths, but, equally, Jourdain never looked likely to make a pass.

Instead he had a more pressing issue on his mind: conservation. The torrid pace resulted in several contenders using more fuel than they had anticipated. Sure enough, Tagliani was forced to make his first pit stop three laps shy of the mandated maximum of 28 laps. Tracy, too, couldn't stretch his first 35 gallons of methanol and ducked into the pits after 27 laps. Their profligacy was to prove costly.

Jourdain, meanwhile, had been able to save fuel by running in Tracy's wake, and the extra lap at speed, coupled with excellent service by Bharat Naran's crew, enabled him to emerge from the pits narrowly ahead of the Canadian. Then he made his Gigante car as *gigante* as it could possibly be as he struggled to maintain his hard-won advantage. This time it was Tracy's turn to cry foul.

"I tried to make a pass on him and he took me over to the wall," claimed the Canadian. "That was a little bit sketchy. We bumped wheels and I was up against the wall. So that was a little bit frustrating. Then the yellow came out right after that."

The first full-course caution of the afternoon (after Patrick Lemarie spun in Turn One) couldn't have come at a better moment for the new race leader – a little more than half a lap after he had emerged from the pits and before Tracy could make a move to reclaim the point.

The next dozen or so laps included three more brief full-course cautions, during which the status quo remained at the front of the field. Behind, however, there was plenty of shuffling as teams sought to take advantage of the pit-stop windows.

The quickest of quick thinkers in the pit lane figured that the

**S**EVERAL new teams graced the scene when the 2003 Bridgestone Presents the Champ Car World Series Powered by Ford convened for the first time at St. Petersburg in February. All of them faced an uphill battle, especially since the season began a full month earlier than in 2002. None was more pressed, however, than American Spirit Team Johansson.

The final go-ahead to form the team wasn't made until January 1, so everything was a battle against the clock. Incredibly, four race-ready Reynard chassis were presented for the opening round in Florida, and both Champ Car veteran Jimmy Vasser, the only former champion in the field, and rookie Ryan Hunter-Reay, a graduate of the CART Ladder System who had progressed through the Barber Dodge Pro Series and Toyota Atlantic, acquitted themselves very respectably during the first two races.

Hopes were high in the runup to Long Beach, and things looked good on Friday when both drivers were among the top ten in each of the first two practice sessions. Provisional qualifying went well, too, with Vasser posting the tenth-fastest time and Hunter-Reay 12th. Saturday was a bit more of a struggle, even though both men improved their times. Hunter-Reay, troubled by excessive understeer, retained 12th on the grid, just over a second adrift of Jourdain's pole time, while a last-minute wing change on Vasser's car did not have the desired effect and the 1996 champion slipped back to 14th.

Still, the mood remained upbeat for the race. "We need to remain focused and bring both cars home at the end of the race," noted team principal Stefan Johansson.

Sure enough, both Vasser and Hunter-Reay made good progress. An inspired call to make a pit stop during a full-course caution on lap 34 enabled Vasser to leap several positions up the order, whereupon a truly spectacular outside-line pass of Mario Dominguez in Turn One showed that his racing skills remained as sharp as ever. He continued the good work to take a strong fourth, while Hunter-Reay secured his best finish to date in seventh place.

"It's a great result for us, especially considering the weekend we have had," said Vasser. "We couldn't buy a break all weekend and our strategy really worked out for us today."

**Right: Mario Dominguez scored his first points of the season with fifth place.**
P. Cocciadeferro/LAT

**Far right: Overcast skies above the Long Beach grid, with Bobby Rahal center stage.**
Mike Levitt/LAT

**Below: A hat trick of wins for Tracy.**
Dan Boyd/LAT

**Below: Adrian Fernandez profited from astute pit-stop strategy to vault from seventh to second, equaling the best result to date for his eponymous team.**
Gavin Lawrence/LAT

earliest opportunity to make a second visit to the pits – and still be able to reach the finish with just one more stop – would be on lap 34. Carpentier, who had been running in fourth, was the highest-placed runner to employ that strategy. Oriol Servia, Mario Dominguez and Jimmy Vasser followed suit. A lap later, Fernandez made his second visit to the pits for fuel and fresh Bridgestone Potenza tires. On lap 37, following a very brief period of green-flag racing, Bourdais, Tagliani (who had slipped to fifth) and a few others headed into the pit lane.

When the race resumed after 41 laps, Jourdain remained in the lead ahead of Tracy and Junqueira. All three still would require two more pit stops. Everyone else, led initially by Servia, needed just one more stop. Interesting. The leaders knew they needed to run absolutely flat out to have any chance of winning.

Jourdain stretched away to around a two-second lead over Tracy before making his next pit stop, on lap 56, along with Junqueira, who had been a similar distance behind in third. Tracy, as before, had been obliged to stop one lap earlier. When the trio rejoined they were temporarily in 11th, 12th and 13th places.

Servia, meanwhile, took over the lead, having passed Carpentier superbly under braking for Turn One immediately after the earlier restart on lap 42. Fernandez remained close behind the French-Canadian in third. These three made what would be their final visits to the pit lane on laps 62 (Servia and Carpentier) and 63 (Fernandez). Once again, the advantage of running an extra lap at speed provided dividends for Fernandez, who was able to overtake Servia.

The latest round of pit stops elevated Jourdain once more to the catbird seat on lap 66. Tracy and Junqueira still chased along behind, and all three continued to drive flat out in the knowledge that they needed a gap of at least 32 seconds over Fernandez & Co., if they were to successfully make their final pit stops without losing positions. It was going to be close.

Junqueira was the first of the three leaders to make his final

stop. It came on lap 79. At that stage he was around 30 seconds clear of Fernandez. The stop was quick, at 9.4 seconds, but it wasn't enough. He resumed behind Fernandez in fourth. Tracy was next in after 82 laps. He emerged still in second place, albeit with Fernandez charging hard to close the gap – and looking to take advantage of his already-hot tires.

Now the pressure was on Jourdain and Team Rahal. Everyone did their job perfectly, but then the gearbox broke. Jourdain was virtually inconsolable.

"I did everything right and the crew did everything right," he said, after regaining his composure. "It just wasn't meant to happen." At least not this day.

So it was that Tracy found himself in the lead once more. For the first time in 2003, however, he had a real fight on his hands. Fernandez was hot on his heels and seeking to become the first owner/driver to win a Champ Car race since Bobby Rahal at Nazareth Speedway in 1992.

Tracy, though, was up to the task, and Fernandez was content with second.

"I was very fast on my last set of tires and I was pushing very hard," said Fernandez. "The Bridgestone tires were very consistent. Unfortunately I just overused them, and at the end my rear tires were just gone. Then I was not close enough to Paul when he came out of the pits. Once you give him the chance of at least a lap, I mean, it's over. He had new tires, or newer tires than I had. So at the end, I was just trying to stay there – it was very important to finish the race on the podium."

Junqueira had a relatively uneventful day, but he managed to keep within shouting distance of Tracy in the points standings by virtue of another top-three finish. Jimmy Vasser, meanwhile, claimed a well-deserved fourth place for American Spirit Team Johansson after the luckless Servia ran out of fuel with three laps remaining.

*Jeremy Shaw*

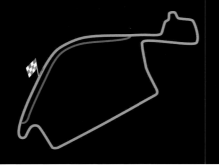

# TOYOTA
# GRAND PRIX OF LONG BEACH

**ROUND 3**

## LONG BEACH STREET CIRCUIT, CALIFORNIA
### APRIL 13, 90 laps of 1.968 miles – 177.120 miles

| Pl. | Driver (Nat.) | No. | Team Sponsors Engine/Car | Tires | Q Speed | Q Time | Q Pos. | Laps | Time/Status | Ave. (mph) | Pts. |
|---|---|---|---|---|---|---|---|---|---|---|---|
| 1 | Paul Tracy (CDN) | 3 | Forsythe Racing Player's/Indeck Ford Cosworth/Lola B02/00 | BS | 102.561 | 1m 09.079s | 2 | 90 | 1h 56m 01.792s | 91.590 | 21 |
| 2 | Adrian Fernandez (MEX) | 51 | Fernandez Tecate/Quaker State/Telmex Ford Cosworth/Lola B02/00 | BS | 103.001 | 1m 08.784s | 7 | 90 | 1h 56m 06.336s | 91.530 | 16 |
| 3 | Bruno Junqueira (BR) | 1 | Newman/Haas Racing PacifiCare Ford Cosworth/Lola B02/00 | BS | 103.372 | 1m 08.537s | 4 | 90 | 1h 56m 15.443s | 91.411 | 14 |
| 4 | Jimmy Vasser (USA) | 12 | American Spirit Team Johansson Ford Cosworth/Reynard 2KI | BS | 101.552 | 1m 09.765s | 14 | 90 | 1h 56m 22.832s | 91.314 | 12 |
| 5 | Mario Dominguez (MEX) | 55 | Herdez Competition Ford Cosworth/Lola B03/00 | BS | 102.349 | 1m 09.222s | 11 | 90 | 1h 56m 23.983s | 91.299 | 10 |
| 6 | Patrick Carpentier (CDN) | 32 | Forsythe Racing Player's/Indeck Ford Cosworth/Lola B02/00 | BS | 103.187 | 1m 08.660s | 6 | 90 | 1h 56m 24.452s | 91.293 | 8 |
| 7 | *Ryan Hunter-Reay (USA) | 31 | American Spirit Team Johansson Ford Cosworth/Reynard 02I | BS | 102.147 | 1m 09.359s | 12 | 90 | 1h 56m 27.495s | 91.253 | 6 |
| 8 | *Darren Manning (GB) | 15 | Walker Racing RAC/Autowindscreens Ford Cosworth/Reynard 02I | BS | 102.478 | 1m 09.135s | 10 | 90 | 1h 56m 35.165s | 91.153 | 5 |
| 9 | *Mario Haberfeld (BR) | 34 | Mi-Jack Conquest Racing Ford Cosworth/Reynard 02I | BS | 101.191 | 1m 10.014s | 15 | 90 | 1h 56m 50.363s | 90.956 | 4 |
| 10 | Alex Tagliani (CDN) | 33 | Rocketsports Racing Johnson Controls Ford Cosworth/Lola B01/00 | BS | 103.623 | 1m 08.371s | 3 | 89 | Running | | 3 |
| 11 | *Tiago Monteiro (P) | 7 | Fittipaldi-Dingman Racing Ford Cosworth/Reynard 02I | BS | 101.079 | 1m 10.092s | 16 | 88 | Running | | 2 |
| 12 | Oriol Servia (E) | 20 | Patrick Racing Visteon Ford Cosworth/Lola B02/00 | BS | 102.945 | 1m 08.821s | 8 | 87 | Out of fuel | | 1 |
| 13 | *Patrick Lemarie (F) | 27 | PK Racing Ford Cosworth/Lola B02/00 | BS | 101.595 | 1m 09.736s | 13 | 87 | Running | | |
| 14 | *Joel Camathias (CH) | 19 | Dale Coyne Racing Ford Cosworth/Lola B01/00 | BS | 99.362 | 1m 11.303s | 18 | 84 | Running | | |
| 15 | Michel Jourdain Jr. (MEX) | 9 | Team Rahal Gigante Ford Cosworth/Lola B01/00 | BS | 103.918 | 1m 08.177s | 1 | 83 | Gearbox | | 2 |
| 16 | *Sébastien Bourdais (F) | 2 | Newman/Haas Racing Lilly Ford Cosworth/Lola B01/00 | BS | 103.354 | 1m 08.549s | 5 | 70 | Engine | | |
| 17 | Roberto Moreno (BR) | 4 | Herdez Competition Ford Cosworth/Lola B01/00 | BS | 102.637 | 1m 09.028s | 9 | 36 | Accident | | |
| 18 | *Rodolfo Lavin (MEX) | 5 | Walker Racing Corona Competition Ford Cosworth/Reynard 01I | BS | 99.671 | 1m 11.082s | 17 | 35 | Accident | | |
| 19 | *Alex Yoong (MAL) | 11 | Dale Coyne Racing Ford Cosworth/Lola B2K/00 | BS | 98.997 | 1m 11.566s | 19 | 32 | Accident | | |

*\* denotes rookie driver*

**Caution flags:** Laps 28–30, tow/Lemarie; laps 33–35, accident/Yoong; laps 37–40, accident/Lavin & Moreno. **Total: Three for 10 laps.**

**Lap leaders:** Paul Tracy, 1–26 (26 laps); Michel Jourdain Jr., 27–56 (30 laps); Oriol Servia, 57–61 (5 laps); Adrian Fernandez, 62 (1 lap); Sébastien Bourdais, 63–65 (3 laps); Jourdain, 66–83 (18 laps); Tracy, 84–90 (7 laps). Totals: Jourdain, 48 laps; Tracy, 33 laps; Servia, 5 laps; Bourdais, 3 laps; Fernandez, 1 lap.

**Fastest race lap:** Michel Jourdain Jr., 1m 09.050s, 102.604 mph on lap 77.

**Championship positions:** 1 Tracy, 64; 2 Junqueira, 38; 3 Jourdain Jr., 34; 4 Fernandez, 28; 5 Vasser, 20; 6 Moreno & Carpentier, 18; 8 Tagliani, 17; 9 Haberfeld, 16; 10 Manning, 11; 11 Dominguez, 10; 12 Monteiro, 8; 13 Hunter-Reay, 7; 14 Camathias & Lemarie, 6; 16 Bourdais, 5; 17 Yoong, 4; 18 Servia, 2.

# LONG BEACH SNIPPETS

• A few days after the 29th Annual Toyota Grand Prix of Long Beach, the Bridgestone Presents the Champ Car World Series Powered by Ford was featured on one of the nation's most popular TELEVISION shows, FOX channel's "American Idol." Invited by the Ford Motor Company, the seven finalists on the hit music reality show were shown meeting and talking with Champ Car drivers Michel Jourdain Jr. and Oriol Servia along with their teams.

• As usual, a long list of CELEBRITIES took the time to savor the sights and sounds of the famed Southern California "beach party." In addition to the "American Idol" finalists, other notables included Luke Perry, best known for his role as Dillon McKay on the TV hit series "90210," George Eads, who plays crime investigator Nick Stokes on "CSI," Larry Wilcox, well known for his portrayal of California Highway Patrol officer Jon Baker in "CHiPs," and movie stars Luke Wilson ("Legally Blonde" and both "Charlie's Angels" films) and Owen Wilson ("Shanghai Noon," "Behind Enemy Lines" and "Blade").

• Yet more well-known names were featured in the 27th Annual Toyota Pro-Celebrity race, which in the previous dozen years had raised more than $1 million for the national "Racing for Kids" CHARITY. An enthralling contest saw "Days of Our Lives" TV star Peter Reckell fight off a determined late challenge from "Monster

Garage" host Jesse James. Seven-time AMA Supercross Champion Jeremy McGrath finished fourth overall and won the professional category.

• A mouth-watering selection of Historic Grand Prix cars, honoring the FORMULA 1 heritage of Long Beach, featured on the support card. First across the finish line was Danny Baker's ex-Brett Lunger 1976 Chesterfield McLaren M23, followed by Charles Nearburg's ex-Alan Jones 1981 Long Beach Grand Prix-winning Williams FW07 and Erich Joiner's ex-Keke Rosberg 1983 Williams FW08C.

• Fittipaldi-Dingman Racing, owned by former Champ Car and Formula 1 champion Emerson Fittipaldi and businessman James Dingman, sported ALLEGIANCE to the World Childhood Foundation on the flanks of Tiago Monteiro's #7 Reynard (below). The charity had been founded by Queen Silvia of Sweden as a means of promoting better living conditions for vulnerable and exploited children.

• Despite a fine run to third place in Monterrey by Alex Tagliani, the ROCKETSPORTS RACING team lost the services of race engineer Andy

Borme, who preferred to make his family's home in Indianapolis, rather than Lansing, Michigan. Borme's place was filled by Will Phillips, formerly of PacWest Racing and Reynard Racing Cars, and Adam Schaeckter, who had worked with Mo Nunn Racing in 2002. The change of regime clearly didn't have any detrimental effect, since Tagliani was second quickest in qualifying. "Right now I'm really happy with the way the car is," said Tagliani. "I'm working with pretty much the same setup every race weekend. We try little things, but not anything really weird on the car right now."

• ANDY BORME had landed a job with Eric Bachelart's Mi-Jack/Conquest Racing team, working on the Reynard of Mario Haberfeld. Amazingly this marked the third engineering change of the season for the Brazilian rookie. Andy Miller, who had worked with Haberfeld in Europe, parted company with the team prior to the first race. Then Todd Malloy left after the first race to take up a position with Paul Tracy at Team Player's. Veteran John Ward stepped in to assist the team at Monterrey, prior to Borme's arrival.

• Long Beach marked the final race for Team Rahal crew chief BHARAT NARAN. He was leaving the Hilliard, Ohio-based organization to return to his former base in Southern California to run an off-road truck program for ex-Champ Car racers, and brothers, Mike and Robbie Groff.

Phil Abbott/LAT

BRIDGESTONE PRESENTS THE CHAMP CAR WORLD SERIES POWERED BY FORD · ROUND 4

# BRANDS HATCH

Main photograph: **Sébastien Bourdais leads Newman/Haas teammate Bruno Junqueira and Alex Tagliani up the hill toward the Druids hairpin.**
Malcolm Griffiths/LAT

Above right: **A moment to savor for Bourdais following his first Champ Car win.**
Kevin Wood/LAT

## THE FIRST WIN IS THE SWEETEST

SÉBASTIEN Bourdais etched his name in the record books by qualifying on pole for both of his first two Champ Car races, at St. Petersburg and Monterrey, only to be stymied each time by a strategic miscue and a driving error. Consequently he had just five championship points to his credit — two for being fastest qualifier on each day in Florida, two more for an 11th-place finish in the opener and one for snaring the pole in Mexico. Then, at Long Beach, after starting fifth, his Lilly Lola was forced out by a rare Ford Cosworth engine failure. No points again.

At Brands Hatch, however, Bourdais put all those disappointments firmly behind him. He had never been to the short, challenging circuit before, but Bourdais was second fastest in practice and was only narrowly edged by Paul Tracy and his own Newman/Haas Racing teammate, Bruno Junqueira, in provisional qualifying. Not bad at all for his first experience of single-car qualifying.

"It is a different exercise than we are used to," he said. "My first lap was pretty quick, but it's always a compromise between pushing hard and not taking too many chances."

Bourdais was fastest in practice on Sunday morning and felt confident of being able to attack Tracy's provisional pole time. The ambient temperature in the afternoon was significantly higher, however, and less conducive to outright speed. He came excruciatingly close to beating Tracy, but on his final lap carried much more speed than before into Paddock Hill Bend (Turn One) and almost crashed. He had to be content with second.

The Frenchman chased after Tracy in the early stages of the 165-lap race. His proximity to the race leader also enabled him to save a little fuel, which proved to be crucial as he completed one more lap than Tracy before making his first stop. Bourdais duly emerged with the lead, then controlled the remainder of the race after Tracy succumbed to a gearbox failure.

"I am very pleased about the win," said Bourdais, whose only "mistake" came after the checkered flag when he stalled the engine in a dismal attempt at donuts. "I knew coming into the race that I really needed just to make it to the finish and score some points, and I told myself that I was not going to bust my car up running like hell for the win, and it came to us anyway. I think, as a Frenchman, I will appreciate the champagne tonight!"

SÉBASTIEN Bourdais displayed scintillating speed in his first three Champ Car races, but received precious little reward. Finally, however, in the inaugural London Champ Car Trophy at the famed Brands Hatch road course, just 20 miles or so from the British capital, the Frenchman emerged to score a fine victory for Newman/Haas Racing.

Once again the race boiled down to a duel between Bourdais and Paul Tracy, who was seeking his fourth consecutive win. Tracy gave himself the best possible opportunity by snaring the pole, but this time Lady Luck was not looking his way. He lost out to Bourdais at the first round of pit stops and later succumbed to a gearbox meltdown, leaving the way clear for the Newman/Haas driver to take his first checkered flag.

"We should have won a couple of races earlier in the year, but had troubles, so this is very satisfying for me and the Lilly team," said Bourdais. "It's been a frustrating year until now."

A large crowd had assembled under mostly sunny skies in the amphitheater-like setting on a Bank Holiday Monday, and although everyone realized that overtaking would be difficult on the serpentine 1.192-mile layout, expectations were high for a spectacular show. The first attempt at a start was aborted when the field was not lined up to the satisfaction of Starter J.D. Wilbur, but the green flag was shown the next time around for the first of 165 laps.

Tracy took advantage of his pole position to lead the way into the daunting Paddock Hill Bend. Bourdais and teammate Bruno Junqueira slotted in dutifully behind the Player's Lola, while Alex Tagliani (Johnson Controls Lola) contrived to edge out Oriol

Servia's Visteon car for fourth place. In their wake, Adrian Fernandez found himself jostled into a huge sideways drift midway through the tricky first corner and instantly lost several positions as he struggled to maintain control of his Tecate/Quaker State/Telmex Lola.

Tracy, meanwhile, quickly established a good rhythm, stretching his lead over Bourdais and Junqueira to almost two seconds within the first ten laps. Tagliani was a similar distance behind the two Newman/Haas Lolas, while Servia headed a closely matched group comprising Mario Dominguez (Herdez Lola), Darren Manning (RAC/Autowindscreens Reynard), Patrick Carpentier (Player's Lola) and the recovered Fernandez, who was ruing that first-corner mishap.

"I had a great start and something happened," related the Mexican, who had spent a lot of time at Brands Hatch when racing in the British Formula Ford series during the formative stages of his career. "I am not sure if I was hit or not. I almost lost it and went into the sand [trap]. That cost us a few positions. I tried to push, but it was very difficult to pass."

The pit stops, indeed, provided the best opportunity to make up positions, so strategy assumed an even greater importance than usual. The extremely narrow pit lane led officials to adopt a slightly different rule for this event, the usual minimum number of laps between pit stops being replaced by a simple mandate that every car should make at least two stops. The timing of those stops was left up to the teams. Unfortunately, fuel consumption also played a prominent role. Several drivers struggled to achieve adequate fuel mileage, which, due to the absence of yellow-flag

Druids," related the Malaysian. "I got into the dirty stuff and sailed in slow motion into the tires."

Yoong's departure left 12 drivers on the lead lap. Two of them, Tagliani and Manning, elected to make pit stops during the caution, thereby committing themselves to a three-stop strategy.

Bourdais turned the two fastest laps of the race thus far immediately after the restart, but Tracy countered with an even quicker lap on his 91st circuit. There was still precious little to choose between them. Junqueira couldn't match their pace and had slipped some four seconds in arrears at this stage, with Dominguez charging along in his wake.

Dominguez and Servia were the first to make their second and final pit stops, on lap 109. Tracy relinquished second place after 113 laps, while race leader Bourdais waited four more laps before taking his final service. Already, though, there was an ominous wisp of smoke from the rear of Tracy's car. The haze gradually worsened for the next couple of laps, then the rear end burst into flames as he negotiated Paddock Hill Bend for the 118th time. He pulled off the road at the bottom of the hill, his race over.

"We had issues with the gearbox during the race," acknowledged Tracy. "Sometimes it was shifting by itself. Three or four laps before the car caught fire, I heard a noise and the car started to smoke a bit. It's disappointing to have a failure like that."

An out-of-sequence Tagliani took the lead when Bourdais made his final visit to the pits, but the French-Canadian still required an extra pit stop. It came on lap 133. Tagliani resumed in eighth.

Bourdais was left with a comfortable cushion over Junqueira, which he had no problem in maintaining until the finish. It was not the first British success for the 24-year-old Frenchman.

"I won my first F3000 race in England, at Silverstone [in 2001], and to win my first Champ Car race at Brands Hatch is special," he said. "It is also good to win so close to my home [at Le Mans]."

Junqueira ensured a banner day for team owners Carl Haas and Paul Newman by taking second in his similar PacifiCare Lola.

"This track is very, very good for our cars, but I burned too much fuel trying to catch Sébastien and Paul to win today," reckoned the Brazilian. "I was trying to save fuel, but I just couldn't go one more lap like Sébastien. It's a good result, and good to get another podium."

The early final pit stop cost Dominguez time to the Newman/Haas cars, but the Mexican was still delighted to claim a first podium finish of the year for the Herdez Competition team.

"The team has worked very hard for this and I am very pleased with how things went today," he said. "This is probably more satisfying for me than the win in Australia [in 2002] because myself and the team had to earn it by running hard all day."

Servia drove well, too, earning a season-best fourth for Patrick Racing, while Carpentier remained hard on his heels in the closing stages. Jourdain was never particularly happy with his Gigante car, but he soldiered on to score useful championship points in sixth, while Moreno and Tagliani were the final unlapped finishers.

*Jeremy Shaw*

## QUALIFYING

**Englishman Darren Manning thrilled both himself and the enthusiastic Brands Hatch crowd when he set the fastest time during the first practice session on Saturday morning. Local knowledge no doubt played a part in Manning's early success, although normal business was resumed later in the day as Paul Tracy and Sébastien Bourdais led the way in second practice and vied for the honor of provisional pole position later in the afternoon.**

**The short, tortuous nature of the Brands Hatch "Indy" circuit (so named after the visit of the USAC National Championship in 1978) led Champ Car officials to adopt a modified single-car format for qualifying, with cars venturing out one at a time for a warm-up lap followed by four timed laps, the fastest of which would count. The drivers praised the decision, since it negated any "traffic" concerns, although it made little difference to the status quo. For the third race in a row, Tracy took the first-day honors to secure himself a position on the front row of the grid.**

**"Team Player's did a great job again today," said Tracy. "We've been fortunate to start on the front row for every race this year. It's a real bonus to be able to do that."**

**When no one managed to beat his Saturday time in final qualifying, held in decidedly warmer temperatures, Tracy elected merely to complete one lap to scrub in a fresh set of Bridgestone Potenza tires for the race, secure in the knowledge that his pole position was assured. Amazingly it represented his first pole in 52 starts, since Michigan in 2000, and even more incredibly, his first on a road course since Laguna Seca in 1994!**

**Bourdais came within 0.038s of Tracy's time but had to be content with a position on the outside of the front row. "I'm between satisfied and frustrated right now," he said. "My best time was on my third lap, so I would probably have been faster on my fourth lap. I was much quicker in Turn One – so much quicker that I had to shift [gear] sooner and I tried to hold the steering wheel with one hand while shifting, and then I lost the steering wheel and got off course."**

**Despite the error, Bourdais remained just clear of teammate Junqueira. Oriol Servia was fourth ahead of Alex Tagliani and Adrian Fernandez. Local hero Manning was comfortably the fastest Reynard qualifier in eighth.**

caution periods, meant they were obliged to make three visits to the pit lane.

Tagliani was the first of the leaders to make a pit stop, on lap 49. Other top-ten runners to stop early included Manning, Fernandez and Carpentier, who peeled off after 51 laps. Servia waited two laps longer before taking on service, while Tracy and Junqueira completed 55 laps on their first tank of methanol. The most frugal of all were Bourdais, who had closed up onto Tracy's tail before the Canadian made his first pit stop, and Michel Jourdain Jr., who had run a distant tenth during the opening stint.

The race took on a slightly different complexion after the first round of stops. Great work by Bourdais and his Newman/Haas team enabled the Frenchman to emerge in the lead, followed closely by erstwhile pacesetter Tracy. Junqueira was now some 3.5 seconds adrift, with Dominguez up into fourth, a further five seconds or so back. Then there was a four-second gap to Servia, who was chased by Tagliani and Carpentier.

The middle stages of the race saw the entire 18-car field running amazingly similar lap times. Perhaps the most impressive performer was Dominguez, who gradually edged closer to the third-placed Junqueira. But in general the race had turned into little more than a high-speed procession – albeit a spectacular high-speed procession.

The only full-course caution of the afternoon came after 79 laps, when rookie Alex Yoong, who had been running a creditable 11th, paid the price for a slight mistake in his Dale Coyne Racing Lola.

"I was right up there with [Roberto] Moreno, with Jourdain some distance behind, when I locked up [the brakes] going into

Right: **Fuel economy and the difficulty of overtaking were the main talking points in the post-race press conference.**
Kevin Wood/LAT

Below: **Opening-lap drama as Adrian Fernandez fights a lurid slide through Paddock Hill Bend; Mario Dominguez and Darren Manning prepare to pounce.**
Phil Abbott/LAT

## BOUNCING BACK

I T was with a mixture of pleasure, satisfaction and relief that Oriol Servia (right) finished a solid fourth in the London Champ Car Trophy. The likable Spaniard and his Patrick Racing team had garnered a measly two points from the first three races of the season – not at all representative of the combination's potency. Finally, at Brands Hatch, the result came close to mirroring his competitiveness.

"The Visteon/Patrick Racing team had a good race today," reflected Servia. "I am happy and excited that we scored our first real points. It feels good to have a top-five result after what has happened to us the first three races. Hopefully this will get us started on a string of good results."

Entering the closing stages of the race, Servia and his team could have been forgiven for wondering what might have gone wrong. After all, he had run well at some stage or another in each of the first three events, only for something to go awry. At St. Petersburg, Servia was third quickest on Friday, but slipped to ninth on the grid when he made a mistake in final qualifying and had to forfeit his best lap (which would have been good enough for the top four) after sliding off and causing a red-flag stoppage. Even so, he bounced back to run fourth at half-distance before losing many laps to an electrical glitch. He started fourth in Monterrey, but missed an opportunity to make an early pit stop and then committed another error. In Long Beach, he ran fourth until a malfunction during his final pit stop resulted in his Visteon Lola running out of fuel three laps shy of the finish.

Happily there was no last-minute hiccup at Brands Hatch.

"Today the Visteon/Patrick Racing team began to show what we are capable of doing in the races," declared Servia. "We have had some bad luck this season, but today we didn't have any major problems and the car ran very well. This should provide us with some momentum going into the next race. The engineering staff and crew did a fantastic job preparing the car for this race, and I am really looking forward to going to Germany and racing on the oval."

Kevin Wood/LAT

# THE LONDON CHAMP CAR TROPHY

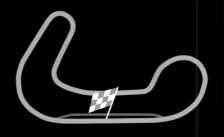

## BRANDS HATCH, FAWKHAM, KENT, ENGLAND

**MAY 5, 165 laps of 1.192 miles – 196.680 miles**

| Pl. | Driver (Nat.) | No. | Team Sponsors Engine/Car | Tires | Q Speed | Q Time | Q Pos. | Laps | Time/Status | Ave. (mph) | Pts. |
|---|---|---|---|---|---|---|---|---|---|---|---|
| 1 | *Sébastien Bourdais (F) | 2 | Newman/Haas Racing Lilly Ford Cosworth/Lola B01/00 | BS | 115.841 | 37.044s | 2 | 165 | 1h 51m 56.987s | 105.412 | 22 |
| 2 | Bruno Junqueira (BR) | 1 | Newman/Haas Racing PacifiCare Ford Cosworth/Lola B02/00 | BS | 115.909 | 37.022s | 3 | 165 | 1h 52m 04.822s | 105.289 | 16 |
| 3 | Mario Dominguez (MEX) | 55 | Herdez Competition Ford Cosworth/Lola B03/00 | BS | 114.298 | 37.544s | 7 | 165 | 1h 52m 08.511s | 105.231 | 14 |
| 4 | Oriol Servia (E) | 20 | Patrick Racing Visteon Ford Cosworth/Lola B02/00 | BS | 115.188 | 37.254s | 4 | 165 | 1h 52m 11.372s | 105.186 | 12 |
| 5 | Patrick Carpentier (CDN) | 32 | Forsythe Racing Player's/Indeck Ford Cosworth/Lola B02/00 | BS | 114.188 | 37.580s | 9 | 165 | 1h 52m 12.022s | 105.176 | 10 |
| 6 | Michel Jourdain Jr. (MEX) | 9 | Team Rahal Gigante Ford Cosworth/Lola B01/00 | BS | 113.810 | 37.705s | 10 | 165 | 1h 52m 27.690s | 104.932 | 8 |
| 7 | Roberto Moreno (BR) | 4 | Herdez Competition Ford Cosworth/Lola B03/00 | BS | 113.734 | 37.730s | 12 | 165 | 1h 52m 33.984s | 104.834 | 6 |
| 8 | Alex Tagliani (CDN) | 33 | Rocketsports Racing Johnson Controls Ford Cosworth/Lola B02/00 | BS | 114.671 | 37.422s | 5 | 165 | 1h 52m 35.749s | 104.807 | 5 |
| 9 | *Mario Haberfeld (BR) | 34 | Mi-Jack Conquest Racing Ford Cosworth/Reynard 02I | BS | 113.768 | 37.719s | 11 | 164 | Running | | 4 |
| 10 | *Darren Manning (GB) | 15 | Walker Racing RAC/Autowindscreens Ford Cosworth/Reynard 02I | BS | 114.234 | 37.565s | 8 | 164 | Running | | 3 |
| 11 | *Patrick Lemarie (F) | 27 | PK Racing Ford Cosworth/Lola B02/00 | BS | 112.083 | 38.286s | 17 | 163 | Running | | 2 |
| 12 | Adrian Fernandez (MEX) | 51 | Fernandez Tecate/Quaker State/Telmex Ford Cosworth/Lola B02/00 | BS | 114.530 | 37.468s | 6 | 163 | Running | | 1 |
| 13 | *Joel Camathias (CH) | 19 | Dale Coyne Racing Ford Cosworth/Lola B01/00 | BS | 112.071 | 38.290s | 18 | 163 | Running | | |
| 14 | *Tiago Monteiro (P) | 7 | Fittipaldi-Dingman Racing Ford Cosworth/Reynard 02I | BS | 112.710 | 38.073s | 15 | 163 | Running | | |
| 15 | *Rodolfo Lavin (MEX) | 5 | Walker Racing Corona Competition Ford Cosworth/Reynard 02I | BS | 111.683 | 38.423s | 19 | 162 | Running | | |
| 16 | *Ryan Hunter-Reay (USA) | 31 | American Spirit Team Johansson Ford Cosworth/Reynard 02I | BS | 112.586 | 38.115s | 16 | 162 | Running | | |
| 17 | Paul Tracy (CDN) | 3 | Forsythe Racing Player's/Indeck Ford Cosworth/Lola B02/00 | BS | 115.960 | 37.006s | 1 | 118 | Gearbox | | 1 |
| 18 | *Alex Yoong (MAL) | 11 | Dale Coyne Racing Ford Cosworth/Lola B2K/00 | BS | 113.329 | 37.865s | 13 | 78 | Accident | | |
| 19 | Jimmy Vasser (USA) | 12 | American Spirit Team Johansson Ford Cosworth/Reynard 2KI | BS | 112.980 | 37.982s | 14 | 1 | Suspension | | |

* denotes rookie driver

Caution flags: Laps 0–1, yellow start; laps 79–83, tow/Yoong. Total: Two for 6 laps.

Lap leaders: Paul Tracy, 1–54 (54 laps); Sébastien Bourdais, 55–116 (62 laps); Alex Tagliiani, 117–132 (16 laps); Bourdais, 133–165 (33 laps). Totals: Bourdais, 95 laps; Tracy, 54 laps; Tagliani, 16 laps.

Fastest race lap: Adrian Fernandez, 38.210s, 112.306 mph on lap 152 (record).

Championship positions: 1 Tracy, 65; 2 Junqueira, 54; 3 Jourdain Jr., 42; 4 Fernandez, 29; 5 Carpentier, 28; 6 Bourdais, 27; 7 Dominguez & Moreno, 24; 9 Tagliani, 22; 10 Vasser & Haberfeld, 20; 12 Servia & Manning, 14; 14 Monteiro & Lemarie, 8; 16 Hunter-Reay, 7; 17 Camathias, 6; 18 Yoong, 4.

# BRANDS HATCH SNIPPETS

• The time-honored COMMAND to fire up the engines prior to the start was given in chorus by an illustrious trio of Formula 1 World Championship-winning Grand Marshals: Damon Hill, Mario Andretti and Emerson Fittipaldi (above).

• JIMMY VASSER has visited Brands Hatch on two occasions and still has yet to complete a racing lap. In 1990, after being selected as the first winner of the Team USA Scholarship, Vasser's prize was a drive in the prestigious Formula Ford Festival & World Cup. Unfortunately he was taken out in an incident at the second corner, Druids. This time the American felt that something was awry with his American Spirit Team Johansson Reynard as soon as he left the grid, so he headed directly back to the pit lane. A suspension problem was discovered,

and once again his day was over almost before it had begun.

• Aside from Jimmy Vasser, who retired on the first lap, all 18 drivers posted a FASTEST LAP within 0.8s of each other during an intensely competitive race.

• The Champ Cars had visited BRANDS HATCH once before, in 1978, and had left an indelible impression. Pacesetter Danny Ongais had reached an astonishing top speed of 173 mph at the start/finish line – substantially faster than Formula 1 cars of the day – despite running on the short, 1.2-mile "club circuit" rather than the full 2.65-mile "Grand Prix" layout, which permitted a much faster exit from the final corner, Clearways. A quarter-century on, the top speed was only slightly higher, but technological development allowed greatly increased cornering speeds. Consequently, despite a tightening of the third corner, Graham Hill Bend (or Bottom Bend as it used to be known), lap times tumbled from 39.95s, an average speed of 105.811 mph, set by polesitter Al Unser in 1978, to the new record of 37.006s/115.960 mph established by Paul Tracy.

• It was a good event for the FRENCH. Sébastien Bourdais won, of course, while fellow countryman Patrick Lemarie enjoyed his most competitive outing to date for the PK Racing team. The

former BAR Formula 1 test driver qualified only 17th, but made up more positions than anyone else in the race to finish 11th. "We knew after warmup that the car was much better than in qualifying," he reported. "We did well, with a good strategy and good pit stops, so we're happy and we're making progress."

• Darren Manning was hoping for a good RESULT in front of his home crowd. The Englishman was obliged to make three pit stops, however, and under the circumstances did well to bring his Walker Racing Reynard home in tenth spot.

• En route to England, ADRIAN FERNANDEZ enjoyed a brief vacation in Paris, France, where he took the time to propose to longtime girlfriend

Michelle Davis. She accepted. No wedding date was announced, although the happy couple said they were in no hurry to tie the knot. Unfortunately the race didn't go so well for Fernandez, who was involved in a couple of scrapes, but he showed what might have been by posting the fastest lap.

• Several tweaks were made to the COMPETITION RULES in deference to the extremely tight nature of the circuit, and especially the pit lane. In addition to single-car qualifying, the pit-lane speed limit was set at just 35 mph, rather than the usual 50 mph, and the normal maximum number of laps between pit stops during the race was replaced by a simple requirement to make a minimum of two pit stops – under greenflag conditions – during the 165-lap contest.

# LAUSITZ

**Above: Winner Sébastien Bourdais is congratulated by racelong rivals Michel Jourdain Jr. and Mario Dominguez (right).**

**Above right: Bourdais is chased all the way to the line by Dominguez and Jourdain, ensuring a near-perfect photo finish.**
Photographs: Gavin Lawrence/LAT

**Right: Symbolically completing the "missing" 13 laps from that fateful afternoon at Eurospeedway Lausitz in 2001, Alex Zanardi takes the checker after an inspirational display of willpower – and speed.**

**Far right: Zanardi and the Simple Green Safety Team, which was instrumental in saving his life.**
Photographs: Phil Abbott/LAT

## ZANARDI'S MOMENTOUS RETURN

**T**HE German 500 was a spectacular motor race, featuring a no-holds-barred battle for the lead throughout the 154-lap contest. But there's no doubt the biggest cheer of the day from the 68,000-strong crowd was reserved for two-time Champ Car title winner Alex Zanardi, who made an emotional return to the track that almost took his life in 2001.

On that fateful day in September, little more than a week after the tragic terrorist attacks on the World Trade Center in New York and the Pentagon in Washington, Zanardi had enjoyed by far his most competitive race during a disappointing season with Mo Nunn Racing. Then came disaster. With just 12 laps to go, he lost control of his car as he exited the pit lane and slid sideways, directly into the path of Alex Tagliani. The impact was catastrophic. Zanardi lost both legs in the crash, and only magnificent work by the CART Simple Green Safety Team and the doctors at Klinikum Berlin-Marzahn saved his life.

Remarkably, Zanardi bounced back from that devastating day with a zest that will remain an inspiration to many in the future. He returned to the Champ Car scene to serve as Grand Marshall of the Molson Indy

Toronto in 2002, less than a year after his crash, and agreed to do so again for the German 500. Not only that, he drove a Ford Cosworth-powered Reynard Champ Car, fitted with special hand controls and decked out in the same Pioneer colors as when he led the race in 2001. Predictably, Zanardi wasn't content merely to lolly around. Oh no. He had gained a brief taste of the car during a shakedown test in England the previous week, and he was full-throttle on his first flying lap around the 2.023-mile oval. Clearly he had lost none of his bravado! Indeed, in his 13-lap run prior to the race on Sunday, accompanied by chants of "Zanardi! Zanardi!" from the crowd and a cacophony of airhorns, he turned a fastest lap at 37.487s, an average speed of 194.275 mph.

"It was great again to feel the speed, to feel the downforce," said Zanardi. "Most of all what made it particularly enjoyable was the love of all the people in the Champ Car community, in particular the drivers, and certainly the fans. It was just awesome."

After receiving rapturous applause, Zanardi composed himself in time to utter the famous pre-race command — albeit with a slight twist: "Friends, Start Your Engines!"

Below: **Bruno Junqueira was nonplussed by a slight but critical performance deficit to his precocious teammate, Bourdais.**
Gavin Lawrence/LAT

## QUALIFYING

The Champ Car teams had little chance to relax between the races at Brands Hatch and EuroSpeedway Lausitz, especially since the race in England had been held on a Monday. Sensibly, however, the German 500 was slated to be just a two-day affair, with practice and qualifying on Saturday and the race on Sunday afternoon. Furthermore, in a bid to restrict costs, CART had decreed that teams had to use a very similar aerodynamic package for the two events – even though they could hardly have been held on two more disparate racetracks. Still the crews had plenty of work to do in changing their cars' suspension settings from road-course to superspeedway specification.

Rookie sensation Sébastien Bourdais, taking part in his very first oval race, continued where he had left off in England by topping the charts at 36.794s, 197.934 mph, in the first and only practice session of the weekend. He was also fastest in qualifying, securing his third pole in just five attempts.

"It's great to win the pole on my first trip to an oval," said Bourdais, who was quick to pin the credit on his team. "It was not really my job – the engineers did a wonderful job to make the car where I could run flat out."

Amazingly, since the high-downforce package meant that everyone could run easily flat-foot around the 2.023-mile oval, Bourdais ended up well clear of teammate Bruno Junqueira.

"We were two-tenths [of a second] off of the pole time and I was flat out, and I have no idea why," said the Brazilian of the discrepancy. "Two-tenths is like a lifetime around here."

Michel Jourdain Jr. maintained his recent competitiveness by setting the third-fastest time for Team Rahal. "I am happy, although it is such a long race tomorrow that qualifying doesn't matter so much," he opined, before adding, "but it is better to be in the front than the back."

Mario Haberfeld qualified an impressive fourth, despite having to use the Mi-Jack/Conquest Racing team's backup Reynard following an engine problem during practice. He also had posted the previous best qualifying performance by a Reynard in '03 when he annexed sixth on the grid at St. Petersburg.

"I have to credit my engineer, Andy Borme," said Haberfeld. "He made a lot of [setup] changes for qualifying and it worked out well."

Darren Manning made it two Reynards among the top five, while Walker Racing teammate Rodolfo Lavin qualified a career-best eighth in his Corona entry.

SÉBASTIEN Bourdais ensured a clean sweep of the 2003 Bridgestone Presents the Champ Car World Series Powered by Ford's two-race European foray, edging out Mario Dominguez in a photo-finish at the German 500. The Frenchman and the steadily improving Mexican fought an outstanding battle during the 500-kilometer race at the magnificent EuroSpeedway Lausitz. First one, then the other appeared to have the upper hand on the high-speed tri-oval, but it was Bourdais who held the crucial advantage at the checkered flag, nosing ahead to win by a scant 0.084s in Newman/Haas Racing's Lilly Ford Cosworth/Lola.

"It was a lot of fun, for sure," said an exhausted Bourdais. "It was a lot of stress, too. It was very fair, but so tight. I mean, it was just really difficult to keep out of trouble."

There had been controversy during the early stages when Dominguez was assessed a penalty for allegedly blocking his rival. The Mexican fought back, however, and rewarded his Herdez Competition team with a second podium finish in as many races.

"Sébastien and I had a lot of fun out there," he said. "It was very clean racing, but very aggressive too."

The huge crowd went into raptures when two-time champion Alex Zanardi performed an amazing demonstration prior to the start. It was the perfect curtain-raiser to what turned out to be a thrilling race. The start was clean, with Bruno Junqueira drafting around the outside of his polesitting teammate, Bourdais, in Turn One. Michel Jourdain Jr. held on to third in Team Rahal's Gigante Lola, followed by Dominguez who immediately leapt ahead of Mario Haberfeld's Mi-Jack Reynard and Darren Manning's similar RAC entry. Farther back, points leader Paul Tracy posted one of his characteristic first-lap charges. The #3 Player's Lola stormed around the high line in Turn One and continued to make up ground all around the opening 2.023-mile lap as Tracy rose inside the top ten after starting a dismal 16th.

The Player's team, however, had drastically miscalculated its aerodynamic package. Tracy and teammate Patrick Carpentier snuck ahead of the struggling Haberfeld on lap two, but were unable to keep pace with the leading pack.

Bourdais relieved Junqueira of the point on lap three and was repassed on lap 19, but the two Newman/Haas Lolas were unable to shake off their pursuers. By lap 20, the top eight cars remained in one long train. Dominguez had moved up to third ahead of Oriol Servia (Visteon Lola), Jourdain, Alex Tagliani (Johnson Controls Lola) and the two Walker Racing Reynards of a fired-up Rodolfo Lavin and Manning.

The first chance to catch breath came on lap 25, when a full-course caution was called due to some debris on the racing surface in Turn Two. Everyone took the opportunity to make the first of an anticipated five pit stops.

Little changed at the head of the order, but there was disaster for Patrick Lemarie. The Frenchman had vaulted into ninth place, ahead of both Player's cars, immediately before the caution. Good work by Chris Schofield's PK Racing crew seemed likely to gain another position or two in the pit lane – until Lemarie was unwittingly sideswiped by Lavin. He, in turn, had been broadsided by Jourdain, catapulting out of his pit box following slightly slower

than usual service by Team Rahal. Lemarie's awful run of misfortune continued as he pulled off at the pit exit with broken suspension. Lavin resumed at the back of the pack after making an additional visit to the pits to check for damage to his Corona Reynard, while Jourdain continued with minimal delay. At least for the time being…

After the restart, Dominguez lost no time in making his presence felt. He passed Bourdais effortlessly when the green flag came out, and five laps later made his move for the lead in Turn Two. The top four soon distanced themselves from Jourdain, who similarly pulled clear of Carpentier and Manning.

The real focus, however, was on the battle up front between Dominguez and Bourdais. Time and again Bourdais tried to wrest away the lead, but Dominguez's car was working to perfection on the inside line and he clung doggedly to his advantage. On one occasion, on lap 51, Bourdais moved to the inside coming off Turn One. Dominguez, though, maintained his usual tight line, and the Frenchman suddenly realized he was headed directly for some cones that served to separate the oval from the infield road course. Instinctively he jinked to his left, onto the road course, then veered across the grass – at over 200 mph – to rejoin the oval!

Controversially, after a lengthy review of the video tape, the offi-

cials assessed a five-second penalty, which Dominguez served during a regular pit stop on lap 81. Also, during the previous round of stops, on lap 53, Jourdain was held in his pit box for 15 seconds as punishment for causing the earlier melee in the pit lane.

Fortunately for both miscreants, there was a brief caution period on lap 83 – again because of debris after Alex Yoong suffered a broken driveshaft – which enabled them to make up the lost ground. The order at this stage saw Bourdais back in the lead, having taken over the point due to Dominguez's enforced stay in the pit lane. Servia was running in second ahead of Junqueira, Dominguez, Jourdain, Manning, Jimmy Vasser and Carpentier. Everyone else, led by Roberto Moreno, Lavin and Tracy, already was a lap in arrears.

Bourdais enjoyed a slight cushion at the restart, there being three lapped cars between him and his immediate pursuers. Still, by lap 99, Junqueira had worked his way back onto his teammate's tail before drafting past into the lead once again. The top five swapped places regularly before making their next pit stops on lap 109. Carpentier and Vasser, who had topped off with fuel prior to the earlier restart, each took a brief turn in front before stopping again five laps later.

As the 154-lap race drew toward its climax, it appeared that

**Above: Action stations at the pit-lane exit as the Newman/Haas pair jostle for position. Behind, Jourdain gets too much wheelspin and is about to make contact with the Walker Racing Reynard of Rodolfo Lavin – an indiscretion that would not go unnoticed by the officials…**

**Left: Jourdain came up just 0.245s short at the finish, but had to settle for third.**
**Photographs: Gavin Lawrence/LAT**

## DOMINGUEZ ON A ROLL

**M**ARIO Dominguez showed that his performance at Brands Hatch had been no fluke by snaring his second straight podium appearance. The 28-year-old Mexican, who had scored a fortuitous maiden victory in the rain-marred race at Surfers Paradise in 2002, started his sophomore campaign by displaying a new-found confidence as he finished fifth in St. Petersburg. Then he earned a career-best seventh spot on the grid at Brands Hatch, which he parlayed into an excellent third-place finish.

His first foray into Continental Europe carried on in the same vein as he set the third-fastest time in the first practice session at EuroSpeedway Lausitz. He slipped to sixth in qualifying, but was still in no doubt that he could be a factor in the German 500.

"I am a bit surprised at how fast people are going overall, but we were flat out and gave it our best shot," he said. "I think the race will be very busy with the traffic and will be very interesting to watch. I really feel that we are on our way up as a team. We are right in there every weekend, consistently fighting with the leaders. That's what it's all about."

He was right on every score. Dominguez was embroiled in a tense battle with polesitter Sébastien Bourdais throughout a thrilling race that had the crowd on the edges of their seats. He was also involved in controversy after being adjudged to have unlawfully "blocked" his rival in the early stages, earning himself a five-second stop-and-wait penalty. Afterward he pleaded innocence.

"I'm just very disappointed with the officials because as far as I'm concerned, I didn't do anything wrong," he claimed. "Sébastien, when I was behind him [in the closing stages], he was doing exactly the same thing I was doing, which is OK with me. But, you know, why should I get a penalty? I didn't do anything wrong."

That aside, Dominguez was delighted with his result: "I'm just very pleased, especially with the whole Herdez Competition team. I think they've been doing a great job all year. Today they saved me because my pit stops weren't the best. I didn't come in very well, but they still managed to adjust and get me out of the pits very fast. They were definitely my guardian angels today. I've got to give them a lot of credit."

**Left: Dominguez and Bourdais fought a thrilling to-and-fro duel.**
Mike Weston/LAT

**Below: Lemarie, Lavin, Jourdain and Tagliani squabble over the asphalt on their way out of the pits. It would end in tears – and broken suspension – for Lemarie.**
Guenter Reinhold/LAT

Bourdais and Dominguez had the fastest cars, although Jourdain also was hanging in there as best he could. Servia and Junqueira had slipped a few seconds in arrears prior to the final pit stops on lap 137. Barring a late caution, it seemed unlikely that they would challenge the leading trio.

Excellent final service by Team Rahal enabled Jourdain to leapfrog ahead of the other two main contenders, but the Mexican had been bundled back to third place again by the time Carpentier – still a little out of sequence with the other leaders – pulled into the pit lane for the final time. Dominguez zapped past Jourdain around the outside of Turn Two on lap 141, only to be inadvertently and momentarily blocked by the lapped Reynard of Haberfeld. He was obliged to lift from the throttle for an instant, but that was all Bourdais needed to regain the upper hand. For the final 13 laps, Dominguez ducked and weaved around in Bourdais' slipstream, but to no avail. The Frenchman refused to be distracted. He clung doggedly to the inside groove, and even though Dominguez towed alongside on numerous occasions in the final stages, he was unable to find enough momentum to wrest away the advantage.

"I had never raced on an oval, so it was very tough," said Bourdais, still quivering excitedly in Victory Lane. "I was just building up my confidence. That was just the secret of the day. We adjust the car a bit after the first [pit] stop, and after it was just perfect.

"I learned a lot behind Mario [in the early stages]," continued Bourdais. "[Toward the end] when I had the inside line, that was just to try to put him a little in dirty air to build a bit of understeer on his car – not to allow him to be side by side with me. So that was very much a thinking game. And I think I did pretty well on that."

"If you take the shorter way around the track on the inside, it's hard to pass," said Dominguez. "My mistake was to show him which way to go early in the race, and of course he's a quick learner. We've all seen that this year. He learns fast."

Jourdain set the fastest lap of the race, running in the draft of the other two, but had to settle for third. Junqueira snuck past Servia on the final lap to claim fourth, while Manning completed a strong day for Walker Racing by being the final unlapped finisher in sixth.

*Jeremy Shaw*

# GERMAN 500

## EUROSPEEDWAY LAUSITZ, KLETTWITZ, GERMANY

**MAY 11, 154 laps of 2.023 miles – 311.542 miles**

**ROUND 5**

| Pl. | Driver (Nat.) | No. | Team Sponsors Engine/Car | Tires | Q Speed | Q Time | Q Pos. | Laps | Time/Status | Ave. (mph) | Pts. |
|---|---|---|---|---|---|---|---|---|---|---|---|
| 1 | *Sébastien Bourdais (F) | 2 | Newman/Haas Racing Lilly Ford Cosworth/Lola B02/00 | BS | 196.832 | 37.000s | 1 | 154 | 1h 49m 22.498s | 170.903 | 22 |
| 2 | Mario Dominguez (MEX) | 55 | Herdez Competition Ford Cosworth/Lola B03/00 | BS | 193.229 | 37.690s | 6 | 154 | 1h 49m 22.582s | 170.901 | 16 |
| 3 | Michel Jourdain Jr. (MEX) | 9 | Team Rahal Gigante Ford Cosworth/Lola B01/00 | BS | 195.386 | 37.274s | 3 | 154 | 1h 49m 22.743s | 170.897 | 14 |
| 4 | Bruno Junqueira (BR) | 1 | Newman/Haas Racing PacifiCare Ford Cosworth/Lola B02/00 | BS | 195.716 | 37.211s | 2 | 154 | 1h 49m 34.540s | 170.590 | 12 |
| 5 | Oriol Servia (E) | 20 | Patrick Racing Visteon Ford Cosworth/Lola B02/00 | BS | 193.167 | 37.702s | 7 | 154 | 1h 49m 34.553s | 170.590 | 10 |
| 6 | *Darren Manning (GB) | 15 | Walker Racing RAC/Autowindscreens Ford Cosworth/Reynard 02I | BS | 194.042 | 37.532s | 5 | 154 | 1h 49m 47.100s | 170.265 | 8 |
| 7 | Patrick Carpentier (CDN) | 32 | Forsythe Racing Player's/Indeck Ford Cosworth/Lola B02/00 | BS | 190.221 | 38.286s | 17 | 153 | Running | | 6 |
| 8 | Jimmy Vasser (USA) | 12 | American Spirit Team Johansson Ford Cosworth/Reynard 2KI | BS | 192.103 | 37.911s | 11 | 153 | Running | | 5 |
| 9 | *Rodolfo Lavin (MEX) | 5 | Walker Racing Corona Competition Ford Cosworth/Reynard 02I | BS | 193.091 | 37.717s | 8 | 153 | Running | | 4 |
| 10 | Roberto Moreno (BR) | 4 | Herdez Competition Ford Cosworth/Lola B03/00 | BS | 191.366 | 38.057s | 12 | 153 | Running | | 3 |
| 11 | *Ryan Hunter-Reay (USA) | 31 | American Spirit Team Johansson Ford Cosworth/Reynard 02I | BS | 190.549 | 38.220s | 15 | 152 | Running | | 2 |
| 12 | Paul Tracy (CDN) | 3 | Forsythe Racing Player's/Indeck Ford Cosworth/Lola B02/00 | BS | 190.430 | 38.244s | 16 | 152 | Running | | 1 |
| 13 | *Tiago Monteiro (P) | 7 | Fittipaldi-Dingman Racing Ford Cosworth/Reynard 02I | BS | 190.669 | 38.196s | 14 | 152 | Running | | |
| 14 | *Mario Haberfeld (BR) | 34 | Mi-Jack Conquest Racing Ford Cosworth/Reynard 2KI | BS | 194.769 | 37.392s | 4 | 152 | Running | | |
| 15 | Adrian Fernandez (MEX) | 51 | Fernandez Tecate/Quaker State/Telmex Ford Cosworth/Lola B02/00 | BS | 188.352 | 38.666s | 19 | 152 | Running | | |
| 16 | *Joel Camathias (CH) | 19 | Dale Coyne Racing Ford Cosworth/Lola B01/00 | BS | 188.879 | 38.558s | 18 | 152 | Running | | |
| 17 | *Alex Yoong (MAL) | 11 | Dale Coyne Racing Ford Cosworth/Lola B2K/00 | BS | 190.889 | 38.152s | 13 | 81 | Driveshaft | | |
| 18 | Alex Tagliani (CDN) | 33 | Rocketsports Racing Johnson Controls Ford Cosworth/Lola B02/00 | BS | 193.014 | 37.732s | 9 | 28 | Shift linkage | | |
| 19 | *Patrick Lemarie (F) | 27 | PK Racing Ford Cosworth/Lola B02/00 | BS | 192.636 | 37.806s | 10 | 25 | Accident | | |

\* denotes rookie driver

**Caution flags:** Laps 23–27, debris; laps 83–88, debris. Total: Two for 11 laps.

**Lap leaders:** Bruno Junqueira, 1–3 (3 laps); Sébastien Bourdais, 4–18 (15 laps); Junqueira, 19–34 (16 laps); Mario Dominguez, 35–81 (47 laps); Bourdais, 82–98 (17 laps); Junqueira, 99–101 (3 laps); Bourdais, 102 (1 lap); Junqueira, 103 (1 lap); Bourdais, 104–108 (5 laps); Patrick Carpentier, 109–111 (3 laps); Jimmy Vasser, 112–114 (3 laps); Bourdais, 115–137 (23 laps); Carpentier, 138–141 (4 laps); Bourdais, 142–154 (13 laps). Totals: Bourdais, 74 laps; Dominguez, 47 laps; Junqueira, 23 laps; Carpentier, 7 laps; Vasser, 3 laps.

**Fastest race lap:** Michel Jourdain Jr., 36.721s, 198.328 mph on lap 133.

**Championship positions:** 1 Tracy & Junqueira, 66; 3 Jourdain Jr., 56; 4 Bourdais, 49; 5 Dominguez, 40; 6 Carpentier, 34; 7 Fernandez, 29; 8 Moreno, 27; 9 Vasser, 25; 10 Servia, 24; 11 Tagliani & Manning, 22; 13 Haberfeld, 20; 14 Hunter-Reay, 9; 15 Monteiro & Lemarie, 8; 17 Camathias, 6; 18 Lavin & Yoong, 4.

# LAUSITZ SNIPPETS

• Sébastien Bourdais had been LOOKING FORWARD to his first-ever oval track race. "I tested for two days in Phoenix and it was quite an eye-opening experience," he related. "I watched the oval races on TV, but I didn't fully appreciate the skill needed until I did it for myself. Before, I thought, 'Wow, how hard can it be?' But it is a real test of ability and it's definitely mentally challenging. It requires 110 percent concentration 110 percent of the time."

• Rodolfo Lavin (below) drove by far his most IMPRESSIVE race to date in the Champ Car ranks. The 25-year-old from San Luis Potosi, Mexico, ran comfortably among the top eight until being involved in an incident – not of his making – during the first round of pit stops. He lost more time in the course of his third visit to the pit lane, thanks to a refueling glitch, which eventually caused him to fall a lap down. Lavin rebounded, however, to finish ninth, and he set the seventh-fastest race lap for good measure.

• Bourdais became the FIRST driver since Juan Pablo Montoya in 1999 to win back-to-back races as a rookie, and the first to win his debut oval-track race from the pole. Scott Dixon won his first oval race in a Champ Car, at Nazareth Speedway in 2001, but had started a distant 23rd. Coincidentally fellow rookie Bruno Junqueira started from pole in that very same event – his first on an oval – but faded to seventh in the race.

• The Champ Cars ran with a completely different AERODYNAMIC PACKAGE by comparison to the series' last visit to EuroSpeedway Lausitz in 2001. The change to a high-downforce setup led to a significant reduction in speeds, as evidenced by Bourdais' pole-winning effort at 196.832 mph (37.000s), compared to Tony Kanaan's best of 210.340 mph (34.623s) set with the traditional tiny "superspeedway" wings during practice in 2001. The new package provided a much greater draft, however, which meant that the fastest lap all weekend was set in the race by Michel Jourdain Jr. at 198.328 mph (36.721s).

• A large and massively enthusiastic CROWD ensured a sensational atmosphere for the German 500. All the drivers were impressed, especially those making their first visit to the magnificent Eurospeedway facility situated between Berlin and Dresden. "The German fans are the best!"

declared Mario Dominguez. "You can hear them cheering, and the airhorns, every time you come down the front straight. This is for sure my new favorite track!"

• The German 500 marked the first superspeedway event for the LATEST Ford Cosworth XFE engine. To control speeds, turbocharger boost pressure was reduced from 41.5 inches of mercury to 39 inches, resulting in a power output in the 700-hp range – down from around 755 hp in regular road-course trim. As usual, the motors performed absolutely flawlessly.

• Malaysian Alex Yoong also RAN WELL, rising into the top ten before being ousted by a broken driveshaft after 81 laps. "This result definitely does not reflect the good work done by the team," he said.

• Team Rahal survived a SCARE on Saturday evening after Michel Jourdain Jr. (below) had his qualifying time disallowed following post-qualifying inspection. Officials declared that the Gigante Lola's turbocharger inlet was in violation of Rule 9.5.2H2 of the Champ Car Rule Book, which states, "No addition of air ducts or modification of the filter mounting is allowed." The team also was assessed a $10,000 fine. A protest was lodged immediately, however, and after lengthy deliberations through the evening, a panel of three judges overturned the earlier verdict after determining that the team had not intended deliberately to circumvent the rules.

BRIDGESTONE PRESENTS
THE CHAMP CAR WORLD SERIES POWERED BY FORD    ROUND 6

# MILWAUKEE

THE venerable Wisconsin State Fair Park in suburban Milwaukee had an altogether different feel compared to the previous visit by the Champ Cars in 2002. For starters, the trademark old grandstand, a staple since the 1930s, had been replaced by a magnificent new aluminum and steel structure that stretched virtually the length of the front straightaway. New, too, at the facility that had hosted its very first auto race on September 11, 1903, and had been visited regularly by the Champ Cars since 1933, was a spectacular illumination system provided by Musco Lighting.

Even the cars were different. A variety of aerodynamic configurations had been run at the venue over the years, but since 1998, when Patrick Carpentier had used the ultimate high-downforce setup to establish a new track record in qualifying at 185.500 mph, CART had adopted a package of much smaller wings aimed at curtailing the escalation in speed. The new measures were successful. In 1999, Helio Castroneves snared the pole at a "mere" 169.404 mph average. Since then, however, concern had shifted from excessive speed to a lack of wheel-to-wheel competition, for which The Milwaukee Mile had been famous.

For 2003, therefore, CART adopted new aerodynamic rules aimed at promoting side-by-side racing. CART Chief Steward Chris Kneifel also introduced new regulations that effectively outlawed "defensive driving." No longer would any kind of "blocking" be tolerated. The combination of these changes produced a spectacular show, and afterward the drivers were unanimous in their praise.

"CART made a lot of changes to a lot of things for this weekend," noted track record holder Carpentier. "We have new wings, more downforce, and Bridgestone came up with the right set of tires and everything was really good. Often CART gets criticized about decisions they make, but tonight they made all the right decisions. I hope people enjoyed the show because I really did. I really loved it. It was a great race."

"I think it was good that they made that rule, so at least you can see some passing," added Oriol Servia, who had battled long and hard – and cleanly – with Paul Tracy. "I think it was much better for the show." No doubt about it.

**Inset far left: Victory at last for Michel Jourdain Jr., while Oriol Servia finally gained a tangible result to back up his consistent pace. The sense of relief, as much as joy, is written on their faces as they hoist their trophies.**

**Inset left: The impressive new grandstand towering above the front straightaway.**

**Main photograph: Floodlights gave the Milwaukee Mile a new look in 2003.**
**Photographs: Gavin Lawrence/LAT**

Mike Levitt/LAT

## QUALIFYING

The entire Champ Car community had been eagerly awaiting the first ever qualifying session to be run at night. Not so the weather gods, apparently. A persistent drizzle set in on Friday morning, and although there was a brief dry window during the afternoon that allowed the final practice to go ahead, the rain returned as the evening progressed and qualifying was canceled. The grid instead was set according to practice times and no championship bonus point was awarded.

Alex Tagliani (above) made light of gusting winds during the final practice session aboard Paul Gentilozzi's Johnson Controls Lola to post the fastest time and claim the fourth pole of his career. It was also the first for Rocketsports Racing since switching to the Champ Car ranks at the beginning of the season.

"It's great," said the French-Canadian. "The winds were fluctuating a lot out there and I think we may have been lucky to catch a lap with no wind. But we made a good run and it was very important to us to do well here because it is one of the major headquarters for Johnson Controls, and the team was really excited to do well for them here in Milwaukee."

Michel Jourdain Jr. had been fastest the previous evening with Team Rahal's Gigante Lola, and that time proved good enough for him to secure the outside-front-row starting position.

"Today we didn't want to make too many laps," noted the Mexican. "It was really windy and we didn't want to change the car much for the conditions the track was in."

Series leader Paul Tracy, who set the third-fastest time, spoke for all the drivers when he paid tribute to the hardy fans who had waited in vain for the rain to abate: "It's disappointing because we wanted to put on a good show for the fans, and Mother Nature didn't allow us to."

Tracy's teammate, Patrick Carpentier, was just a few ticks of the watch slower in practice, followed by owner/driver Adrian Fernandez and the only past series champion in the field, Jimmy Vasser, who was fastest of the Reynard contingent for American Spirit Team Johansson.

"I have had a lot of success here," said the 1998 winner, "and I am looking forward to a good race tomorrow night."

Oriol Servia maintained his run of top-ten starts for Patrick Racing, while one of the biggest surprises was the fact that title contender Bruno Junqueira was only eighth quickest for Newman/Haas Racing.

A THRILLING Milwaukee Mile Centennial 250 Presented by Miller Lite and Argent Mortgage at the newly renovated Wisconsin State Fair Park saw Michel Jourdain Jr. gain a well-deserved maiden Champ Car victory. The young Mexican gave a stunning performance in the first CART-sanctioned event ever to be run under lights on a Saturday evening. He started Team Rahal's Gigante Ford Cosworth/Lola from the outside of the front row, snuck past polesitter Alex Tagliani as soon as the green flag waved, and controlled the pace for the remainder of the night.

"I couldn't have asked for more from the team," said an emotional Jourdain. "The car was just perfect. This is probably the best thing that ever happened to me in my whole life."

Championship leader Paul Tracy ran second for much of the evening and looked set to extend his points advantage, but that hope evaporated when his Player's Lola shed its left rear wheel immediately after his final pit stop. Second suddenly became 12th. The other major contender, Bruno Junqueira, also struck trouble, crashing on the opening lap. The miscues further played into the hands of Jourdain, who parlayed his fourth podium visit of the year into a ten-point championship lead.

After qualifying had been rained out on Friday evening, much to everyone's dismay, Saturday dawned cool and clear. Conditions remained decidedly chilly when race time rolled around, and the officials wisely decided to delay the green flag for a few laps to allow the drivers time to build some heat into their Bridgestone Potenza tires.

For the second year running in Milwaukee, the polesitter was beaten away from the start by the outside-front-row qualifier. In 2002, Paul Tracy had stolen a march on Adrian Fernandez. This time, it was Jourdain who took advantage of Tagliani lighting up the rear wheels of Rocketsports Racing's Johnson Controls Lola as the green flag flew. Tracy, starting third this time around, also jumped ahead of Tagliani as the field swept into Turn One. Patrick Carpentier, in the second Player's car, slotted into fourth while Oriol Servia and Jimmy Vasser both managed to usurp Fernandez, who had started fifth. Behind there was mayhem as Junqueira lost control in between Turns One and Two. When the dust had settled, Roberto Moreno and the luckless Patrick Lemarie had joined Junqueira on the sidelines. Moreno's teammate, Mario Dominguez, also was involved, but managed to escape merely with a damaged nose, which Daryl Fox and the boys replaced during a sequence of visits to the pit lane.

The race finally got under way properly with 19 laps in the books. Jourdain again leapt into the lead and quickly opened up a margin to Tracy. Servia, meanwhile, also found a way past Tagliani on lap 21.

Above: **Jimmy Vasser waits impassively as American Spirit Team Johansson performs routine service on the #12 Reynard.**

Far left: **A blur of color as Servia's orange Visteon Lola flashes past the scenery.**
Photographs: Gavin Lawrence/LAT

Center left: **The fluorescent decals aglow on Bruno Junqueira's Newman/Haas Lola.**

Left: **A cauldron of light illuminates Adrian Fernandez's car as his pit crew goes to work. The nighttime format was popular with teams, drivers and fans alike.**
Photographs: Mike Levitt/LAT

Below left: **Bagged to go. Ryan Hunter-Reay is towed away. The rookie was one of several drivers to find the wall in the chilly evening conditions.**
Phil Abbott/LAT

The Catalan, seeking to build on a pair of top-five finishes in the two most recent races, continued to charge. On lap 46, he got a run on Tracy exiting Turn Four to take over second place behind the fleeing Jourdain. Others moving up included English rookie Darren Manning, who rose superbly from 11th on the grid to fourth before the first round of pit stops, and Carpentier, who elected to pit during the early caution and was back in 12th at the restart. The French-Canadian passed Vasser for seventh on lap 56, then took a turn in the lead when all the other front-runners pulled in for routine service three laps later. Carpentier remained on the point until pitting, on schedule, after 73 laps.

As darkness enveloped the surrounding neighborhood – but not the racetrack, of course, courtesy of the sensational Musco lighting system – Jourdain continued to dominate the show, leaving Tracy and Servia to battle over second. Manning, too, should have been in the thick of the fight. Superb work in the pits by Neil Brown's crew saw the #15 Walker Racing Reynard emerge ahead of Servia, whereupon the cool evening temperatures almost

**Below: Jourdain was rewarded with a richly deserved maiden Champ Car win. Here, he shows Paul Tracy the way.**
Phil Abbott/LAT

**Bottom: Jourdain is nabbed for a quick interview by SPEED Channel's Derek Daly before heading for the podium ceremonies.**
Mike Levitt/LAT

## JOURDAIN'S FIRST WIN

IT had been a long time coming. A total of 126 races, to be precise. Michel Jourdain Jr. had displayed much flair since becoming the youngest driver ever to start a Champ Car race – at Long Beach in 1996 – and especially since splitting with longtime supporters Herdez and joining Team Rahal prior to the 2002 campaign. But a victory had continued to elude him. Until now.

"I am so proud of the job Michel has done this season," said car owner and three-time series champion Bobby Rahal. "I always felt that there was untapped potential in Michel, and he has proved me right numerous times since we signed him. This is a special moment for any driver and I am glad this moment came so soon for him after the heartbreak at Long Beach."

A couple of months earlier, indeed, the 26-year-old Mexico City native had been on the verge of a momentous triumph on the famed Californian street circuit, only to be robbed at almost the last moment by a transmission failure. This time, there was nothing to stand in his way. The victory was even more meaningful given the fact that Jourdain had always struggled on the Milwaukee Mile – never qualifying better than 18th and with only one point-scoring finish (a fifth in '02) in seven previous attempts.

"It means a lot to get my first win here at Milwaukee," said Jourdain, "especially because I have had so much trouble here in the past. Someday I will be able to tell my grandchildren that I won the first night race in CART and that I won the 100th [anniversary] race at the Milwaukee Mile. This is so sweet, especially after the disappointment at Long Beach. We had a dominant car there just like we did tonight. There are so many things that can go wrong on a short oval that I just kept thinking to myself, 'What will go wrong tonight?' But nothing did. The car was so good and we were able to pull out a big lead on everybody, so I just had to concentrate and not make a mistake. I knew we had the fastest car and so if I didn't make a mistake no one would get past me."

Jourdain's drive was, indeed, flawless. And even his rivals were pleased to see this likable, down-to-earth young man finally tasting the fruit of success.

"I am very happy for Michel," said fellow countryman Adrian Fernandez. "He drove a fantastic race and really drove like a champion."

"He's been working toward this for nine years and he did a great job out there tonight," added Mario Dominguez. "I'm very happy for him."

caught out Manning in Turn Two as he switched off the speed limiter at the pit-lane exit. Somehow the Briton managed to contain a lurid slide, but by then both Servia and Fernandez had stolen past.

"That was close," admitted a chastened Manning. "The tires were just so cold and I almost crashed."

Carpentier also rejoined ahead of the Englishman after making his second pit stop. Tagliani ran seventh at the 85-lap mark, despite having difficulty in traffic.

"The car performed well on its own," he related, "but when I got too close to the car ahead of me, it was too loose and I felt it slipping away from me. I decided to keep it steady and keep my distance, rather than lose it."

Rookie Ryan Hunter-Reay was the last car on the lead lap – until lap 86, when his American Spirit Team Johansson Reynard got away from him in Turn Two.

"We fought the car all weekend," said Hunter-Reay, who also had crashed during practice on Thursday evening. "It was a tough weekend for us and I'm glad it's behind us."

All of the leaders made pit stops during the lengthy caution, after which Jourdain resumed in the lead ahead of Servia, Tracy, Fernandez, Carpentier, Manning and Tagliani.

The two Player's cars swept forward at the restart. Tracy shot past Servia for second and Carpentier displaced Fernandez from fourth as Jourdain once again set sail out in front. Tracy was unable to shake off the Visteon/Patrick Racing car of Servia, however, and on lap 138, the positions changed again as the latter got the power down a little bit better coming off Turn Four.

A similar scenario played out following another caution on lap 154, when Joel Camathias hit the wall in Turn Two. Again Servia lost out to Tracy at the restart, the Canadian surging around the outside of Turns One and Two in a characteristically bold maneuver. Servia once more remained glued to the Player's Lola's gearbox, and finally, on lap 207, made his move to regain the position – this time going into Turn Three.

The pace of this duel was such that, for the first time all evening, Jourdain began to come under pressure. The handling of his Gigante car wasn't quite as good as it had been earlier, especially when he was trying to get around some lapped traffic. Indeed, by lap 210, the top eight cars once again were running in nose-to-tail formation, with Jourdain only narrowly ahead of Servia, Tracy, Carpentier, Fernandez, Manning, Tagliani and Mario Haberfeld, who had contrived to work his way right back into contention. Rodolfo Lavin, too, was back on the lead lap in ninth. This was building toward a sensational climax!

All the leaders were obliged to make their final pit stop together on lap 213. Team Rahal performed its usual exemplary service for Jourdain, who remained in the lead. Servia's Patrick Racing crew also was flawless. Tracy wasn't so fortunate. A problem with the airjack meant that his left rear wheel wasn't properly affixed, and it duly worked its way loose as he rejoined the fray. Wheel and hub finally parted company in Turn Four, leaving Tracy to limp back into the pits and ensuring another full-course caution.

"You can't win championships with things like that happening," said Tracy pointedly, after losing a lap and falling to his second 12th-place finish in a row. "We need to do a better job as a team. To get 64 points in the first three races and only three points in the next three, it's bitterly disappointing."

There was one more caution, after Lavin's strong run ended prematurely when he crashed the Corona Reynard immediately after the restart on lap 226. Afterward there was time for a ten-lap shootout to the checkered flag, and Jourdain had no difficulty in hanging on to score a hugely popular victory.

"It was very emotional for me," he admitted. "I was almost crying in the car those last few laps."

Servia also was delighted with his career-best second, having thoroughly enjoyed his battle with Tracy.

"It was good racing – as it should be," said Servia. "It was close. I tell you, Paul didn't give me one millimeter extra, any corner; we were side by side. And I think I did the same with him. We were fair to each other and it was…it is nice to race like that."

Manning also claimed a career-best fourth, mere inches behind Carpentier, while Tagliani slipped past Fernandez at the final round of pit stops to take fifth ahead of Haberfeld, Dominguez and the rest.

*Jeremy Shaw*

# MILWAUKEE MILE CENTENNIAL 250
## PRESENTED BY MILLER LITE AND ARGENT MORTGAGE

**ROUND 6**

### THE MILWAUKEE MILE, W. ALLIS, WISCONSIN
**MAY 31, 250 laps of 1.032 miles – 258.000 miles**

| Pl. | Driver (Nat.) | No. | Team Sponsors Engine/Car | Tires | Q Speed | Q Time † | Q Pos. | Laps | Time/Status | Ave. (mph) | Pts. |
|---|---|---|---|---|---|---|---|---|---|---|---|
| 1 | Michel Jourdain Jr. (MEX) | 9 | Team Rahal Gigante Ford Cosworth/Lola B01/00 | BS | 176.578 | 21.040s | 2 | 250 | 2h 16m 45.692s | 113.190 | 21 |
| 2 | Oriol Servia (E) | 20 | Patrick Racing Visteon Ford Cosworth/Lola B02/00 | BS | 174.923 | 21.239s | 7 | 250 | 2h 16m 46.160s | 113.183 | 16 |
| 3 | Patrick Carpentier (CDN) | 32 | Forsythe Racing Player's/Indeck Ford Cosworth/Lola B03/00 | BS | 175.693 | 21.146s | 4 | 250 | 2h 16m 46.396s | 113.180 | 14 |
| 4 | *Darren Manning (GB) | 15 | Walker Racing RAC/Autowindscreens Ford Cosworth/Reynard 02I | BS | 174.112 | 21.338s | 11 | 250 | 2h 16m 46.865s | 113.174 | 12 |
| 5 | Alex Tagliani (CDN) | 33 | Rocketsports Racing Johnson Controls Ford Cosworth/Lola B02/00 | BS | 177.914 | 20.882s | 1 | 250 | 2h 16m 47.884s | 113.159 | 10 |
| 6 | Adrian Fernandez (MEX) | 51 | Fernandez Tecate/Quaker State/Telmex Ford Cosworth/Lola B02/00 | BS | 175.618 | 21.155s | 5 | 250 | 2h 16m 48.798s | 113.147 | 8 |
| 7 | *Mario Haberfeld (BR) | 34 | Mi-Jack Conquest Racing Ford Cosworth/Reynard 2KI | BS | 174.316 | 21.313s | 10 | 250 | 2h 16m 49.918s | 113.131 | 6 |
| 8 | Mario Dominguez (MEX) | 55 | Herdez Competition Ford Cosworth/Lola B03/00 | BS | 173.543 | 21.408s | 12 | 250 | 2h 16m 51.281s | 113.113 | 5 |
| 9 | *Sébastien Bourdais (F) | 2 | Newman/Haas Racing Lilly Ford Cosworth/Lola B01/00 | BS | 172.969 | 21.479s | 13 | 250 | 2h 16m 51.575s | 113.109 | 4 |
| 10 | *Tiago Monteiro (P) | 7 | Fittipaldi-Dingman Racing Ford Cosworth/Reynard 02I | BS | 174.570 | 21.282s | 9 | 250 | 2h 16m 53.379s | 113.084 | 3 |
| 11 | Jimmy Vasser (USA) | 12 | American Spirit Team Johansson Ford Cosworth/Reynard 2KI | BS | 175.146 | 21.212s | 6 | 250 | 2h 16m 54.769s | 113.065 | 2 |
| 12 | Paul Tracy (CDN) | 3 | Forsythe Racing Player's/Indeck Ford Cosworth/Lola B02/00 | BS | 176.285 | 21.075s | 3 | 249 | Running | | 1 |
| 13 | Gualter Salles (BR) | 11 | Dale Coyne Racing Alpina/Golden Cross Ford Cosworth/Lola B2K/00 | BS | 168.177 | 22.091s | 18 | 240 | Accident | | |
| 14 | *Rodolfo Lavin (MEX) | 5 | Walker Racing Corona Competition Ford Cosworth/Reynard 02I | BS | 171.310 | 21.687s | 14 | 225 | Accident | | |
| 15 | *Joel Camathias (CH) | 19 | Dale Coyne Racing Ford Cosworth/Lola B01/00 | BS | 166.504 | 22.313s | 19 | 150 | Accident | | |
| 16 | *Ryan Hunter-Reay (USA) | 31 | American Spirit Team Johansson Ford Cosworth/Reynard 02I | BS | 168.926 | 21.993s | 17 | 85 | Accident | | |
| 17 | Bruno Junqueira (BR) | 1 | Newman/Haas Racing PacifiCare Ford Cosworth/Lola B02/00 | BS | 174.841 | 21.249s | 8 | 3 | Accident | | |
| 18 | *Patrick Lemarie (F) | 27 | PK Racing Ford Cosworth/Lola B02/00 | BS | 169.049 | 21.977s | 16 | 3 | Accident | | |
| 19 | Roberto Moreno (BR) | 4 | Herdez Competition Ford Cosworth/Lola B01/00 | BS | 171.263 | 21.693s | 15 | 3 | Accident | | |

* denotes rookie driver    † qualifying rained out, so grid established according to practice times; no championship point awarded

**Caution flags:** Laps 1–2, yellow start; laps 4–18, accident/Junqueira, Moreno & Lemarie; laps 86–107, accident/Hunter-Reay; laps 154–168, accident/Camathias; laps 214–224, loose wheel/Tracy; laps 226–238, accident/Lavin; lap 239, yellow restart. Total: Seven for 79 laps.

**Lap leaders:** Alex Tagliani, 1–2 (2 laps); Michel Jourdain Jr., 3–59 (57 laps); Patrick Carpentier, 60–72 (13 laps); Mario Dominguez, 73 (1 lap); Jourdain, 74–250 (177 laps). Totals: Jourdain, 234 laps; Carpentier, 13 laps; Tagliani, 2 laps; Dominguez, 1 lap.

**Fastest race lap:** Patrick Carpentier, 21.820s, 170.266 mph on lap 246.

**Championship positions:** 1 Jourdain Jr., 77; 2 Tracy, 67; 3 Junqueira, 66; 4 Bourdais, 53; 5 Carpentier, 48; 6 Dominguez, 45; 7 Servia, 40; 8 Fernandez, 37; 9 Manning, 34; 10 Tagliani, 32; 11 Vasser & Moreno, 27; 13 Haberfeld, 26; 14 Monteiro, 11; 15 Hunter-Reay, 9; 16 Lemarie, 8; 17 Camathias, 6; 18 Lavin & Yoong, 4.

## MILWAUKEE SNIPPETS

• In addition to the "no blocking" rule (see sidebar, page 87), a new SPARE-CAR POLICY also took effect in Milwaukee. Virtually all teams traditionally provide a pair of cars for each of their drivers, and in the past, teams had been permitted to switch between those cars as required during the race weekend. Not any longer. Henceforth teams were required to nominate their primary car for each driver, which would go through technical inspection prior to official practice. Teams would only be permitted to run the backup chassis if the primary car was deemed by the Champ Car stewards to be damaged beyond repair. Ryan Hunter-Reay was the first to test the new rule, badly damaging his primary chassis in a heavy crash during practice on Thursday evening. He was allowed to switch to the backup for the balance of the weekend.

• Happily, the rain clouds had moved out of the Milwaukee area by Saturday morning and the sky was clear in time for the 8 p.m. start. But temperatures remained unseasonably COOL, which led to some concerns about being able to build sufficient heat in the Bridgestone Potenza tires. Champ Car officials wisely allowed a few extra pace laps before unleashing the field. The new high-downforce aero package also proved beneficial. "It wasn't that big a deal," said Oriol Servia. "Going out of the pits on cold tires, the first turn was a little slippery, but by the next turn they were already working well." Added race

winner Michel Jourdain Jr., "The engineers from Bridgestone told us to be careful on cold tires, but they build a much better tire than even they think they do."

• A lack of SPONSORSHIP sidelined Alex Yoong from Dale Coyne Racing's #11 Ford Cosworth/Lola. Veteran Gualter Salles took over the ride after securing support from Brazilian high-tech equipment supplier Alpina and medical plan provider Golden Cross.

• DARREN MANNING (below) was one of the stars of the show, working his way from 11th on the grid to fourth in Derrick Walker's RAC/Autowindscreens Reynard. "I knew the first day that

we had a great car for the night conditions," said the Briton. "It's a shame we didn't get to put in a qualifying run because I had a perfect car, which I think showed in the race." Manning, whose best lap of 21.842s, set on lap 148, stood as the race's fastest until the closing stages, made just one slip, when he almost crashed at the pit-lane exit on lap 60. "I'm just so frustrated with that mistake," he said. "The car was great though, and the guys gave me fantastic stops throughout the race. Finishing fourth is another improvement for the team, so overall I have to be happy."

• Sébastien Bourdais was never happy with the HANDLING of his Newman/Haas Racing Lola. "I

didn't have much grip for the entire race," said the Frenchman. "We kept working on it as the race went on, but it never improved. It was just hang on, hang on for the entire race." Bourdais hung on well, securing ninth place at the finish.

• A quick glance at the cars in the pit lane showed a VARIETY of interpretations of the new aerodynamic regulations. The various Lola teams employed just about every conceivable permutation of two- and three-plane front wings, high- and low-downforce sidepods and assorted "flip-ups" in front of the rear wheels. Fascinating.

• Paul Tracy arrived in Milwaukee with HIGH EXPECTATIONS and confident of putting a disappointing two-race European swing – from which he had garnered a measly two championship points – behind him. Tracy, who had three previous Champ Car wins to his credit on the famed Mile, plus a victory in Indy Lights, came out of the box strong on Thursday by posting the fastest practice time in the first session. He lost some track time in the evening after glancing the wall at the exit of Turn Four and tweaking his Lola's right rear suspension, but was a strong contender in the race until a pit-lane miscue dropped him a lap off the pace. "We were poised for a great battle to the finish and I believe we could have pulled it out at the end," he declared, "but fate intervened."

Gavin Lawrence/LAT

BRIDGESTONE PRESENTS
THE CHAMP CAR WORLD SERIES POWERED BY FORD • ROUND 7

# LAGUNA SECA

PATRICK Carpentier was never headed in the Grand Prix of Monterey at Mazda Raceway Laguna Seca. Not that he had an easy time of it. Oh, no. Carpentier's mirrors were filled by the sight of Paul Tracy's identical Team Player's Ford Cosworth/Lola for the first two-thirds of the 87-lap race, and in the late stages he had to contend with a determined challenge from the PacifiCare Lola of Bruno Junqueira, who finished less than a second behind.

"It felt like I stole a car and I had a bunch of policemen running after me," said Carpentier, grinning broadly. "I was looking in the mirrors and these guys were really, really close."

Junqueira put the disappointment of Milwaukee firmly behind him by finishing second, while Tracy fell off the pace in the middle stages and had to be content with third. Championship leader Michel Jourdain Jr. drove brilliantly from 13th to fourth after what would have been a polewinning qualifying time was disallowed when his Gigante Lola was found to be below the minimum weight limit.

Beautifully clear and sunny conditions greeted the Champ Car World Series contenders on raceday. All was not picture-perfect, however, at the first attempt to get the race under way. Indeed it almost spelled disaster for the Player's pair as Carpentier sought to maintain his advantage over Junqueira.

"Bruno was behind me and I knew he was trying to play a game there and to get a good start," explained Carpentier, "so I just kind of slowed down when he accelerated. I wanted to make it obvious, but Paul [Tracy, third on the grid] helped me to make it really obvious. He hit me at the back and my car went up in the air."

No green flag was forthcoming, and both drivers were fortunate to escape unscathed. The order at the front of the field wasn't much better following an extra pace lap – "I left a little bit early," admitted Carpentier – but Starter J.D. Wilbur elected to display the green anyway. The race was under way.

Carpentier duly led the 19-car field over the brow of the hill and down toward the Mario Andretti Hairpin. Junqueira and Tracy squabbled over second place until Junqueira locked up his brakes at the Corkscrew and slid slightly off course. Tracy needed no second bidding and moved past the Brazilian into the number-two spot. The other Newman/Haas car of Sébastien Bourdais also had been shuffled out, losing a couple of positions to Adrian Fernandez and Mario Haberfeld.

## CARPENTIER'S COMEBACK

AFTER being overshadowed in the early part of the season by Player's teammate Paul Tracy, Patrick Carpentier hit his stride at Mazda Raceway Laguna Seca. He outpaced his fellow Canadian all weekend, withstood intense pressure for much of the race distance and came away with a well-deserved first victory of 2003.

"My guys did a really, really good job in the pits," said Carpentier. "The series is so competitive now and there's so many good drivers and these guys are really aggressive, and to win, it takes everything to happen right and we had it today."

Carpentier had to overcome a few miscues in the early part of the season. He made a mistake and hit the wall in the first race at St. Petersburg, while in second behind Tracy, and took another off-track excursion in Monterrey while running well despite suffering a nasty bout of stomach cramps. Throughout he was never far from the ultimate pace, even though faced with having to get to grips with the Player's/Forsythe team's new Lola chassis. (All of his 108 starts prior to the 2003 season had been made at the wheel of Reynard chassis.)

"For me, the beginning of the season is always a little bit slow," he admitted. "It's the same this year. We had to learn the Lola. Over the last few weeks, we're getting much better at it."

The new-found confidence showed right away in California. Carpentier was second fastest in both Friday-morning practice sessions and second again in provisional qualifying. He was also second in final qualifying, but moved up to secure the pole after Michel Jourdain Jr.'s car failed technical inspection. His performance on raceday was exemplary. Carpentier led the whole way and posted the race's fastest lap for good measure. Even so, he had had to work hard to fend off the attentions of, first, Tracy and then Junqueira.

"I was looking in the mirrors and just trying to drive hard to get away, and it was not working," said Carpentier. "I think starting position was pretty important and we pretty much finished the way we started. It's hard for Michel, but for us it was a little bit of luck to get the pole position and it helped us tremendously today. So we got it and managed to stay ahead.

"At one stage, Paul and Bruno were faster than me. So I was just trying to stay ahead of them, and there were a few backmarkers which made it more interesting. It was a fun race; I really liked it. And it feels good right now."

Carpentier completed the first racing lap with a comfortable 1.6-second margin over his pursuers and, little by little, continued to stretch that lead. The gap had reached as much as three seconds by lap nine. Then Tracy found his rhythm. Over the next ten laps, he drew rapidly away from Junqueira and homed in again on his teammate. By lap 20, the two blue, white and gold cars were in nose-to-tail formation, while Junqueira, struggling with a flat-spotted left front tire, had slipped nine seconds back, within reach of a tight battle between Fernandez, Haberfeld and Bourdais.

The first round of pit stops came at the end of the Champ Car-mandated limit, after 24 laps. There was no change at the front as Carpentier rejoined narrowly ahead of Tracy, with Junqueira some way adrift in third. There was some shuffling behind, however, as Bourdais gained two places and Fernandez lost two, while Haberfeld contrived to maintain station in fifth. There was a change for seventh, too, as Oriol Servia vaulted ahead of Jimmy Vasser after the pit stops. Jourdain also moved up to ninth at the expense of Roberto Moreno.

A brand-new set of Bridgestone Potenza tires transformed the handling of Junqueira's PacifiCare Lola, and soon he began to take large bites out of the substantial deficit between himself and the two Player's cars. By lap 42, the gap had shrunk to just a couple of car lengths.

"The car was very, very fast," said Junqueira, "but it was tough to pass, so I was waiting for the pit stops."

He almost didn't have to wait that long. Carpentier struggled toward the end of each stint as he worked his tires to the limit, and on one occasion almost lost control in Turn Three. He clung on,

Above: Mario Haberfeld was at home on the swooping Californian road course, finishing an excellent fifth.
Paul Mounce/LAT

Right: Michel Jourdain Jr. (here tracking down Mario Dominguez) scythed through the field in impressive fashion.

Far right: Jimmy Vasser concentrates.
Photographs: Gavin Lawrence/LAT

Below right: The fleet of pace cars leads the field around the track prior to the start.
Mike Levitt/LAT

## QUALIFYING

In light of Cristiano da Matta's dominant victory in 2002, and the fact that Bruno Junqueira and Sébastien Bourdais had set a torrid pace during a major preseason test in January, Newman/Haas Racing arrived at the scenic Monterey Peninsula venue as hot favorite. Sure enough, Junqueira was fastest in the first practice session on Friday morning, while teammate Bourdais set the pace in the second period. Junqueira also was quickest in provisional qualifying at 1m 10.040s.

Lap times tumbled on Saturday, however, and when the checkered flag fell it was Michel Jourdain Jr. who was credited with the best time after a stellar lap aboard Team Rahal's Gigante Lola. It seemed the perfect way for the popular Mexican to ram home his message after scoring a long-overdue maiden victory and taking the championship lead in the previous race at Milwaukee.

Sadly the story was too good to be true. Post-qualifying technical inspection revealed that Jourdain's car was a few pounds below the minimum weight limit. His time was disallowed and he was obliged to rely on his Friday time, good enough only for 13th on the grid.

Subsequently the team admitted that it had simply made a mistake. "We feel bad for Michel who did a fantastic job," read a team statement. "We hate to see his success taken away from him because of an error by the team."

Pole instead was grabbed by Patrick Carpentier, following a fine effort in his familiar #32 Player's Lola.

"We had a good car today, but it did understeer a bit," he noted. "We will have to make it better for the race."

Junqueira, meanwhile, had to be content with second on the grid, courtesy of his Friday time, after making an injudicious setup change midway through the final session.

"The car was really loose, really difficult to drive," he lamented. "It's a shame because the PacifiCare car has been good all weekend. Just when I needed it most, I made a mistake when I asked for the change from the team."

A rare engine problem cost Junqueira's teammate, Bourdais, any opportunity to improve his time when the track was at its fastest, although he had still done enough to earn fourth on the grid ahead of Adrian Fernandez and top Reynard runner Mario Haberfeld.

though, and repeated the feat immediately after the second round of pit stops, on lap 49, when Tracy mounted an attempt to usurp his teammate in Turn Two.

"I tried to go on the outside of Pat on cold tires, and I locked both front tires up really badly and made a huge flat spot on the tires," related Tracy. "I was struggling from there on. I had very bad braking and very bad handling and a bad vibration."

Carpentier quickly stretched his advantage as Tracy came under increasing pressure from Junqueira.

"I tried to hang on as long as I could," said Tracy, "and I ended up understeering right off the track in Turn Six going up the hill and almost hit the wall."

Junqueira took the opportunity to nip past, immediately setting his sights on race leader Carpentier. The gap came down steadily. By lap 70, with the final round of pit stops looming, Junqueira was in a position to challenge.

Meanwhile, his teammate, Bourdais, had not been so fortunate, having fallen victim to a turbo boost problem after 77 laps. Now, aside from the newly resurrected battle for the lead, attention also was focused on the progress of Jourdain. The fired-up Mexican had passed Fernandez impressively at the Corkscrew on lap 49, and ten laps later had overtaken Servia for sixth. Next in his sights was Haberfeld, doing an excellent job in the Mi-Jack/Conquest Racing Reynard.

First came the pit stops. Carpentier peeled off the track, right on schedule, after 72 laps, but in his haste almost collected the barriers at the pit entrance.

"I said [to myself], 'Oh, this time I am really going to come in hard,' and I couldn't make the turn," admitted Carpentier. "I almost hit the tires, and Bruno almost got me to the inside. So I was pretty happy there was no more pit stops after that."

"It was close," agreed Junqueira. "I almost crashed behind him because there was no space.

"The only time he made a mistake and there was no room for me to pass him," lamented the Brazilian.

No such errors were made by the pit crews. Carpentier duly rejoined with a narrow margin over Junqueira, which he was able to

retain until the checkered flag to score his first win of the season and the fourth of his Champ Car career. His margin of victory was a mere 0.844s.

"It feels great," said the French-Canadian. "One thing to note is we finished that close and there was no yellow flags, so it was a pretty good race."

"Patrick was driving very well," praised Junqueira. "He made no mistakes. We were a little bit faster, but on this track it was difficult to pass. It wasn't worth the risk because we want to win the championship."

Tracy, too, had an eye on the championship after winning the first three races of the season and mustering just three points from the next three.

"The last three races have been pretty difficult to swallow because we have given up 30, 40 points," he reflected. "Our goal this weekend was to stop the bleeding and finish in the top five. [Toward the end] I ran the same time as the leaders, but I was 20-something seconds behind. I had a big gap to Michel and basically just settled for third and get some solid points."

Jourdain had passed Haberfeld during the final round of pit stops to cement a fine fourth place – pretty good after starting in 13th spot on the grid.

"The car was fantastic today and the Team Rahal crew did a great job on the pit stops," said Jourdain, who continued to lead the championship. "It was a tough race. I am so tired. But we were able to pass some people on the track and in the pits. And considering what happened yesterday, fourth place isn't too bad."

Haberfeld was the first rookie – and the top Reynard – finisher in fifth place. "We could have used some more downforce and we struggled with cold tires, but I think we did the best we could," he concluded. "The crew did a great job. I'm very happy with the result."

Servia took sixth after an eventful weekend, which had included a crash in qualifying, while Fernandez was disappointed to secure only seventh after losing time on each of his pit stops. Vasser was the final unlapped finisher.

*Jeremy Shaw*

**Below: Carpentier climbs out of his car – and out of Tracy's shadow – in Victory Lane.**

**Bottom: Adrian Fernandez and Oriol Servia indulge in a late-braking contest as they crest the rise approaching the Corkscrew.**
Photographs: Mike Levitt/LAT

## ALL CHANGE AT PKR

A COUPLE of days before the Champ Car teams assembled at Mazda Raceway Laguna Seca, PK Racing announced that circuit expert Bryan Herta (below) had been contracted to drive its #27 Lola for the weekend in place of previous incumbent Patrick Lemarie. Then, on Saturday, it was confirmed that Herta's deal would be merely a one-off and that Max Papis would take over the ride beginning with the following weekend's G.I. Joe's 200 at Portland. Curious.

To be honest, no one was really surprised at Lemarie's departure. The Frenchman had raced only sporadically since his previous full-time ride in Formula 3000 in 1997, and had gained the Champ Car place largely because of his close friendship with Jacques Villeneuve and his manager, Craig Pollock, who was also one of the partners in PK Racing.

Lemarie had been a test driver for the BAR F1 team, of which Pollock was one of the founders.

PKR, which had been established very late in the off-season by Pollock and Australian-born businessman Kevin Kalkhoven, had struggled to be competitive in the early races. In six starts, Lemarie had mustered a best qualifying performance of tenth at EuroSpeedway Lausitz and had finished in tenth place in each of the first two races.

In search of better results, the team had hired Papis. The Italian, however, already had a prior commitment to the Panoz team for the Le Mans 24-hour race, which clashed with the Grand Prix of Monterey. Herta was a logical stopgap, having previously earned two Champ Car victories and three poles at the Californian road course.

"PK Racing is dedicated to winning races and we will continue to do whatever it takes to achieve that goal," said Kalkhoven. "I want to experience the podium – I want that feeling, and I have confidence that both Bryan and Max can get us there."

Herta, like Lemarie before him, struggled to find a good balance with the car during practice and qualifying – hardly surprising given that he had had no opportunity to test the car beforehand. Nevertheless he was seventh fastest in practice on Saturday and, after qualifying 12th, enjoyed a fine tussle with championship leader Michel Jourdain Jr. in the early stages of the race before finishing 11th.

Gavin Lawrence/LAT

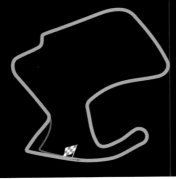

# GRAND PRIX OF MONTEREY

**MAZDA RACEWAY LAGUNA SECA, MONTEREY, CALIFORNIA**

**JUNE 15, 87 laps of 2.238 miles – 194.706 miles**

**ROUND 7**

| Pl. | Driver (Nat.) | No. | Team Sponsors Engine/Car | Tires | Q Speed | Q Time | Q Pos. | Laps | Time/Status | Ave. (mph) | Pts. |
|---|---|---|---|---|---|---|---|---|---|---|---|
| 1 | Patrick Carpentier (CDN) | 32 | Forsythe Racing Player's/Indeck Ford Cosworth/Lola B03/00 | BS | 115.800 | 1m 09.575s | 1 | 87 | 1h 48m 11.023s | 107.986 | 22 |
| 2 | Bruno Junqueira (BR) | 1 | Newman/Haas Racing PacifiCare Ford Cosworth/Lola B02/00 | BS | 115.437 | 1m 09.794s | 2 | 87 | 1h 48m 11.867s | 107.764 | 17 |
| 3 | Paul Tracy (CDN) | 3 | Forsythe Racing Player's/Indeck Ford Cosworth/Lola B02/00 | BS | 115.641 | 1m 09.671s | 3 | 87 | 1h 48m 39.598s | 107.513 | 14 |
| 4 | Michel Jourdain Jr. (MEX) | 9 | Team Rahal Gigante Ford Cosworth/Lola B01/00 | BS | 113.524 | 1m 10.970s | 13 | 87 | 1h 48m 51.842s | 107.311 | 12 |
| 5 | *Mario Haberfeld (BR) | 34 | Mi-Jack Conquest Racing Ford Cosworth/Reynard 02I | BS | 114.697 | 1m 10.244s | 6 | 87 | 1h 48m 53.135s | 107.290 | 10 |
| 6 | Oriol Servia (E) | 20 | Patrick Racing Visteon Ford Cosworth/Lola B02/00 | BS | 114.124 | 1m 10.597s | 10 | 87 | 1h 49m 11.180s | 106.995 | 8 |
| 7 | Adrian Fernandez (MEX) | 51 | Fernandez Tecate/Quaker State/Telmex Ford Cosworth/Lola B02/00 | BS | 114.723 | 1m 10.228s | 5 | 87 | 1h 49m 12.451s | 106.974 | 6 |
| 8 | Jimmy Vasser (USA) | 12 | American Spirit Team Johansson Ford Cosworth/Reynard 2KI | BS | 114.219 | 1m 10.538s | 8 | 87 | 1h 49m 12.851s | 106.967 | 5 |
| 9 | *Tiago Monteiro (P) | 7 | Fittipaldi-Dingman Racing Ford Cosworth/Reynard 02I | BS | 112.913 | 1m 11.354s | 15 | 86 | Running | | 4 |
| 10 | Mario Dominguez (MEX) | 55 | Herdez Competition Ford Cosworth/Lola B03/00 | BS | 113.797 | 1m 10.800s | 11 | 86 | Running | | 3 |
| 11 | Bryan Herta (USA) | 27 | PK Racing Ford Cosworth/Lola B02/00 | BS | 113.567 | 1m 10.943s | 12 | 86 | Running | | 2 |
| 12 | *Ryan Hunter-Reay (USA) | 31 | American Spirit Team Johansson Ford Cosworth/Reynard 01I | BS | 112.761 | 1m 11.450s | 17 | 86 | Running | | 1 |
| 13 | *Joel Camathias (CH) | 19 | Dale Coyne Racing Ford Cosworth/Lola B2K/00 | BS | 112.753 | 1m 11.455s | 18 | 85 | Running | | |
| 14 | Alex Tagliani (CDN) | 33 | Rocketsports Racing Johnson Controls Ford Cosworth/Lola B02/00 | BS | 113.436 | 1m 11.025s | 14 | 85 | Running | | |
| 15 | Roberto Moreno (BR) | 4 | Herdez Competition Ford Cosworth/Lola B03/00 | BS | 114.163 | 1m 10.573s | 9 | 85 | Running | | |
| 16 | *Geoff Boss (USA) | 11 | Dale Coyne Racing Cross Pens Ford Cosworth/Lola B01/00 | BS | 110.667 | 1m 12.802s | 19 | 83 | Driveshaft | | |
| 17 | *Sébastien Bourdais (F) | 2 | Newman/Haas Racing Lilly Ford Cosworth/Lola B2K/00 | BS | 114.935 | 1m 10.099s | 4 | 77 | Pop-off valve | | |
| 18 | *Darren Manning (GB) | 15 | Walker Racing RAC/Autowindscreens Ford Cosworth/Reynard 02I | BS | 114.231 | 1m 10.531s | 7 | 12 | Oil pump | | |
| 19 | *Rodolfo Lavin (MEX) | 5 | Walker Racing Corona Competition Ford Cosworth/Reynard 01I | BS | 112.793 | 1m 11.430s | 16 | 10 | Gearbox | | |

\* denotes rookie driver

Caution flags: **Lap 1,** yellow start. Total: **One for 1 lap.**

Lap leader: **Patrick Carpentier, 1–87 (87 laps).** Total: **Carpentier, 87 laps.**

Fastest race lap: **Patrick Carpentier, 1m 11.898s, 112.059 mph on lap 81.**

Championship positions: 1 Jourdain Jr., 89; 2 Junqueira, 83; 3 Tracy, 81; 4 Carpentier, 70; 5 Bourdais, 53; 6 Dominguez & Servia, 48; 8 Fernandez, 43; 9 Haberfeld, 36; 10 Manning, 34; 11 Tagliani & Vasser, 32; 13 Moreno, 27; 14 Monteiro, 15; 15 Hunter-Reay, 10; 16 Lemarie, 8; 17 Camathias, 6; 18 Lavin & Yoong, 4; 20 Herta, 2.

# LAGUNA SECA SNIPPETS

• The Association of Hole In The Wall Camps was named as the OFFICIAL CHARITY of CART. The first camp had been created by Academy Award-winning actor and Newman/Haas Racing co-owner Paul Newman in 1988. By 2002, the organization had grown to encompass five locations that combined to provide an opportunity for almost 7,000 children with life-threatening illnesses to experience the joy of attending a real camp.

• A prior COMMITMENT to the Brazilian Stock Car Championship, in which he was running his own two-car team, prevented Gualter Salles from taking his place with Dale Coyne Racing at Mazda Raceway Laguna Seca. (Salles also would be obliged to skip the races later in the season in Toronto and Miami.) Instead Geoff Boss (below) stepped into the ride for his Champ Car

debut. Boss, 34, from Narragansett, Rhode Island, had been a front-runner in the Barber Dodge Pro Series and Dayton Indy Lights Championship in the 1990s.

• The ADDITION of Bryan Herta and Geoff Boss to the field for the Grand Prix of Monterey doubled the number of American drivers taking part.

• BRUNO JUNQUEIRA admitted to being a little stiff and sore following his crash in the previous race at Milwaukee. He said he hadn't resumed his usual workout routine, but had been cycling to prepare himself as much as possible. Junqueira drove well, recording his sixth top-five finish in seven starts to take him to within six points of the championship lead. But still he had yet to win a race in 2003. "Yeah, it's kind of strange," he agreed. "Everybody thought that I would be winning a lot of

poles and winning a lot of races. So far, I think, at least half of the races I was fast enough to get the poles and fast enough to win the races, but it didn't happen. The luck just didn't knock on my door, but at least we're working hard, and if we keep being consistently fast and consistent in finishing the races, we're going to win some races this year and we're going to get some poles."

• NTN Bearing Corporation signed on as an associate SPONSOR for the remainder of Englishman Darren Manning's rookie campaign with Walker Racing. NTN, based in Osaka, Japan, also boasted a strong presence in Canada and since 1995 had supported various Canadian drivers in the CART Toyota Atlantic Championship.

• PAUL TRACY qualified third (his equal-worst starting position of the season thus far, aside from a dismal showing at EuroSpeedway Lausitz), but was focused on regaining the championship lead after his recent slump. "The key is to make a good start," reckoned the Canadian. "I must overtake my teammate, but I must also be smart because it's a long race and I need to score a lot of points."

• The Grand Prix of Monterey weekend coincided with a MASSIVE EVENT being staged at Ford World Headquarters in Dearborn, Michigan, to celebrate the 100th anniversary of the formation of Ford Motor Company on June 16, 1903.

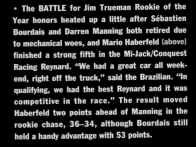

• The BATTLE for Jim Trueman Rookie of the Year honors heated up a little after Sébastien Bourdais and Darren Manning both retired due to mechanical woes, and Mario Haberfeld (above) finished a strong fifth in the Mi-Jack/Conquest Racing Reynard. "We had a great car all weekend, right off the truck," said the Brazilian. "In qualifying, we had the best Reynard and it was competitive in the race." The result moved Haberfeld two points ahead of Manning in the rookie chase, 36–34, although Bourdais still held a handy advantage with 53 points.

103

# PORTLAND

## A MOMENTOUS VICTORY

**W**HEN Adrian Fernandez decided at the end of a successful 2000 season to establish his own team, in partnership with Tom Anderson, some people thought he had lost his mind. After all, he had just finished a career-best second in the FedEx-backed Champ Car World Series, driving for Patrick Racing. Anderson, meanwhile, as managing director of Target/Chip Ganassi Racing, had had a hand in winning four of the previous five championship titles. Yet both men were intent upon starting a brand-new team from scratch!

The first year was difficult, highlighted by a couple of podium finishes. The '02 campaign was better, but still a victory proved elusive. And prior to the G.I. Joe's 200, the first seven races of 2003 had produced only a couple of top-fives, including a second at Long Beach.

"I was having a lot of pressure with the sponsors," Fernandez admitted, "and when you are not getting the results that you plan to do…I mean, it's not like you suddenly forgot how to drive, but I was suddenly faced with a lot of things that I didn't expect. That was the hard part."

No wonder he was bursting with pride after securing his first victory: "It's fantastic because this team started from nothing. We didn't have anything. We didn't have any people. It was just Tom, myself and obviously at that time it was Honda, which was a big part of what we did."

"We started hiring people, good people, and from there we started to build it to the point that we have 50 people now. It's not easy, sometimes a lot of work – you know, it's like having a lot of kids sometimes," he chuckled. "Sometimes their personalities don't match, but obviously results like this are going to make them believe in themselves more and believe in what we have."

Even more satisfying for Fernandez was the manner in which he achieved the victory – by passing Paul Tracy in a head-to-head battle.

"My car was really good on the last set of tires," related the Mexican, "and when I saw Paul make a slight mistake, I knew that was my chance – and probably my only chance. I said, 'Whenever he brakes, I am going to brake later.'

"To be able to win against teams like Newman/Haas and Jerry Forsythe and Bobby Rahal, teams that have been there for so many years, for me, it's fantastic. A lot of people told me that I should retire, and things like that, but I wanted to continue to be a driver and to have a team that can give me the tools eventually to win races, like now. So I may be 40 years old, but [I feel] 20 years in the heart, and I still want to win and want to do it for many years more."

**Main photograph: Adrian Fernandez**
secured a hard-earned first win as an
owner/driver with a superlative
performance at Portland.

**Inset: A proud Fernandez is feted by a trio**
of Tecate lovelies on the podium.
Photographs: Gavin Lawrence/LAT

**Above right: Alex Tagliani posted the fastest lap en route to a strong third place for the fledgling Rocketsports team.**
Gavin Lawrence/LAT

**Above far right: Oriol Servia's car is readied for action by the Patrick Racing crew.**
Mike Levitt/LAT

**Right: Rain in the Pacific Northwest falls mainly on Portland International Raceway it often seems. Paul Tracy braves the elements during practice, throwing up great rooster tails of spray from the wheels of his Player's/Forsythe Lola.**
Gavin Lawrence/LAT

## QUALIFYING

Typically changeable weather conditions in the Pacific Northwest set the scene for a couple of exciting qualifying sessions. In the provisional period on Friday, a rain shower shortly before the end left several drivers wishing they had ventured out earlier. Michel Jourdain Jr. was not one of them, however. His confidence at an all-time high, the personable Mexican led the way with Team Rahal's Gigante Lola after posting a lap at 59.397s.

The rain on Saturday came a half-hour or so prior to the final session. The ensuing bright sunshine dried the track quickly, however, and Alex Tagliani set the stage by dipping beneath Jourdain's Friday best during the usual brief pre-qualifying practice. Typically drivers wait several minutes after the start of qualifying before beginning their allotment of 15 laps, but with more dark clouds threatening, there was a virtual stampede as soon as the green flag was displayed.

Early-season points leader Paul Tracy was the first to make his mark, moving to the top of the charts at 58.793s on only his third flying lap. That time remained good for the pole, and Tracy backed it up with two more laps that were quicker than anyone else could manage.

"I had a lot of motivation going into the session," said Tracy, who had been only seventh quickest on Friday, "and I guess sometimes it helps to drive angry."

Jourdain, with a front-row grid position already assured, was the only driver to sit out the opening minutes, although it wasn't long before Tracy's efforts spurred him into action. Jourdain came close, but couldn't quite eclipse the Canadian.

"We waited a little while, but we may have waited a little too long," reckoned Jourdain. "Paul did a fantastic job. I am still very happy to be in the front row."

Adrian Fernandez was quick in the final session too, posting a time that was good enough for third on the grid to equal his best starting position of the season (he had been third also in St. Petersburg): "I actually thought I had a chance at the pole. The track improved tremendously [from Friday]. There was more grip than we expected. I did not have enough to catch Paul, but we're still happy with third."

Sébastien Bourdais was fourth fastest among a closely matched field that saw the top 15 cars covered by less than a second. Ryan Hunter-Reay was best of the Reynards in seventh.

THE battle for the 2003 Bridgestone Presents the Champ Car World Series Powered by Ford reached boiling point in the G.I. Joe's 200 at Portland International Raceway. After qualifying on the front row of the grid, two of the primary contenders, Paul Tracy and Michel Jourdain Jr., were involved in a controversial incident in which Jourdain, much to his disgust, came off worst.

Tracy continued, only to find himself under pressure from yet another rapid Mexican.

Adrian Fernandez, the doyen of race fans "South of the Border," then steeled himself for a brave pass with 15 laps remaining and consolidated his position in the closing stages to score his first victory since forming his own team, in partnership with Tom Anderson, prior to the 2001 campaign. It was the first win by a Champ Car owner/driver since Bobby Rahal achieved the feat at Nazareth Speedway in 1992. No wonder Fernandez was over the moon.

"It feels great to get the win," he said after taking the checkered flag in his Tecate/Quaker State/Telmex Ford Cosworth/Lola. "We built this team from nothing and we were starting to get some pressure from our sponsors, but this is great."

Tracy was upset with himself for losing the race, but had the consolation of regaining the championship lead after finishing second ahead of Alex Tagliani.

Champ Car drivers always seem to have difficulty in getting the race under way at P.I.R. Presumably it's because the long front straightaway funnels directly into the tight and notorious Festival Curves, which provide the best overtaking opportunity on the flat 1.969-mile road course, and everyone wants to try to get a jump on their rivals. Indeed, for the second straight year, it took three attempts before the starter was satisfied that the 19-car field was in an acceptable order. Even then, Tracy, the polesitter, was extremely displeased after losing the advantage to Jourdain.

"Everybody is trying to make the good starts, but [Starter J.D. Wilbur] throws the green when it's maybe not appropriate," declared the Canadian. "I thought the second and the third ones were good starts, but I guess the field behind us was ragged,

they said on the radio; it's not the front row's fault that the field is ragged. We were lined up good, so…"

Tracy's protestations fell on deaf ears. Jourdain snuck ahead into the first turn and the Canadian was obliged to tuck in behind. Fernandez maintained third ahead of Tagliani, Sébastien Bourdais, Oriol Servia and the first of the Reynards, driven by rookie Darren Manning.

Jourdain held a small but secure cushion through the opening laps. Tracy was generally around 1.3 seconds behind, followed by Fernandez almost three seconds adrift. Tagliani, Bourdais & Co. were a similar distance back after ten laps, whereupon the Frenchman informed his Newman/Haas crew that the Lilly Lola was beginning to oversteer. His engineers examined the telemetry data in the pit lane and diagnosed a slowly deflating left rear tire. On lap 13, they called him in for a pit stop, changing all four tires and topping off the fuel.

Three laps later came the first full-course caution of the day, when Geoff Boss spun and stalled in Turn 11. There was a flurry of activity as everyone took the opportunity to take on service for the first time. The top six positions remained unchanged. Jourdain continued to lead Tracy, Fernandez, Tagliani, Servia and Manning. Mario Haberfeld moved up to seventh at the expense of both Bruno Junqueira, who lost a little time in the pits, and Patrick Carpentier, who spun, apparently on oil. Not coincidentally, Gualter Salles retired during the caution due to a broken gearbox oil line, while Dale Coyne Racing teammate Boss continued after being restarted by the Simple Green Safety Team.

Junqueira, who had qualified a disappointing 11th, passed both Haberfeld, on lap 24, and Manning, on lap 41. Otherwise, the status quo remained at the front of the field until the second round of pit stops, made under green-flag conditions, after 44 laps. Sensational work by Team Player's saw Tracy blast out of his pit box fractionally ahead of Jourdain. The Canadian immediately veered over into the fast lane, forcing Jourdain to lift off momentarily to avoid contact. The race stewards reviewed video tape of the incident and decreed that Tracy had been at fault – drivers are supposed to proceed through the intermediate

"speed-up" lane, not dive directly out of their pit box into the outside "fast" lane. Tracy would be held for five seconds at his next pit stop.

Before that news was passed on, however, Jourdain – angered by Tracy's blatant "block" in the pit lane – saw an opportunity to regain the lead under braking for the Festival Curves. On lap 46, he dived to the inside. Tracy, though, hung on gamely to the outside line through the first right-handed part of the complex, which gave him the inside line for the ensuing left-hander. Then there was contact, and Jourdain's Gigante Lola was sent spinning.

"I had him on the pass," claimed Jourdain. "We were on cold tires, and he lifted early and I just dived in. It was quite easy. I went to the line and he touched me and he kept pushing, pushing and pushing, and then he spun me."

Tracy, predictably, saw the incident from an altogether different perspective.

"I looked in the mirror and saw that he was coming, and I didn't move over or block or anything," he explained. "I left him room to go and we went into Turn One side by side; when we got to the next corner, he just turned across in front of me. When I was there, we locked up [wheels] and he spun around and I kept going. You know, it was really just one of those things."

Tracy was fortunate to be able to continue, albeit with a damaged front wing. Jourdain wasn't so lucky, stalling his motor and losing a lap before he could be restarted.

After a brief full-course caution, Tracy was informed of his impending penalty. He knew what he had to do. The gap to Fernandez in second place opened quickly to over three seconds, then stabilized for a while. But Tracy pushed again, posting a string of fastest laps to open out his advantage to right around five seconds. Tagliani was a further seven seconds adrift in third place by lap 71, chased by Servia and the two Newman/Haas cars, Bourdais having driven extremely well to work his way back into sixth following his early delay.

The leaders made their final pit stops after 72 laps. Tracy appeared to have done just enough. Despite being held for an extra five seconds, he rejoined narrowly ahead of Fernandez. Bourdais,

meanwhile, took advantage of pitting a couple of laps later than the others, resuming in third place ahead of Tagliani, Junqueira and Servia.

A couple of full-course cautions served to keep the pack in tight order, and it was soon after one of the restarts, on lap 86, that Fernandez made his move – again under braking for the Festival Curves after Tracy had lost just a little momentum coming onto the straightaway. The pass was clean and incisive. Tracy was powerless to defend.

"Paul made a mistake and I knew I had to take advantage of it because he probably would not make another one," related the Mexican driver.

Fernandez made no hint of a mistake in the closing laps, despite the threat of rain. In fact, there were a few sprinkles just before the finish, but he edged clear to take the checkers a little more than two seconds ahead of Tracy.

"I'm a little disappointed in myself because I felt like I gave it away, making a mistake which allowed Adrian to pass me," commented Tracy.

Bourdais' misfortunes continued when the rear wing support on his Newman/Haas Lola failed abruptly just ten laps from the finish. Tagliani took advantage by reclaiming third pace for Rocketsports Racing.

"We had a great car," said the French-Canadian. "It took a little while for it to come up to temperature, but it worked really well for a fast-paced race."

Junqueira, too, did well to take fourth, just ahead of Servia, while Manning fought off a late challenge from Jimmy Vasser to finish in sixth.

"My car wasn't very good on the brakes going into the last turn toward the end of the race, and that allowed Jimmy to get up alongside me at the end there to make me work really hard for sixth," summarized the Briton. "It was a good result and about where we deserved to be based on our speeds."

Haberfeld and the two Herdez cars of Roberto Moreno and Mario Dominguez rounded out the top ten ahead of the final unlapped finisher, Rodolfo Lavin.

*Jeremy Shaw*

**Above: CART Chief Operating Officer David Clare (left) confers with Carl Haas.**
Mike Levitt/LAT

**Top: No quarter given as Herdez teammates Roberto Moreno and Mario Dominguez dispute the same piece of road. They were blanketed by less than 0.5s at the finish.**
Phil Abbott/LAT

# MR. CONSISTENCY

Gavin Lawrence/LAT

**C**ONSISTENCY was one of the traits Bruno Junqueira (left) was hoping, and expecting, to exhibit in 2003 after joining Newman/Haas Racing. He was also expecting to be fast. After all, he had finished second in the 2002 title chase and was about to embark on his third season of Champ Car competition, driving for the same team that had taken Cristiano da Matta to the 2002 crown.

In most respects, Junqueira had done a good job in the first seven races. He had qualified among the top ten in all of them and finished among the top five in all except one, at Milwaukee, where he had crashed on the opening lap. Surprisingly, however, the 26-year-old Brazilian had been outperformed quite regularly by his rookie teammate, Sébastien Bourdais. Four times out of seven, he had qualified behind the Frenchman, while at Portland Junqueira languished a disappointing 11th on the grid.

"I had traffic on every lap," he lamented. "I couldn't believe it. It was impossible to put together a quick lap. I think we had a car capable of pole, but Paul Tracy blocked me every lap on my first stint. I don't know what he was doing. On my second stint [and second set of fresh Bridgestone Potenza tires], I got traffic every lap as well."

To say that he was frustrated would be a massive understatement.

"I'm going to start really far back, but the PacifiCare car is good," said Junqueira, "so I'm going to get by people and catch up to Tracy and show him what he did to me and pay him back."

Bold words. Some would say not too mature, either.

Fortunately, Junqueira didn't need to do anything unruly. He moved up steadily, made a couple of good passes in the middle stages to dispatch rookies Mario Haberfeld and Darren Manning, and took advantage of other people's errors or misfortunes so that he was up into fourth place by the checkered flag.

"It was great to finish fourth from where we started," said Junqueira, who held on to second place in the points table, just four markers behind his nemesis, Tracy. "We didn't win yet this year, but we have been consistent enough to finish in the top five in all but one race so far. It's a shame about Milwaukee, but you have to be consistent to win the championship and we have done a good job of that so far. We're going to get a win sooner or later."

**Above:** Bruno Junqueira racked up more useful points, but a win continued to prove frustratingly elusive for the Brazilian.
Mike Levitt/LAT

**Right:** Early leader Michel Jourdain Jr. tangled with Paul Tracy at the notorious Festival chicane and came off second best.
Phil Abbott/LAT

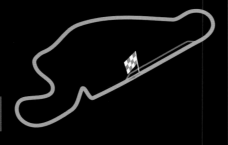

# 20TH
# G.I. JOE'S 200

ROUND 8

## PORTLAND INTERNATIONAL RACEWAY
## PORTLAND, OREGON

JUNE 22, 100 laps of 1.969 miles – 196.900 miles

| Pl. | Driver (Nat.) | No. | Team Sponsors Engine/Car | Tires | Q Speed | Q Time | Q Pos. | Laps | Time/Status | Ave. (mph) | Pts. |
|---|---|---|---|---|---|---|---|---|---|---|---|
| 1 | Adrian Fernandez (MEX) | 51 | Fernandez Tecate/Quaker State/Telmex Ford Cosworth/Lola B02/00 | BS | 120.248 | 58.948s | 3 | 100 | 1h 56m 16.626s | 101.602 | 20 |
| 2 | Paul Tracy (CDN) | 3 | Forsythe Racing Player's/Indeck Ford Cosworth/Lola B02/00 | BS | 120.565 | 58.793s | 1 | 100 | 1h 56m 18.899s | 101.569 | 18 |
| 3 | Alex Tagliani (CDN) | 33 | Rocketsports Racing Johnson Controls Ford Cosworth/Lola B02/00 | BS | 120.018 | 59.061s | 5 | 100 | 1h 56m 21.083s | 101.537 | 14 |
| 4 | Bruno Junqueira (BR) | 1 | Newman/Haas Racing PacifiCare Ford Cosworth/Lola B02/00 | BS | 119.205 | 59.464s | 11 | 100 | 1h 56m 25.211s | 101.477 | 12 |
| 5 | Oriol Servia (E) | 20 | Patrick Racing Visteon Ford Cosworth/Lola B02/00 | BS | 119.700 | 59.218s | 6 | 100 | 1h 56m 26.653s | 101.456 | 10 |
| 6 | *Darren Manning (GB) | 15 | Walker Racing RAC/Autowindscreens Ford Cosworth/Reynard 02I | BS | 119.686 | 59.225s | 8 | 100 | 1h 56m 27.516s | 101.444 | 8 |
| 7 | Jimmy Vasser (USA) | 12 | American Spirit Team Johansson Ford Cosworth/Reynard 2KI | BS | 119.349 | 59.392s | 9 | 100 | 1h 56m 27.811s | 101.439 | 6 |
| 8 | *Mario Haberfeld (BR) | 34 | Mi-Jack Conquest Racing Ford Cosworth/Reynard 02I | BS | 119.123 | 59.505s | 12 | 100 | 1h 56m 29.885s | 101.409 | 5 |
| 9 | Roberto Moreno (BR) | 4 | Herdez Competition Ford Cosworth/Lola B03/00 | BS | 118.901 | 59.616s | 14 | 100 | 1h 56m 31.097s | 101.392 | 4 |
| 10 | Mario Dominguez (MEX) | 55 | Herdez Competition Ford Cosworth/Lola B03/00 | BS | 118.513 | 59.811s | 16 | 100 | 1h 56m 31.565s | 101.385 | 3 |
| 11 | *Rodolfo Lavin (MEX) | 5 | Walker Racing Corona Competition Ford Cosworth/Reynard 02I | BS | 119.089 | 59.522s | 13 | 100 | 1h 56m 34.572s | 101.341 | 2 |
| 12 | Michel Jourdain Jr. (MEX) | 9 | Team Rahal Gigante Ford Cosworth/Lola B01/00 | BS | 120.473 | 58.838s | 2 | 99 | Running | | 2 |
| 13 | *Geoff Boss (USA) | 11 | Dale Coyne Racing Cross Pens Ford Cosworth/Lola B01/00 | BS | 116.780 | 1m 00.699s | 18 | 96 | Running | | |
| 14 | *Sébastien Bourdais (F) | 2 | Newman/Haas Racing Lilly Ford Cosworth/Lola B2K/00 | BS | 120.191 | 58.976s | 4 | 91 | Rear wing | | |
| 15 | Max Papis (I) | 27 | PK Racing Ford Cosworth/Lola B02/00 | BS | 118.726 | 59.704s | 15 | 87 | Accident | | |
| 16 | Patrick Carpentier (CDN) | 32 | Forsythe Racing Player's/Indeck Ford Cosworth/Lola B02/00 | BS | 119.223 | 59.455s | 10 | 73 | Accident | | |
| 17 | *Ryan Hunter-Reay (USA) | 31 | American Spirit Team Johansson Ford Cosworth/Reynard 01I | BS | 119.698 | 59.219s | 7 | 21 | Clutch | | |
| 18 | Gualter Salles (BR) | 19 | Dale Coyne Racing Alpina/Golden Cross Ford Cosworth/Lola B2K/00 | BS | 116.699 | 1m 00.741s | 19 | 16 | Gearbox oil line | | |
| 19 | *Tiago Monteiro (P) | 7 | Fittipaldi-Dingman Racing Ford Cosworth/Reynard 02I | BS | 117.414 | 1m 00.371s | 17 | 5 | Gearbox | | |

* denotes rookie driver

Caution flags: Laps 1–2, yellow start; laps 15–18, tow/Boss; laps 45–47, accident/Tracy & Jourdain Jr.; laps 74–77, accident/Carpentier; laps 82–83, debris; laps 88–89, accident/Papis. Total: Six for 17 laps.

Lap leaders: Paul Tracy, 1–2 (2 laps); Michel Jourdain Jr., 3–44 (42 laps); Tracy, 45–72 (28 laps); Sébastien Bourdais, 73 (1 lap); Tracy, 74–85 (12 laps); Adrian Fernandez, 86–100 (15 laps). Totals: Tracy & Jourdain Jr, 42 laps; Fernandez, 15 laps; Bourdais, 1 lap.

Fastest race lap: Alex Tagliani, 1m 00.875s, 116.442 mph on lap 95.

Championship positions: 1 Tracy, 99; 2 Junqueira, 95; 3 Jourdain Jr., 91; 4 Carpentier, 70; 5 Fernandez, 63; 6 Servia, 58; 7 Bourdais, 53; 8 Dominguez, 51; 9 Tagliani, 46; 10 Manning, 42; 11 Haberfeld, 41; 12 Vasser, 38; 13 Moreno, 31; 14 Monteiro, 15; 15 Hunter-Reay, 10; 16 Lemarie, 8; 17 Camathias & Lavin, 6; 19 Yoong, 4; 20 Herta, 2.

## PORTLAND SNIPPETS

Gavin Lawrence/LAT

• Walker Racing spread its WINGS, literally, during the P.I.R. weekend by announcing a new "marketing and business development agreement" with Air China. "This is a great opportunity to partner with one of the most recognized brands both inside and outside of China," said team owner Derrick Walker. "Our relationship will allow Walker Racing to partner with other companies that want to do business with Air China and open the door to those who want to do business in the world's fastest growing market."

• Michel Jourdain Jr. couldn't resist a DIG at Paul Tracy after his attempted pass on lap 46 ended with a controversial collision. "He hit me in the rear of the sidepod, so I think I had him cleanly," reckoned Jourdain. "Away from the track, Paul and I are very good friends, but on the track nobody is your friend. Hey, that was the way he had to beat me today."

• PK Racing also unveiled a couple of new SUPPORTERS, Japhiro Swiss Watches and Prosperco, a Swiss finance company, as well as a new driver, Max Papis.

• The battle for NATION'S CUP honors between Mexico and Canada continued to ebb and flow. Canada had taken an early lead by virtue of Paul Tracy's three wins at the start of the season. Then Mexico fought back to claim the advantage following consecutive podium finishes for Mario Dominguez in Europe and Michel Jourdain Jr. in Milwaukee. After Patrick Carpentier swung the balance back in Canada's favor by winning at Mazda Raceway Laguna Seca, Adrian Fernandez's triumph in Oregon enabled Mexico to rebound and lead by just two points, 115–113, after nine races.

• Champ Car Starter J.D. Wilbur, responsible for throwing the green flag at the beginning of the races, came in for renewed CRITICISM after the first three attempts at getting the G.I. Joe's 200 under way were aborted. There had been problems earlier in the season, too, most obviously at Long Beach. "Really, I don't mean to throw down, but he's done five bad starts out of seven or eight races so far this year," declared polesitter Paul Tracy, who was irate after being beaten into the first corner by outside-front-row starter Michel Jourdain Jr. "You know, we tried at it four times and the fourth one I got screwed. So we're going to have to sit down with the chief steward and talk about it."

• Alex Tagliani (below) qualified fifth and finished a strong third for Rocketsports Racing, marking a welcome TURNAROUND after a disappointing weekend at Mazda Raceway Laguna Seca. "We worked really hard on analyzing every bit of data from the car and we found some major prob-

lems," declared Tagliani. "After that, we were confident coming here that we were going to be quick and we worked on the car all weekend long. At the end, I was able to run a really quick lap time. We're definitely improving race by race and I am sure that if we keep at knocking on the door like this, we'll have our chances."

• There was yet ANOTHER SHUFFLE within the Dale Coyne Racing ranks between the races in California and Oregon. Lanky and personable Swiss Joel Camathias, sadly, had run out of funding – a shame after his very respectable seventh-fastest lap during the race at Mazda Raceway Laguna Seca. His place in the #19 Lola was taken by Gualter Salles, back in action after being forced to skip the previous weekend's race, while Geoff Boss remained in the #11 car. The crews, however, had been shifted around, Orlando Ledesma & Co. moving across to take care of Boss' entry and Wayne Hill's crew looking after Salles.

• American Spirit Team Johansson delivered a STUNNING PERFORMANCE in qualifying on Friday, the Reynards of rookie Ryan Hunter-Reay and veteran Jimmy Vasser ending the session beaten only by Michel Jourdain Jr.'s Lola. Sadly the team's joy was tempered when Hunter-Reay's car was found to be just three pounds below the minimum weight limit and his time was disallowed.

Mike Levitt/LAT

# CLEVELAND

Inset left: Paul Newman, Sébastien Bourdais, Carl Haas and Bruno Junqueira celebrate a magnificent Cleveland 1-3.
Gavin Lawrence/LAT

Main photograph: The full drama of pit stops at night is captured as Paul Tracy takes on service.
Mike Levitt/LAT

**T**HE annual thrash around Cleveland's Burke Lakefront Airport always offers first-rate entertainment value for spectators. The latest event served up more of the same, only with the added dimension of the race taking place at night, under floodlights, for the first time in the history of open-wheel road racing.

Musco Lighting, the Iowa-based company assigned the task of illuminating the circuit, had accumulated a wealth of experience with all manner of sporting and entertainment events, from the Olympic Games to rock concerts, over a quarter-century. It had also handled CART's inaugural night race at Milwaukee at the end of May, universally deemed a resounding success. But lighting a 2.106-mile airport-cum-racetrack represented an altogether more Herculean task.

"This is by far the largest mobile lighting job we've ever taken on," confirmed the company's president, Joe Crookham. "The 21 trucks, generators and lighting systems we've brought here create as much light as nearly a half-million car headlights."

The logistical challenge was heightened by the makeshift nature of the Cleveland venue. Because Burke Lakefront is an active airport, it only closes for a strictly limited period to accommodate the race, and Musco's crews had to work to an extremely tight timetable.

The verdict from organizers, teams and drivers alike was overwhelmingly positive. Naturally there were one or two teething difficulties. After a couple of exploratory practice sessions on Thursday night, drivers reported a few dark spots around the east end of the track, where it hadn't been possible to install lighting units until Thursday morning, when the airfield had finally been shut down.

Musco's technicians labored into the small hours adjusting the positioning of the lights, while CART and track officials attended to such details as painting the tire bundles at corner apexes fluorescent orange and tying the bundles with glo-lights to aid visibility on a track notoriously devoid of natural reference points. The various tweaks worked a treat, and come Saturday night there were precious few complaints to be heard.

The experiment helped draw the largest three-day attendance in years, while the cars were a sight to behold, silhouetted against the night sky, their turbo engines spitting flame out of the wastegates at pit stops. "You see the sparks coming off the cars ahead of you, the brake rotors glowing red – it is fun to be a part of this," enthused Oriol Servia.

Facing page: **Bourdais and Junqueira lead the way into the braking area for Turn One.**

Below: **Bourdais celebrates his fourth pole.**
Photographs: Mike Levitt/LAT

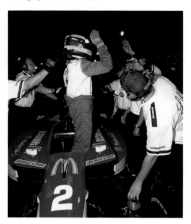

## QUALIFYING

The unique Burke Lakefront Airport temporary road course, with its rough transitions between runways and taxiways, could be expected to favor the more well-heeled teams with the benefit of substantial development budgets to hone the fine points of shock-absorber settings and suspension geometry. So it was no surprise to find Newman/Haas Racing and Player's/Forsythe once again making the running in the lead-up to the race.

For much of final qualifying – played out before packed grandstands on Friday night – Paul Tracy's provisional time of 58.405s, which had topped the charts by nearly a half-second on Thursday, looked unassailable. When Tracy spun and stalled midway through the session, bringing out the red flag, paradoxically his pole seemed more, not less secure, since time was running out for his competitors. But in the dying minutes, Sébastien Bourdais uncorked a pair of flyers, the second of which eclipsed Tracy's benchmark by 0.391s.

"Yesterday we found we had a very good car for these conditions," said Bourdais after pacing the field for the fourth time in nine events. "We really didn't make any changes today. I knew it was going to be OK as long as we had good conditions and a clear lap."

Bourdais freely admitted that waiting for optimal track conditions before showing his hand had been a high-risk strategy – and it appeared to have backfired when Patrick Carpentier emulated his teammate by spinning in Turn Four with four minutes to go. But Carpentier kept the engine running and a red flag was averted. After a lap to clean up his tires, the 2002 Cleveland winner snared third spot on the grid on his final allotted lap, just 0.044s adrift of Tracy's Thursday standard.

Mindful of the fact that he would have to forfeit his fastest time as penance for causing a stoppage, Tracy shrewdly elected to fall back on his guaranteed front-row starting berth and sit out the balance of the session, thereby conserving an extra set of fresh "sticker" tires for the race.

Oriol Servia lined up fourth for Patrick Racing, equaling his best qualifying performance of the year, while Bruno Junqueira was left to rue a mid-session setup change after being bumped from second to fifth in the last minute.

Right: **Michel Jourdain Jr.'s Gigante Lola at full speed as the sun sets over Lake Erie.**
Gavin Lawrence/LAT

SOMEHOW it seemed fitting that Sébastien Bourdais should emerge as victor of the floodlit US Bank Presents the Cleveland Grand Prix, after an intense duel with Paul Tracy, which left both drivers physically and mentally spent. Bourdais is an old hand at night races, having competed in the classic Le Mans 24-hour sports car race on three occasions, in addition to winning the 2002 Spa 24-hour enduro aboard a Chrysler Viper. Ultimately, however, it wasn't his experience of racing under the stars but his sheer pace that accounted for his third win of the season and first on American soil. That and an inspired tactical gambit by Newman/Haas Racing.

After ceding the lead at the outset, Bourdais spent most of the 115-lap contest in the wheel tracks of Tracy's Player's/Forsythe machine, matching him fastest lap for fastest lap, but never getting close enough to mount a challenge. By half-distance, a stalemate appeared to have been reached. But at the penultimate round of fuel stops, Bourdais' crew elected to "short-fill" their charge, and the vital couple of seconds saved enabled him to leapfrog Tracy in the pit lane. It proved to be the turning point. Bourdais sprinted away like a scalded cat and looked set to canter home to the checkered flag until a last-minute yellow presented the famously opportunistic Tracy with a chance to counterattack. Instead, however, the Canadian found his hands full repelling a spirited challenge from Bruno Junqueira, leaving Bourdais to win by 2.2 seconds.

"I'm very proud to score my first victory in the United States," said the 24-year-old. "Paul and I pushed as hard as possible – that means 100 percent and even more – all through the race, so this result is really satisfying."

Burke Lakefront's 100-foot-wide main runway funneling into a tight hairpin traditionally invites the most optimistic of lunges in the braking area, especially on the opening lap, but for the first time anyone could remember the entire field made it through without a major pile-up. Bourdais forfeited the lead after opting to take a defensive line down the inside – "…it was the safest thing to do…" – while Tracy laid claim to the far outside and gave himself a much better angle of attack for the corner.

Junqueira got the jump on both Patrick Carpentier and Oriol Servia to slot into third place, but Michel Jourdain Jr. quickly found himself going in the opposite direction. He hustled around the outside of Carpentier at Turn Three, only to lose control of the Gigante Lola on acceleration out of Turn Four and spin across the bows of the onrushing pack. The Mexican had the presence of mind to floor the throttle and allow the car to slide backward onto the grass, whereupon he quickly righted the spin and set about a dogged recovery drive from the tail of the field.

Initially it looked as if Tracy was going to run and hide, as he established a 2.8-second cushion in the space of two laps. But Bourdais soon got into his stride, and by the fifth lap was beginning to chip away at the deficit. On the eighth time around, he clocked the first sub-60s lap of the evening, and a lap later he was a mere 1.4 seconds in arrears. We had a race on our hands.

Third-placed Junqueira wasn't quite able to match the leaders' pace, finding that his PacifiCare Lola was understeering more than he would have liked. Nonetheless he pulled out a useful margin over Servia and Carpentier, while Roberto Moreno was enjoying his best outing of the season in sixth place, fending off the attentions of Jimmy Vasser in the leading Reynard. Sadly the little Brazilian's race came to an abrupt end when Vasser attempted a dive-bomb pass at the hairpin and punted the Herdez Competition Lola into retirement.

A full-course yellow ensued while Moreno's stricken machine was pulled out of harm's way, triggering the first spate of pit stops at the conclusion of lap 16. By now Bourdais had closed to within 0.9s of Tracy, but the top three cars emerged from the pit lane in the same order. A slow stop for Servia enabled Carpentier to move up to fourth, with Mario Dominguez, Ryan Hunter-Reay, Adrian Fernandez, and the recovering Vasser and Jourdain completing the top ten.

As the sun began to set over Lake Erie, the race's second stint settled into a familiar pattern – Tracy eking out a slight advantage on cold tires and a full fuel load, before Bourdais steadily began to reel him in. The gap hovered around the one-second mark as the pair traded fastest laps all the way up to the next round of pit stops on lap 42. It was an absorbing duel, both drivers scratching for every last hundredth of a second and occasionally throwing up a wisp of dust from the track's edges to emphasize the point.

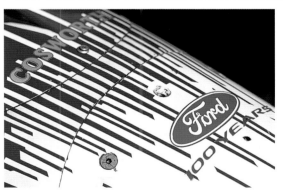

**Above:** The capacity crowd watches as Carpentier leads Servia into the chicane.
Dan Boyd/LAT

**Left:** The 2003 season marked a major milestone for the Ford Motor Company.
Gavin Lawrence/LAT

113

A slight front wing adjustment helped Bourdais to keep pace with Tracy in the race's third segment, while a tardy pit stop for Junqueira dashed any hopes he had of keeping the two leaders in sight. Fourth-placed Carpentier now was in close attendance, well clear of Servia and Jourdain, who had passed Vasser, Fernandez and Hunter-Reay in the previous stint before relieving Dominguez of sixth on lap 46.

Servia's pulse was sent skyward on lap 57, when he encountered a spinning Rodolfo Lavin on the racing line as he swept through Turn Eight and narrowly avoided contact with the Mexican rookie. Lavin's stalled Corona Reynard brought out the caution. A lap after the restart, Servia – who had been struggling with the brake balance on his Visteon Lola – locked up the rears going into Turn One and ran wide. A grateful Jourdain slipped past the Spaniard, while Dominguez followed suit at Turn Five as Servia struggled to clean his tires and regain his rhythm.

Next came the pivotal third round of pit stops, and the short-fill by the Newman/Haas crew that finally released Bourdais' McDonald's/Lilly Lola into clear air.

Just as crucial as the brisk service was Bourdais' rapid in-lap and committed assault on the pit-lane entrance, followed by an equally stunning out-lap that propelled him into an immediate 1.6-second lead over Tracy. One more lap and the margin was up to 2.4 seconds. By lap 74, the Frenchman had four seconds in hand.

"It took me five or six laps to get back into the 59-second range, and by that time he was too far down the road," noted Tracy afterward.

By the time an out-of-sequence Vasser – who had temporarily assumed the lead – pitted on lap 83, Bourdais had an eight-second advantage over Tracy. He lost a couple of seconds lapping an uncooperative Max Papis, but then proceeded to reel off a succession of laps in the very low 59s bracket, comfortably quicker than anyone else. It appeared to be game over for his pursuers.

The final flurry of pit stops, on lap 94, saw Dominguez swap places with Jourdain, thanks to sterling work from Daryl Fox's crew, but otherwise the status quo prevailed. Attention now focused on the intensifying scrap for fourth between Carpentier – who was struggling with a damaged front wing endplate – Dominguez, Jourdain and Servia. After a lively seesaw exchange on lap 98, Servia had the final say on sixth place by dint of an opportunistic move going into Turn Four a few laps later, when Jourdain was blocked by the obstructive Papis.

Meanwhile Junqueira appeared to have acquired a new lease of life on his final set of tires and was starting to turn up the heat on Tracy. Then, on lap 112, the yellow flags flew after Vasser spun and stalled in Turn One. It was unwelcome news for Bourdais, who had just survived a scare when he banged wheels with Fernandez while lapping the Portland winner at Turn Three, apparently having failed to anticipate that the owner/driver would lift off to let him by. Fortunately damage was limited to a broken "flugelhorn" in front of the left rear wheel, and Bourdais radioed to his pit that nothing felt amiss.

The Simple Green Safety Team managed to clear the way for a one-lap shootout to the finish. Tracy scented blood. But Bourdais' restart was exemplary, and Tracy had to pull out all the stops to keep Junqueira at bay. "Junky" outbraked Tracy into Turn Three, but went in a little too deep, allowing the Canadian to gain the upper hand around the outside in Turn Four. Great stuff, and in the time-honored, no-holds-barred Cleveland mold of passing and repassing.

"I think Paul made a great maneuver to get around me on the outside," acknowledged Junqueira magnanimously. "I said to myself, 'Oh, there is one driver in the world who could do that, and that guy is Paul Tracy!'"

Tracy had indeed done himself proud. But, on this day, neither he nor anyone else was a match for the raw speed of Bourdais, whose performance was the most convincing to date of a thoroughly impressive rookie campaign, and the tactical acumen and teamwork of Newman/Haas Racing.

*Alex Sabine*

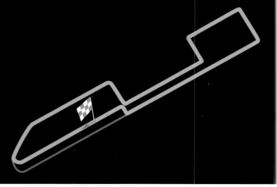

# US BANK PRESENTS
# THE CLEVELAND GRAND PRIX

## BURKE LAKEFRONT AIRPORT, CLEVELAND, OHIO

### JULY 5, 115 laps of 2.106 miles – 242.190 miles

| Pl. | Driver (Nat.) | No. | Team Sponsors Engine/Car | Tires | Q Speed | Q Time | Q Pos. | Laps | Time/Status | Ave. (mph) | Pts. |
|---|---|---|---|---|---|---|---|---|---|---|---|
| 1 | *Sébastien Bourdais (F) | 2 | Newman/Haas Racing McDonald's/Lilly Ford Cosworth/Lola B01/00 | BS | 130.686 | 58.014s | 1 | 115 | 2h 03m 51.974s | 117.315 | 22 |
| 2 | Paul Tracy (CDN) | 3 | Forsythe Racing Player's/Indeck Ford Cosworth/Lola B02/00 | BS | 129.811 | 58.405s | 2 | 115 | 2h 03m 54.215s | 117.280 | 17 |
| 3 | Bruno Junqueira (BR) | 1 | Newman/Haas Racing PacifiCare Ford Cosworth/Lola B02/00 | BS | 129.587 | 58.506s | 5 | 115 | 2h 03m 54.952s | 117.268 | 14 |
| 4 | Patrick Carpentier (CDN) | 32 | Forsythe Racing Player's/Indeck Ford Cosworth/Lola B03/00 | BS | 129.713 | 58.449s | 3 | 115 | 2h 03m 59.811s | 117.192 | 12 |
| 5 | Mario Dominguez (MEX) | 55 | Herdez Competition Ford Cosworth/Lola B03/00 | BS | 129.106 | 58.724s | 8 | 115 | 2h 04m 00.209s | 117.185 | 10 |
| 6 | Oriol Servia (E) | 20 | Patrick Racing Visteon Ford Cosworth/Lola B02/00 | BS | 129.596 | 58.502s | 4 | 115 | 2h 04m 01.839s | 117.160 | 8 |
| 7 | Michel Jourdain Jr. (MEX) | 9 | Team Rahal Gigante Ford Cosworth/Lola B01/00 | BS | 129.158 | 58.700s | 6 | 115 | 2h 04m 02.500s | 117.149 | 6 |
| 8 | Alex Tagliani (CDN) | 33 | Rocketsports Racing Johnson Controls Ford Cosworth/Lola B02/00 | BS | 129.119 | 59.718s | 7 | 115 | 2h 04m 04.935s | 117.111 | 5 |
| 9 | *Ryan Hunter-Reay (USA) | 31 | American Spirit Team Johansson Ford Cosworth/Reynard 01I | BS | 128.343 | 59.073s | 11 | 115 | 2h 04m 07.333s | 117.073 | 4 |
| 10 | *Darren Manning (GB) | 15 | Walker Racing RAC/Autowindscreens Ford Cosworth/Reynard 02I | BS | 128.139 | 59.167s | 13 | 115 | 2h 04m 14.197s | 116.966 | 3 |
| 11 | Adrian Fernandez (MEX) | 51 | Fernandez Tecate/Quaker State/Telmex Ford Cosworth/Lola B02/00 | BS | 127.839 | 59.306s | 14 | 114 | Running | | 2 |
| 12 | Max Papis (I) | 27 | PK Racing Ford Cosworth/Lola B02/00 | BS | 126.318 | 1m 00.020s | 18 | 114 | Running | | 1 |
| 13 | Jimmy Vasser (USA) | 12 | American Spirit Team Johansson Ford Cosworth/Reynard 02I | BS | 128.805 | 58.861s | 10 | 113 | Running | | |
| 14 | *Rodolfo Lavin (MEX) | 5 | Walker Racing Corona Competition Ford Cosworth/Reynard 02I | BS | 127.355 | 59.531s | 15 | 112 | Running | | |
| 15 | *Mario Haberfeld (BR) | 34 | Mi-Jack Conquest Racing Ford Cosworth/Reynard 02I | BS | 128.195 | 59.141s | 12 | 110 | Running | | |
| 16 | *Geoff Boss (USA) | 11 | Dale Coyne Racing Cross Pens Ford Cosworth/Lola B01/00 | BS | 124.079 | 1m 01.103s | 19 | 36 | Suspension | | |
| 17 | Gualter Salles (BR) | 19 | Dale Coyne Racing Alpina/Golden Cross Ford Cosworth/Lola B2K/00 | BS | 126.427 | 59.968s | 17 | 18 | Throttle cable | | |
| 18 | Roberto Moreno (BR) | 4 | Herdez Competition Ford Cosworth/Lola B01/00 | BS | 128.840 | 58.845s | 9 | 16 | Accident | | |
| DNS | *Tiago Monteiro (P) | 7 | Fittipaldi-Dingman Racing Ford Cosworth/Reynard 02I | BS | 126.736 | 59.822s | 16 | – | Withdrawn | | |

\* denotes rookie driver

Caution flags: Laps 15–17, accident/Vasser & Moreno; laps 20–21, tow/Salles; laps 57–59, tow/Lavin; laps 112–113, tow/Vasser. Total: Four for 10 laps.

Lap leaders: Paul Tracy, 1–67 (67 laps); Jimmy Vasser, 68–82 (15 laps); Sébastien Bourdais, 83–115 (33 laps). Totals: Tracy, 67 laps; Bourdais, 33 laps; Vasser, 12 laps.

Fastest race lap: Sébastien Bourdais, 58.949s, 128.613 mph on lap 41.

Championship positions: 1 Tracy, 117; 2 Junqueira, 109; 3 Jourdain Jr., 97; 4 Carpentier, 82; 5 Bourdais, 74; 6 Servia, 66; 7 Fernandez, 65; 8 Dominguez, 61; 9 Tagliani, 51; 10 Manning, 45; 11 Haberfeld, 41; 12 Vasser, 38; 13 Moreno, 31; 14 Monteiro, 15; 15 Hunter-Reay, 14; 16 Lemarie, 8; 17 Camathias & Lavin, 6; 19 Yoong, 4; 20 Herta, 2; 21 Papis, 1.

# CLEVELAND SNIPPETS

• The switch to a nighttime format passed the most important test – it was A HIT with the paying customers. The raceday attendance of 58,471 represented a modest improvement on the last few years, while the three-day throng of 112,232 comfortably surpassed the customary total of 100,000 or so. Smart promotion (the admission price was cut to $5 after 6 p.m.) boosted the Friday-night crowd and contributed to by far the healthiest turnout for any CART qualifying session at a US venue in recent memory, apart from Long Beach. The city of Cleveland's annual Fourth of July fireworks display provided a fitting climax to an atmospheric evening.

• Racing at night, rather than in the sweltering heat of the day, provided welcome respite for the drivers in what is the longest and one of the most physically demanding road races on the CART calendar. Even so, both Sébastien Bourdais and Paul Tracy were EXHAUSTED by the strain of wrestling their Ford Cosworth/Lolas around the bumpy circuit for 115 laps and by the intensity of their battle for the lead. "My hands got really tired the last 15 laps," said Tracy. "The steering got really heavy with all the rubber being laid down and it was hard to hold on to the wheel at the end."

• The endearingly ACCIDENT-PRONE Patrick Carpentier had been in the wars since Portland. The 31-year-old miraculously emerged without serious injury from a harrowing encounter with a pickup truck towing a trailer while out on a bicycle ride with motorbike ace Miguel DuHamel, near his home in Las Vegas. Carpentier's bike hit the trailer, but he managed to dislodge himself from the pedals and scramble to safety, sustaining a hairline fracture in his right arm and assorted bumps and bruises.

• One car attracted more attention at Cleveland than all the combined racing machinery on hand – a production-ready PROTOTYPE of the 2005 Ford GT supercar (below), a modern-day rendition of the GT40 sports car that delivered Ford four consecutive Le Mans victories from 1966 to '69. The dark blue beauty doubled as the pace car and was driven by none other than Mario Andretti.

• Paul Tracy reached another MILESTONE at Cleveland, racking up the 200th start of an illustrious but checkered Champ Car career. Ever the pot-stirrer, PT couldn't resist a waspish swipe at CART officialdom: "Actually this would be my 201st start if Wally [former Chief Steward Wally Dallenbach] hadn't sat me down for a race [the '99 season-opener at Homestead]. Portland should have been my 200th start."

• Points leader Tracy was also at the center of CONTROVERSY after provisional qualifying, when you could have cut the atmosphere in the paddock with the proverbial knife. An irate Michel Jourdain Jr. claimed that Tracy had deliberately blocked him to protect his position at the top of the time sheets. "Every lap he backed off before the last chicane when I was coming up to him on a fast lap," fumed the Mexican, resuming a war of words with Tracy after their travails at Portland. Meanwhile Patrick Carpentier incurred the wrath of Jimmy Vasser by cutting him off while rejoining the track after a spin, although the Québecois later apologized publicly for his transgression.

• Tiago Monteiro was RULED OUT of Saturday night's race following a hefty crash in the afternoon warmup session. The Fittipaldi-Dingman Racing Reynard, which Monteiro had deposited in the tire wall in Turn Eight, was repaired in time for the start, but CART's medical staff would not authorize the Portuguese rookie to drive, since he had suffered a slight concussion in the impact.

• Sébastien Bourdais' victory kicked off a new three-race SPONSORSHIP deal with fast-food giant McDonald's in the best possible fashion. The hamburger chain would join pharmaceutical company Eli Lilly as co-primary sponsor of the #2 Newman/Haas entry for Cleveland, Denver and Miami in a deal brokered by Paul Newman. "My car turned red this weekend with the arrival of the McDonald's sponsorship," said the winner. "I'm very glad of that because the black car seemed to be a synonym of bad luck and now it's gone!"

**P**AUL Tracy's Champ Car career had been anything but dull since he'd made his debut for Dale Coyne Racing at Long Beach in 1991. Hence the former resident of the West Hill area of Scarborough, Ontario, had earned an appropriate soubriquet, "The Thrill from West Hill."

He had won on home ground once before, in 1993, driving for Roger Penske, but his latest victory, the 23rd of his career (moving him to fifth on the all-time CART win list, just one shy of Bobby Rahal's standard), represented a new high-water mark.

"This means maybe ten times more than my first win here in 1993," declared Tracy. "I've been breaking my back ever since then to get back to Victory Lane here, and today it paid off."

The triumph took on greater significance with the realization that Player's had never before won a Champ Car race on home soil. Furthermore Player's confirmed during the Molson Indy weekend that impending, and controversial, new tobacco legislation in Canada would force the company to curtail its sponsorship at the conclusion of the current season. Indeed, from October 1, the team would no longer be permitted to carry Player's identification on the cars.

"This is a product that is still a legal product all around the world," declared Tracy. "You know, to be limited by what they can do to advertise the product, I think that's wrong. If you have a product that's a legal product, you should be allowed to advertise that product.

"This is a place that they have chosen to do that for 42 years. They've created a lot of jobs, they've done a lot of things for charities, done a lot of great things for this city and all across Canada. You know, it's just a shame. They don't want to be in any other type of sports or entertainment. Motor racing is what they love to do."

It's no wonder the victory meant so much.

"It's a great day for the whole team," continued Tracy. "I can't be happier. It hasn't really sunk in yet. The race in Toronto has always been the biggest win of my career. This is the most important race for me in the world. To come back ten years later and win it again with a Canadian sponsor, Canadian team, a lot of Canadian guys on the team, it's probably the defining moment of my career."

**Above:** A dominant performance by Tracy, who started on the pole, led the whole way and set fastest lap for good measure.
Phil Abbott/LAT

**Main photograph:** One of many memorable '03 moments for Tracy as he acknowledges the cheers of a massive hometown crowd.
Gavin Lawrence/LAT

## QUALIFYING

Changeable weather conditions hampered everyone's progress during practice and qualifying, so it was no surprise to see the rookies struggling to match the performance of the veterans. It was also no surprise to see the name of local favorite Paul Tracy toward the top of the order. Tracy, who had raced around Exhibition Place 11 times previously in a Champ Car, was fastest in the first session, and even though he was pipped to the provisional pole by Bruno Junqueira, he bounced back on Saturday to claim his third pole of the campaign for Team Player's.

"This one is for what Player's has done for motorsport in Canada," said Tracy, who twice before had started from the front row, including in 2002. "I've never been on the pole here, and it's great for Player's to come here and score the pole. This is very sweet."

Tracy had timed his run between rain showers to perfection. Junqueira wasn't so lucky. He posted only the fourth-fastest time in the final session, but already had done enough to secure a front-row starting position by being fastest of all on Friday.

"We were waiting until ten minutes to go before going out, but right then it started raining again," related Junqueira. "I could have gone much faster, and it's very frustrating because the rain took my chance to go for the pole."

Michel Jourdain Jr., third in the point standings when the Champ Car contenders arrived in Ontario, ensured that the three leading protagonists would fill their corresponding positions on the starting grid. That in itself represented a substantial improvement on his prior form in Toronto, having netted a best starting position of a measly 15th in six previous attempts.

Alex Tagliani also did well to dodge the rain showers, third fastest overall and fourth on the final grid, followed by fellow Québecois Patrick Carpentier in the second Player's Lola.

"It's a bit disappointing because we had a much better car," reckoned Carpentier. "I was caught in traffic on my second stint just when the track and the tires were at the right temperature. You have to do it on the right lap, otherwise it's not going to be good enough for the pole."

Sébastien Bourdais was fastest of the rookies in sixth, while next among the first-time visitors to Toronto was Darren Manning in 11th. The Briton also was second best among the Reynards, beaten only by ninth-placed Jimmy Vasser.

**Above: Adrian Fernandez's crew finds time for lunch before qualifying.**
Dan Boyd/LAT

PAUL Tracy's challenge for the 2003 Bridgestone Presents the Champ Car World Series Powered by Ford title moved into high gear at the Molson Indy Toronto. The hometown hero was in dominant form aboard Player's/Forsythe Racing's Ford Cosworth/Lola, qualifying on the pole and leading throughout the 112-lap race. The result stretched Tracy's championship advantage to 15 points over Bruno Junqueira, who finished third behind fellow title aspirant Michel Jourdain Jr.

"It's unbelievable to win here because of the importance of the race," said Tracy, who also won at Toronto in 1993 and was brought up in Scarborough, Ontario, just a few miles from the demanding Exhibition Place temporary street course. "It's the most dominant race of my career, and to do it I had to have a great car, and Team Player's gave me a perfect car."

Tracy made his presence felt right from the start, jumping into a clear lead while those behind jostled for position. Fellow Canadian Alex Tagliani went on a tear, moving past joint second-row starter Jourdain at the first corner, then diving inside Junqueira at the end of Lakeshore Boulevard to take over second place in Rocketsports Racing's Johnson Controls Lola. Patrick Carpentier made it three Canadians among the top five, much to the delight of the decidedly partisan crowd of 73,255, while Oriol Servia also got a good jump to sneak ahead of Roberto Moreno and Sébastien Bourdais. Behind, though, there was mayhem at Turn Three as the cars of Adrian Fernandez and Jimmy Vasser became entangled while scrapping over ninth.

Fernandez was able to continue at the back of the pack during the ensuing full-course caution, sporting only slight damage to one of the "flugelhorns" on the side of his Tecate/Quaker State/Telmex Lola. Vasser wasn't so fortunate, losing a lap before his American Spirit Team Johansson Reynard could be restarted by the Simple Green Safety Team. Even worse, teammate Ryan Hunter-Reay was involved in the melee and also rejoined a lap in arrears.

The restart, after four laps under yellow, was similarly short-lived due to another incident in Turn Three. This time it was caused when Mario Haberfeld's attempt to wrest 13th place from Tiago Monteiro went awry, the Brazilian taking out Champ Car debutant Alex Sperafico, who had been minding his own business in Dale Coyne Racing's #19 Lola.

"It was a short race," said a disappointed Sperafico. "The few

## THE CASE FOR PIT WINDOWS

CART had announced a variety of competition rule changes prior to the 2002 season, including the introduction of a "pit window," which mandated a maximum number of laps to be completed between pit stops during the races. Right from the outset, the rule was praised by drivers, teams and fans alike, since it provided an effective end to the "fuel economy" runs that had tended to prevail as teams sought to improve fuel mileage and reduce the amount of fuel taken on during each pit visit.

For the race at Brands Hatch in May, however, mindful of the extremely narrow pit lane at the famed British venue, CART officials had decided to rescind the pit-window rule. The effect, sadly, was predictable, as the race turned into little more than a procession. Incredibly, since then, there has been more talk of eliminating the pit window, but when the subject was raised in one of the regular conferences during the Molson Indy Toronto weekend, the drivers were unanimous in maintaining that the rule should remain as is.

"I think the mandatory window is very good," declared Bruno Junqueira. "If you go back to the race at Brands Hatch, me, Tracy and Sébastien [Bourdais] were lapping slower than we could, just to see who could go one lap farther. That's not the race that the fans want to see. The fans want to see you going as fast as you can and pushing hard. I think the pit windows allow those, obligate us to go as fast as we can."

"Yeah, I agree with Bruno," added series leader Paul Tracy. "Because the way it's set up now, you have to drive the cars to the limit because, if you're all coming in [to the pits] on the same lap, you want to get a lead over the guy behind you, and everybody's going as hard as they can go. You see a lot more action in the car, with the in-car cameras, the cars are sliding more sideways and guys are working really hard to try to not have a whole line of cars behind them because, you know, that's where the difference is, in the pits. You want to have a lead on somebody."

"The rule is meant to be so that the fastest guy wins," reckoned Michel Jourdain Jr. "That's what racing is all about. I think it's a good rule."

laps I had, the car was feeling good, so I thought it would be a good race. Unfortunately Haberfeld missed his braking and collected me."

After another brief interruption while the damaged cars of Sperafico and Haberfeld were removed, the race finally began in earnest. And Tracy lost no time in asserting his superiority. Within four laps of the green, Tagliani already was almost four seconds in arrears. By lap 20, the deficit had grown to over ten seconds.

Tagliani, troubled by excessive understeer, still managed to maintain a small but distinct advantage over Junqueira. Jourdain followed a further 3.6 seconds in arrears, chased by Carpentier. Servia couldn't quite match their pace in sixth as he fought to remain ahead of Moreno. Farther back, Herdez teammate Mario Dominguez had slipped past Darren Manning to run ninth, while Fernandez had made quick work of the tail-enders to move up into 11th after his earlier delay.

Dominguez's day took a turn for the worse on lap 24, when he spun in Turn Three and damaged his rear wing. Then he earned the ire of Fernandez by rejoining directly ahead of his countryman, who was obliged to take evasive action. Dominguez was involved in another scrape later on with Vasser before finishing 12th.

"That had to be the worst race of the season for us," admitted Dominguez.

Four laps later, there was yet another incident in Turn Three, when Tagliani left his braking a tad too late for the right-hand hairpin and ran wide at the apex. In a desperate attempt to hang on to second place, he lunged back across the road, directly into the path of Junqueira.

"At the time, I think my car was faster than his, but I wasn't going to be able to get around him so I was just saving fuel and my tires," related Junqueira. "Alex looked like he was going to go into the tires [barrier] and miss the turn, but at the last minute he came right [back] on the racing line where I already was."

The pair of Lolas made smart contact. Junqueira emerged relatively unscathed, but Tagliani wasn't so fortunate, retiring to the pits with damaged suspension.

"It's frustrating, but we're getting closer [to the front] and success will come," assured the French-Canadian.

Left: **Darren Manning presses on through the streets in Derrick Walker's Reynard.**

Below: **A miscue on his final pit stop forced Junqueira to settle for third.**
Photographs: Gavin Lawrence/LAT

**Right: Tagliani limps toward the pits after damaging his Lola's right rear wheel.**
Mike Levitt/LAT

**Far right: Jourdain drove another forceful race for Team Rahal to earn second place.**
Phil Abbott/LAT

**Above: Trouble at Turn Three on the opening lap as Vasser and Fernandez lock wheels. Monteiro, Hunter-Reay and Papis have nowhere to go, while Lavin (5) squeezes through unscathed on the inside.**
Gregg Feistman/LAT

This time there was no need for a full-course caution, so Tracy proceeded on his merry way, now with an expanded margin of 17 seconds over Junqueira. Shortly afterward, on lap 31, came the first round of pit stops. Again the status quo remained. Tracy resumed 17.7 seconds clear of the Brazilian, with Jourdain a further three seconds or so back in third and soon to come under pressure from Carpentier. Servia was a little way behind in fifth, pursued by Bourdais, Moreno, Manning and Fernandez. Rodolfo Lavin led the rest in tenth, his Corona Reynard already a lap in arrears of the race leader.

The middle stages were largely uneventful. Tracy ran serenely out in front, extending his lead to more than 20 seconds before making his second routine pit stop on lap 62. Teammate Carpentier wasn't nearly so comfortable. His rear tires lost grip as each stint progressed, leaving him to battle extreme oversteer. Carpentier's crew elected to bring him in one lap before everyone else on the second round of pit stops, but that, too, worked against him as he lost out to Servia, Bourdais, Moreno and Manning. Carpentier made up one of those spots when he passed the Englishman neatly going into Turn One on lap 64, but that was as good as it was to get for the Canadian.

Tracy had no such problems, although he did lose his massive advantage – which he had extended to almost 33 seconds – due to a full-course caution on lap 78 after Vasser spun to a halt in Turn Three (again), following contact with Dominguez.

"It was kind of frustrating when the yellow came out because we had such a lead on second place," noted Tracy.

But the interruption had no effect on his rhythm. He quickly settled into a fast pace at the restart, after making his final pit stop of the day, and pulled away gradually before easing off in the last couple of laps and taking the checkered flag 4.533 seconds to the good.

"I could see the crowd in the last couple laps, they were all standing and waving," said Tracy. "You know, it just gave me goose bumps out there. It's just a great, great feeling."

The car in his mirrors, however, was not the purple and white PacifiCare Lola of Junqueira but the red and white Gigante car of Jourdain. The Mexican had taken full advantage of a miscue by Junqueira at the final round of pit stops, when the Brazilian had locked up his brakes and parked too close to the pit wall, costing a few vital seconds as his crew scrambled to adjust their positions. Junqueira put the pressure on Jourdain for a while after the restart, but then the Mexican turned up the wick and edged clear.

"Second is like a win today because Paul was so dominant," declared Jourdain. "When I saw how strong and fast he was, our goal became to lose the least amount of points possible. We did that by finishing second."

Junqueira had to settle for third.

"I really think that if I had been ahead of Jourdain after the last stop, I would have been able to pressure Paul," he reckoned. "I was close to Jourdain to see if he would make a mistake, but then I got some pickup on my tires and it slowed me down a little."

Newman/Haas Racing teammate Bourdais trailed at a respectful distance following an unusually subdued performance.

"The car was pretty good," he related, "but we were at a disadvantage as a rookie because I had to use my tires up more in the practice and only had one set of new ones for the race compared to the others, who probably had two or three. They started the race with bigger potential and more rubber on their rear tires. The last ten laps of each stint were very, very hard for me."

Servia marked his 29th birthday with a solid run to fifth, hot on Bourdais' heels at the finish, while Moreno earned his first top-six finish since the race at Monterrey in March.

*Jeremy Shaw*

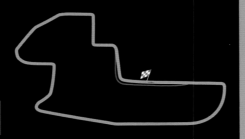

# MOLSON
# INDY TORONTO

**ROUND 10**

## EXHIBITION PLACE, TORONTO, ONTARIO, CANADA

**JULY 13, 112 laps of 1.755 miles – 196.560 miles**

| Pl. | Driver (Nat.) | No. | Team Sponsors Engine/Car | Tires | Q Speed | Q Time | Q Pos. | Laps | Time/Status | Ave. (mph) | Pts. |
|---|---|---|---|---|---|---|---|---|---|---|---|
| 1 | Paul Tracy (CDN) | 3 | Forsythe Racing Player's/Indeck Ford Cosworth/Lola B02/00 | BS | 107.378 | 58.839s | 1 | 112 | 2h 02m 36.488s | 96.189 | 22 |
| 2 | Michel Jourdain Jr. (MEX) | 9 | Team Rahal Gigante Ford Cosworth/Lola B01/00 | BS | 106.691 | 59.218s | 3 | 112 | 2h 02m 41.021s | 96.130 | 16 |
| 3 | Bruno Junqueira (BR) | 1 | Newman/Haas Racing PacifiCare Ford Cosworth/Lola B02/00 | BS | 106.210 | 59.486s | 2 | 112 | 2h 02m 45.114s | 96.077 | 15 |
| 4 | *Sébastien Bourdais (F) | 2 | Newman/Haas Racing McDonald's/Lilly Ford Cosworth/Lola B01/00 | BS | 106.326 | 59.421s | 6 | 112 | 2h 02m 47.141s | 96.050 | 12 |
| 5 | Oriol Servia (E) | 20 | Patrick Racing Visteon Ford Cosworth/Lola B02/00 | BS | 105.520 | 59.875s | 8 | 112 | 2h 02m 47.812s | 96.042 | 10 |
| 6 | Roberto Moreno (BR) | 4 | Herdez Competition Ford Cosworth/Lola B01/00 | BS | 105.529 | 59.870s | 7 | 112 | 2h 02m 50.789s | 96.003 | 8 |
| 7 | Patrick Carpentier (CDN) | 32 | Forsythe Racing Player's/Indeck Ford Cosworth/Lola B03/00 | BS | 106.428 | 59.364s | 5 | 112 | 2h 02m 51.843s | 95.989 | 6 |
| 8 | *Darren Manning (GB) | 15 | Walker Racing RAC/Autowindscreens Ford Cosworth/Reynard 02I | BS | 104.806 | 1m 00.283s | 11 | 112 | 2h 02m 52.224s | 95.984 | 5 |
| 9 | Adrian Fernandez (MEX) | 51 | Fernandez Tecate/Quaker State/Telmex Ford Cosworth/Lola B02/00 | BS | 105.134 | 1m 00.095s | 10 | 112 | 2h 03m 37.465s | 95.399 | 4 |
| 10 | *Tiago Monteiro (P) | 7 | Fittipaldi-Dingman Racing Ford Cosworth/Reynard 02I | BS | 104.232 | 1m 00.615s | 13 | 110 | Running | | 3 |
| 11 | *Ryan Hunter-Reay (USA) | 31 | American Spirit Team Johansson Ford Cosworth/Reynard 01I | BS | 103.669 | 1m 00.944s | 14 | 110 | Running | | 2 |
| 12 | Mario Dominguez (MEX) | 55 | Herdez Competition Ford Cosworth/Lola B03/00 | BS | 104.452 | 1m 00.487s | 12 | 109 | Running | | 1 |
| 13 | Jimmy Vasser (USA) | 12 | American Spirit Team Johansson Ford Cosworth/Reynard 2KI | BS | 105.221 | 1m 00.045s | 9 | 109 | Running | | |
| 14 | *Geoff Boss (USA) | 11 | Dale Coyne Racing Cross Pens Ford Cosworth/Lola B01/00 | BS | 100.985 | 1m 02.564s | 19 | 106 | Running | | |
| 15 | *Rodolfo Lavin (MEX) | 5 | Walker Racing Corona Competition Ford Cosworth/Reynard 02I | BS | 102.640 | 1m 01.555s | 17 | 105 | Running | | |
| 16 | Max Papis (I) | 27 | PK Racing Ford Cosworth/Lola B02/00 | BS | 103.596 | 1m 00.987s | 15 | 36 | Suspension | | |
| 17 | Alex Tagliani (CDN) | 33 | Rocketsports Racing Johnson Controls Ford Cosworth/Lola B02/00 | BS | 106.613 | 59.261s | 4 | 28 | Accident | | |
| 18 | *Alex Sperafico (BR) | 19 | Dale Coyne Racing Alpina/Golden Cross Ford Cosworth/Lola B2K/00 | BS | 102.018 | 1m 01.930s | 18 | 5 | Accident | | |
| 19 | *Mario Haberfeld (BR) | 34 | Mi-Jack Conquest Racing Ford Cosworth/Reynard 02I | BS | 103.535 | 1m 01.023s | 16 | 5 | Accident | | |

\* denotes rookie driver

**Caution flags:** Laps 1–3, accident/Vasser & Fernandez; lap 6, accident/Haberfeld & Sperafico; laps 77–83, accident/Vasser & Dominguez; lap 84, yellow restart. **Total: Four for 12 laps.**

**Lap leader:** Paul Tracy, 1–112 (112 laps). **Total: Tracy, 112 laps.**

**Fastest race lap:** Paul Tracy, 1m 00.527s, 104.383 mph on lap 11.

**Championship positions:** 1 Tracy, 139; 2 Junqueira, 124; 3 Jourdain Jr., 113; 4 Carpentier, 88; 5 Bourdais, 86; 6 Servia, 76; 7 Fernandez, 69; 8 Dominguez, 62; 9 Tagliani, 51; 10 Manning, 50; 11 Haberfeld, 41; 12 Moreno, 39; 13 Vasser, 38; 14 Monteiro, 18; 15 Hunter-Reay, 16; 16 Lemarie, 8; 17 Camathias & Lavin, 6; 19 Yoong, 4; 20 Herta, 2; 21 Papis, 1.

# TORONTO SNIPPETS

• The absence once again of Gualter Salles, previously committed to a Brazilian Stock Car Championship race in São Paulo, provided an opportunity for countryman Alex Sperafico (above) to make his Champ Car DEBUT for Dale Coyne Racing. Aged 29, from Toledo Parana, Sperafico had enjoyed some success in the Champ Car Ladder System, winning a Barber Dodge Pro Series race at Sebring in 2001, and was making his return to North American competition after a disappointing foray to Europe in Formula 3000. Sperafico acquitted himself respectably and was unfortunate to be taken out by an errant Mario Haberfeld in the early stages.

• Rodolfo Lavin enjoyed one of his BETTER forays aboard Derrick Walker's Corona Reynard, running as high as tenth before encountering dif-

ficulties. The Mexican lost some time during his second pit stop due to an airjack failure, then endured a lengthy delay after his car's rear wing mounting developed a crack.

• Talking of cracks, Paul Tracy was NOT AMUSED when title rival Bruno Junqueira said after qualifying that he wasn't worried about losing his provisional pole because he reckoned the Canadian was liable to crack under pressure. "When I heard what Junqueira said, that he was going to make me crack, that kind of p****d me off a little bit," said Tracy after his faultless drive to victory. "I said, 'I'm going to show him crack. He's going to look at my ass crack all day.'"

• By leading all 112 laps, Tracy took his career TALLY of laps led to 3,176, propelling him to third on the all-time CART Champ Car list, ahead of Al Unser Jr. (3,113), Bobby Rahal (3,107) and Mario Andretti (3,064).

• The race could hardly have started out worse for American Spirit Team Johansson, as both its drivers, JIMMY VASSER and Ryan Hunter-Reay, lost a lap in the first-lap skirmish. Nonetheless Vasser worked his way back to tenth before being involved in another incident with Mario Dominguez. "I was trying to chase down Fernandez for ninth, and a lapped car, Dominguez, was holding me up terribly. Finally I thought he was going to let me by, so I went for it and I hit him

I guess he wasn't moving over," added Vasser with a wry smile. The good news was that Vasser clearly had a fast car, as evidenced by his posting of the second-fastest race lap.

• Earlier in the year, Toronto had been hard-hit by the effects of the Severe Acute Respiratory Syndrome (SARS) virus, which brought the tourism industry in the region to its knees. Happily, despite inclement weather in the days leading up to the race, the usual STELLAR JOB of promotion by Molstar Entertainment ensured almost record crowds for the 18th annual Molson Indy Toronto.

• American broadcast giant CBS Sports announced PLANS during the Toronto Molson Indy weekend to expand its relationship with the Champ Car World Series in 2004. "Sports fans

as well as racing fans are showing that they enjoy the tight racing action provided by the CART Champ Car World Series," said CBS Sports Senior Vice President of Programming Rob Correa when confirming that his network would televise up to ten races in 2004, an increase from seven in the current season. "We will continue to develop new methods to take the fans even closer to the action, and intend to provide those fans with the finest open-wheel racing coverage anywhere."

• A seventh consecutive top-six finish for Oriol Servia (below) equaled a RECORD for Patrick Racing. The winner of the very first CART-sanctioned event, Gordon Johncock, established the standard on two different occasions while driving for veteran owner U.E. "Pat" Patrick during the early 1980s.

## TRACY SHOOTS FROM THE HIP

THE thorny issue of driver etiquette reared its head once more following provisional qualifying on Friday, and again Paul Tracy was the catalyst. Champ Car's *enfant terrible* stood accused of deliberately blocking Bruno Junqueira and Alex Tagliani to safeguard his place at the top of the timing charts in the waning moments of the 40-minute session.

"[Tracy] did a lap of 1m 06s and I was in the 1m 02s, but he wouldn't let me by," railed Tagliani. "He'll do whatever it takes to preserve his position."

The Newman/Haas and Rocketsports teams immediately lodged verbal protests, and officials spent four hours reviewing the video evidence and telemetry data before electing to disallow Tracy's fastest time. The verdict handed the overnight pole – and the coveted guaranteed front-row starting spot that went with it – to Junqueira and brought about a two-point swing in the Brazilian's favor in the championship standings.

An aggrieved Tracy kept his own counsel about the penalty until the post-qualifying press conference on Saturday afternoon – by which time he had taken the wind out of the sails of his critics by emphatically reclaiming the pole. Then he launched a scathing attack on the series' sanctioning body, reeling off a list of transgressions for which he felt he had been unfairly singled out.

"I feel that I've supported CART when they had nobody else to support them," commented Tracy. "My frustration level doesn't just stem from yesterday. At Portland, I received a stop-and-hold penalty, I felt for no reason. At Cleveland, I received a $15,000 fine for wearing shorts to a PR function [actually a media conference]. Then in Toronto, I was leading the race by 33–34 seconds and there was a full-course yellow for no apparent reason, for a car in the run-off area that was still running and needed to be turned around. So it's a cumulative thing."

Tracy's charge of officiating inconsistencies was by no means groundless. Indeed it had been voiced in a variety of quarters over many years. But the implication that he was the victim of some kind of vendetta smacked of paranoia to most dispassionate observers.

# VANCOUVER

**Above: Lavin steered clear of trouble to claim a career-best eighth-place finish.**
Dan Boyd/LAT

**Below: Moreno earned his season-best qualifying position, third for Herdez.**
Gavin Lawrence/LAT

THERE was no mistaking who was the star turn at the Molson Indy Vancouver. Whether it was triggering controversy over blocking, which erupted in the wake of Friday's provisional qualifying session, subsequently venting his frustration at what he perceived as unjust treatment by the sport's powers-that-be, or thrilling the assembled throng with his driving prowess, Paul Tracy more than lived up to his advance billing when the Champ Car fraternity reconvened amid the scenic delights of British Columbia.

A fortnight after a *tour de force* in his native Ontario, the mercurial Canadian was in similarly dominant form on the West Coast. While he monopolized the headlines throughout the weekend, Tracy's on-track exploits spoke volumes for his sky-high self-assurance in 2003. Indeed his winning margin – a whisker under 18 seconds – was the largest registered in the season thus far.

The bald statistics may be a little misleading, since Bruno Junqueira paced the first 21 green-flag laps before he was adjudged to have jumped the start and ordered to cede the lead to the pursuing Tracy. As it turned out, that belated ruling snuffed out all suspense over the identity of the victor. Junqueira's spirit was broken and he lost concentration at a critical juncture, effectively handing the trophy to his championship protagonist on a plate.

"To win two races in a row in Canada is an awesome feeling," exclaimed Tracy, whose brace of victories helped launch a dream send-off for sponsor Player's, which was set to withdraw from motorsport in October once new Canadian tobacco advertising laws took effect. "Being a Canadian and driving for a Canadian team, the pressure is always very high."

The proceedings kicked off on a bizarre note when *both* the Dale Coyne Racing entries – Geoff Boss and Gualter Salles – accounted for themselves in separate incidents during the parade laps. Salles deposited his Lola in the tire wall at the final chicane, ensuring that the first two laps would be run under caution.

There was some consternation when the green flag eventually flew at the start of lap three, since – to put it mildly – Junqueira got the drop on polesitter Tracy. That much was clear as soon as the front "row" came into view out of the chicane, and Junqueira held a clear advantage by the time the pair passed under the starting gantry.

"I came out of the [last] corner in second gear, waited for [Junqueira] to get lined up, to make it a nice, even start," related Tracy. "I was in second [gear]…I think Bruno went by in fourth. He was going about 60 mph quicker than me."

Junqueira countered plaintively that he had been trying to prevent a repeat of the Toronto race, where Tracy had left him for dead at the start. In that he certainly succeeded.

The first-lap drama was not confined to the vexed issue of the start itself. Sébastien Bourdais tried to go three-abreast into the first corner with Roberto Moreno and Michel Jourdain Jr., but succeeded only in tapping the luckless Moreno into the tire barriers. The Brazilian veteran was out on the spot, and was left to rue the loss of his best opportunity to score a podium finish since his halcyon days with Patrick Racing at the end of 2001.

"We all know how hard it is to start this race cleanly, so I was being very careful, making sure I stayed out of trouble," said Moreno. "And then someone who has never been here before and doesn't realize, tries the impossible and hits me… There's nothing you can do then; the day is over."

A couple of corners farther on, the sister Herdez Competition Lola of Mario Dominguez was caught up in an incident between Oriol Servia and Tiago Monteiro, which sidelined the Spaniard's Visteon Lola. Meanwhile Bourdais pitted to replace a wheel damaged in his collision with Moreno and, unaware that the yellows were now out, arrived on the scene just in time to plough into the back of Dominguez's stalled car! Bourdais managed to find reverse gear and extricate himself from the melee, resuming in 11th place after another couple of visits to the pit lane, while Dominguez and Monteiro were restarted and continued several laps behind the leaders. Both were to play all-too-prominent roles as the afternoon wore on.

The race was rapidly coming to resemble a French farce, and not just because of Bourdais' antics; but to a collective intake of breath, it finally got under way in earnest on lap seven. Surprisingly the officials had passed up the opportunity presented by the

## QUALIFYING

Paul Tracy's body language on and off the track during final qualifying left not a shadow of a doubt that he was out to prove a point after being stripped of his provisional pole late the previous evening. He produced the best possible riposte, throwing down the gauntlet to his rivals with a devastating lap of 1m 00.926s (105.236 mph) midway through the session before taking refuge in the pits, as if goading any would-be pretenders to usurp him from the top of the timing charts. No one did, and Tracy duly claimed his fourth pole of the season.

"We wanted to go out and set our time early so there was no room for anybody to complain about anything," declared Tracy pointedly, adding that he felt vindicated by the day's events.

Patrick Carpentier unwittingly aided his Player's/Forsythe teammate's cause when he clouted the wall exiting the last corner and brought out the red flag with only nine minutes to go. Once the track was clear, just over four minutes remained – not quite enough time to spool up for a serious run at Tracy's benchmark. Amid the final flurry of activity, Bruno Junqueira looked to be the man most likely to threaten the Canadian – as he had been throughout most of the weekend's practice – but came up 0.144s short.

Next up was the evergreen Roberto Moreno, who posted a splendid 1m 01.172s effort in the early going. The 44-year-old had won at Vancouver in 2001 and had been gradually finding his form in recent weeks after an indifferent start to the 2003 campaign, attributing his progress to improved "chemistry" in the Herdez Competition team: "My engineer [Chris Gorne] and I both have very strong personalities, and in the first four races we clashed a little bit. In Germany we sat down and fixed that. From that day on, we just started to gel, and the results are beginning to show."

Michel Jourdain Jr. vaulted from ninth on Friday's grid to fourth in the final reckoning for Team Rahal, shading Sébastien Bourdais and a red-faced Carpentier, who had to forfeit his best time for causing the session stoppage. Walker Racing's Darren Manning paced the Reynard contingent in eighth.

**Above:** Tracy maintained his perfect '03 record in Canada for Team Player's.
Phil Abbott/LAT

**Left:** Bourdais locks up his brakes and punts the unfortunate Moreno into a spin.
Lesley Ann Miller/LAT

**Below left:** Hunter-Reay continued his progress by finishing in a solid sixth place.
Phil Abbott/LAT

**Below:** Manning is the meat in a Tagliani-Servia sandwich during the early stages.
Gavin Lawrence/LAT

caution period to reset the order at the front of the field, despite the predictable – and apparently justified – complaint lodged by Player's/Forsythe Racing. Thus Junqueira led away from an irate Tracy, Patrick Carpentier, Alex Tagliani, Michel Jourdain Jr. and a trio of Reynards, comprising Darren Manning, Mario Haberfeld and Jimmy Vasser.

The two leaders appeared evenly matched, trading fastest laps and pulling away steadily from Carpentier who, in turn, put some distance between himself and a tightening battle for fourth place between Tagliani and Jourdain. Then, almost a half-hour after the initial green flag, came word from Race Control instructing Junqueira to allow Tracy past. The stewards finally had reached the conclusion that the Newman/Haas driver had jumped the start…

Junqueira obliged on lap 24, to a roar of approval from the Canadian crowd. By his own admission, he promptly lost his rhythm and over the next half-dozen laps, up to the first spate of pit stops, fell six seconds adrift of Tracy.

"When the team told me that I had to let Tracy by, I couldn't believe it," said Junqueira. "I didn't get angry, just disappointed. I completely lost concentration. Tracy pulled away from me – not because he was faster, just because I was slower."

To add insult to injury, Junqueira stalled exiting the pits, promoting Carpentier to second place and making it a Player's/Forsythe 1-2. Lest the partisan fans should have things too much their own way, the script then took a cruel twist as Tagliani was bundled out of contention on his out-lap, courtesy of an ill-advised maneuver by Monteiro – who was four laps down – in the claustrophobically tight Science World complex.

The ensuing full-course yellow was perfectly timed for Bourdais, who was able to make his first routine pit visit (and fourth in total!) while the leaders were circulating behind the pace car. He emerged in sixth place and made further progress at the restart with an incisive move inside fellow rookie Manning at Turn One. Half a lap later, Jourdain took advantage of a momentum-sapping sideways moment for Junqueira through the 150-mph Turn Five to outbrake the Brazilian for third place at the end of the back straightaway.

Through the race's second stint, Tracy streaked away at a prodigious rate, lapping with exemplary consistency in the mid-1m 02s range. By the second round of pit stops, on lap 60, he had 14 seconds in hand over Carpentier. The Québecois established a comfortable cushion over an intense tussle for third place between Jourdain and the Newman/Haas pair, only to slip back into their clutches when he began to struggle with excessive tire wear, just as he had done in Toronto.

Such minor concerns were rendered academic on lap 61, when, in a virtual replay of the Tagliani/Monteiro situation – albeit at a different part of the circuit – Carpentier was rudely punted into retirement by an over-eager Dominguez, who was several laps in arrears following his earlier drama. The Mexican was going quickly on hot tires, while Carpentier was striving to bring his fresh set of Bridgestone Potenzas up to operating temperature. Monteiro could at least plead inexperience, but, as Carpentier observed, "Dominguez is no rookie and he should know better."

Carpentier's demise might have been expected to elevate Jourdain to second place, but the Team Rahal Lola was displaced by both Newman/Haas examples during the pit-stop exchange. Junqueira benefited from ultra-slick service from Don Hoevel's crew, while Bourdais capitalized on the two extra hot laps afforded by his slightly out-of-sequence schedule to make the difference on the racetrack.

The closing laps were a mere formality as Tracy stroked it home to the 24th victory of his career, equaling Bobby Rahal's tally. Junqueira, meanwhile, had snapped out of his despondent frame of mind, and both he and third-placed Bourdais were lapping quickly – witness Bourdais' fastest lap of the race on the 98th tour – but Tracy had them easily covered.

Jourdain crossed the line a distant fourth, his car having lost its edge toward the end, while Manning finished fifth after a dogged drive that included an unscheduled pit stop to replace a broken front wing, the legacy of a botched passing attempt on Adrian Fernandez. The fact that the Englishman bagged ten points despite trailing two laps behind the winner gave some indication of the race's high attrition.

*Alex Sabine*

## CART LOOKS FOR WHITE KNIGHT

**R**UMORS surrounding CART's future had been rife for months, and had gained momentum in mid-June with the announcement that it had retained the investment banking firm Bear, Stearns & Co. to explore "alternative funding options," including the sale of the publicly traded company. Speculation reached fever pitch in Vancouver after the organization issued revised financial guidance admitting that it would be unlikely to see out the 2004 season unless a private buyer and/or a major series sponsor could be found. Moreover, management warned, it could not realistically expect to turn a profit until 2006.

The downgrading of earlier projections reflected lower than expected revenue during the first half of the season from sanction fees, sponsorship sales and television advertising, as well as higher than anticipated legal expenses.

The underlying cause of the cash-flow crisis was that CART had depleted its reserves by subsidizing teams through the Entrant Support Program – an initiative that provided a lifeline to outfits struggling to procure sponsorship in a difficult economic climate. Without this expedient, the sanctioning body would have been unable to fulfil its commitment to race promoters to field a minimum of 18 cars. Its undertaking to "self-promote" six events represented a major additional drain on resources, especially since this included footing the bill for the flyaway tour to Europe.

Insofar as it pointed to the need for an urgent financial transfusion, the latest statement merely spelt out what had been taken for granted by insiders for weeks – and indeed was readily apparent from a cursory glance at the company's quarterly results. Inevitably, however, it prompted a media feeding frenzy regarding the future complexion of the series and the identity of potential buyers/investors.

All manner of people were said to be in the frame, but as the dust began to settle it became clear that team owners Gerald Forsythe (co-owner of Player's/Forsythe and CART's largest shareholder), Kevin Kalkhoven (the "K" of PK Racing) and Paul Gentilozzi (of Rocketsports), pictured above right, constituted the nucleus of a group seriously contemplating a bid to acquire the organization. Suggestions that Formula 1 impresario Bernie Ecclestone would seek to purchase a controlling stake were understood to be wide of the mark.

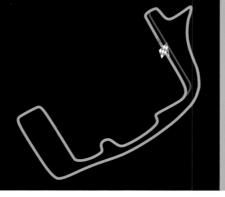

# MOLSON
# INDY VANCOUVER

## CONCORD PACIFIC PLACE, VANCOUVER, BRITISH COLUMBIA, CANADA

**JULY 27, 100 laps of 1.781 miles – 178.100 miles**

ROUND 11

| Pl. | Driver (Nat.) | No. | Team Sponsors Engine/Car | Tires | Q Speed | Q Time | Q Pos. | Laps | Time/Status | Ave. (mph) | Pts. |
|---|---|---|---|---|---|---|---|---|---|---|---|
| 1 | Paul Tracy (CDN) | 3 | Forsythe Racing Player's/Indeck Ford Cosworth/Lola B02/00 | BS | 105.236 | 1m 00.926s | 1 | 100 | 1h 57m 54.322s | 90.632 | 22 |
| 2 | Bruno Junqueira (BR) | 1 | Newman/Haas Racing PacifiCare Ford Cosworth/Lola B02/00 | BS | 104.988 | 1m 01.070s | 2 | 100 | 1h 58m 12.142s | 90.404 | 17 |
| 3 | *Sébastien Bourdais (F) | 2 | Newman/Haas Racing Lilly Ford Cosworth/Lola B2K/00 | BS | 104.056 | 1m 01.617s | 5 | 100 | 1h 58m 20.042s | 90.304 | 14 |
| 4 | Michel Jourdain Jr. (MEX) | 9 | Team Rahal Gigante Ford Cosworth/Lola B01/00 | BS | 104.115 | 1m 01.582s | 4 | 100 | 1h 58m 39.737s | 90.054 | 12 |
| 5 | *Darren Manning (GB) | 15 | Walker Racing RAC/Autowindscreens Ford Cosworth/Reynard 02I | BS | 103.360 | 1m 02.032s | 8 | 98 | Running | | 10 |
| 6 | *Ryan Hunter-Reay (USA) | 31 | American Spirit Team Johansson Ford Cosworth/Reynard 01I | BS | 101.262 | 1m 03.317s | 16 | 98 | Running | | 8 |
| 7 | *Mario Haberfeld (BR) | 34 | Mi-Jack Conquest Racing Ford Cosworth/Reynard 02I | BS | 102.842 | 1m 02.344s | 10 | 98 | Running | | 6 |
| 8 | *Rodolfo Lavin (MEX) | 5 | Walker Racing Corona Competition Ford Cosworth/Reynard 02I | BS | 101.070 | 1m 03.437s | 18 | 98 | Running | | 5 |
| 9 | Max Papis (I) | 27 | PK Racing Ford Cosworth/Lola B02/00 | BS | 102.096 | 1m 02.800s | 15 | 98 | Running | | 4 |
| 10 | Mario Dominguez (MEX) | 55 | Herdez Competition Ford Cosworth/Lola B03/00 | BS | 102.794 | 1m 02.373s | 12 | 96 | Running | | 3 |
| 11 | Jimmy Vasser (USA) | 12 | American Spirit Team Johansson Ford Cosworth/Reynard 2KI | BS | 102.655 | 1m 02.458s | 13 | 90 | Gearbox | | 2 |
| 12 | Adrian Fernandez (MEX) | 51 | Fernandez Tecate/Quaker State/Telmex Ford Cosworth/Lola B02/00 | BS | 102.637 | 1m 02.469s | 14 | 72 | Oil cooler | | 1 |
| 13 | Patrick Carpentier (CDN) | 32 | Forsythe Racing Player's/Indeck Ford Cosworth/Lola B03/00 | BS | 103.931 | 1m 01.691s | 6 | 60 | Accident | | |
| 14 | Alex Tagliani (CDN) | 33 | Rocketsports Racing Johnson Controls Ford Cosworth/Lola B02/00 | BS | 103.721 | 1m 01.816s | 7 | 30 | Accident | | |
| 15 | *Tiago Monteiro (P) | 7 | Fittipaldi-Dingman Racing Ford Cosworth/Reynard 02I | BS | 102.831 | 1m 02.351s | 11 | 27 | Accident | | |
| 16 | Oriol Servia (E) | 20 | Patrick Racing Visteon Ford Cosworth/Lola B02/00 | BS | 103.308 | 1m 02.063s | 9 | 4 | Accident | | |
| 17 | Roberto Moreno (BR) | 4 | Herdez Competition Ford Cosworth/Lola B01/00 | BS | 104.813 | 1m 01.172s | 3 | 3 | Accident | | |
| DNS | Gualter Salles (BR) | 19 | Dale Coyne Racing Alpina/Golden Cross Ford Cosworth/Lola B2K/00 | BS | 101.148 | 1m 03.388s | 17 | – | Accident | | |
| DNS | *Geoff Boss (USA) | 11 | Dale Coyne Racing Cross Pens Ford Cosworth/Lola B01/00 | BS | 99.777 | 1m 04.259s | 19 | – | Accident | | |

*denotes rookie driver*

**Caution flags:** Laps 1–2, accident/Salles; laps 4–6, accident/Bourdais/Moreno & Monteiro/Dominguez; laps 31–36, accident/Monteiro & Tagliani. **Total: Three for 11 laps.**

**Lap leaders:** Paul Tracy, 1–2 (12 laps); Bruno Junqueira, 3–23 (21 laps); Tracy, 24–60 (37 laps); Sébastien Bourdais, 61–62 (2 laps); Tracy, 63–100 (38 laps). Totals: Tracy, 77 laps; Junqueira, 21 laps; Bourdais, 2 laps.

**Fastest race lap:** Sébastien Bourdais, 1m 02.011s, 103.395 mph on lap 98.

**Championship positions:** 1 Tracy, 161; 2 Junqueira, 141; 3 Jourdain Jr., 125; 4 Bourdais, 100; 5 Carpentier, 88; 6 Servia, 76; 7 Fernandez, 70; 8 Dominguez, 65; 9 Manning, 60; 10 Tagliani, 51; 11 Haberfeld, 47; 12 Vasser, 40; 13 Moreno, 39; 14 Hunter-Reay, 24; 15 Monteiro, 18; 16 Lavin, 11; 17 Lemarie, 8; 18 Camathias, 6; 19 Papis, 5; 20 Yoong, 4; 21 Herta, 2.

# VANCOUVER SNIPPETS

Dan Boyd/LAT

• Mario Haberfeld deserved better than seventh place after a fine weekend's endeavor for Mi-Jack/Conquest Racing. The '98 British Formula 3 champion was running a handy fifth before encountering GEARBOX WOES. "We're having problems making the gearbox reliable and we don't know why," lamented the Brazilian rookie. "At Cleveland, I lost third, fourth and fifth gears; here I lost second and third."

• Fellow Reynard campaigner Jimmy Vasser could sympathize with Haberfeld's plight after falling VICTIM to a similar gearbox malaise. In Vasser's case, the problem was serious enough to sideline him altogether on lap 90. American Spirit Team Johansson stablemate Ryan Hunter-Reay at least provided some cheer, recording the best finish of his young Champ Car career in sixth.

• Derrick Walker and Toyota Atlantic STANDOUT Michael Valiante (right) held a joint press conference on Friday in Vancouver to announce that they had signed a contract that would see the 23-year-old graduate to the Champ Car ranks in 2004 – provided the necessary sponsorship could be secured. Valiante had tried to put together a deal with Walker for the 2003 season, but had run out of time, settling instead for another year of Atlantic competition with Lynx Racing. "He hasn't got a penny," said Walker, "but he has lots of talent." Valiante, who hails from the Vancouver suburb of New Westminster, was reminded that he hadn't made it to the big time just yet when an overzealous security guard denied him access to the media center upon his arrival for the press conference! As luck would have it, Stu Ballantyne, the general manager of the Molson Indy Vancouver, was standing nearby and convinced the skeptical doorman of Valiante's bona fides.

• In an ironic postscript to the ongoing SAGA involving Paul Tracy and blocking, officials voided Gualter Salles' best lap in final qualifying for impeding the progress of a faster car – driven by, you guessed it, Tracy!

• Notwithstanding the obvious falling-out between himself and CART, Tracy was at pains to deny RUMORS that he was involved in a shoving match with the series' president/CEO Chris Pook upon learning of his penalty at a sponsor function on Friday evening. "There was no pushing," Tracy insisted. "A lot of things get blown up out of proportion. We had a talk, but not a physical confrontation." CART's Vice President of Communications Adam Saal characterized the pair's impromptu meeting as "professional."

• An impressive total of 162,271 fans filed through the turnstiles over the three days of the Molson Indy Vancouver, giving further proof of Champ Car racing's POPULARITY north of the border. Friday's attendance of 45,023 was the best first-day turnout in the event's 14-year history.

Phil Abbott/LAT

Mike Levitt/LAT

# ROAD AMERICA

Mike Weston/LAT

## ANDRETTI TO THE RESCUE

**F**OR more than a month, it seemed as though the demanding and universally favored Road America venue would be missing from the 2003 Bridgestone Presents the Champ Car World Series Powered by Ford calendar for the first time since 1981. The event originally had been slated to be held August 17, then was shifted to August 3 following a shuffle involving the race at Mid-Ohio. On March 10, however, a few weeks after filing a lawsuit relating to financial disagreements following the previous year's race, CART issued a statement to say that the 2003 Road America Grand Prix had been canceled.

Both sides blamed the other for the dispute, although on April 8, after the track had filed a countersuit claiming to be in full compliance with its previous financial commitments to CART, Road America President and General Manager George Bruggentheis said in a statement, "We remain hopeful that we can resolve the issues, put the differences behind us, and develop a mutually beneficial contract for 2003 and beyond."

By then, auto racing legend Mario Andretti had entered the picture as a mediator. Needless to say, both sides took Andretti's involvement seriously, and by April 23 a middle ground had been secured and the race reinstated on the Champ Car schedule.

Andretti echoed the sentiments of both race fans and participants when he said, "Road America has always been one of the premier tracks in the United States and is probably the most popular venue among drivers on the CART Champ Car circuit. It was a track that we needed to have on our schedule to maintain the series' standing as the truest challenge in open-wheel racing."

Andretti's statesmanship was duly recognized when the event was renamed in his honor as the Mario Andretti Grand Prix at Road America.

"I must thank Mario Andretti for his tireless efforts toward getting Road America back on our schedule," said CART Champ Car President and CEO Chris Pook. "It is great to see that he has the same level of passion for the heritage of CART Champ Car racing that he did when he was behind the wheel."

**Above and above right: Mario Andretti remains as popular with the fans as ever – especially after keeping Elkhart Lake on the calendar.**

**Main photograph: Junqueira never put a wheel wrong in appalling conditions to secure his first win of the season for Newman/Haas Racing.**
Phil Abbott/LAT

# JUNQUEIRA...AT LAST

**B**RUNO Junqueira arrived in Wisconsin all too aware that he had not yet won a race in 2003, despite beginning the season as a hot championship favorite. He was not out of the title reckoning by any means, but with primary rival Paul Tracy having won back-to-back races in Toronto and Vancouver, Junqueira had fallen 20 points in arrears. The pressure was on.

"Tracy did very well and got a lead on me on the championship," he acknowledged. "I knew that I had to win a race [soon] to keep motivated and keep the team believing that we can win the championship. I knew that my best shot to win a pole and win a race was this racetrack because I always did well here. Tracy was, for sure, after winning two races in Canada, really strong in his head, and you know that in any sport it is very important if you're very strong in the head. I think he came here very confident that he could win again, especially because of his success in the past. And I was very confident I could win, as well, because of my success in the past."

Junqueira had developed a close affinity for Elkhart Lake's Road America from the first time he visited the scenic road course as a rookie in 2001 – and won. In addition to securing his first Champ Car victory at the fast and challenging four-mile track, Junqueira also snared the pole in 2002. On both visits, he set the fastest race lap.

"I love this track," he declared after taking the provisional pole on Friday. "I'm very, very happy that Mario Andretti and some other people put the effort to bring back this race to Road America because for me it's my favorite racetrack in the championship. It's the highest point of the season for me. I have so much fun driving around here, even more because I always perform well. But even so, I like every corner. I like a lot to drive here."

It showed. Junqueira became the first driver in 2003 to extract the maximum 23-point haul from a weekend by virtue of being fastest in qualifying on both days, winning the race and leading most laps. Furthermore, with Tracy failing to finish, Junqueira moved to the top of the championship standings for the first time in his young career.

"I was pressuring myself extra this weekend to do very well," he admitted. "I knew I had to turn the table and start to do better than [Tracy]. Everything came great for me this weekend."

**Above:** Junqueira, flanked on the podium by Tagliani and Bourdais, was both happy and relieved to take the win in Wisconsin.
Mike Levitt/LAT

## QUALIFYING

Bruno Junqueira left everyone shaking their heads in disbelief following a sensational display in the first qualifying period on Friday afternoon, when his PacifiCare Lola was a full 0.805s clear of the pack at 1m 43.917s.

"Road courses have always been my favorite," he explained. "This track is my favorite on the CART circuit. It reminds me a lot of tracks like Spa and Barcelona, where I used to do well when I raced Formula 3000 [in Europe]. We are very happy to have such a big advantage today, but we don't know how the track will be tomorrow."

Junqueira wasn't quite so dominant in final qualifying; even so, he remained the only driver to dip below the 1m 44s barrier. The wiry Brazilian's best of 1m 43.703s, an average speed of 140.524 mph, was still more than a half-second clear of the rest, led by Newman/Haas teammate Sébastien Bourdais.

"I think we had two good runs," reckoned Bourdais. "Unfortunately I didn't put either of my laps together. I made some mistakes every time. But we closed the gap a lot with Bruno. The Lilly crew did a good job. I think we're pretty much there."

Patrick Carpentier had managed no better than 12th on the grid in six previous attempts at the challenging Wisconsin road course, so a third place represented a substantial improvement of which he was justifiably proud. "We could have done a time good enough for second place, but I was caught in traffic at the end," he said. "That's part of the game. Team Player's did a great job today. We have been struggling the last two races in Canada, so this is good."

Oriol Servia matched his best starting position in 2003, fourth for Patrick Racing, while the ever-improving Mario Dominguez secured a career-best fifth for the Herdez Competition team, despite struggling early in the weekend with some braking difficulties.

"I have to give credit to the engineering team," said the Mexican. "We didn't have much time to work on [the setup], but we haven't had to make many changes – the car was good off the truck."

Series leader Paul Tracy was far from happy with his Player's Lola. He was only sixth on the grid and just ahead of the two American Spirit Team Johansson Reynards, Jimmy Vasser having marginally outpaced rookie teammate Ryan Hunter-Reay.

THE on-off nature of CART's annual pilgrimage to Elkhart Lake's Road America continued until the bitter end. The event had been removed from the 2003 calendar in March due to a financial dispute following the 2002 race, and there was widespread excitement when Champ Car legend Mario Andretti acted as an intermediary and arranged for the popular fixture to be reinstated. Unfortunately this turned to abject disappointment after a heavy rainstorm brought chaos shortly before the scheduled start time.

Two attempts to get the newly monikered Mario Andretti Grand Prix Presented by Briggs & Stratton under way were aborted due to the track conditions. Finally, almost three-and-a-half hours behind schedule, the track was deemed fit for action. Even then, various incidents broke up the proceedings and the race was stopped after only 34 of the slated 60 laps had been completed.

Nothing, though, could distract Bruno Junqueira from his mission. The preseason championship favorite had claimed his first pole of the campaign – on his favorite track – and in the truncated race he drove flawlessly to a well-deserved victory for Newman/Haas Racing. Paul Tracy having crashed out in the saturated early stages, Junqueira's win put the 26-year-old Brazilian atop the championship points table. And as if that wasn't enough, teammate Sébastien Bourdais finished hot on his tail in second place.

"It was a perfect way to end a perfect weekend," said a delighted Junqueira, apparently oblivious to the confused nature of the preceding few hours. "We were struggling to get our first win and pole, and we got it done this weekend."

The weather, which had been predominantly fair during two days of practice and qualifying, was fine for the warmup on race morning, but took a distinct turn for the worse about an hour before the scheduled 2.00 p.m. start. A short, sharp cloudburst left the track virtually awash. Unfortunately the rain returned just as the cars were leaving the grid for the first parade lap. Officials still had hopes of getting the race under way – after CART Champ Car Chief Steward Chris Kneifel declared that the first few laps would be run behind the pace car.

Rodolfo Lavin was the first driver to discover just how treacherous were the conditions when he lost control of Derrick Walker's Corona Reynard on the exit of Turn Five – under yellow. The Simple Green Safety Team was despatched to remove the stricken car, which had suffered some rear wing damage.

At the same time, with the rain falling again, many drivers radioed to their pits to say that the track conditions were too dangerous to contemplate a green flag. Kneifel wisely heeded their warnings and displayed the red, and the competitors duly filed into the pit road while the jet driers were summoned to facilitate the drying process.

A little over 20 minutes later, the Ford Cosworth XFE race engines were refired and the decision was made to shorten the race to 47 laps. Once again, though, weather and track conditions promptly deteriorated. After six more laps run behind the pace car, Race Control displayed the red flag for a second time.

"The safety of our drivers and the fans are our primary concerns," explained Kneifel. "The track is simply too wet to go racing right now."

Finally, just after 5.30 p.m., many disappointed fans already having departed, the order to restart the engines was given once again. By then the race had been further shortened to 34 laps. Third time proved a charm – albeit not for Oriol Servia, who, just before the green flag was set to be shown, lost control of Pat Patrick's Visteon Lola under braking for Turn 12 and skated into the barriers. Cue another delay.

The track was still wet, and all the remaining competitors were on grooved Bridgestone Potenza tires when the race at last began in earnest with ten laps already in the books. The 17 cars slithered through the first few corners without drama, Junqueira taking full advantage of clear visibility to maintain his lead. Bourdais immediately went into defensive mode as he strove to stay ahead of Patrick Carpentier. Tracy, meanwhile, glimpsed an opportunity to use his massive experience to good effect in the treacherous conditions. The Canadian quickly snuck past Mario Dominguez into

fifth place, but it all went wrong for the championship leader when he left his braking too late for the downhill approach to Turn Eight (which is difficult enough in the dry) in an ambitious bid to oust Carpentier on the outside line. Tracy speared off the road, through the gravel trap and out of the race.

"I tried to power my way out of the gravel trap," related Tracy, "but it just pushed me toward the tire barrier."

Behind, there was more carnage in the same turn as Michel Jourdain Jr. lost control and came into contact with Tiago Monteiro and Darren Manning. Roberto Moreno also was badly delayed. Only the Englishman continued as the race once more came under the control of a full-course caution.

Even though less than one lap had been completed at racing speeds, it was almost time for the first mandatory round of pit stops. Sure enough, after 13 laps, with the field still under caution, the crews leapt into action. The Newman/Haas pair continued out front, while Dominguez moved into third ahead of Carpentier. Amazingly, both American Spirit Team Johansson Reynards suffered airjack problems, causing Jimmy Vasser to fall from fifth to tenth and teammate Ryan Hunter-Reay to slip from sixth to 14th.

The restart came after 14 laps, Junqueira still leading from Bourdais. Dominguez, who had qualified his Herdez Lola a career-best fifth in the dry, was not nearly so happy in the wet and soon lost a place to Carpentier in Turn Five. A few corners later, he slithered off the road again and fell to 14th. On lap 19, Dominguez's attempts to pass Geoff Boss ended with yet another off-course excursion, which finally ended his day.

Alex Tagliani, meanwhile, had been moving in the opposite direction. Equipped with a full wet-weather setup, Tagliani had taken advantage of the various early shenanigans to move from 13th to sixth for Rocketsports Racing. Then he made short work of Adrian Fernandez following the restart on lap 15 and was piling the pressure on fellow French-Canadian Carpentier when the yellow flags waved for one final time after Dominguez's visit to the gravel trap at Canada Corner.

The timing of the caution enabled everyone to make their final scheduled pit stop before the action was resumed after 22 laps. This time it had been Carpentier's turn to hit difficulty – another airjack problem caused him to slip from third to sixth. Manning, meanwhile, took advantage of the usual excellent work by Neil Brown's crew to vault up to fourth in Derrick Walker's RAC/Autowindscreens Reynard.

Junqueira took off once more at the green flag, with teammate Bourdais in hot pursuit. The Frenchman remained in close contact for the next couple of laps before Junqueira asserted his superiority. The gap had stretched out almost to five seconds by lap 29, whereupon Junqueira adopted a more conservative strategy and cruised home to the finish. Bourdais had closed to within less than a second at the checkered flag, and set the race's fastest lap for good measure, but this was to be Junqueira's day.

"After Vancouver, something happen to me," said the Brazilian in his stilted English. "I was a little bit shaken by everything that happen. I said, 'I'm going to be strong.' Nothing could be better than my favorite racetrack, Road America, and to have a perfect weekend – 23 points, pole on both days, lead all laps. I'm quite happy."

Bourdais was equally pleased, his second-place finish moving him to fourth in the points chase, while Tagliani struggled a little in the closing stages as the track finally began to dry, but still finished a strong third. Manning looked set for a fine fourth until his Reynard lost third gear in the closing stages. Max Papis moved past with two laps remaining to score a best-yet result for PK Racing, while Carpentier took advantage of Manning's problem at the final corner to sneak past into fifth.

"What a great race," exclaimed Manning, in spite of his disappointment. "I've been itching to have a wet race because I knew we could have a strong finish, and we nearly matched our best effort of the year [fourth at Milwaukee]. The crew gave me two fantastic pit stops and then I was holding my own until I lost third gear. It's a great finish for the team though – our fifth consecutive top-ten finish."

*Jeremy Shaw*

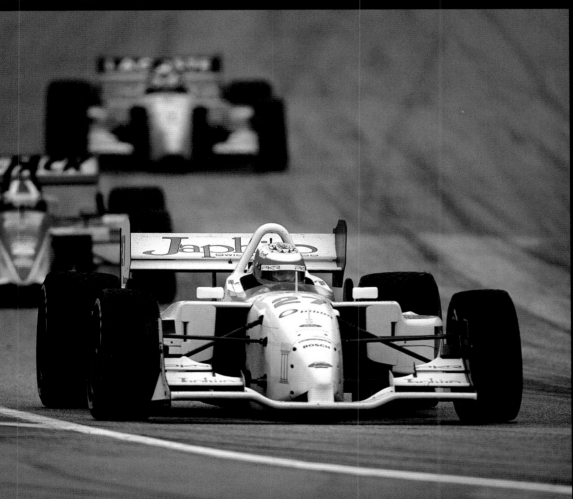

**Top:** Boudais set fastest lap of the race while ensuring a 1-2 for Newman/Haas.
Phil Abbott/LAT

**Above:** Tagliani makes certain to keep his driving shoes dry during a red-flag delay.
Maria Grady/LAT

**Left:** Papis qualified poorly, but moved steadily forward to finish fourth for PKR.
Mike Weston/LAT

**Main photograph:** Manning posted another fine drive for Walker Racing, but lost fourth place because of a late-race gearbox malady.
Mike Weston/LAT

**Right:** Tagliani took advantage of a full wet-weather setup for Rocketsports.
Phil Abbott/LAT

**Above:** The unfortunate Lavin was out of the race even before the green flag flew.

**Right:** Haberfeld speeds under the bridge in Turn Six en route to eighth position.
Photographs: Maria Grady/LAT

# MARIO ANDRETTI GRAND PRIX
## PRESENTED BY BRIGGS & STRATTON

### ROAD AMERICA, ELKHART LAKE, WISCONSIN

**AUGUST 3, 34 laps of 4.048 miles – 137.632 miles**

| Pl. | Driver (Nat.) | No. | Team Sponsors Engine/Car | Tires | Q Speed | Q Time | Q Pos. | Laps | Time/Status | Ave. (mph) | Pts. |
|---|---|---|---|---|---|---|---|---|---|---|---|
| 1 | Bruno Junqueira (BR) | 1 | Newman/Haas Racing PacifiCare Ford Cosworth/Lola B02/00 | BS | 140.524 | 1m 43.703s | 1 | 34 | 1h 35m 28.491s | 86.493 | 23 |
| 2 | *Sébastien Bourdais (F) | 2 | Newman/Haas Racing Lilly Ford Cosworth/Lola B2K/00 | BS | 139.798 | 1m 44.242s | 2 | 34 | 1h 35m 29.194s | 86.483 | 16 |
| 3 | Alex Tagliani (CDN) | 33 | Rocketsports Racing Johnson Controls Ford Cosworth/Lola B02/00 | BS | 138.730 | 1m 45.044s | 13 | 34 | 1h 35m 39.374s | 86.329 | 14 |
| 4 | Max Papis (I) | 27 | PK Racing Ford Cosworth/Lola B02/00 | BS | 137.833 | 1m 45.728s | 16 | 34 | 1h 35m 43.434s | 86.268 | 12 |
| 5 | Patrick Carpentier (CDN) | 32 | Forsythe Racing Player's/Indeck Ford Cosworth/Lola B02/00 | BS | 139.712 | 1m 44.306s | 3 | 34 | 1h 35m 47.985s | 86.200 | 10 |
| 6 | *Darren Manning (GB) | 15 | Walker Racing RAC/Autowindscreens Ford Cosworth/Reynard 02I | BS | 138.688 | 1m 45.076s | 14 | 34 | 1h 35m 48.083s | 86.198 | 8 |
| 7 | Roberto Moreno (BR) | 4 | Herdez Competition Ford Cosworth/Lola B03/00 | BS | 138.761 | 1m 45.021s | 12 | 34 | 1h 35m 59.789s | 86.023 | 6 |
| 8 | *Mario Haberfeld (BR) | 34 | Mi-Jack Conquest Racing Ford Cosworth/Reynard 02I | BS | 138.560 | 1m 45.173s | 15 | 34 | 1h 36m 00.032s | 86.020 | 5 |
| 9 | Jimmy Vasser (USA) | 12 | American Spirit Team Johansson Ford Cosworth/Reynard 2KI | BS | 139.393 | 1m 44.545s | 7 | 34 | 1h 36m 03.473s | 85.968 | 4 |
| 10 | *Ryan Hunter-Reay (USA) | 31 | American Spirit Team Johansson Ford Cosworth/Reynard 01I | BS | 139.385 | 1m 44.551s | 8 | 34 | 1h 36m 09.516s | 85.878 | 3 |
| 11 | Gualter Salles (BR) | 19 | Dale Coyne Racing Alpina/Golden Cross Ford Cosworth/Lola B2K/00 | BS | 136.191 | 1m 47.003s | 18 | 34 | 1h 36m 13.769s | 85.815 | 2 |
| 12 | Adrian Fernandez (MEX) | 51 | Fernandez Tecate/Quaker State/Telmex Ford Cosworth/Lola B02/00 | BS | 139.293 | 1m 44.620s | 9 | 34 | 1h 36m 28.067s | 85.603 | 1 |
| 13 | *Geoff Boss (USA) | 11 | Dale Coyne Racing Cross Pens Ford Cosworth/Lola B01/00 | BS | 135.629 | 1m 47.446s | 19 | 34 | 1h 37m 03.509s | 85.082 | |
| 14 | Mario Dominguez (MEX) | 55 | Herdez Competition Ford Cosworth/Lola B03/00 | BS | 139.616 | 1m 44.378s | 5 | 18 | Accident | | |
| 15 | Paul Tracy (CDN) | 3 | Forsythe Racing Player's/Indeck Ford Cosworth/Lola B02/00 | BS | 139.427 | 1m 44.519s | 6 | 10 | Accident | | |
| 16 | Michel Jourdain Jr. (MEX) | 9 | Team Rahal Gigante Ford Cosworth/Lola B01/00 | BS | 139.117 | 1m 44.752s | 10 | 10 | Accident | | |
| 17 | *Tiago Monteiro (P) | 7 | Fittipaldi-Dingman Racing Ford Cosworth/Reynard 02I | BS | 139.083 | 1m 44.778s | 11 | 10 | Accident | | |
| 18 | Oriol Servia (E) | 20 | Patrick Racing Visteon Ford Cosworth/Lola B02/00 | BS | 139.701 | 1m 44.314s | 4 | 7 | Accident | | |
| 19 | *Rodolfo Lavin (MEX) | 5 | Walker Racing Corona Competition Ford Cosworth/Reynard 02I | BS | 137.462 | 1m 46.013s | 17 | 0 | Accident | | |

* denotes rookie driver

**Caution flags:** Lap 1, yellow start; laps 2–7, yellow restart after 20m 44s red flag; laps 8–9, yellow restart after 2h 40m 56s red flag; laps 11–13, accidents/Tracy & Jourdain/Monteiro/Manning/Moreno; laps 19–21, tow/Dominguez. Total: **Five for 15 laps.**

**Lap leader:** Bruno Junqueira, 1–34 (34 laps). Total: Junqueira, 34 laps.

**Fastest race lap:** Sébastien Bourdais, 1m 58.187s, 123.303 mph on lap 33.

**Championship positions:** 1 Junqueira, 164; 2 Tracy, 161; 3 Jourdain Jr., 125; 4 Bourdais, 116; 5 Carpentier, 98; 6 Servia, 76; 7 Fernandez, 71; 8 Manning, 68; 9 Dominguez & Tagliani, 65; 11 Haberfeld, 52; 12 Moreno, 45; 13 Vasser, 44; 14 Hunter-Reay, 27; 15 Monteiro, 18; 16 Papis, 17; 17 Lavin, 11; 18 Lemarie, 8; 19 Camathias, 6; 20 Yoong, 4; 21 Salles & Herta, 2.

## ROAD AMERICA SNIPPETS

• A new rule was brought into effect at the beginning of the season whereby the minimum WEIGHT of each car was determined according to a sliding scale depending on the weight of the individual drivers. Thus, theoretically, the lighter drivers would no longer have an advantage, since the combined weight of the cars and drivers had been equalized. Every participant was weighed prior to the first race, and the process was repeated during the Vancouver weekend in case any adjustments were necessary. Interestingly only two drivers had gained a little weight in the interim period (Paul Tracy and Mario Haberfeld), while no fewer than 11 had lost a few pounds – or in Darren Manning's case, 15 pounds. The differential between the heaviest (Tracy) and lightest (Moreno) drivers was a whopping 62 pounds.

• The CART Champ Car Stewards came in for a lot of CRITICISM for delaying the start several times due to the weather conditions (below). Event Grand Marshall Mario Andretti was among many who reckoned the race could have been started much earlier, if not even on time. The vast majority of drivers, however, disagreed, claiming the conditions were far too dangerous.

"I think the decision was good because at least today everybody goes home in one piece," said race winner Junqueira.

• In the aftermath of the Molson Indy Vancouver, both Tiago Monteiro and Mario Dominguez were placed on PROBATION by the CART Champ Car Stewards as a result of separate incidents in which they were at least a lap down and lead-lap cars were eliminated.

• Patrick Carpentier's long-time race engineer, Michael Cannon, was REASSIGNED to a new shop-based position within the Team Player's organization prior to the Road America weekend. His place was taken by Eric Zeto, who had served as Cannon's assistant for the previous three years.

• Alex Tagliani was forced to SWITCH to Rocketsports Racing's backup Lola following a nasty-looking accident on Friday afternoon, in which he caromed over the top of Mario Haberfeld's car in Turn 14 after the Brazilian had slowed abruptly to avoid a spinning Tiago Monteiro.

• Junqueira topped the timing charts in provisional qualifying for the third consecutive event (and fourth overall in 2003), and finally was able to repeat the feat in final qualifying to secure his FIRST POLE of the season. It was also his first pole for Newman/Haas Racing and the team's

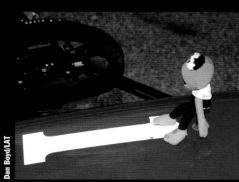

75th since its formation in 1983. The race victory was Newman/Haas' 72nd, the first of which also came at Road America when Mario Andretti triumphed – from the pole.

• While Paul Tracy had won the two previous races in his HOME country, Bruno Junqueira did not have the opportunity to do the same in Brazil, but found the next best thing in rural Wisconsin which, like his home state of Minas Gerais, is well-known for its dairy products. "I like the cheese-heads. I think here is my home in the US, so I got my win at home," he quipped, adding, "but I also consider Mid-Ohio my home...and Denver and Miami, and California as well!"

# MID-OHIO

## HISTORIC 1-2 PUNCH FOR TEAM PLAYER'S

F the heroics performed by American Spirit Team Johansson demonstrated the exciting potential of some of the new blood in the Champ Car World Series, Player's/Forsythe Racing's sweep of the top two rungs of the podium suggested that the marquee teams weren't about to make way for a changing of the guard just yet.

"A fantastic day for Team Player's," was Tracy's succinct summary on Sunday afternoon. "It was an extremely tough race; I was going as quick as I could in the middle stages and Patrick [Carpentier] kept catching me. He had a really fast car today."

Indeed, in terms of ultimate race pace, Carpentier for once appeared to have the legs of Tracy, who had hogged the limelight since joining the Player's/Forsythe fold at the beginning of the season, leaving Carpentier – the sitting tenant – to enjoy only fleeting moments in the sun. But at Mid-Ohio, the Québécois gave his teammate a genuine run for his money, aided by crackerjack pit work from Jason Weatherford's crew.

"I just went flat-out every lap, and I told myself that if I didn't finish, I didn't finish, that's all there was to it," trilled the irrepressible Carpentier. "The guys said to me, 'Give us one spot on the track and we'll gain you some positions on your pit stops.' And that's what happened. I passed Sébastien Bourdais and the crew got me two places in the pits."

The resulting 1-2 finish was the first in Forsythe Racing's 12 years of CART competition. That somewhat surprising statistic merely underscored the point that the Phil LePan-managed organization, ably overseen on behalf of Gerald Forsythe by Vice-President of Operations Neil Mickewright, had finally developed into a bona fide title contender after years of sporadic success and gnawing inconsistency.

One of the keys to the team's blossoming in 2003 was the "chemistry" between Tracy and highly respected technical guru Tony Cicale. The pair had worked together to good effect at Team KOOL Green during 1999–2000, and Cicale's wealth of experience and phlegmatic temperament once again exercised a calming influence on Tracy, harnessing his mercurial talents to the task of maintaining a consistent season-long championship challenge. The results spoke volumes for the efficacy of the partnership.

**Above: Paul Tracy has learned a great deal from Tony Cicale.**

**Left: The Player's pair proved to be a dominant force.**
Photographs: Mike Levitt/LAT

**Top: Tracy compares notes with Carpentier after their 1-2 sweep.**
Mike Weston/LAT

THE pressure had shifted onto Paul Tracy when the Champ Car fraternity alighted at the Mid-Ohio Sports Car Course. Bruno Junqueira's peerless display at Road America a week earlier, together with Tracy's ignominious excursion among the Wisconsin scenery, had swung the championship pendulum in the Brazilian's favor, giving him a slender three-point advantage as the title chase began to crystallize into a two-horse contest.

Tracy turned the tables in emphatic fashion at Mid-Ohio, however, stamping his authority on the meeting and emulating Junqueira's Elkhart Lake feat by netting all 23 available points. And, just to complete an uncanny reversal of fortunes, Junqueira went home empty-handed after being pitched into a gravel trap by Oriol Servia in the early going.

"I had a long talk with Tony Cicale [Player's/Forsythe technical advisor and longtime mentor] this week," related Tracy in the afterglow of his sixth victory of the year and maiden Mid-Ohio triumph. "He said, 'We're not going to win the championship at Mid-Ohio, but we can definitely lose it there if we don't have a good race. We can't afford to have a bad race from here on out.'"

The pep talk obviously had the desired effect. Tracy took matters into his own hands and left as little as possible to chance – by sticking to a firm game plan for qualifying around the busy, traffic-strewn, 2.258-mile road course, duly claiming pole position and then controlling the race from the front. He had to work hard for his laurels, however, seeing off a strong challenge from teammate Patrick Carpentier, as well as a valiant chase from more unexpected quarters in the form of American Spirit Team Johansson, whose young charger, Ryan Hunter-Reay, qualified brilliantly on the outside of the front row.

As the field snaked its way through the roller-coaster Esses on the opening lap, Tracy led from Hunter-Reay and Michel Jourdain Jr., who took advantage of the favorable camber in the first right-hander to execute a neat outside-line pass on Sébastien Bourdais. Carpentier survived a ragged grass-cutting moment to hold on to fifth place ahead of Junqueira and Servia, who squeezed past Alex Tagliani over the crest of the hill in Turn Five.

Tracy made an early break from the chasing pack and was soon circulating in the mid-1m 09s range, while most others were unable to crack the 1m 10s barrier. Aside from a few minor skirmishes in the midfield, the opening stages were fairly uneventful – until Roberto Moreno spun his Herdez Competition Lola into the Turn Nine tire wall on (coincidentally) lap nine, triggering a full-course yellow.

The caution served to erase Tracy's 4.5-second advantage, but another interruption immediately following the restart brought altogether more welcome news for the Canadian. His title protagonist, Junqueira, was gesticulating furiously from the cockpit of his PacifiCare Lola, which was beached in the sand trap at the Keyhole after sustaining a hefty thump in the right rear corner from Servia's Visteon machine.

"You need to take advantage of any opportunity, especially at Mid-Ohio," pleaded Servia after his third shunt in as many races. "Bruno was sitting on the right, playing a little bit, and then when I was committed he turned in on me."

Junqueira, not surprisingly, begged to differ: "He wasn't even side by side and he hit my rear wheel. It was too early in the race for him to try something like that."

Broken suspension rendered Servia hors de combat, but Junqueira was able to resume 17th and last, two laps in arrears, once the Newman/Haas team had fitted a replacement front wing. The erstwhile championship leader soldiered on manfully, but fell one place short of a points-paying finish in 13th.

Tracy set a torrid pace from the restart. By the first round of scheduled pit stops on lap 24, he had reestablished a five-second buffer over Hunter-Reay, who, in turn, appeared to have the measure of Jourdain, Bourdais, Carpentier et al. But typically slick service from Greg Cates' crew enabled Jourdain to leapfrog Hunter-Reay in the pit lane, and Team Rahal's charge led the pursuit of Tracy through the race's second stint.

The leaderboard took on a novel complexion at this point, as a quartet of cars that had stopped during the earlier pace-car interludes, comprising Adrian Fernandez, Tiago Monteiro, Rodolfo Lavin and Gualter Salles, temporarily occupied the top four spots. Tracy was unperturbed, however – he remained the de facto leader and, with the luxury of a seven-second cushion over Jourdain, could afford to bide his time and wait for the out-of-sequence traffic in front of him to peel off into the pits.

## QUALIFYING

**Paul Tracy was the man to beat all weekend at Mid-Ohio. A variety of pretenders – some familiar, others less probable (Sébastien Bourdais, Patrick Carpentier, Darren Manning and Tiago Monteiro) – paced the free practice sessions, but it was Tracy who delivered the goods when it mattered, vaulting to the top of the Friday grid and then sealing his fifth pole of the season on Saturday afternoon.**

**Judicious timing and a slice of good fortune aided the Canadian's cause. On each day he took advantage of a relatively clear track to set an impressive benchmark time on his first set of tires, before retiring to the pits to await further developments. In both sessions, his opening salvo proved good enough, as heavy traffic around the serpentine 2.258-mile circuit, coupled with red-flag stoppages in the dying moments, stymied the last-ditch efforts of his rivals.**

**One man who very nearly upset the applecart was rookie Ryan Hunter-Reay, who produced a sensational lap just 0.016s slower than Tracy's polewinning effort to annex the other front-row spot in Stefan Johansson's Reynard.**

**"Awesome!" exclaimed the Florida-domiciled 22-year-old, whose achievement was even more meritorious than it appeared on paper, since he hadn't participated in CART's recent open test at Mid-Ohio. In fact, his last experience of the demanding parkland layout had occurred while competing in the 2001 Barber Dodge Pro Series! Talk about jumping in at the deep end...**

**"The difference between the Barber Dodge car and the Champ Car is unbelievable," affirmed a wide-eyed Hunter-Reay. "I mean, this place seems so much shorter, it feels like a slot-car track! It's definitely a roller-coaster ride, and it's a lot of fun. When the car is working well, it's even that much better."**

**Fellow freshman Bourdais was a mere 0.056s farther back in third, and the faster of the Newman/Haas duo, but felt he had left a few crumbs on the table. "We definitely had a very good setup, but the red flag hurt us for the second day running," he lamented.**

**Michel Jourdain Jr. lined up fourth for Team Rahal's home race, ahead of defending Mid-Ohio winner Carpentier and a disgruntled Bruno Junqueira, who consistently was unable to find – or create – the necessary gaps in the traffic.**

Fernandez duly obliged on lap 37, rejoining the fray in the thick of the Bourdais/Carpentier scrap for fourth place, only to be hung out to dry as he struggled to bring his tires up to working temperature. One lap later, a slight miscue by Bourdais through the Keyhole was just the invitation Carpentier needed to draft past the Newman/Haas Lola along the back straightaway.

The second bout of pit stops, on lap 48, produced a wholesale shuffle of the order behind Tracy. Hunter-Reay regained the place he had lost to Jourdain during the previous exchange, while Player's/Forsythe Racing employed a blend of shrewd tactics – taking on slightly less than a full tank of methanol – and nifty pit work to catapult Carpentier past both of them. It was a close-run thing, however, and the French-Canadian only just dropped the clutch in time to slot in front of Hunter-Reay in the course of his wheelspinning exit.

Fernandez elected to move back into synch with the front-runners during this pit-stop cycle, but fellow interloper Monteiro persisted with his original schedule and enjoyed a ten-lap spell in the lead. Tracy appeared content to hold a watching brief behind the Portuguese rookie, who was turning very respectable lap times and remained more than a second up the road. All the same, Paul reckoned that his pace was being dictated by the Fittipaldi-Dingman Reynard – and, indeed, teammate Carpentier started to make significant inroads into his advantage.

## AMERICAN SPIRIT RESONATES THROUGH MID-OHIO

AMERICAN Spirit Team Johansson's giant-killing performance was a revelation. The first-year outfit rocked the Champ Car establishment by overshadowing all bar the Player's/Forsythe behemoth and coming within spitting distance of a remarkable 3-4 finish. As it was, Ryan Hunter-Reay's fine third place represented a watershed for the enthusiastic all-American squad, which hitherto had endured a tough baptism.

The learning curve was bound to be steep, not to say vertical, given ASTJ's 11th-hour genesis. Under the impetus of Formula 1 and Champ Car alumnus Stefan Johansson and investors Chris James and Dan Benton, the new team had come to fruition on January 2 – just seven weeks before the opening race at St. Petersburg! Its year-old Reynard chassis, purchased from Jerry Forsythe, didn't so much as turn a wheel until Spring Training in early February, and with in-season testing at a premium, the team had to endure the inevitable teething troubles in the full glare of publicity.

Happily, while financial resources were scarce, ASTJ boasted a wealth of experience among its key personnel, notably Ed Nathman, Rob Hill and Graham Taylor. It took some time – and a fair amount of reshuffling – before the various elements began to gel into a cohesive unit, however. On balance, the Reynard chassis was clearly a handicap, too – although on its day it was more than capable of embarrassing the more fashionable Lolas, particularly at permanent road courses where a reasonably low ride height was feasible.

Mid-Ohio was one such track. Both ASTJ Reynards were among the out-and-out fastest cars all weekend – although Jimmy Vasser's pace was masked initially by a broken gearbox input shaft immediately prior to final qualifying, which consigned him to an unrepresentative 14th-place starting berth. Come Sunday evening, Johansson was wearing an ear-to-ear grin, and lavished effusive praise on his two charges: "I think if Jimmy had started up front, he'd have just checked out... And Ryan drove a helluva race. He didn't put a wheel wrong all day."

For his part, Hunter-Reay found his first taste of life at the sharp end of the Champ Car field something of a wake-up call: "It was like running qualifying laps every lap! I hadn't really experienced that level of intensity before."

In which case, one had to say, his driving hadn't shown it.

The man cutting the biggest swathe through the lap chart was Jimmy Vasser, who had climbed from 14th on the grid to seventh inside 13 laps courtesy of the assorted mishaps that had befallen those in front of him and a couple of incisive passing moves. After demoting sixth-placed Tagliani at the second round of pit stops, he tracked down Bourdais and promptly dispatched the series' *wunderkind* with a textbook outbraking maneuver into the Esses on lap 54. Vasser made equally light work of Jourdain at the same location three laps later, before disappearing over the horizon in pursuit of American Spirit Team Johansson stable-mate Hunter-Reay.

A succession of scintillating laps – culminating in a 1m 08.366s orbit on lap 60, which would stand as the fastest lap of the race – ensured that Vasser was soon looming large in Hunter-Reay's mirrors, but the youngster got the message and responded with a new personal best of 1m 08.851s. That was rapid enough to enable the red, white and blue-liveried Reynards to begin to home in on the mighty Player's/Forsythe Lolas – to the cheers of the heartland crowd, which clearly warmed to the David-and-Goliath theme.

Carpentier, meanwhile, was in the midst of an inspired spurt of his own, whittling the deficit to Tracy from nine seconds immediately after the pit stops to a scant 0.889s by lap 65 (six tours after Monteiro had relinquished the lead).

"My car was really fast today," declared Carpentier with a glint

in his eye. "I caught up to Paul, but to pass him would have been another story."

Tracy, however, showed that he was equal to the challenge by eking out a three-second margin prior to the final pit stops on lap 72, whereupon the gap grew by a further second. The intra-team contest had been settled decisively.

Sadly the same could be said with even greater certainty about the ASTJ pair on lap 83, when Vasser's magnificent drive came to an abrupt end against the tire barrier at Turn Nine. The veteran had been walking the tightrope of on-the-limit adhesion, and simply lost the back end of his Reynard through the preceding tricky off-camber right-hander.

"I'd just done two 1m 08.4s [laps] in a row and it just stepped out on me," confessed Vasser. "I thought, 'You gotta be kiddin' me.' I don't usually make mental mistakes like that – that's what really ticks me off."

The ensuing caution paved the way for a six-lap sprint to the checkered flag. Tracy comfortably held sway over Carpentier and Hunter-Reay, who upheld ASTJ's honor admirably by securing the fledgling outfit's first podium. Jourdain managed to stave off the attentions of a rejuvenated Bourdais, while Tagliani rounded out the top six after a workmanlike, if low-key, day at the office for Rocketsports Racing.

*Alex Sabine*

**Above left and top: American Spirit Team Johansson displayed tremendous form, with Ryan Hunter-Reay leading the way.**
Photographs: Mike Levitt/LAT

**Above: Jimmy Vasser took advantage of great pit stops to move up into fourth before making a mistake in the late stages of the race.**
Gregg Feistmann/LAT

Left: Jourdain drove hard to keep
Bourdais in his mirrors.
Mike Weston/LAT

FINISH

START

# CHAMP CAR
# GRAND PRIX OF MID-OHIO

## MID-OHIO SPORTS CAR COURSE, LEXINGTON, OHIO

### AUGUST 10, 92 laps of 2.258 miles – 206.769 miles

| Pl. | Driver (Nat.) | No. | Team Sponsors Engine/Car | Tires | Q Speed | Q Time | Q Pos. | Laps | Time/Status | Ave. (mph) | Pts. |
|---|---|---|---|---|---|---|---|---|---|---|---|
| 1 | Paul Tracy (CDN) | 3 | Forsythe Racing Player's/Indeck Ford Cosworth/Lola B02/00 | BS | 121.220 | 1m 07.058s | 1 | 92 | 1h 56m 45.737s | 106.251 | 23 |
| 2 | Patrick Carpentier (CDN) | 32 | Forsythe Racing Player's/Indeck Ford Cosworth/Lola B03/00 | BS | 120.792 | 1m 07.296s | 5 | 92 | 1h 56m 46.347s | 106.242 | 16 |
| 3 | *Ryan Hunter-Reay (USA) | 31 | American Spirit Team Johansson Ford Cosworth/Reynard 01I | BS | 121.192 | 1m 07.074s | 2 | 92 | 1h 56m 47.709s | 106.221 | 14 |
| 4 | Michel Jourdain Jr. (MEX) | 9 | Team Rahal Gigante Ford Cosworth/Lola B01/00 | BS | 120.900 | 1m 07.236s | 4 | 92 | 1h 56m 48.942s | 106.203 | 12 |
| 5 | *Sébastien Bourdais (F) | 2 | Newman/Haas Racing Lilly Ford Cosworth/Lola B01/00 | BS | 121.090 | 1m 07.130s | 3 | 92 | 1h 56m 49.791s | 106.190 | 10 |
| 6 | Alex Tagliani (CDN) | 33 | Rocketsports Racing Johnson Controls Ford Cosworth/Lola B02/00 | BS | 120.468 | 1m 07.477s | 7 | 92 | 1h 56m 53.662s | 106.131 | 8 |
| 7 | Adrian Fernandez (MEX) | 51 | Fernandez Tecate/Quaker State/Telmex Ford Cosworth/Lola B02/00 | BS | 120.110 | 1m 07.678s | 10 | 92 | 1h 56m 54.450s | 106.119 | 6 |
| 8 | *Darren Manning (GB) | 15 | Walker Racing RAC/Autowindscreens Ford Cosworth/Reynard 02I | BS | 119.604 | 1m 07.964s | 13 | 92 | 1h 56m 54.899s | 106.112 | 5 |
| 9 | Max Papis (I) | 27 | PK Racing Ford Cosworth/Lola B02/00 | BS | 118.913 | 1m 08.359s | 16 | 92 | 1h 56m 56.245s | 106.092 | 4 |
| 10 | *Mario Haberfeld (BR) | 34 | Mi-Jack Conquest Racing Ford Cosworth/Reynard 02I | BS | 119.273 | 1m 08.153s | 15 | 92 | 1h 56m 58.151s | 106.063 | 3 |
| 11 | *Tiago Monteiro (P) | 7 | Fittipaldi-Dingman Racing Ford Cosworth/Reynard 02I | BS | 119.693 | 1m 07.914s | 12 | 91 | Running | | 2 |
| 12 | *Rodolfo Lavin (MEX) | 5 | Walker Racing Corona Competition Ford Cosworth/Reynard 02I | BS | 118.736 | 1m 08.461s | 17 | 91 | Running | | 1 |
| 13 | Bruno Junqueira (BR) | 1 | Newman/Haas Racing PacifiCare Ford Cosworth/Lola B02/00 | BS | 120.785 | 1m 07.300s | 6 | 90 | Running | | |
| 14 | *Geoff Boss (USA) | 11 | Dale Coyne Racing Cross Pens Ford Cosworth/Lola B01/00 | BS | 118.191 | 1m 08.777s | 18 | 90 | Running | | |
| 15 | Jimmy Vasser (USA) | 12 | American Spirit Team Johansson Ford Cosworth/Reynard 2KI | BS | 119.322 | 1m 08.125s | 14 | 82 | Accident | | |
| 16 | Mario Dominguez (MEX) | 55 | Herdez Competition Ford Cosworth/Lola B03/00 | BS | 120.156 | 1m 07.652s | 9 | 71 | Out of fuel | | |
| 17 | Gualter Salles (BR) | 19 | Dale Coyne Racing Alpina/Golden Cross Ford Cosworth/Lola B2K/00 | BS | 118.177 | 1m 08.785s | 19 | 46 | Electrical fire | | |
| 18 | Oriol Servia (E) | 20 | Patrick Racing Visteon Ford Cosworth/Lola B02/00 | BS | 120.375 | 1m 07.529s | 8 | 13 | Accident | | |
| 19 | Roberto Moreno (BR) | 4 | Herdez Competition Ford Cosworth/Lola B03/00 | BS | 119.887 | 1m 07.804s | 11 | 9 | Accident | | |

\* denotes rookie driver

Caution flags: Lap 9–11, accident/Moreno; laps 13–16, accident/Servia & Junqueira; laps 83–86, accident/Vasser. Total: **Three** for **11** laps.

Lap leaders: Paul Tracy, 1–24 (24 laps); Adrian Fernandez, 25–37 (13 laps); Tracy, 38–48 (11 laps); Tiago Monteiro, 49–58 (10 laps); Tracy, 59–92 (34 laps). Totals: Tracy, **69** laps; Fernandez, **13** laps; Monteiro, **10** laps.

Fastest race lap: Jimmy Vasser, 1m 08.366s, 118.901 mph on lap 60.

Championship positions: 1 Tracy, 184; 2 Junqueira, 164; 3 Jourdain Jr., 137; 4 Bourdais, 126; 5 Carpentier, 114; 6 Fernandez, 77; 7 Servia, 76; 8 Tagliani & Manning, 73; 10 Dominguez, 65; 11 Haberfeld, 55; 12 Moreno, 45; 13 Vasser, 44; 14 Hunter-Reay, 41; 15 Papis, 21; 16 Monteiro, 20; 17 Lavin, 12; 18 Lemarie, 8; 19 Camathias, 6; 20 Yoong, 4; 21 Salles & Herta, 2.

# MID-OHIO SNIPPETS

• In the wake of persistent mutterings about blocking in qualifying sessions, CART announced that it would adopt a single-car qualifying FOR-MAT for the upcoming street races at Denver and Miami, owing to the furiously short and tight nature of the downtown layouts. Single-car qualifying had been adopted for the London Champ Car Trophy at Brands Hatch to general satisfaction.

• Ryan Hunter-Reay's podium finish was the FIRST for an American rookie since Eddie Cheever – by then a Formula 1 veteran – placed third at the rain-sodden Molson Indy Toronto in 1990. It also marked the first time a Reynard driver had scaled the rostrum in '03.

• Fresh from a famous victory for Bentley in the Le Mans 24-hour race, Englishman Guy Smith was doing the rounds of the Mid-Ohio paddock in PUR-SUIT of a Champ Car drive for 2004. "I've got a bit of sponsorship money and I've had some interesting meetings this weekend," claimed the former Indy Lights standout.

• Paul Tracy and Patrick Carpentier (above) CELEBRATED their 1-2 in the style patented by Carpentier when he won at Mid-Ohio in 2002. Which is to say that they draped checkered flags around their otherwise naked frames and ran a victory lap around the paddock, much to the mirth of the assembled Team Player's crew.

• Fernandez Racing had conducted another SHAKEUP of its engineering department since the race at Road America, race engineer David Watson having been relieved of his duties in favor of Chris Finch, who had held the post of assistant race engineer since the team's inception in 2001. "It was felt that a change of di-

rection was needed," stated the team's co-owner and managing director, Tom Anderson, alluding to a mediocre mid-season run of form punctuated only by victory at Portland.

• Sébastien Bourdais had been BUSY in the week since Road America, stopping off in London, Paris, Charlotte and Miami en route to Mid-Ohio. The purpose of his whistle-stop tour? A sponsor appearance for Eli Lilly, as well as a visit to a Hole in the Wall Gang camp – for children with life-threatening illnesses – in Fontainebleau, France, with Newman/Haas Racing co-owner and HITWG camp founder Paul Newman. Bourdais found it a humbling experience: "It's amazing to see all these kids with so many troubles so happy. I tell you, after being there I realize I am not allowed to complain about anything in my life."

• Bourdais' fifth-place finish was a GRITTY EFFORT given that he had to make do with negligible fluid intake over 92 laps of one of the most physically demanding racetracks on the calendar. "I was a bit dry [dehydrated] because the water bottle in my car didn't work, but the team did a good job to get me some water during the pit stops," he said. Notwithstanding this handicap, the Frenchman clocked the race's second-fastest lap.

• CART responded to criticism of its handling of recent races by announcing a shuffling of DUTIES

within its Competition department, effective immediately. The reorganization, designed to streamline decision making, resulted in Chief Steward Chris Kneifel (below) being rechristened Race Director, while experienced former team manager John Anderson moved up from the pit lane to the control tower. Anderson would hold any necessary "post-event meetings" with competitors in addition to carrying out his existing technical inspection duties.

Mike Weston/LAT

il Abbott/LAT

BRIDGESTONE PRESENTS
THE CHAMP CAR WORLD SERIES POWERED BY FORD · ROUND 14

# MONTREAL

**Above: All smiles on the podium for Servia, winner Jourdain and Carpentier.**
Mike Levitt/LAT

**Main photograph: After being the man to beat all weekend, Tagliani was desperately unlucky not to score an overdue Champ Car win.**
Gavin Lawrence/LAT

**S**INCE making his Champ Car debut at Homestead-Miami Speedway in 2000, French-Canadian Alex Tagliani had competed in 72 races and finished second on three occasions – at Toronto in '01, and both Motegi and Road America one year later. He had added a handful of thirds – Surfers Paradise and Fontana in 2001, plus three times already in 2003 at Monterrey, Portland and Road America – and four times had started from the pole. Tagliani could have dreamed of no better place than Montreal to end his lengthy quest for a maiden Champ Car victory.

For much of the weekend, Tagliani looked set to achieve his goal. He qualified Paul Gentilozzi's Johnson Controls/Rocketsports Racing Ford Cosworth/Lola on the pole and led 52 of the first 57 laps. Ultimately, however, the team's strategy was to prove his downfall.

Prior to the race, fuel consumption was widely regarded as a critical issue. The stop-start nature of the Circuit-Gilles Villeneuve is notorious for providing poor fuel economy, and all of the teams realized their drivers would have to adopt a conservative approach if they wanted to complete the maximum 20 laps allowed between pit stops. Midway through the first stint, however, the Rocketsports engineers instructed Tagliani to go for broke. He responded in style, pulling out a lead of almost four seconds before his first visit to the pit lane. Even though he was obliged to stop one lap sooner than the other front-runners, Tagliani extended his advantage to almost six seconds before making his second pit stop after 38 laps.

Unfortunately a pair of full-course cautions proved to be his undoing. Tagliani's lead was slashed to just a few car lengths, and the handicap of making his final pit stop before chief rival Michel Jourdain Jr., who was able to run two more laps at full speed before taking on service, was too great to overcome. Tagliani slipped to an unrepresentative fourth place at the checkered flag.

To his credit, Tagliani remained upbeat: "The team was awesome. My engineers were super and this was the best car of my Champ Car career. It was perfect."

"We went with a strategy to save fuel in the beginning and Servia was not catching me, so I went for it," he continued. "We changed the strategy and just raced. In the end, with the yellow, it didn't work and we didn't get the results we wanted. We learned a lot and are convinced now more than ever that a win for Rocketsports is going to happen soon."

**Above:** The pit suites in Montreal afford an excellent view as the crews ply their trade.

**Top right:** Tagliani claims his second pole of the year and the first in his hometown.
Photographs: Gavin Lawrence/LAT

**Center right:** Race engineer Craig Hampson tried his best, but it was a weekend to forget for Sébastien Bourdais.
Mike Levitt/LAT

**Right:** A timely pass and great pitwork paved the way for Jourdain's second win.
Gavin Lawrence/LAT

THE ebb and flow of emotions continued unchecked as the 2003 Bridgestone Presents the Champ Car World Series Powered by Ford paid its second annual visit to the famed Circuit Gilles-Villeneuve for the Molson Indy Montreal. Paul Tracy arrived with high hopes of maintaining his 100-percent record on Canadian soil in 2003 after winning in Toronto and Vancouver. He was to be disappointed, unable to match the front-running pace and then losing a hard-earned fourth place when his Player's Lola ran out of fuel exiting the final corner. Primary title rival Bruno Junqueira fared even worse, spinning not once but twice and finishing out of the points for the second successive race. It fell to Michel Jourdain Jr. to take the checkered flag, earning a superb second victory of the season aboard Team Rahal's Gigante Ford Cosworth/Lola.

"We had a quiet weekend until raceday," noted Jourdain, who had qualified fourth on the grid, after closing to within seven points of second-placed Junqueira in the championship standings. "The team did a fantastic job in the pits and they deserved this win as much as anyone."

But spare a thought for Alex Tagliani. The local hero qualified Paul Gentilozzi's Johnson Controls/Rocketsports Racing Lola on the pole and dominated the race until his quest for victory was ended by inferior fuel mileage, causing him to lose crucial time at his final pit stop.

Tagliani, from Lachenaie, Quebec, held off a challenge from outside-front-row starter Oriol Servia's Visteon/Patrick Racing Lola into the first corner and, to the delight of his hometown crowd, held an appreciable advantage at the end of the first of 75 laps. The remainder of the top five followed in grid formation, Junqueira slotting into third ahead of Jourdain and another Quebec native, Patrick Carpentier, in the leading Player's car. Teammate Tracy posted one of his patented first-lap charges to vault from eighth on

the grid to sixth at the expense of Sébastien Bourdais and Reynard standard bearer Jimmy Vasser. Mario Dominguez and Darren Manning also exchanged places on the opening lap as the Mexican found a way around the Englishman's Reynard.

Two laps later, Dominguez made up another position when he slipped inside Vasser under braking for the hairpin. Farther back, on lap seven, Vasser's teammate, Ryan Hunter-Reay, tried a similar maneuver on Mario Haberfeld for 12th, but succeeded only in locking up his rear wheels and spinning. Worse, Hunter-Reay stalled his motor, necessitating the first full-course caution of the afternoon while his American Spirit Team Johansson Reynard was restarted by the Simple Green Safety Team.

The order at the front of the field remained unchanged as Tagliani once again resisted pressure from Servia at the restart. Junqueira continued in third, but only briefly. On lap 12, he spun under braking for the hairpin. The Brazilian lost five positions and was fortunate to emerge unscathed.

Tagliani set a torrid pace, posting a succession of fastest laps as he extended his margin over Servia to 3.6 seconds by lap 18. But such profligacy would come back to haunt him.

On lap 19, Tagliani brought his Rocketsports car into the pit lane for the first time. All of the other front-runners waited until the CART-mandated limit of 20 laps before taking on service. On this occasion, the early stop didn't cause him any concern. Tagliani resumed still in the lead, albeit under pressure from the Herdez car of Roberto Moreno, who, in common with Max Papis, Adrian Fernandez and Rodolfo Lavin, had opted to make pit stops during the earlier caution period. All four would be obliged to pit again after 29 laps.

In the meantime, Fernandez ran a strong third and actually began to home in on the two leaders. Behind, Jourdain charged hard after Servia following his first pit stop and, on lap 21, with

both men still bringing their fresh Bridgestone Potenza tires up to temperature, the Mexican dived for the inside line under braking for the final chicane. It was a great move, and one that paved the way for his eventual victory.

"Oriol was very fast – he was probably the fastest guy all weekend – but I saw an opportunity and I went for it," declared Jourdain, who soon moved up into the number-two spot when Moreno and Fernandez made their second pit stops.

The gap between the two leading cars remained fairly constant at around five seconds. Once again, though, Tagliani completed one less lap than the other front-runners before making his second visit to the pit lane. And when Jourdain exited the pits, on schedule after 40 laps, the deficit to Tagliani had shrunk to just 2.1 seconds, thanks to the benefit of running two extra laps on hot tires.

Servia remained in third, around 1.5 seconds behind his good buddy Jourdain, while Carpentier had fallen almost ten seconds farther back in fourth place. Tracy ran fifth at this stage, another couple of seconds adrift, chased by Fernandez (still out of sequence to the other pace-setters), then Dominguez and Junqueira, who, incredibly, locked up his rear brakes and spun for a second time at the hairpin on lap 45.

"I am frustrated more than I can explain," the Brazilian said later. "I was too close to the guy in front of me and lost the downforce. I locked my rear tires and spun twice."

Junqueira's second error – and another incident at the hairpin on lap 49, between Tiago Monteiro and Hunter-Reay – also proved massively detrimental to Tagliani's victory hopes. As long as the race remained green, it appeared as though the French-Canadian's pace would enable him to remain far enough clear of Jourdain to overcome the inevitable handicap of making his final pit stop sooner than his closest challengers. But the two caution periods in quick succession erased Tagliani's 2.5-second lead and left him looking extremely vulnerable.

The French-Canadian pushed hard when the green flags

A thrilling final 40-minute qualifying session for the Molson Indy Montreal ended with the top six contenders blanketed by a scant 0.153s. Even more exciting for the enthusiastic crowd was the fact that hometown hero Alex Tagliani, who had been fastest in practice on Friday, but secured only fifth on the provisional grid, posted a dramatic improvement to snare the pole with a superb lap in 1m 19.665s.

"I am the same guy who drove yesterday," quipped Tagliani, "but I must have a faster car today to get such good results. Thanks to my engineers, Will Phillips and Adam Schaechter, the car is great. The guys did such a good job on it all weekend. They have worked hard all season and to have this pole for the race tomorrow is rewarding."

Oriol Servia managed only fourth in the final session aboard Pat Patrick's Visteon Lola, less than a tenth of a second shy of Tagliani's polewinning effort, but the personable Spaniard already had secured his first ever front-row starting position by virtue of pacing the field in provisional qualifying on Friday.

"We knew it was going to be tight today in qualifying – and it was," noted Servia. "I needed to give all that I had, and actually on the last lap I was almost 0.2s quicker than my best time, but I knew I had to go for more and I guess I asked for a little too much in the hairpin and I lost it there. But that is qualifying for you. You need to go for everything. I did it yesterday, but today we were a little short."

Bruno Junqueira, a mere 0.006s slower than Tagliani on Saturday, had to be content with a position on the inside of the second row of the grid for Newman/Haas Racing, alongside Michel Jourdain Jr.'s similar Gigante/Team Rahal Lola. Patrick Carpentier (Team Player's) and Sébastien Bourdais (Newman/Haas Racing) shared row three of the grid, the Frenchman just 0.153s away from the pole on his first visit to the Circuit Gilles-Villeneuve, while Jimmy Vasser was fastest of the Reynards, seventh for American Spirit Team Johansson.

Points leader Paul Tracy was a disappointed eighth. "The car was good on old tires, but when the Team Player's crew put on new tires, the car became unstable," he related. "It was also nervous under braking and jumping around. Some days are going to be tougher than others. Today we just couldn't put it together. We know it can't be perfect every weekend, so now we are going to have to fight to get a good result."

## FULL OF ZEST

ROBERTO Moreno might be the elder statesman among the Champ Car drivers, at 44, but you'd never know it from the boyish enthusiasm he routinely displays at the racetracks. Quite simply, he loves to drive fast. The popular Brazilian sat on the sidelines throughout the 2002 campaign after losing his ride with Patrick Racing, but he never lost faith that he would find suitable alternate employment. Finally, having spent a great deal of time working with Mario Dominguez during his rookie season with the Herdez Competition team, Moreno was signed up to pilot a second Lola as the Indianapolis-based team stepped up to a two-car operation for 2003.

It was an astute choice by team principal Keith Wiggins. Moreno's vast experience was invaluable as the ambitious team came to grips with its expansion, and he celebrated his return with a solid fifth-place finish the St. Petersburg opener.

The veteran racer's setup knowledge paid major dividends both for the engineering staff, led by Tom Brown, and for series sophomore Dominguez, whose confidence blossomed as a result of not having the full weight of responsibility laid on his shoulders.

More often than not, Moreno was outpaced by his more youthful teammate, although from time to time he showed real flashes of speed – notably in Vancouver, where the old hand qualified an excellent third, only to be involved in an incident at the first corner.

The Molson Indy Montreal was another such occasion. Moreno qualified only 13th, then lost a position on the first lap to rookie Ryan Hunter-Reay, but he benefited from a smart strategic call by race engineer Chris Gorne by making his first pit stop during a full-course caution on lap nine. He remained out of sequence for the balance of the afternoon – and made one more pit stop than most of the front-runners – but he enjoyed his first laps in the lead of a Champ Car race since Fontana in 2001 before eventually finishing a creditable seventh.

"I'll take that with pleasure," he said with his characteristic broad grin. "The car was awesome and the team's strategy of pitting me during the first caution period paid off. Initially I wasn't so sure because I came out of that first stop behind the yellow [Dale Coyne Racing] cars. But after the third stop, I ended up in the lead of the race and was able to set some quick lap times. That's when the strategy really showed."

waved again after 52 laps, knowing full well that he had only six laps to build up a margin before taking on service for the final time. But he could circulate no better than in the low 1m 21s range, and the gap to Jourdain was a mere 1.5 seconds when he ducked into the pits after 58 laps. The next time around, Jourdain toured the 2.709 miles in 1m 20.89s, then turned another quick lap on his way into the pits. When the Mexican emerged from the pit lane – behind Moreno, Fernandez and Papis, who had not yet made their final stops – he was comfortably ahead of the erstwhile pacesetter. Indeed Tagliani also had been leapfrogged by Servia, Carpentier and Tracy.

"We had the car to win," lamented Tagliani, still seeking his maiden Champ Car victory after 73 starts. "Montreal was the best place for it to happen, but that second yellow destroyed our strategy and our day."

Moreno enjoyed a handful of laps in the lead (see sidebar) before making his final pit stop and handing back the advantage to Jourdain. Typically brisk work by Don Oldenburg's Patrick Racing crew saw Servia hot on Jourdain's heels after the final round of pit stops, but that was as close as he got. Jourdain even managed to stretch his lead to almost two seconds when Servia was forced to switch his attention from attempting to make a move on him to defending his own position from a charging Carpentier.

"I'm not as happy now as I was when I took second in Milwaukee," admitted Servia, "but it is still a good weekend for us, especially after the last three races didn't go so well."

"I was having a great time out there pushing Oriol, trying to make him make a mistake," said Carpentier. "The car was great and Team Player's did a wonderful job all weekend, especially today. We did have minor problems with the brakes because they were overheating, but we managed to nurse them enough to finish on the podium."

Carpentier's teammate, Tracy, seemed set for fourth until his engine sputtered, out of fuel, as he went to accelerate out of the very last corner. Instead he coasted across the line an angry sixth.

"I didn't know I was low on fuel until the last lap in the hairpin [when he was informed over the radio by his crew]," he raged. "It's just points given away for no reason."

Jourdain, meanwhile, was celebrating the second win of his career – without losing his customary sense of perspective: "I feel bad for Alex [Tagliani] because I know what it's like to dominate a race – like in Long Beach – but not win."

*Jeremy Shaw*

# MOLSON
# INDY MONTREAL

## CIRCUIT GILLES-VILLENEUVE, MONTREAL, QUEBEC, CANADA

### AUGUST 24, 75 laps of 2.709 miles – 203.175 miles

**ROUND 14**

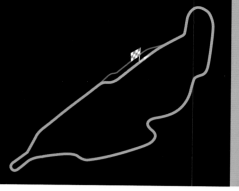

| Pl. | Driver (Nat.) | No. | Team Sponsors Engine/Car | Tires | Q Speed | Q Time | Q Pos. | Laps | Time/Status | Ave. (mph) | Pts. |
|---|---|---|---|---|---|---|---|---|---|---|---|
| 1 | Michel Jourdain Jr. (MEX) | 9 | Team Rahal Gigante Ford Cosworth/Lola B01/00 | BS | 122.286 | 1m 19.751s | 4 | 75 | 1h 54m 23.210s | 106.573 | 20 |
| 2 | Oriol Servia (E) | 20 | Patrick Racing Visteon Ford Cosworth/Lola B02/00 | BS | 122.276 | 1m 19.757s | 2 | 75 | 1h 54m 24.487s | 106.553 | 17 |
| 3 | Patrick Carpentier (CDN) | 32 | Forsythe Racing Player's/Indeck Ford Cosworth/Lola B02/00 | BS | 122.195 | 1m 19.810s | 5 | 75 | 1h 54m 25.309s | 106.540 | 14 |
| 4 | Alex Tagliani (CDN) | 33 | Rocketsports Racing Johnson Controls Ford Cosworth/Lola B02/00 | BS | 122.418 | 1m 19.665s | 1 | 75 | 1h 54m 30.429s | 106.461 | 14 |
| 5 | Mario Dominguez (MEX) | 55 | Herdez Competition Ford Cosworth/Lola B03/00 | BS | 121.359 | 1m 20.360s | 10 | 75 | 1h 54m 33.220s | 106.417 | 10 |
| 6 | Paul Tracy (CDN) | 3 | Forsythe Racing Player's/Indeck Ford Cosworth/Lola B02/00 | BS | 121.882 | 1m 20.015s | 8 | 75 | 1h 54m 38.121s | 106.342 | 8 |
| 7 | Roberto Moreno (BR) | 4 | Herdez Competition Ford Cosworth/Lola B2K/00 | BS | 120.659 | 1m 20.826s | 13 | 75 | 1h 54m 40.043s | 106.312 | 6 |
| 8 | Adrian Fernandez (MEX) | 51 | Fernandez Tecate/Quaker State/Telmex Ford Cosworth/Lola B02/00 | BS | 120.049 | 1m 21.237s | 16 | 75 | 1h 55m 00.405s | 105.998 | 5 |
| 9 | Max Papis (I) | 27 | PK Racing Ford Cosworth/Lola B02/00 | BS | 120.228 | 1m 21.116s | 15 | 75 | 1h 55m 00.753s | 105.993 | 4 |
| 10 | *Darren Manning (GB) | 15 | Walker Racing RAC/Autowindscreens Ford Cosworth/Reynard 02I | BS | 121.437 | 1m 20.308s | 9 | 75 | 1h 55m 01.627s | 105.979 | 3 |
| 11 | *Mario Haberfeld (BR) | 34 | Mi-Jack Conquest Racing Ford Cosworth/Reynard 02I | BS | 120.939 | 1m 20.639s | 12 | 75 | 1h 55m 02.037s | 105.973 | 2 |
| 12 | Gualter Salles (BR) | 19 | Dale Coyne Racing Alpina/Golden Cross Ford Cosworth/Lola B2K/00 | BS | 119.666 | 1m 21.497s | 17 | 75 | 1h 55m 13.756s | 105.793 | 1 |
| 13 | Bruno Junqueira (BR) | 1 | Newman/Haas Racing PacifiCare Ford Cosworth/Lola B02/00 | BS | 122.408 | 1m 19.671s | 3 | 74 | Running | | |
| 14 | *Geoff Boss (USA) | 11 | Dale Coyne Racing Cross Pens Ford Cosworth/Lola B01/00 | BS | 118.676 | 1m 22.177s | 19 | 74 | Running | | |
| 15 | *Rodolfo Lavin (MEX) | 5 | Walker Racing Corona Competition Ford Cosworth/Reynard 02I | BS | 119.342 | 1m 21.718s | 18 | 74 | Running | | |
| 16 | Jimmy Vasser (USA) | 12 | American Spirit Team Johansson Ford Cosworth/Reynard 01I | BS | 122.085 | 1m 19.882s | 7 | 72 | Gearbox | | |
| 17 | *Ryan Hunter-Reay (USA) | 31 | American Spirit Team Johansson Ford Cosworth/Reynard 02I | BS | 120.455 | 1m 20.963s | 14 | 60 | Gearbox | | |
| 18 | *Tiago Monteiro (P) | 7 | Fittipaldi-Dingman Racing Ford Cosworth/Reynard 02I | BS | 121.359 | 1m 20.360s | 11 | 49 | Accident | | |
| 19 | *Sébastien Bourdais (F) | 2 | Newman/Haas Racing Lilly Ford Cosworth/Lola B01/00 | BS | 122.183 | 1m 19.818s | 6 | 28 | Differential | | |

\* denotes rookie driver

**Caution flags:** Lap 7–9, tow/Hunter-Reay; laps 45–47, tow/Junqueira; laps 50–51, accident/Monteiro & Hunter-Reay. Total: **Three for 8 laps.**

**Lap leaders:** Alex Tagliani, 1–18 (18 laps); Oriol Servia, 19–20 (2 laps); Tagliani, 21–37 (17 laps); Michel Jourdain Jr., 38–40 (3 laps); Tagliani, 41–57 (17 laps); Jourdain, 58–59 (2 laps); Roberto Moreno, 60–65 (6 laps); Jourdain, 66–75 (10 laps). Totals: Tagliani, 52 laps; Jourdain, 15 laps; Moreno, 6 laps; Servia, 2 laps.

**Fastest race lap:** Bruno Junqueira, 1m 20.634s, 120.946 mph on lap 69.

**Championship positions:** 1 Tracy, **192**; 2 Junqueira, **164**; 3 Jourdain Jr., **157**; 4 Carpentier, **128**; 5 Bourdais, **126**; 6 Servia, **93**; 7 Tagliani, **87**; 8 Fernandez, **82**; 9 Manning, **76**; 10 Dominguez, **75**; 11 Haberfeld, **57**; 12 Moreno, **51**; 13 Vasser, **44**; 14 Hunter-Reay, **41**; 15 Papis, **25**; 16 Monteiro, **20**; 17 Lavin, **12**; 18 Lemarie, **8**; 19 Camathias, **6**; 20 Yoong, **4**; 21 Salles, **3**; 22 Herta, **2**.

# MONTREAL SNIPPETS

Dan Boyd/LAT

• American Spirit Team Johansson threw a PARTY for Jimmy Vasser (above) on Saturday to commemorate his 200th Champ Car start. Close friend Alex Zanardi couldn't be present, but sent his best wishes along with a specially composed song that he relayed via telephone from Europe. Vasser was fastest of the Reynard contingent virtually all weekend, although, sadly, his car was stricken with gearbox woes and finally dropped out of eighth place just three laps shy of the finish.

• The challenging Circuit-Gilles Villeneuve on Montreal's Ile de Notre Dame, situated in the middle of the majestic St. Lawrence River, once again proved a POPULAR VENUE for fans and teams alike. The raceday crowd of 58,000 pushed the weekend attendance above 148,000 – not as high as for the inaugural visit by the Champ Cars in 2002, but still an extremely respectable turnout.

• Mario Dominguez enhanced his reputation as a burgeoning TALENT by moving up impressively from his tenth starting position to finish a strong fifth for the Herdez Competition team. "I had a really good car," noted the Mexican. "Other than putting fuel in and tires on, we didn't touch it, and we really took advantage of that."

• Bruno Junqueira squandered a good OPPORTUNITY to keep the pressure on series points leader Paul Tracy by spinning twice within the first 45 laps and eventually finishing in 13th. "A good finish was important today," he acknowledged. "It gets more and more important the closer we get to the end of the championship." Junqueira set the fastest lap of the race as he fought, in vain, to make up lost ground. By the end of the day, he trailed Tracy in the championship chase by an ominous 28-point margin, 192–164.

• Junqueira's Newman/Haas teammate, Sébastien Bourdais, saw his HOPES of a sixth consecutive top-five finish evaporate when a broken differential caused him to be the first driver out of the race after 28 laps. "Since the beginning of the year, we have had some mechanical problems. That's just the way it is," the Frenchman noted philosophically. "It's probably not my year."

• Michel Jourdain Jr. became only the SECOND Mexican to win as many as two races in a single season, mirroring the feat of Adrian Fernandez in 1998, '99 and 2000. Incredibly, Jourdain also was only the second non front row qualifier to win a race in 2003. The only other man to do so was Fernandez, who started third before speeding to victory at Portland.

• Briton Darren Manning overcame a PUZZLING lack of straightline speed in the race to record his seventh consecutive top-ten finish for Walker Racing, equaling the record for a rookie established by Canadian John Jones in 1988.

• Gualter Salles (below) finished among the POINTS for the second time in three races, despite experiencing a couple of uncharacteristic slow pit stops by Wayne Hill's #19 Dale Coyne Racing crew. "It's the best car I had all year long," said the Brazilian.

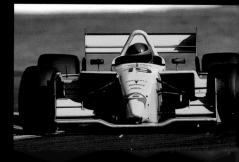

Gavin Lawrence/LAT

BRIDGESTONE PRESENTS
THE CHAMP CAR WORLD SERIES POWERED BY FORD • ROUND 15

# DENVER

BRUNO Junqueira knew exactly what he needed to do in the Centrix Financial Grand Prix of Denver if he was to keep alive his hopes of winning the 2003 Champ Car World Series title. The Brazilian had failed to score in each of the previous two races, but he arrived in the Mile High City in a positive frame of mind after dominating the event in 2002. Sure enough, Junqueira delivered in style. He qualified on the pole for the second time in 2003 and, just as he had done at Road America, led most of the race in Newman/Haas Racing's Pacifi-Care Ford Cosworth/Lola.

But Junqueira had his work cut out. Oriol Servia maintained his recent run of good form by qualifying second and then shadowing the Brazilian through the opening stages of the 106-lap race. Excellent work in the pits enabled Servia to wrest away the lead following the first round of pit stops, although Junqueira kept his cool, regained the advantage when next he took on service, and finally was granted some respite when teammate Sébastien Bourdais emerged in second place ahead of Servia. The pair then held station to ensure a glorious 1-2 finish for Carl Haas and Paul Newman.

"I like Denver more and more each time I come back here," said Junqueira, a twinkle in his eye, after whittling his deficit to series leader Paul Tracy – who finished fourth – to just 18 points with four events remaining on the schedule.

For the umpteenth time in 2003, there was confusion at the start when Servia twice jumped clear of the polesitter, and Starter J.D. Wilbur was obliged to wave the yellow flag instead of the green. Finally, at the third attempt, the right man led the way into Turn One and the race was under way. Servia slotted dutifully into second, chased by Bourdais, Adrian Fernandez and Patrick Carpentier, who quickly hustled past Tiago Monteiro after the Portuguese had qualified a career-best fifth for Fittipaldi-Dingman Racing. Tracy also was on a mission. After starting ninth, he snuck past the Reynards of Mario Haberfeld and Darren Manning within the first couple of turns, then dispensed with Monteiro's similar car under braking for Turn Six. Tracy completed the first lap right on teammate Carpentier's tail in sixth place.

Moments later, out came the yellow flags again: Rodolfo Lavin had been attempting to pass Jimmy Vasser in Turn Five, but he succeeded only in spinning Derrick Walker's Corona Reynard and collecting the wall. The two Herdez Lolas of Mario Dominguez and Roberto Moreno also were involved, although they were able to resume at the back of the pack after a quick visit apiece to the pit lane.

The restart saw no change in the top ten. Farther back, Vasser managed to sneak ahead of Champ Car debutant Mika Salo's PK Racing Lola, while Dominguez quickly worked his way past Moreno and the two Dale Coyne Racing Lolas of Geoff Boss and Gualter Salles.

Junqueira set a torrid pace out front, circulating consistently just a second or so off his pole-winning time. The gap back to Servia fluctuated between a few car lengths and as much as a couple of seconds, as the Spaniard remained under stern pressure from Bourdais. Fernandez couldn't quite match their pace and settled into his own rhythm, edging clear of Carpentier, who, in turn, was unchallenged in the early stages by Tracy.

The sinuous nature of the racetrack made overtaking extremely difficult, so most contenders were content to wait until the pit stops, hoping perhaps that their crews might be able to make a difference to the status quo. Sure enough, a quick stop by Don Oldenburg's Patrick Racing team, combined with a minor glitch in the Newman/Haas pit, enabled Servia to resume narrowly ahead of Junqueira.

The middle stages of the race saw Servia holding a slight edge over the Newman/Haas pair, but he was never able to extend his lead by much more than a second or so. Fernandez continued to run all alone in fourth with his Tecate/Quaker State/Telmex car, while Carpentier came under increasing pressure from Tracy. Finally, on lap 49, Carpentier acceded to the Player's team's wishes and allowed his championship-contending teammate to move through into fifth. Tracy, his car now working far more to his satisfaction, showed his gratitude by posting the fastest lap of the race thus far at 1m 02.349s.

"In clean air I was fast," acknowledged Tracy. Indeed, over the next dozen laps, he whittled the gap to Fernandez from more than 11 seconds to just over three seconds.

The other man on the move was Dominguez, who also had played a starring role one week earlier in Montreal. The Mexican charged past Vasser on lap 19, and elevated himself inside the top ten by virtue of a later stop than everyone else (because he had pitted during the early caution following his fracas with Lavin). Dominguez then executed a nice pass on Monteiro in Turn Eight on lap 67, although he failed to display the same precision when he braked too late while attempting to pass Haberfeld in Turn Five. Their two cars made contact, whereupon the luckless Brazilian was obliged to make an unscheduled pit stop to replace a punctured tire. Dominguez was more fortunate, losing only a couple of places – to Manning and a curiously off-the-pace Michel Jourdain Jr.

Undaunted, Dominguez set about regaining the lost ground. He passed the Englishman after a mighty battle, but Jourdain picked up his pace in the closing stages and just held off his countryman for sixth at the checkered flag.

"I had a lot of fun out there – especially those last 20 laps chasing Michel," related Dominguez. "It was good, clean racing and we were both going for it."

Up at the sharp end, meanwhile, the pace was slowed by a full-course caution on lap 62 when Carpentier, who had been having problems with a locking front brake, lost control and slid into the Turn One wall.

The entire field took the opportunity to make pit stops. For

## QUALIFYING

**The tortuous nature of the Denver track, laid out through the city streets and a portion of the parking lot surrounding the Pepsi Center (home of the National Basketball Association's Denver Nuggets and the National Hockey League's Colorado Avalanche), led CART officials to abandon the usual 40-minute open qualifying sessions in favor of oval-style, single-car qualifying. One session apiece was held on Friday and Saturday, with the usual championship point – and a guaranteed front-row start – up for grabs on each day. The final grid was set according to the fastest lap for each driver, irrespective of when it was established.**

**Mario Haberfeld caused a major surprise by being fastest in practice on both Friday and Saturday with his Mi-Jack/Conquest Racing Reynard, but the Brazilian rookie was unable to translate those results into a top grid placing. To no one's amazement, Bruno Junqueira, who had claimed the pole for Chip Ganassi in 2002, was fastest again for Newman/Haas on Friday. Adrian Fernandez, who, coincidentally, had qualified second in 2002, mirrored that feat one year on, with Darren Manning an excellent third quickest for Walker Racing, ahead of series leader Paul Tracy.**

**Heavy overnight rain and more showers on Saturday saw the track drying steadily during final qualifying, but the top provisional qualifiers soon were biting their fingernails as the sky darkened dramatically. Oriol Servia, who had been only ninth on Friday for Patrick Racing, posted a massive improvement to surge within just 0.039s of Junqueira's provisional pole. Several rivals tried in vain to beat Servia's benchmark, until just Fernandez and Junqueira remained. But then the rain arrived – just as Fernandez was starting his hot lap. The Mexican was forced to abandon his qualifying attempt, so Junqueira's pole was assured and Servia's time remained good enough for the outside-front-row starting position.**

**"I think the only guy that could have beaten me was Adrian," reckoned Junqueira, "but we were both penalized when the rains came. I wanted to try to get another championship point, but the rain didn't let us go out, unfortunately."**

**Fernandez was lucky not to slip any lower than fourth on the final grid, behind Sébastien Bourdais, while Portuguese rookie Tiago Monteiro claimed a career-best fifth starting position aboard his Fittipaldi-Dingman Racing Reynard. Haberfeld was troubled by understeer in the final session and could do no better than eighth, behind Patrick Carpentier and Manning.**

**Facing page: Junqueira jumped out in front of Servia at the start and went on to maintain his 100-percent record on the Denver street circuit.**
Gavin Lawrence/LAT

**Left: Jourdain on the limit for Team Rahal.**
Dan Boyd/LAT

Servia, though, hopes of a long-overdue maiden victory were thwarted by an airgun problem. A couple of vital seconds ticked away before he was able to rejoin, and by then Junqueira had regained the upper hand.

Bourdais also resumed ahead of Servia, who found his Visteon/Patrick Racing Lola coming under intense pressure from Fernandez when the green flag waved again to restart the racing after 65 laps.

"This was a very difficult race," declared Servia. "The track, instead of getting better, just got more slippery."

Servia had slipped more than ten seconds behind the two leading Newman/Haas cars by lap 78, when the yellow flags came out again for another incident, this time involving Moreno who had found the wall in Turn One. Still, Servia remained ahead of Fernandez, who in turn was being pressured by Tracy. Monteiro, too, running an excellent sixth, was in contention. Haberfeld, sadly, was not, having resumed a lap in arrears following his incident with Dominguez.

This latest caution period triggered the final round of pit stops. Junqueira, Bourdais and Servia retained the top three positions, while Tracy took advantage of a great stop by Steve Moore's Player's crew to slip past the Tecate/Quaker State/Telmex car of Fernandez.

After another brief interruption when Salo hit the wall at the restart, a final 20-lap sprint to the finish saw no real change at the front. The two Newman/Haas Lolas ran in lock-step and once again pulled clear of Servia to ensure maximum points in a milestone event for the Lincolnshire, Illinois-based team.

"This is for sure a big win for Newman/Haas Racing," said Junqueira. "Finishing 1-2 in their 350th start is great. Scoring more points for the championship is big too; this is exactly what I needed coming in to Denver."

"I tried as hard as I could, but never had a chance to get Bruno," added Bourdais, after snaring the sixth podium finish of his rookie campaign. "He is tough on street circuits, and the only way I was going to get a chance to pass him was at Turn Five. But I wasn't about to try something stupid and risk ruining Bruno's run at the championship."

Servia finished around 12 seconds back in third, just ahead of Tracy, while Fernandez remained clear of the tussle between fellow Mexicans Jourdain and Dominguez.

"Basically, it was about track position today," declared Fernandez. "Passing was difficult even after the pit stops. You could gain on the pit stops, but unfortunately today wasn't our day. Our stops have been good all year, and today Paul Tracy just beat us by a hair."

*Jeremy Shaw*

## SUPER MARIO

**M**ARIO Haberfeld was the talk of the Champ Car paddock for much of the Denver weekend. The 27-year-old Brazilian rookie, who had accumulated an enviable record of nine top-ten finishes in his first 14 Champ Car races, posted the fastest times in practice on both Friday and Saturday mornings to mark himself as a bona fide front-runner for the first time.

Haberfeld, originally from São Paulo, Brazil, started out racing karts in South America before switching his attention to Europe and progressing in traditional style through the ranks of Formula Ford, Formula Renault and Formula 3. He won six races en route to clinching the coveted British Formula 3 Championship with Paul Stewart Racing in 1998 – following in the footsteps of the likes of fellow Brazilian Gil de Ferran – and was touted as a potential Grand Prix star. Curiously, his fortunes waned when he moved into Formula 3000. Like several other top drivers before and since, Haberfeld struggled to come to grips with the category and notched a solitary podium finish in four seasons – at the A1-Ring in Austria in 2002.

Then, in common with an increasing number of his countrymen, including de Ferran, Tony Kanaan and Helio Castroneves, Haberfeld set his sights on North America. Outwardly calm, urbane and clearly very intelligent, he settled in quickly with Eric Bachelart's Mi-Jack/Conquest Racing team. He finished an excellent fourth on his debut in St. Petersburg, although his early season was blighted by a constantly changing engineering team: Englishman Andy Miller (with whom he had worked successfully at PSR), Todd Malloy, John Ward and Andy Borme all took a turn in charge of his year-old Reynard. Happily, the environment soon became more settled and Haberfeld worked well with Borme, adding a string of promising results that included a fifth at Mazda Raceway Laguna Seca.

Haberfeld wasn't able to translate his practice form at Denver into anything better than eighth on the grid, but he was running well in sixth until being taken out by Dominguez on lap 70. Again, though, Haberfeld showed his speed by posting the fastest lap of the race and climbing back to tenth at the finish.

"I think we had a good race," Haberfeld summarized. "I think we've found our way and we'll be competitive in the next races."

Main photograph: **Once again, Servia was a pacesetter for Visteon Patrick Racing.**
Gavin Lawrence/LAT

Below: **Servia was happy with his third podium of the year – and fourth in all – but oh, how he would have loved that first win.**
Mike Levitt/LAT

## STILL SEARCHING

**O**RIOL Servia went into the Centrix Financial Grand Prix of Denver confident of being able to clinch a long-awaited first Champ Car victory. He had momentum on his side. Servia, whose best result prior to the 2003 campaign had been a third at Detroit in his rookie year, 2000, with Cal Wells' Precision Preparation, Inc. team, had netted a strong second at Milwaukee in June and achieved an impressive streak of seven consecutive top-six finishes before being involved in an early fracas at Vancouver. He was frustrated, too, in the next races at Road America and Mid-Ohio, but bounced back to lead a couple of laps at Montreal, where eventually he finished second to Michel Jourdain Jr. (who, coincidentally, also beat him to the checkered flag at Milwaukee).

"We'll see about the start," said Servia on Saturday evening, "but we need to be consistent and strong, and maybe we'll get that first win."

Servia certainly did everything he could to claim the advantage from polesitter Bruno Junqueira at the beginning of the race. Twice he jumped clear of the Brazilian in anticipation of the green flag, but each time – correctly – CART Starter J.D. Wilbur brandished the yellow instead. At the third attempt, Junqueira duly claimed the upper hand and led until the first round of pit stops, when a slight miscue by Newman/Haas Racing, allied to typically quick service from Don Oldenburg's Visteon/Patrick Racing team, enabled Servia to vault into the lead.

Unfortunately for the personable Catalan, the opposite occurred when it came to the second round of pit stops. This time, Servia was hindered slightly and Newman/Haas was perfect. The result? Junqueira was back in front, chased by teammate Sébastien Bourdais, and Servia was down in third, where, despite his best efforts, he remained until the finish.

"I thought we could win this race, but only one team can win and the Newman/Haas cars were very strong today," said Servia, magnanimously, after coming up just a little short in his 68th Champ Car start.

"I'm actually happier this weekend with third than last weekend in Montreal, where we could have won the race," continued Servia. "This week is different because Friday we struggled, Saturday was better and my guys had great stops today. I felt really good and thought this was our day, but on our second stop we had a slight problem with an airgun. I'm happy with the result and our second straight podium."

Right, below and bottom: A terrifying moment for Ryan Hunter-Reay, but sensational work by his crew saw the methanol fire doused with water and extinguished almost immediately.
Photographs: Dan Streck/LAT

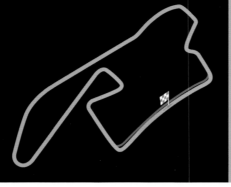

# CENTRIX FINANCIAL
# GRAND PRIX
# OF DENVER

## PEPSI CENTER, DENVER, COLORADO
### AUGUST 31, 106 laps of 1.647 miles – 174.582 miles

| Pl. | Driver (Nat.) | No. | Team Sponsors Engine/Car | Tires | Q Speed | Q Time | Q Pos. | Laps | Time/Status | Ave. (mph) | Pts. |
|---|---|---|---|---|---|---|---|---|---|---|---|
| 1 | Bruno Junqueira (BR) | 1 | Newman/Haas Racing PacifiCare Ford Cosworth/Lola B02/00 | BS | 96.507 | 1m 01.438s | 1 | 106 | 2h 03m 10.259s | 85.044 | 22 |
| 2 | *Sébastien Bourdais (F) | 2 | Newman/Haas Racing Lilly Ford Cosworth/Lola B2K/00 | BS | 96.336 | 1m 01.547s | 3 | 106 | 2h 03m 10.594s | 85.040 | 16 |
| 3 | Oriol Servia (E) | 20 | Patrick Racing Visteon Ford Cosworth/Lola B02/00 | BS | 96.446 | 1m 01.477s | 2 | 106 | 2h 03m 22.754s | 84.900 | 15 |
| 4 | Paul Tracy (CDN) | 3 | Forsythe Racing Player's/Indeck Ford Cosworth/Lola B02/00 | BS | 95.546 | 1m 02.056s | 9 | 106 | 2h 03m 23.577s | 84.891 | 12 |
| 5 | Adrian Fernandez (MEX) | 51 | Fernandez Tecate/Quaker State/Telmex Ford Cosworth/Lola B02/00 | BS | 96.280 | 1m 01.583s | 4 | 106 | 2h 03m 27.974s | 84.840 | 10 |
| 6 | Michel Jourdain Jr. (MEX) | 9 | Team Rahal Gigante Ford Cosworth/Lola B01/00 | BS | 95.415 | 1m 02.141s | 10 | 106 | 2h 03m 29.040s | 84.828 | 8 |
| 7 | Mario Dominguez (MEX) | 55 | Herdez Competition Ford Cosworth/Lola B03/00 | BS | 94.125 | 1m 02.993s | 14 | 106 | 2h 03m 29.522s | 84.823 | 6 |
| 8 | *Darren Manning (GB) | 15 | Walker Racing RAC/Autowindscreens Ford Cosworth/Reynard 02I | BS | 95.835 | 1m 01.869s | 7 | 106 | 2h 03m 35.849s | 84.750 | 5 |
| 9 | Alex Tagliani (CDN) | 33 | Rocketsports Racing Johnson Controls Ford Cosworth/Lola B02/00 | BS | 95.192 | 1m 02.287s | 11 | 106 | 2h 03m 37.175s | 84.735 | 4 |
| 10 | *Mario Haberfeld (BR) | 34 | Mi-Jack Conquest Racing Ford Cosworth/Reynard 02I | BS | 95.555 | 1m 02.050s | 8 | 106 | 2h 04m 00.958s | 84.464 | 3 |
| 11 | Jimmy Vasser (USA) | 12 | American Spirit Team Johansson Ford Cosworth/Reynard 01I | BS | 94.198 | 1m 02.944s | 13 | 106 | 2h 04m 05.492s | 84.413 | 2 |
| 12 | *Geoff Boss (USA) | 11 | Dale Coyne Racing Cross Pens Ford Cosworth/Lola B01/00 | BS | 92.365 | 1m 04.193s | 19 | 101 | Running | | 1 |
| 13 | *Tiago Monteiro (P) | 7 | Fittipaldi-Dingman Racing Ford Cosworth/Reynard 02I | BS | 96.210 | 1m 01.628s | 5 | 86 | Accident | | |
| 14 | *Mika Salo (SF) | 27 | PK Racing Ford Cosworth/Lola B02/00 | BS | 92.825 | 1m 03.875s | 17 | 84 | Accident | | |
| 15 | *Ryan Hunter-Reay (USA) | 31 | American Spirit Team Johansson Ford Cosworth/Reynard 02I | BS | 94.948 | 1m 02.447s | 12 | 80 | Fire | | |
| 16 | Roberto Moreno (BR) | 4 | Herdez Competition Ford Cosworth/Lola B2K/00 | BS | 93.705 | 1m 03.275s | 16 | 77 | Accident | | |
| 17 | Patrick Carpentier (CDN) | 32 | Forsythe Racing Player's/Indeck Ford Cosworth/Lola B02/00 | BS | 95.936 | 1m 01.804s | 6 | 61 | Accident | | |
| 18 | Gualter Salles (BR) | 19 | Dale Coyne Racing Alpina/Golden Cross Ford Cosworth/Lola B2K/00 | BS | 92.802 | 1m 03.891s | 18 | 33 | Driveshaft | | |
| 19 | *Rodolfo Lavin (MEX) | 5 | Walker Racing Corona Competition Ford Cosworth/Reynard 02I | BS | 93.867 | 1m 03.166s | 15 | 2 | Accident | | |

* denotes rookie driver

Caution flags: **Lap 1**, yellow start; **laps 3–5**, accident/Dominguez, Lavin & Moreno; **laps 61–64**, accident/Carpentier; **laps 78–83**, accident/Moreno & pit fire/Hunter-Reay. Total: **Four for 14 laps.**

Lap leaders: **Bruno Junqueira, 1–32 (32 laps)**; Oriol Servia, 33–62 (30 laps); Junqueira, 63–106 (44 laps). Totals: Junqueira, **76 laps**; Servia, **30 laps.**

Fastest race lap: **Mario Haberfeld, 1m 02.082s, 95.506 mph on lap 100.**

Championship positions: **1** Tracy, 204; **2** Junqueira, 186; **3** Jourdain Jr., 165; **4** Bourdais, 142; **5** Carpentier, 128; **6** Servia, 108; **7** Fernandez, 92; **8** Tagliani, 91; **9** Dominguez & Manning, 81; **11** Haberfeld, 60; **12** Moreno, 51; **13** Vasser, 46; **14** Hunter-Reay, 41; **15** Papis, 25; **16** Monteiro, 20; **17** Lavin, 12; **18** Lemarie, 8; **19** Camathias, 6; **20** Yoong, 4; **21** Salles, 3; **22** Herta, 2; **23** Boss, 1.

# DENVER SNIPPETS

• Opinions were divided on whether or not the switch to single-car QUALIFYING was a success. Relatively cool temperatures and a series of rain showers on Saturday meant that most drivers had difficulty in getting their Bridgestone Potenza radial racing tires up to optimal working temperature in just three laps on the short, 1.647-mile circuit – the surface of which was much smoother than for the inaugural event in 2002 – but one thing was certain: None of the drivers could complain about being held up by slower traffic!

• One of the leaders in the on-line sports betting and gaming industry, Sportsbook.com, was introduced in Denver as an associate SPONSOR for Darren Manning's RAC/Autowindscreens/Walker Racing Reynard. The Englishman promptly celebrated the announcement by posting the third-fastest time in provisional qualifying on Friday. Manning also established a new record of eight consecutive top-ten finishes by a rookie driver.

• After struggling more often than not to match the pace of the numerically dominant Lolas in 2003, the REYNARDS were competitive in Denver, with Mario Haberfeld fastest of all in practice (and in the race), Tiago Monteiro taking a personal-best fifth on the grid and Darren Manning also among the top three on the first day of qualifying. "I really can't quantify why the Reynards are successful thus far here," said the Briton. "Maybe it's the high altitude that's contributing to the overall lack of downforce, evening out the field."

• PK Racing made a further SWITCH to its driving strength at Denver, replacing Max Papis with another ex-Formula 1 driver, Mika Salo. The Finn (below) had tested the car at Mid-Ohio prior to the previous race at Montreal, impressing the team with his feedback and enthusiasm. Predictably, however, he struggled to come to terms with a car that lacked an automatic gearbox, traction control, launch control and myriad other driver aids common in Formula 1. Salo qualified a disappointing 17th, but ran as high as 11th before crashing out in the late stages. "I am enjoying myself a lot in Champ Cars," he said after qualifying. "It's a really nice atmosphere here."

• Ryan Hunter-Reay had crashed out of the Toyota Atlantic Championship race at Denver in 2002, and didn't fare much better when he returned to the Champ Cars with American Spirit Team Johansson. He qualified a respectable 12th, but never made any real progress in the race and eventually went out in spectacular style following a major FIRE during his final pit stop after 80 laps. "The Sparco [safety] equipment did a great job for me today," said the rookie gratefully. "I was in the car with everything around me on fire, including me, for about ten or

15 seconds and I have no burns anywhere, and neither does anyone on my crew."

• Fellow rookie Geoff Boss STRUGGLED once again to find a competitive speed in Dale Coyne Racing's #11 Cross Pens Ford Cosworth/Lola, but he kept out of trouble and took advantage of the high rate of attrition to earn his first championship point with a 12th-place finish.

• Patrick Carpentier had a weekend to forget. Both he and Player's teammate Paul Tracy experienced a variety of INCIDENTS in practice and qualifying, damaging at least four rear wings between them. Although Carpentier ran a solid fifth in the early stages, eventually he was caught out by locking brakes and crashed in Turn One.

• Montreal winner Michel Jourdain Jr.'s Gigante/Team Rahal Lola was never a factor in Denver. The Mexican qualified a DISAPPOINTING tenth (only once, at Laguna Seca, did he have a worse starting position), and he struggled in the race, too, although he did well to keep his nose clean and earn eight valuable points for a sixth-place finish. "It was a very long day and we did the best we could hope for," he said. "We lost a few points to Paul [Tracy] in the championship and that is unfortunate, but it could have been a lot worse."

Gavin Lawrence/LAT

BRIDGESTONE PRESENTS
THE CHAMP CAR WORLD SERIES POWERED BY FORD    ROUND 16

# MIAMI

**Above:** F1 convert Mika Salo rewarded PK Racing co-owner Kevin Kalkhoven's trust by taking third in just his second race.
Mike Levitt/LAT

**Above center:** Miami certainly provided a sensational setting for the Champ Cars.
Gavin Lawrence/LAT

## HERDEZ'S FINEST HOUR

**H**ERDEZ Competition scaled new heights of achievement with its 1-2 finish in Miami. The team had begun life as Bettenhausen Motorsports in 1986, but had morphed into its current guise following Tony B's tragic death in a light aircraft accident on Valentine's Day, 2000. The tight-knit but impecunious outfit went through many lean years, yet the partnership with Grupo Herdez, one of Mexico's leading food manufacturing and distribution companies, yielded some much-needed financial security. The team expanded to a two-car program for 2003 and procured the services of veteran Roberto Moreno to join sophomore Mario Dominguez. At last the pieces were in place for a speedy rise to prominence.

Sure enough, the Keith Wiggins-run organization embarked upon a breakthrough season, Dominguez, in particular, emerging as a true force to be reckoned with. Despite scooping Rookie of the Year honors, the Mexican had endured a difficult baptism in '02, but benefited immensely from the guiding hand of Moreno, who – as ever – proved to be the consummate team player.

"Roberto has become such a great teammate and friend," Dominguez said of his mentor. "It's been great having him here, because – I have to be honest with you – the team didn't believe me [last year] when I said the car wasn't working. Then Roberto came in and our opinions matched, so people opened their eyes and said, 'OK, we'd better work on it, develop it.'

"When we started to work this year, there was a whole different mindset within the team...the mindset of developing a car that hadn't been there in the past. We started to take the cars to some post-rig tests and that's made a big, big difference. We obviously have a disadvantage against Newman/Haas or Player's, [as] they've been doing that for many years. But we are on our way."

Moreno offered a generous assessment of his younger teammate's progress: "I think Mario has developed very quickly in just his consistency, because he could see what he was doing was right; he could compare it. His confidence has grown a lot this year and he's shown great pace all season. I've seen some of the best overtaking in a long time in the last few races, and it came from Mario."

## QUALIFYING

**As in Denver, a Formula 1-style single-car qualifying format was employed at the tight Miami street circuit to ensure that slower traffic would not prejudice the outcome. In Friday's provisional session, Bruno Junqueira picked up where he had left off in Colorado a month earlier, blitzing the field by 0.662s – a remarkable margin considering that the revamped Bayfront Park layout measured little over a mile in length.**

**The Newman/Haas star would have cause to be thankful for that performance come final qualifying on Saturday, when he crashed heavily in the tricky fountain complex on his last hot lap, tearing off the right front corner of his PacifiCare Lola and damaging the monocoque. Fortunately, the car was repairable, and (per CART qualifying rules) Junqueira's Friday effort assured him of a front-row starting berth.**

**"I didn't really push on the first two laps and I knew I had to push a little more on the last lap," he explained sheepishly. "Maybe I pushed too hard…"**

**The man who walked the tightrope of adhesion to best effect was Adrian Fernandez, upstaging the fancied runners to secure the fourth pole of his career and the third since founding his eponymous team in 2001. The Mexican had endured an often trying 2003 season, and attributed his recent upturn in form to a new-found stability and focus within the team's engineering department since Chris Finch took over the reins prior to the Mid-Ohio event.**

**"We've taken a much simpler approach since a few races ago and everything is working much better," commented Fernandez. "The results are coming; maybe the consistency is still not there, but I think we're getting more competitive at every race."**

**Fernandez's polewinning lap bettered Oriol Servia's benchmark by a scant 0.036s. With Junqueira already having reserved the other front-row slot, that wafer-thin margin represented the difference between first and third on the grid. Sébastien Bourdais lined up fourth in the second Newman/Haas entry, while Paul Tracy was relieved to start fifth after a veritable comedy of errors had blighted his weekend's endeavor. Perhaps the most embarrassing miscue came during provisional qualifying, when he completed only two of his three allotted flying laps after misunderstanding the countdown over the radio from his Player's/Forsythe team…**

ON a typically sultry afternoon in South Florida, Mario Dominguez finally laid to rest the ghosts that had been circling since his Pyrrhic victory at Surfers Paradise the previous fall. On that occasion, appalling weather conditions had reduced the race to a soggy procession, and it was only the fortuitous – and controversial – timing of the eventual red flag that had given a surprised Dominguez his maiden Champ Car success. Eleven months later, at the Grand Prix Americas in downtown Miami, the ever-improving Mexican needed much less in the way of outside assistance. Instead he relied on a well-judged blend of speed and patience – as well as, to be sure, a sliver of good fortune – to lead Roberto Moreno home in a glorious 1-2 sweep for the Herdez Competition team.

"It just feels amazing, I tell you," said a jubilant Dominguez. "It's a historic moment and a great result for our team. Just crossing the finish line knowing that Roberto and I went 1-2…I can't describe that to you."

"Not too shabby for an old guy!" joked the young-at-heart 44-year-old Moreno, who derived as much satisfaction from his performance as did Dominguez from his win. "I was patient, set a steady pace and here I am, on the podium."

The Bayfront Park street course had been reconfigured since

Jourdain Jr. held an increasingly lonely sixth ahead of a squabbling trio comprising Moreno, Alex Tagliani and Dominguez.

By lap 31, Fernandez had caught a group of tail-enders disputing 15th place. New boy Mika Salo courteously moved aside and allowed the leaders easy passage, but Rodolfo Lavin and Patrick Carpentier were engaged in a frantic dice, and it took Fernandez several laps to dispatch them. The delay temporarily caused the top five cars to bunch up, but the net beneficiary of the traffic was sixth-placed Jourdain, who erased the substantial deficit to Bourdais in one fell swoop.

So far, the 19-strong field had been remarkably well behaved, but the rot began to set in on lap 39 when Geoff Boss spun and stalled his Dale Coyne Racing Lola at Turn One. The ensuing full-course caution ushered in the first spate of scheduled pit stops. The most significant shuffle, as it would turn out, involved the Herdez twins. Moreno's crew lost vital seconds trying to extract a balky fuel nozzle from the #4 car, while Daryl Fox's boys serviced Dominguez in double-quick time and gained him another position at the expense of Tagliani's Rocketsports entry.

No sooner was the restart under way than it had to be aborted, after Servia caromed into the wall coming onto the pit straight-away and comprehensively put paid to his Visteon Lola. The Spaniard was caught out by the combination of cold tires and a notorious bump in the middle of the Turn 13/14 chicane – dubbed a "ski jump" by Salo – which had been ground down by track workers over the weekend but still routinely launched cars into the air at 100 mph.

There followed a relatively uneventful stint of green-flag racing that saw the front-runners circulating in close company. Then,

**Left: Wheel-to-wheel action featuring Dominguez and Tagliani in Turn One.**
Gavin Lawrence/LAT

**Below: Moreno backed up his young teammate superbly by claiming second.**
Mike Levitt/LAT

**Bottom: He wasn't especially quick, but Salo kept out of trouble and brought PK Racing a long-overdue first podium finish.**
Gavin Lawrence/LAT

the previous year's race, eliminating the hated parking-lot section that had afforded zero grip and reducing the track length by a few hundred yards, to just 1.15 miles. But the essential character of the circuit was unchanged: bumpy, narrow and unforgiving. And as if 135 mistake-free laps of the writhing concrete canyon didn't pose enough of a challenge, raceday brought sweltering 90-degree heat and soaking humidity into the bargain.

Fears that there might be a distinct dearth of overtaking initially proved unfounded. Bruno Junqueira outdragged polesitter Adrian Fernandez to steal the lead into the first corner, while Sébastien Bourdais tried in vain to go the long way around Oriol Servia, allowing Paul Tracy to slip by into fourth place. The suspicion that Junqueira's getaway may have been a little *too* eager was swiftly rendered a moot point at the start of the second lap, when Fernandez redressed the balance with a superbly authoritative last-of-the-late-brakers maneuver into Turn One.

Junqueira lurked around 1.5 seconds in arrears through most of the first 30 laps, while Servia gradually lost touch with the lead pair. The Patrick Racing driver looked reasonably secure in third place, however, since Tracy had his hands full fending off Bourdais, who had signaled his pace with an early fastest lap before latching on to the gearbox of the Player's/Forsythe Lola. Michel

## SLIM PICKINGS FOR TITLE HOPEFULS

A ROUGH 'n tumble Grand Prix Americas saw all three main championship contenders score spectacular own-goals. Points leader Paul Tracy was the first to err, knocking himself and Sébastien Bourdais out of the race with a clumsy overtaking attempt just after half-distance. An irate Bourdais promptly made a beeline for Tracy's pit, but any confrontation was headed off at the pass by a CART official and several Player's/Forsythe crew members.

"I tried five times to pass Paul [before eventually succeeding] and he moved over on me every time," the Frenchman said later. "It is something that can be avoided. We are friends and we respect each other, but this was a stupid thing to happen."

To his credit, Tracy freely accepted responsibility for the collision, adding, "I am very fortunate to leave here with my points lead still intact."

Bruno Junqueira squandered a golden opportunity to make hay by locking up his brakes and sliding into race leader Adrian Fernandez when he had an easy second place in the bag. That would have moved him into a virtual dead heat with Tracy in the overall standings; as it was, he trailed home ninth and left Miami 13 points in arrears.

Thus a grateful Michel Jourdain Jr. inherited the lead, and was poised to move into the thick of the points battle when he was penalized for a pit-lane incident in which he had snagged one of Mario Haberfeld's tires and side-swiped Tiago Monteiro's Fittipaldi-Dingman Reynard. The ruling consigned Jourdain to a seventh-place finish and the status of a rank outsider in the title chase with only three rounds remaining.

"Today we were victims of circumstance," claimed a deeply disappointed Jourdain. "From my point of view, we did everything we could to avoid contact."

Team owner Bobby Rahal was equally aggrieved. "I find it difficult to comprehend why the officials would want to interject themselves into the championship," he said. "It should be decided on the track, not in some room. What I find particularly galling is the fact that these pits are at best inappropriate for an event of this stature. To allow such marginal confines to have a potentially devastating effect on a championship is, quite frankly, beyond me."

having spent 68 laps shadowing Tracy's every move, Bourdais broke the stalemate by executing a clean pass under braking for Turn One. He ran a mite wide on the exit of the corner, prompting Tracy to counterattack into Turn Two. The Canadian was nowhere near alongside his Newman/Haas rival at the turn-in point, however, and punted Bourdais unceremoniously into the tire barrier. The impact smashed the McDonald's/Lilly Lola's rear wing and broke the mounting points, ensuring that Bourdais would play no further part in the proceedings. Suffice it to say that the French rookie was not impressed. Tracy, meanwhile, limped back to the pits, where it was found that he had tweaked a suspension wishbone, forcing him to call it a day too.

"It was my fault," confessed Tracy later. "Bourdais made a pass and I tried to get it back right away, but I wasn't close enough."

Tracy's *faux pas* played perfectly into the hands of fellow title protagonists Junqueira and Jourdain (who now lay second and third, respectively) – or so it seemed. But this was a race from which few of the favorites would emerge without a large dollop of egg on their faces. The second and final round of pit stops on lap 90 proved Jourdain's undoing.

Upon the completion of routine service, chief mechanic Greg Cates duly waved the Team Rahal driver out of his pit box – whereupon Jourdain found an inbound Tiago Monteiro on his left and a spare tire, awaiting Mario Haberfeld's arrival in the adjacent Mi-Jack/Conquest Racing pit stall, blocking his path on the right. He tried to thread the needle, but in the cramped Miami pit lane there was no space, and he inadvertently clouted both Monteiro's Fittipaldi-Dingman Reynard and Haberfeld's tire. Jourdain's Gigante Lola survived unscathed, but the incident hadn't escaped the attention of the officials…

Moments later, the script took an even more dramatic twist when Junqueira made an elementary error of judgment and slammed into the back of Fernandez as the leader attempted to lap the hapless Monteiro at Turn Six. All three cars spun to a halt, engines dead – although Fernandez and Junqueira eventually were able to rejoin the fray after being tow-started under the subsequent full-course yellow.

"It was my mistake," acknowledged a contrite Junqueira. "I was on cold tires and I knew I had about five laps to pass him. I tried to follow him [past Monteiro] because I didn't want Tiago to close the door, but I lost traction and hit Adrian."

"It was just a bad mistake on Bruno's part," agreed a philosophical Fernandez, who had turned in a flawless performance only to be cruelly denied a probable second victory as an owner/driver.

Junqueira's blunder appeared to leave Jourdain sitting pretty, but the latter's pit-lane indiscretion came back to haunt him during the next caution period, triggered when fourth-placed Tagliani was rear-ended by backmarker Alex Sperafico at Turn Six. The stewards instructed Jourdain to drop to the tail of the restart line, relegating the disgruntled Mexican to eighth place.

Thus an out-of-sequence Darren Manning headed the field when the green flags fluttered again on lap 107, but he had another mandatory pit visit still to make. In any case, the Englishman was struggling for pace after clipping the wall earlier in the race, and could offer no more than token resistance when Dominguez moved in for the kill one lap later. Moreno – who had lost a spot to Jimmy Vasser by pitting a lap early at the second stops, only to recover it with a bold move at the lap-100 restart – wasted no time in following suit.

Manning's Walker Racing Reynard was promptly engulfed by the chasing pack, which was led now by none other than Salo. The Finn had used astute pit strategy to regain his lost lap, before taking advantage of a minor skirmish between Vasser and Haberfeld in the wake of Moreno's pass to leapfrog both Reynards. All of a sudden he was staring down the barrel of a first-ever podium finish for the fledgling PK Racing team in only his second Champ Car outing.

"The team did a good job for me," said Salo afterward. "They did all of the talking and planning. We pitted under the yellows and got the lap back. I just kept my nose clean today… I can't believe we wound up third!"

Salo's patience had indeed paid unexpected dividends. But, as Dominguez and Moreno could attest, the secret of success in Miami's grueling two-hour-long street fight had been to temper valor with a large measure of discretion.

*Alex Sabine*

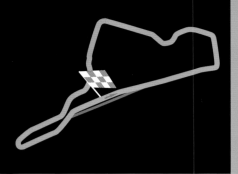

# GRAND PRIX AMERICAS
## PRESENTED BY SPORTSBOOK.COM

**ROUND 16**

**MIAMI BAYFRONT STREET CIRCUIT, MIAMI, FLORIDA**

**SEPTEMBER 28, 135 laps of 1.150 miles – 155.250 miles**

| Pl. | Driver (Nat.) | No. | Team Sponsors Engine/Car | Tires | Q Speed | Q Time | Q Pos. | Laps | Time/Status | Ave. (mph) | Pts. |
|---|---|---|---|---|---|---|---|---|---|---|---|
| 1 | Mario Dominguez (MEX) | 55 | Herdez Competition Ford Cosworth/Lola B03/00 | BS | 91.680 | 45.157s | 8 | 135 | 2h 03m 19.401s | 75.533 | 20 |
| 2 | Roberto Moreno (BR) | 4 | Herdez Competition Ford Cosworth/Lola B01/00 | BS | 91.715 | 45.140s | 7 | 135 | 2h 03m 24.642s | 75.480 | 16 |
| 3 | *Mika Salo (SF) | 27 | PK Racing Ford Cosworth/Lola B02/00 | BS | 90.619 | 45.686s | 15 | 135 | 2h 03m 27.389s | 75.452 | 14 |
| 4 | Jimmy Vasser (USA) | 12 | American Spirit Team Johansson Ford Cosworth/Reynard 01I | BS | 91.230 | 45.380s | 11 | 135 | 2h 03m 28.609s | 75.439 | 12 |
| 5 | *Mario Haberfeld (BR) | 34 | Mi-Jack Conquest Racing Ford Cosworth/Reynard 02I | BS | 91.107 | 45.441s | 13 | 135 | 2h 03m 28.884s | 75.436 | 10 |
| 6 | Patrick Carpentier (CDN) | 32 | Forsythe Racing Player's/Indeck Ford Cosworth/Lola B03/00 | BS | 88.528 | 46.765s | 18 | 135 | 2h 03m 29.658s | 75.429 | 8 |
| 7 | Michel Jourdain Jr. (MEX) | 9 | Team Rahal Gigante Ford Cosworth/Lola B01/00 | BS | 92.125 | 44.939s | 6 | 135 | 2h 03m 38.575s | 75.338 | 6 |
| 8 | Adrian Fernandez (MEX) | 51 | Fernandez Tecate/Quaker State/Telmex Ford Cosworth/Lola B02/00 | BS | 93.553 | 44.253s | 1 | 134 | Running | | 7 |
| 9 | Bruno Junqueira (BR) | 1 | Newman/Haas Racing PacifiCare Ford Cosworth/Lola B02/00 | BS | 91.951 | 45.024s | 2 | 131 | Running | | 5 |
| 10 | *Geoff Boss (USA) | 11 | Dale Coyne Racing Cross Pens Ford Cosworth/Lola B01/00 | BS | 89.136 | 46.446s | 17 | 129 | Running | | 3 |
| 11 | *Darren Manning (GB) | 15 | Walker Racing RAC/Sportsbook.com Ford Cosworth/Reynard 02I | BS | 91.129 | 45.430s | 12 | 123 | Gearbox | | 2 |
| 12 | *Ryan Hunter-Reay (USA) | 31 | American Spirit Team Johansson Ford Cosworth/Reynard 02I | BS | 90.686 | 45.652s | 14 | 114 | Accident | | 1 |
| 13 | Alex Tagliani (CDN) | 33 | Rocketsports Racing Johnson Controls Ford Cosworth/Lola B02/00 | BS | 91.246 | 45.372s | 10 | 101 | Accident | | |
| 14 | *Alex Sperafico (BR) | 19 | Dale Coyne Racing Ford Cosworth/Lola B2K/00 | BS | 84.713 | 48.871s | 19 | 98 | Accident | | |
| 15 | *Tiago Monteiro (P) | 7 | Fittipaldi-Dingman Racing Ford Cosworth/Reynard 02I | BS | 91.354 | 45.318s | 9 | 91 | Accident | | |
| 16 | Paul Tracy (CDN) | 3 | Forsythe Racing Player's/Indeck Ford Cosworth/Lola B02/00 | BS | 92.477 | 44.768s | 5 | 69 | Accident | | |
| 17 | *Sébastien Bourdais (F) | 2 | Newman/Haas Racing McDonald's/Lilly Ford Cosworth/Lola B2K/00 | BS | 92.806 | 44.609s | 4 | 69 | Accident | | |
| 18 | *Rodolfo Lavin (MEX) | 5 | Walker Racing Corona Competition Ford Cosworth/Reynard 02I | BS | 89.380 | 46.319s | 16 | 56 | Accident | | |
| 19 | Oriol Servia (E) | 20 | Patrick Racing Visteon Ford Cosworth/Lola B02/00 | BS | 93.477 | 44.289s | 3 | 43 | Accident | | |

\* denotes rookie driver

**Caution flags: Laps 39–43**, tow/Boss; **laps 44–52**, accident/Servia; **laps 68–72**, accident/Tracy & Bourdais; **laps 93–99**, accident/Junqueira, Fernandez & Monteiro; **laps 100–105**, accident/Sperafico; **laps 118–121**, accident/Hunter-Reay. Total: **Six for 36 laps.**

**Lap leaders: Bruno Junqueira, 1** (1 lap); **Adrian Fernandez, 2–89** (88 laps); **Mika Salo, 90–95** (6 laps); **Michel Jourdain Jr., 96–103** (8 laps); **Darren Manning, 104–107** (4 laps); **Mario Dominguez, 108–135** (28 laps). Totals: **Fernandez**, 88 laps; **Dominguez**, 28 laps; **Jourdain**, 8 laps; **Salo**, 6 laps; **Manning**, 4 laps; **Junqueira**, 1 lap.

**Fastest race lap: Adrian Fernandez, 45.010s,** 91.980 mph on lap 89 (establishes record).

**Championship positions: 1 Tracy, 204; 2 Junqueira, 191; 3 Jourdain Jr., 171; 4 Bourdais, 142; 5 Carpentier, 136; 6 Servia, 108; 7 Dominguez, 101; 8 Fernandez, 99; 9 Tagliani, 91; 10 Manning, 83; 11 Haberfeld, 70; 12 Moreno, 67; 13 Vasser, 58; 14 Hunter-Reay, 42; 15 Papis, 25; 16 Monteiro, 20; 17 Salo, 14; 18 Lavin, 12; 19 Lemarie, 8; 20 Camathias, 6; 21 Yoong, 4; 22 Boss, 4; 23 Salles, 3; 24 Herta, 2.**

# MIAMI SNIPPETS

Mark Elias/LAT

• For the second year running, Champ Cars shared the BILLING with the American Le Mans Series, while Toyota Atlantic and Trans-Am events ensured a strong support race program for the sizeable crowd (announced as 75,000 over the three-day meeting). The "Blast by the Bay" also featured numerous sideshows to keep the fans entertained away from the track, including Kid Rock (above) and Elton John concerts in the adjacent American Airlines Arena. The concerts showcased the much-discussed MotoRock concept – aiming to "synergize cars, stars and guitars" – advocated by Open Wheel Racing Series, the consortium looking to buy CART.

• CART released a preliminary list of events expected to form the basis of its 2004 CALENDAR on Sunday. Although no dates were specified, 15 events were listed as "confirmed," with another six described as "under consideration." Among the former was a new race in Las Vegas, while the unconfirmed category included an opaque reference to "East Asia," which the paddock rumor mill reckoned to be a street circuit in Seoul, South Korea. Both were potentially exciting new ventures – although, worryingly for purists, three of America's traditional road courses (Laguna Seca, Mid-Ohio and Portland) were omitted from the list of confirmed venues.

• Highly esteemed former Williams and McLaren Formula 1 ENGINEER David Brown joined American Spirit Team Johansson in time for Miami to oversee Ryan Hunter-Reay's car. Brown, who had recently worked on the Panther Racing IRL team, thereby became the rookie's third different race engineer (following in the footsteps of Graham Taylor and Paul Burgess).

• Mika Salo took an ADVENTUROUS route to second on Friday's grid. After his original qualifying run was interrupted when Darren Manning spun on his warmup lap, Salo was sent out for a second attempt at the end of the session, whereupon the officials mistakenly called him in after a single flying

lap. Therefore he was granted a third run – and made the most of his opportunity by posting a 0.8s improvement. "For sure, the extra track time helped a lot," admitted the F1 refugee.

• The Arts & Entertainment TV network gave the green light to a DOCUMENTARY of Mario Andretti for its award-winning "Biography" series. Andretti would be the first racing driver and one of very few sportsmen to be profiled, joining such iconic figures as Babe Ruth and Muhammad Ali. According to producer Adam Friedman, the underlying theme of the piece would be Andretti's rise from humble beginnings to sporting legend. The episode, tentatively scheduled to air in February 2004, would be narrated by Paul Newman, with veteran motorsports journalist Gordon Kirby acting as a consultant on the project.

• Quote of the weekend came from Adrian Fernandez, who had the last word in some good-natured REPARTEE with Oriol Servia and Bruno Junqueira during Saturday's post-qualifying press conference. Miami residents Servia and Junqueira traded theories as to whether training early in the morning or in the heat of the day was better preparation for Sunday's exigencies. Polesitter Fernandez chimed in with the perfect riposte: "These guys talk about training, but I went to see Kid Rock last night and I was out until midnight. That seemed to

work pretty well for me, so I'm planning to go to the Elton John show tonight!"

• The Grand Prix Americas marked the LAST OCCASION on which the Player's/Forsythe Lolas bore the distinctive Player's logo, owing to Canadian tobacco legislation set to take effect on October 1. The stalwart sponsor pulled out all the stops to ensure a fitting finale, announcing the launch of a website, lastlap.ca, on which fans could register their names and greetings. Up to 1,200 names would adorn the cars' otherwise naked bodywork during the season-closing races.

Gavin Lawrence/LAT

**Main photograph:** Paul Tracy certainly
excelled in Mexico City, where a dominant
performance enabled him to open up an
appreciable gap over Bruno Junqueira in the
title chase.

**Inset:** The crowd was simply massive, and
the fans were massively enthusiastic.
Photographs: Gavin Lawrence/LAT

BRIDGESTONE PRESENTS
THE CHAMP CAR WORLD SERIES POWERED BY FORD · ROUND 17

# MEXICO CITY

**Right:** Local driver Roberto Gonzalez was invited to run Roberto Moreno's usual car.

**Far right:** For the second year running, Luis Diaz looked good, only to succumb to mechanical problems in the early stages.
Photographs: Gavin Lawrence/LAT

## QUALIFYING

After scrabbling around the tight confines of Denver and Miami, the Champ Car combatants embraced the wide-open challenge of Mexico City's Autódromo Hermanos Rodriguez with a palpable sense of exhilaration. The highlight of the 2.786-mile lap from the standpoints of spectacle and driver satisfaction is undoubtedly the Esses, a sequence of eight interlinked bends entered at 50 mph and left at over 150 mph. A never-ending tightrope act of balanced throttle and settling brakes, this section (aptly nicknamed "The Snake") is further enlivened by some nasty bumps, which are liable to pitch cars into the "kitty litter" if they stray more than a few inches from the preferred racing line. The consensus following the first day's running was that these ripples were considerably more severe than in 2002.

Paul Tracy set the pace in provisional qualifying, circulating in 1m 28.842s to nab a bonus championship point and a guaranteed place on the front row. That was enough to pip Bruno Junqueira by 0.063s, and a fascinating needle match between the title protagonists looked in prospect.

Upon the resumption of hostilities on Saturday, however, both were unexpectedly upstaged by Tiago Monteiro, who spearheaded the strongest Reynard challenge of the season in his Fittipaldi-Dingman entry. Hot on his heels were fellow rookies Ryan Hunter-Reay and Darren Manning in (respectively) the American Spirit Team Johansson and Walker Racing examples. During Friday morning's practice, Manning had clocked a lap of 1m 28.517s, which would stand as comfortably the quickest tour of the weekend. Had he been able to reproduce that time in either of the official sessions, the Englishman would have been a shoe-in for the pole.

There, however, lay the rub. Track conditions were more slippery in the heat of the afternoon, while on Saturday there was the added complication that the surface had been washed clean of rubber by a morning shower.

The upshot was that no one seriously threatened Tracy's Friday benchmark. Monteiro came up exactly two-tenths of a second short, but dislodged Junqueira from a front-row starting berth by virtue of topping the order in final qualifying. The Brazilian would be flanked on the second row by Newman/Haas teammate Sébastien Bourdais, who leapfrogged Hunter-Reay and Manning on the strength of his Friday effort.

AFTER dropping the ball spectacularly in Miami, only to be let off the hook by a corresponding indiscretion from archrival Bruno Junqueira, Paul Tracy took a giant, potentially decisive, stride toward an elusive maiden CART title at the Gran Premio Telmex/Gigante in Mexico City. Pole position and a hardearned but emphatic victory ensured that Tracy racked up a nearperfect tally of 22 points for his weekend's endeavor. Meanwhile, the unfortunate Junqueira had fallen victim to food poisoning and could muster only a plucky seventh-place finish.

"It's great to bounce back like this," declared Tracy. "After Miami, we sat down, had a couple of meetings and really thought about what we had to do here. We brought our best stuff along and the car was good right away. The momentum has been going Bruno's way in the past five races; this will help us build some momentum of our own at just the right time."

Even by the record-breaking standards of the inaugural Mexico City event in 2002, the crowd that descended on the fabled Autódromo Hermanos Rodriguez on raceday had to be seen to be believed. According to promoter GRAND, no fewer than 221,011 fans were on hand, up by nearly 50,000 compared to 2002. The three-day attendance figure of 402,413 comfortably surpassed anything in the history of Champ Car racing, aside from the Indianapolis 500, and ensured an electric atmosphere by the three o'clock start on Sunday afternoon.

Thus it was something of an anti-climax when the first attempt to get the proceedings under way was waved off due to poor alignment. The starter was satisfied at the next time of asking, however, and the first three or four rows seemed to compress as they fanned out across the 60-foot expanse of track on the long drag to Turn One. Tracy immediately found himself under attack from Junqueira – upset stomach or not – but held off his brakes a fraction longer and successfully defended his lead.

For the second year running, that inviting straightaway funneling into a tight chicane-type complex proved a recipe for some entertaining antics – although Darren Manning probably wouldn't see it that way. The Englishman made a cracking getaway from sixth on the grid and had drawn alongside surprise front-row starter Tiago Monteiro when the latter nudged him into a spin that relegated him to the tail end of the order.

Almost simultaneously, Jimmy Vasser performed a similar pirouette all by himself, stalling the engine and needing a towstart from the Simple Green Safety Team. Of greater concern to the locals was the fact that Michel Jourdain Jr. lost a half-dozen places while taking avoiding action on the grass. The dean of the Mexican drivers, Adrian Fernandez, also went for a cross-country jaunt, setting the tone for an uncharacteristically wayward performance that later would see him bundle Oriol Servia out of contention en route to an eventual eighth place.

A brief full-course yellow afforded the opportunity to draw breath and take stock of the revised leaderboard. The top ten now comprised Tracy, Junqueira, Sébastien Bourdais, Monteiro, Ryan Hunter-Reay, Patrick Carpentier, Mario Dominguez, Mika Salo, impressive novice Luis Diaz and Alex Tagliani.

Tracy bolted away at the restart and was leading by the metaphorical country mile when he sped past the main grandstands a minute-and-a-half later. He reeled off a succession of searing laps to establish a 4.5-second advantage by the tenth circuit, then was content to pad his cushion at a more gradual rate before triggering the first round of pit stops on lap 19.

Slick work by the PF Racing (née Player's/Forsythe) crew further aided Tracy's cause, and by lap 21 he was more than eight seconds to the good. Junqueira continued to give valiant chase through the race's second stint and started to match Tracy's lap times, but was unable to make any real headway. Junqueira's teammate, Bourdais, followed at a respectful distance, while no one else was remotely in touch.

All the same, Monteiro was doing a sterling job in fourth place aboard his Fittipaldi-Dingman Reynard, showing a clean pair of heels to man-of-the-moment Dominguez. The Miami victor had passed Carpentier for sixth in the early going before gaining another spot at the expense of Hunter-Reay at the pit-stop exchange. Salo, meanwhile, had leapfrogged both RH-R and Carpentier courtesy of outstanding service from PK Racing, and began to turn up

the heat on Dominguez as the second bout of stops beckoned.

It was at this juncture that what had been threatening to become a rather processional race suddenly came to life. First the Newman/Haas pair swapped positions when Junqueira lost precious seconds with clutch-creep exiting his pit bay. Bourdais immediately put the hammer down, leaving his teammate for dead and chiseling three seconds off Tracy's lead in as many laps. Maybe we had a race on our hands after all...

"My team radioed me and said Sébastien was going really quick," related Tracy afterward. "But I was still a long way ahead."

That state of affairs changed dramatically on lap 41, when Vasser outbraked himself at Turn One (again) and took Tagliani off with him. Out came the pace car, bunching up the field and halving Bourdais's task at a stroke. The Frenchman, though, reckoned it was a mixed blessing.

"It closed the gap to Tracy, obviously," he allowed, "but the tires went from cold to hot back to cold again in a short period of time. It killed the performance advantage we had, and after the restart it was really, really difficult to pass Paul."

For the balance of the afternoon, Tracy had the newly-liveried #2 Cialis-sponsored Lola snapping at his heels, but he would reveal no hint of a chink in his armor. On each lap, he made sure that he put the power down sufficiently early out of the tight final corner (still called the Peraltada after the daunting high-speed sweeper of fond memory) to keep Bourdais just out of overtaking range and dissuade him from trying his luck into Turn One. It wasn't until the last handful of laps that Tracy enjoyed any respite, whereupon he duly stroked it home to win by 1.782 seconds.

The checkered flag couldn't come soon enough as far as Junqueira was concerned. The Brazilian's reserves of morale, as well as energy, had been sapped by the tardy second pit stop, and he promptly began a free fall down the lap chart. Monteiro was the first to pounce, winning an entertaining side-by-side dice through the first couple of corners on the lap-46 restart.

A more conventional outbraking maneuver did the trick for Dominguez nine tours later, sending the partisan crowd into raptures. The Herdez Competition team had shrewdly opted for a lowdownforce setup to facilitate Dominguez's progress from 11th on the grid, giving him prodigious top-end speed with which to slingshot past rivals on the kilometer-long main straightaway.

"We knew that was the only place to get past people," explained Dominguez. "We were very fast there, not so fast in the Esses [as a result], but it was important to be fast where you can overtake. It was a bit of a gamble, but it paid off."

Indeed, Dominguez's charging drive ultimately would be rewarded with a place on the podium, as he was the beneficiary of a delay suffered by Monteiro amid the final flurry of pit-lane activity on lap 57. The Portuguese driver at least fared better than fellow rookie Hunter-Reay, who had been lying sixth but stalled leaving the American Spirit Team Johansson pit and disappeared from the radar screen.

"Everyone has had problems with stalling in the pits all weekend [due to the reduced throttle response experienced at Mexico City's high altitude]," shrugged a crestfallen Hunter-Reay, whose late-race pace was indicated by a fastest lap some 0.491s fleeter than anyone else managed all day.

Into the breach stepped none other than Jourdain, who had recovered well from his opening-lap travails to slot in behind countryman Dominguez. The successful damage-limitation exercise owed much to canny strategy from Team Rahal, which moved its charge out of sequence with the front-runners on his final two pit visits, handing him a clear track on which to make up ground while the midfield dogfight raged.

Salo provided the lion's share of the action in the waning stages, capitalizing on a mistake by the ailing Junqueira at Turn One on lap 62, before breezing past Monteiro at the same location two laps later to secure his second consecutive top-five finish.

For the seventh time in the season, however, the big picture was all about Tracy. The Canadian's flawless display under pressure had brought the Vanderbilt Cup tantalizingly within his grasp as the battle-weary Champ Car contingent limbered up for the long flight to Australia.

*Alex Sabine*

**Far left:** For Mario Dominguez, third in his hometown was almost as good as a win.
Phil Abbott/LAT

**Left:** Patrick Carpentier climbs aboard his PF Racing Lola, newly festooned with the names of hundreds of diehard fans.
Gavin Lawrence/LAT

**Below:** Jim Swintal greets Paul Tracy with an impressive flourish at the finish line.
Dan Boyd/LAT

**Bottom:** Sébastien Bourdais gave another workmanlike performance, taking second.
Gavin Lawrence/LAT

## REYNARDS TO THE FORE

ONE of the talking points of the weekend was the impressive performance of the much-maligned Reynard chassis. The conventional wisdom throughout the season had been that the 02I was no match for the more intensively developed Lola B02/00, yet in Mexico on Saturday a phalanx of Reynards put the horde of Lolas firmly in the shade. The tables were turned come Sunday afternoon, but the 02I undoubtedly exhibited a new level of competitiveness south of the border – witness Ryan Hunter-Reay's stunning fastest lap on raceday, and the fact that Darren Manning paced the field for much of Friday. As it was, four of the top seven starting positions were filled by Reynards.

Tiago Monteiro (pictured leading Hunter-Reay), the marque's standard-bearer in final qualifying, was at a loss to explain the sudden upturn in form. "Honestly I have no idea," he confessed. "There are a few elements of this track that help the Reynard, like the long straightaway [since the 02I was believed to produce less drag than the Lola]. But usually when it's bumpy like it is here and we have to raise the car, it costs us a lot more downforce…"

Hunter-Reay was similarly nonplussed, but suggested that the inexperience of the teams campaigning Reynards (all of whom, bar Walker Racing, were new to CART in 2003) may have exaggerated the real performance disadvantage of the chassis earlier in the year. "I think the Reynard teams are getting a better handle on their cars now, that's part of it," he ventured.

The Reynard, being widely regarded as more sensitive to ride-height changes and less at home on bumpy circuits, might have been expected to struggle over the furrowed surface of the Autódromo Hermanos Rodriguez. One factor, however, appeared to work clearly in its favor: Mexico City's thin air at 7,500 feet above sea level. Judging by the near-parity of the two chassis at Denver, the series' other high-altitude venue – where Monteiro and Mario Haberfeld both showed strongly – the Reynard suffered less than its rival from starvation of downforce in the rarefied atmosphere. Of course, as any good scientist knows, correlation doesn't prove causation, but the black art of aerodynamics seemed to offer the most plausible explanation for the welcome Reynard renaissance.

Phil Abbott/LAT

## MONTEIRO TURNS HEADS

ROOKIE Tiago Monteiro and the first-year Fittipaldi-Dingman Racing team enjoyed a morale-boosting outing in Mexico. In one sense, sixth place was a disappointing outcome, as a podium had looked to be on the cards until a fumbled wheel nut on the final pit stop cost Monteiro two spots, whereupon he fell into the clutches of a charging Mika Salo. But Monteiro understandably preferred to accentuate the positives after running in exalted company all weekend.

"I think it's great when you're disappointed with a sixth-place finish," he remarked. "This is our best result so far and we're on the way to even better things."

Topping the timing charts in Saturday's qualifying session was a real feather in the cap for the Portuguese driver, although his inexperience told at the start when he was outgunned by the Newman/Haas pair. There was nothing wrong with the racecraft he displayed in his mid-race mano a mano tussle with Bruno Junqueira, however, and afterward team co-owner Emerson Fittipaldi showered plaudits on his young protégé.

"Tiago's performance today was outstanding," beamed a proud Emmo. "His overtaking move on Bruno showed the maturity he has gained over the course of this year."

A veteran of French Formula 3, Monteiro had graduated to F3000 in 2002 with the crack Super Nova squad, but he was comprehensively overshadowed by title-winning teammate Sébastien Bourdais. A character-building maiden Champ Car campaign hitherto had yielded more heartache than success for Monteiro. He landed the Fittipaldi-Dingman seat at the 11th hour and had only a shakedown test under his belt prior to the season-opener at St. Petersburg, in which he finished a creditable seventh. Subsequently, he got into hot water on several occasions, notably in Vancouver, where he T-boned Alex Tagliani while trailing several laps in arrears, and at Montreal, where he speared into Ryan Hunter-Reay and faced a dressing-down from a none-too-impressed Fittipaldi on his return to the pits. But a calmer approach had surfaced in recent races, allied to a promising turn of speed that ensured he was now regularly vying for "top Reynard" bragging rights.

"I'm learning all the time, and the communication with my engineer [Don Bricker] is getting better and better," declared the determined 27-year-old.

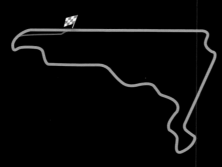

# GRAN PREMIO TELMEX-GIGANTE
## PRESENTED BY BANAMEX/VISA

**AUTÓDROMO HERMANOS RODRIGUEZ, MEXICO CITY, D.F. MEXICO**

**OCTOBER 12, 70 laps of 2.786 miles – 195.020 miles**

ROUND 17

| Pl. | Driver (Nat.) | No. | Team Sponsors Engine/Car | Tires | Q Speed | Q Time | Q Pos. | Laps | Time/Status | Ave. (mph) | Pts. |
|---|---|---|---|---|---|---|---|---|---|---|---|
| 1 | Paul Tracy (CDN) | 3 | Forsythe Racing Indeck Ford Cosworth/Lola B02/00 | BS | 112.893 | 1m 28.842s | 1 | 70 | 1h 56m 51.396s | 100.133 | 22 |
| 2 | *Sébastien Bourdais (F) | 2 | Newman/Haas Racing Cialis/Lilly Ford Cosworth/Lola B2K/00 | BS | 112.553 | 1m 29.110s | 4 | 70 | 1h 56m 53.178s | 100.108 | 16 |
| 3 | Mario Dominguez (MEX) | 55 | Herdez Competition Ford Cosworth/Lola B03/00 | BS | 111.924 | 1m 29.611s | 11 | 70 | 1h 56m 54.650s | 100.087 | 14 |
| 4 | Michel Jourdain Jr. (MEX) | 9 | Team Rahal Gigante Ford Cosworth/Lola B01/00 | BS | 112.219 | 1m 29.375s | 8 | 70 | 1h 57m 03.514s | 99.960 | 12 |
| 5 | *Mika Salo (SF) | 27 | PK Racing Ford Cosworth/Lola B02/00 | BS | 111.737 | 1m 29.761s | 12 | 70 | 1h 57m 05.183s | 99.936 | 10 |
| 6 | *Tiago Monteiro (P) | 7 | Fittipaldi-Dingman Racing Ford Cosworth/Reynard 02I | BS | 112.639 | 1m 29.042s | 2 | 70 | 1h 57m 09.140s | 99.880 | 9 |
| 7 | Bruno Junqueira (BR) | 1 | Newman/Haas Racing PacifiCare Ford Cosworth/Lola B02/00 | BS | 112.813 | 1m 28.905s | 3 | 70 | 1h 57m 09.476s | 99.875 | 6 |
| 8 | Adrian Fernandez (MEX) | 51 | Fernandez Tecate/Quaker State/Telmex Ford Cosworth/Lola B02/00 | BS | 111.386 | 1m 30.044s | 15 | 70 | 1h 57m 11.075s | 99.853 | 5 |
| 9 | *Darren Manning (GB) | 15 | Walker Racing RAC/Sportsbook.com Ford Cosworth/Reynard 02I | BS | 112.448 | 1m 29.193s | 6 | 70 | 1h 57m 18.872s | 99.742 | 4 |
| 10 | *Roberto Gonzalez (MEX) | 4 | Herdez Competition Ford Cosworth/Lola B01/00 | BS | 110.020 | 1m 31.162s | 18 | 70 | 1h 57m 34.385s | 99.523 | 3 |
| 11 | *Ryan Hunter-Reay (USA) | 31 | American Spirit Team Johansson Ford Cosworth/Reynard 02I | BS | 112.451 | 1m 29.191s | 5 | 70 | 1h 57m 43.586s | 99.393 | 2 |
| 12 | *Mario Haberfeld (BR) | 34 | Mi-Jack Conquest Racing Ford Cosworth/Reynard 02I | BS | 111.492 | 1m 29.958s | 14 | 70 | 1h 57m 48.392s | 99.326 | 1 |
| 13 | Oriol Servia (E) | 20 | Patrick Racing Visteon Ford Cosworth/Lola B02/00 | BS | 110.968 | 1m 30.383s | 16 | 69 | Running | | |
| 14 | Patrick Carpentier (CDN) | 32 | Forsythe Racing Indeck Ford Cosworth/Lola B03/00 | BS | 112.126 | 1m 29.449s | 9 | 68 | Out of fuel | | |
| 15 | Gualter Salles (BR) | 19 | Dale Coyne Racing Alpina/Golden Cross Ford Cosworth/Lola B2K/00 | BS | 109.683 | 1m 31.442s | 19 | 53 | Gearbox | | |
| 16 | Alex Tagliani (CDN) | 33 | Rocketsports Racing Johnson Controls Ford Cosworth/Lola B02/00 | BS | 111.586 | 1m 29.882s | 13 | 40 | Accident | | |
| 17 | Jimmy Vasser (USA) | 12 | American Spirit Team Johansson Ford Cosworth/Reynard 01I | BS | 112.295 | 1m 29.315s | 7 | 40 | Accident | | |
| 18 | *Rodolfo Lavin (MEX) | 5 | Walker Racing Corona Competition Ford Cosworth/Reynard 02I | BS | 110.722 | 1m 30.584s | 17 | 20 | Gearbox | | |
| 19 | *Luis Diaz (MEX) | 25 | Walker Racing Sun/Telcel/Motorola Ford Cosworth/Reynard 01I | BS | 112.005 | 1m 29.546s | 10 | 12 | Gearbox | | |
| 20 | *Geoff Boss (USA) | 11 | Dale Coyne Racing Cross Pens Ford Cosworth/Lola B01/00 | BS | 109.462 | 1m 31.626s | 20 | 4 | Off course | | |

\* denotes rookie driver

**Caution flags:** Lap 1, yellow start; lap 2, accident/Vasser, Manning & Fernandez; laps 40–44, accident/Vasser & Tagliani; laps 46–47, accident/Manning & Gonzalez. **Total: Four for 9 laps.**

**Lap leaders:** Paul Tracy, 1–57 (57 laps); Adrian Fernandez, 58–63 (6 laps); Tracy, 64–70 (7 laps). Totals: Tracy, 64 laps; Fernandez, 6 laps.

**Fastest race lap:** Ryan Hunter-Reay, 1m 29.066s, 112.609 mph on lap 63.

**Championship positions:** 1 Tracy, 226; 2 Junqueira, 197; 3 Jourdain Jr., 183; 4 Bourdais, 158; 5 Carpentier, 136; 6 Dominguez, 115; 7 Servia, 108; 8 Fernandez, 104; 9 Tagliani, 91; 10 Manning, 87; 11 Haberfeld, 71; 12 Moreno, 67; 13 Vasser, 58; 14 Hunter-Reay, 44; 15 Monteiro, 29; 16 Papis, 25; 17 Salo, 24; 18 Lavin, 12; 19 Lemarie, 8; 20 Camathias, 6; 21 Yoong & Boss, 4; 23 Salles & Gonzalez, 3; 25 Herta, 2.

# MEXICO CITY SNIPPETS

• A jubilant Mario Dominguez celebrated his fine third-place finish with a series of Alex Zanardi-style tire-smoking DONUTS. Later on Sunday night, authorities shut down one of the main thoroughfares in Mexico City so that Dominguez could perform a demonstration run – cheered to the echo by 15,000 of his countrymen! "This podium is the biggest moment in my life," exclaimed the 27-year-old. "I could hear the crowd chanting from inside the cockpit...it felt like everyone at the racetrack was in the car with me the whole time."

• The quota of MEXICAN DRIVERS increased from four to six thanks to the participation of Luis Diaz, in a third Walker Racing entry, and Roberto Gonzalez, who was drafted into the Herdez Competition squad in place of regular incumbent Roberto Moreno to maximize Herdez's domestic exposure. Toyota Atlantic front-runner Diaz, who had subbed for the injured Adrian Fernandez at the same event in 2002, acquitted himself admirably, qualifying an excellent tenth and running ninth in the race's early stages before succumbing to mechanical woes. Gonzalez made steady progress to finish tenth, although he blotted his copybook by punting Darren Manning into a spin just after half-distance.

• Sébastien Bourdais' runner-up finish was ENOUGH to sew up the Jim Trueman Rookie of the Year Award. "That was the main target for

us this season, and we got it with two races to go, so I'm very happy," said the Frenchman, who emulated one N. Mansell by claiming rookie honors as a Newman/Haas driver.

• Bourdais' car sported an unfamiliar bright green paint job in Mexico, as SPONSOR Eli Lilly took the opportunity to market Cialis, a drug designed to combat erectile dysfunction. The Federal Drug Administration's seal of approval was still pending in the US, but Lilly was free to advertise the product

south of the border. Meanwhile American Spirit Team Johansson had secured a one-off sponsorship deal with Mexican auto parts supply chain Gonher de Mexico for Ryan Hunter-Reay.

• It was announced during the week after Miami that Carl Haas had RESIGNED from CART's Board of Directors. Although Newman/Haas Racing had recently confirmed its plans to test an IRL IndyCar with a view to contesting the 2004 Indy 500, Haas insisted, "My resignation should

not be construed as a current lack of support for CART. I am committed to the series, that's the end of the discussion."

• The Gran Premio Telmex/Gigante saw the resurrection of a TRADITION that had been in abeyance since Mark Donohue won the 1971 Pocono 500. The 13 finishers were greeted by a checkered flag waved trackside (by former CART Starter Jim Swintal) in addition to the customary set of checkers brandished from the starter's gantry.

• The organizers had installed a row of CONES and a white line to narrow the usable width of track on the exit of the final corner after an unusual problem had come to light during the inaugural Mexico City event in 2002. Evidently, the towering grandstands were so close to the racing surface that fans in the lower rows obscured the line of sight from the seats in peanut heaven!

• Bridgestone signaled its intention to continue its DUAL ROLE as presenting sponsor and official tire supplier of the Champ Car World Series in 2004 at a press conference (left) on Friday afternoon. A spokesman said, "We fully intend to continue in CART with at least the status we've had this year. The final details are being negotiated."

Phil Abbott/LAT

BRIDGESTONE PRESENTS THE CHAMP CAR WORLD SERIES POWERED BY FORD • ROUND 18

# SURFERS
# PARADISE

## HUNTER-REAY'S SPIRIT SHINES THROUGH

A COMBINATION of inspired strategy, excellent driving and a stroke of good fortune allowed Ryan Hunter-Reay to become the season's eighth different winner – and, incredibly, the first American to win a Champ Car race in his rookie season since John Paul Jr. achieved the feat at Michigan International Speedway in 1983 (when Hunter-Reay was a mere two years old!).

Sure, the contentious decision by CART officials to close the pits on lap 31, when most of the front-runners were intending to make their final visit to the pit lane, played into Hunter-Reay's hands. It certainly cost Michel Jourdain Jr. the chance to take on service and cement his hard-won advantage. On this occasion, the stewards' intent – to ensure that the overall race leaders were not hindered by the timing of the full-course caution – backfired. But take nothing away from Hunter-Reay, or the American Spirit Team Johansson brains trust that made the bold decision to signal both RH-R and teammate Jimmy Vasser into the pit lane at the earliest opportunity.

The 22-year-old from Boca Raton, Florida, still had to negotiate the final stages of the race while under increasing pressure from fellow rookie Darren Manning, who, let's face it, possessed a great deal more wet-weather experience gleaned during the formative stages of his career in England. Hunter-Reay was up to the task.

A prototypical product of the CART Ladder System, having progressed from karts via various scholarships through the Formula Dodge National Championship presented by RACER, the Barber Dodge Pro Series and the CART Toyota Atlantic Championship, Hunter-Reay was clearly destined for the top. His opportunity to move up into the Champ Cars, however, was cemented only at the very last minute – ASTJ was formed just seven weeks prior to the first race at St. Petersburg – so he had the bare minimum of testing under his belt. Still, Hunter-Reay knuckled down to the task at hand. He made some mistakes, yes, but he proved to be a fast learner. He was generally very close to the pace of team leader Vasser and made a breakthrough effort at Mid-Ohio in August. Thereafter, he was a regular force to be reckoned with, and even set the fastest lap of the race in Mexico City. The maiden victory was no more than he deserved.

**Above left:** "Well, Ryan, what do you think?" asks Jimmy Vasser after teammate Hunter-Reay had swept to an unlikely maiden victory. Darren Manning, meanwhile, seems to be pondering what might have been.
Gavin Lawrence/LAT

**Above:** Given the treacherous conditions, RH-R's win was all the more impressive.
Dan Boyd/LAT

**Left:** This was just the beginning of a very well-deserved victory celebration for Tracy.
Gavin Lawrence/LAT

**Far left:** The Gold Coast oozes glamor.
Dan Boyd/LAT

**Right:** The moment it all went wrong for Junqueira as he loses control under braking for Turn One and slams into the trackside barrier.
Mark Horsburgh/LAT

**Above:** Typically excellent strategy – and pit work – by Walker Racing set the stage for Manning to finish a strong second.
Gavin Lawrence/LAT

**Left:** Surfers Paradise veteran Jimmy Vasser hops over the curbs at the ultra-fast VB Chicane along Main Beach Parade.
Phil Abbott/LAT

ROOKIE Ryan Hunter-Reay emerged with a fairytale victory for American Spirit Team Johansson and Paul Tracy was hailed as the new champion of the 2003 Bridgestone Presents the Champ Car World Series Powered by Ford following a dramatic and at times downright chaotic Lexmark Indy 300 in Australia.

What is it about the massively popular and charismatic event at Surfers Paradise? For the second year in a row, inclement weather brought the race to its knees. A sudden hailstorm wrought havoc after a dozen laps, causing Sébastien Bourdais to crash heavily out of second place and ensuring a red-flag stoppage. At that stage, Tracy's hopes of clinching the title looked slim at best. His PF Racing Lola had been controversially punted into a spin at the first corner by polesitter Bourdais, whereupon Newman/Haas teammate Bruno Junqueira had inherited the lead and seemed set fair for a victory that would ensure the championship battle remained undecided until the scheduled final round at California Speedway.

Later, however, after the race had been restarted, Junqueira lost control of his PacifiCare Lola and crashed heavily. Tracy also was involved in another incident, but his rival's miscue meant that the championship outcome was settled.

"I don't know how to feel right now," admitted Tracy, who, uncharacteristically, broke down in tears when he was presented with the coveted Vanderbilt Cup trophy in Victory Circle. "I went through a roller coaster of emotions today. If God wanted to test me today, he did. But I'll take it any way I can."

Hunter-Reay, too, was struggling to find words after his first Champ Car victory: "It feels great to be up here with a win, although it probably hasn't sunk in yet. It was a crazy day for sure."

The craziness started even before the green flag when the all-Newman/Haas Racing front row of the grid made a clumsy attempt to manipulate the start. Bourdais had inadvertently cost teammate Junqueira a valuable championship point by snaring the pole, and the Frenchman clearly was hellbent on redressing the balance as soon as possible. He led the field toward the starter's gantry in a slow, tight formation, whereupon Junqueira blatantly jumped the start, giving J.D. Wilbur little option but to display the yellow flag. The second attempt wasn't much better, although at least this time the green was brandished. Again Bourdais failed to seize the advantage, accelerating languidly and allowing Junqueira to snatch the upper hand. Initially, championship rival Tracy, who had qualified third, was bottled up behind Bourdais, but quickly broke clear and held second place as he braked for the first chicane.

Bourdais, meanwhile, wasn't planning on making things easy for the Canadian, and when Tracy turned into the corner, he did so without fully clearing the Frenchman's car. The result was a brief brush of wheels, Tracy's left rear against Bourdais' right front. It was just enough to tip Tracy into a spin. Miraculously, he managed to retrieve the situation without making any solid contact. Behind, Oriol Servia wasn't so fortunate, finding himself inadvertently nudged into the wall when Adrian Fernandez instinctively darted to his right as he saw the incident unfold.

When the dust had settled, Servia was out of the race and an irate Tracy had rejoined at the tail of the field.

"I was just disgusted," said Tracy later. "I thought, well, we are not going to get any points today, so we will have to set our minds for the next race."

The restart after three laps was clean, with Junqueira quickly jumping out ahead of Bourdais and Alex Tagliani, who remained under intense pressure from Fernandez and surprise 2002 Surfers Paradise winner Mario Dominguez. The Herdez driver's teammate, Roberto Moreno, ran sixth, followed by Michel Jourdain Jr., who headed a snarling pack comprising Patrick Carpentier, Mika Salo and Hunter-Reay in the best placed of the Reynards.

As the opening stages unfolded, dark storm clouds could be seen gathering menacingly to the west, whipped up by a strong breeze. On lap 12 they began to unleash their fury. Bourdais was the first to be caught out, losing the back end of his Cialis/Lilly Lola as he attempted to accelerate out of the first chicane. In vain he fought to catch the slide and made heavy contact with the wall. Moments later the track was awash. Out

came the yellow flags, and everyone made their first scheduled pit stops. The red flag followed shortly afterward when large hailstones rendered the situation extremely hazardous.

After a delay of around 40 minutes, the race was restarted (albeit now shortened from 65 laps to 47). Junqueira remained out in front, chased by Fernandez and Dominguez. Tagliani had slipped to fourth after a slight delay during his pit stop.

The track was still wet, however, which resulted in several more incidents. Salo spun off even before the restart, then Tagliani revolved his Rocketsports Lola at Turn Three, triggering a chain-reaction incident that also involved Moreno, Tracy and Darren Manning. Tracy, who had already charged back up to seventh, effectively ended his hopes of a finish among the points when he attempted to extricate himself from the melee and succeeded only in breaking his Lola's right rear suspension.

By contrast, everything seemed to be going according to plan for Junqueira. The Brazilian edged clear of Fernandez at the next restart, and by lap 25 he had established a useful cushion of over 3.5 seconds. Jourdain, meanwhile, was reveling in the tricky, drying conditions. He stormed past Dominguez on lap 22 and quickly homed in on Fernandez. Together, the two Mexicans reeled in the race leader. On lap 29, Jourdain outbraked Fernandez neatly into the tight Bartercard Chicane. Next time around, he expertly dispatched Junqueira in Turn Three, while Fernandez quickly followed his countryman into second place.

At virtually the same time, with the track drying steadily, American Spirit Team Johansson made an astute call, having realized that the window of opportunity to make a final visit to the pit lane had opened. Hunter-Reay and teammate Jimmy Vasser duly took on fresh dry-weather Bridgestone Potenza tires and a full load of methanol. They were now good to go. Tagliani also had switched to slick tires one lap earlier, but promptly spun as he attempted to build some heat into the cold rubber.

Moments later, out came the yellow flags one more time – in addition to Tagliani's stalled car, Mario Haberfeld's Mi-Jack Conquest Reynard had ground to a halt with a faulty ECU. The zany nature of the event continued when CART officials misguidedly called for the pit lane to be closed until everyone had taken up a position behind the pace car. Thus the leaders were denied the opportunity of making immediate pit stops. Furthermore, when they were allowed to take on service one lap later, they were duly leapfrogged by those who had had the wisdom/good fortune to pit before the yellow – namely the ASTJ pair, plus Manning and Walker Racing teammate Rodolfo Lavin.

Thus did Hunter-Reay find himself in the lead of a Champ Car race for the very first time. He was chased by Vasser, Manning and Lavin, then Jourdain, Fernandez and Junqueira, who was under pressure from Carpentier and now had some work to do if he was to keep his title hopes alive. One lap after the restart, however, Junqueira crashed heavily under braking for Turn One.

"On the lap before I crashed, Carpentier hit me," claimed Junqueira. "On the next lap, I'm not sure if I locked up the wheels and lost control of the car on water... I tried my best."

Whatever, his title aspirations had been shattered.

There was yet another caution when Fernandez lost his chance at a good position by spinning at the exit of Turn Three. All the while, Hunter-Reay kept his cool. The young American put his head down when the race went green again for a four-lap dash to the checkered flag, and even though Manning used the damp conditions to his benefit by charging past Vasser into second place, Hunter-Reay resisted the pressure and held on for the victory.

"I've led before late in the race in [Toyota] Atlantic, so that wasn't new, but it was a challenge," he admitted.

Manning was content with a magnificent second for Walker Racing, while Vasser compounded the Johansson team's joy by claiming third ahead of an unfortunate Jourdain.

"I raced hard today and I passed everyone clean and earned the lead on the track, and then they go and close the pits on me and cost us another chance to win," summarized Jourdain.

The Mexican had every right to feel aggrieved after a fine drive. Then again, nothing, it seems, is predictable when the Champ Cars visit Australia's Gold Coast...

*Jeremy Shaw*

## QUALIFYING

The battle for top championship honors showed no signs of abating at Surfers Paradise, as Bruno Junqueira bounced back from his Mexican malaise to top the timing charts in provisional qualifying.

"This is a really important weekend for me," explained the Brazilian, who turned a best lap at 1m 32.708s, trimming more than two seconds from the best practice time set earlier in the day by Adrian Fernandez. "I hope to get out of this weekend close enough to [Paul] Tracy to have a chance at winning the championship. That is my goal."

Tracy was almost 1.5 seconds slower than his rival on Friday, although he stepped up his game dramatically during an exciting final session of qualifying on Saturday. In front of a massive crowd of 83,913, Tracy and Junqueira both spent some time atop the timing charts, and at the end of the session they were separated by scant 0.006s. Both were eclipsed, however, by Junqueira's Newman/Haas teammate, Sébastien Bourdais, who recorded his fifth pole of the year (and his first since Round Nine at Cleveland) and established a new rookie record by annexing his 12th consecutive top-six starting position.

"There was so much pressure to put in a good lap here," said Bourdais. "You had to keep the speed, keep patient and watch traffic. It was a very tough qualifying session. I was still shaking after I got out of the car."

Junqueira felt the pressure, too, and reckoned he had been held up by the slower car of Rodolfo Lavin on what would have been his fastest lap.

"To be fast again and lose the pole here for the second straight year is very frustrating," said Junqueira, who in '02 lost out to newly-crowned Cristiano da Matta by a mere 0.01s.

Under the circumstances, Tracy was delighted to be third quickest, especially given that Bourdais had unwittingly aided his cause by snatching the bonus championship point from his teammate's grasp.

"We made a big improvement today," said the Canadian. "I went 12 mph faster through the last chicane than I did yesterday, so that's where we found our speed this afternoon."

Alex Tagliani secured a position on the outside of the second row, bouncing back from a disappointment on Friday when his second-quickest time was erased after the Johnson Controls/Rocketsports Lola was found to be slightly underweight. Fernandez continued his strong street-course form by rounding out the top five, while Ryan Hunter-Reay was the fastest Reynard runner in 12th.

## A FLIP OF THE COYNE

**N**O team owner has worked harder over the years to keep his operation afloat than Dale Coyne. He never enjoyed the level of resources that might have enabled him to contend regularly at the front of the field, but he remained intensely loyal to the CART cause and even briefly took the helm of the sanctioning organization – to good effect – during one of its seemingly frequent leadership transitions in the 1990s.

Coyne, who ran a successful landscaping business in the Chicago area before pursuing his passion for auto racing, and later headed a group of businessmen who established the impressive Route 66 Raceway/Chicagoland Speedway complex in Joliet, Illinois, resisted some calls to lead CART on a full-time basis in favor of continuing his own Champ Car team. A lack of sponsorship, or sponsored drivers, saw him sit out most of the 2002 campaign, but Coyne never considered calling it quits. Instead he provided the equipment and most of the know-how for Team St. George's patriotic foray at the Rockingham 500 in England, where Darren Manning produced an impressive debut performance, leading several laps and eventually finishing a solid ninth. Then at the season finale in Mexico City, he returned with the same car under the more familiar Dale Coyne Racing moniker and guided German rookie Andre Lotterer to a similarly strong result.

Those outings paved the way for a concerted return in 2003, although once again funding deficits obliged him to run a variety of different drivers. Several of them showed promise, but Coyne's patience and persistence finally paid off in what turned out to be the season finale, when Gualter Salles guided the #19 Lola to a solid sixth-place finish and Geoff Boss persevered despite a race-long wastegate problem to claim ninth. For both drivers, those results represented career bests.

"This is my favorite race of the year and the car was running good," said Salles, who performed especially well in the difficult middle stages of the race and then held off determined challenges from Mario Dominguez and Alex Tagliani in the closing laps.

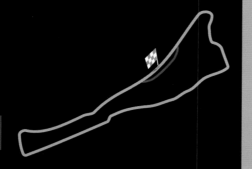

# LEXMARK INDY 300

## SURFERS PARADISE STREET CIRCUIT, QUEENSLAND, AUSTRALIA

**OCTOBER 26, 47 laps of 2.795 miles – 131.365 miles**

ROUND 18

| Pl. | Driver (Nat.) | No. | Team Sponsors Engine/Car | Tires | Q Speed | Q Time | Q Pos. | Laps | Time/Status | Ave. (mph) | Pts. |
|---|---|---|---|---|---|---|---|---|---|---|---|
| 1 | *Ryan Hunter-Reay (USA) | 31 | American Spirit Team Johansson Ford Cosworth/Reynard 02I | BS | 107.567 | 1m 33.542s | 12 | 47 | 1h 49m 02.803s | 72.280 | 20 |
| 2 | *Darren Manning (GB) | 15 | Walker Racing RAC/Sportsbook.com Ford Cosworth/Reynard 02I | BS | 107.131 | 1m 33.922s | 14 | 47 | 1h 49m 04.349s | 72.263 | 16 |
| 3 | Jimmy Vasser (USA) | 12 | American Spirit Team Johansson Ford Cosworth/Reynard 01I | BS | 106.741 | 1m 34.266s | 15 | 47 | 1h 49m 06.595s | 72.238 | 14 |
| 4 | Michel Jourdain Jr. (MEX) | 9 | Team Rahal Gigante Ford Cosworth/Lola B01/00 | BS | 108.063 | 1m 33.112s | 9 | 47 | 1h 49m 08.118s | 72.221 | 12 |
| 5 | Patrick Carpentier (CDN) | 32 | Forsythe Racing Indeck Ford Cosworth/Lola B02/00 | BS | 107.688 | 1m 33.437s | 11 | 47 | 1h 49m 08.640s | 72.216 | 10 |
| 6 | Gualter Salles (BR) | 19 | Dale Coyne Racing Alpina/Golden Cross Ford Cosworth/Lola B2K/00 | BS | 106.312 | 1m 34.646s | 17 | 47 | 1h 49m 10.983s | 72.190 | 8 |
| 7 | Alex Tagliani (CDN) | 33 | Rocketsports Racing Johnson Controls Ford Cosworth/Lola B02/00 | BS | 109.209 | 1m 32.135s | 4 | 47 | 1h 49m 12.934s | 72.168 | 6 |
| 8 | *Rodolfo Lavin (MEX) | 5 | Walker Racing Corona Competition Ford Cosworth/Reynard 02I | BS | 104.731 | 1m 36.075s | 18 | 47 | 1h 49m 14.476s | 72.151 | 5 |
| 9 | *Geoff Boss (USA) | 11 | Dale Coyne Racing Cross Pens Ford Cosworth/Lola B01/00 | BS | 103.468 | 1m 37.247s | 19 | 47 | 1h 49m 53.531s | 71.724 | 4 |
| 10 | Mario Dominguez (MEX) | 55 | Herdez Competition Ford Cosworth/Lola B03/00 | BS | 108.301 | 1m 32.908s | 8 | 46 | Running | | 3 |
| 11 | *Mika Salo (SF) | 27 | PK Racing Ford Cosworth/Lola B02/00 | BS | 107.976 | 1m 33.187s | 10 | 46 | Running | | 2 |
| 12 | Adrian Fernandez (MEX) | 51 | Fernandez Tecate/Quaker State/Telmex Ford Cosworth/Lola B02/00 | BS | 108.854 | 1m 32.436s | 5 | 46 | Running | | 1 |
| 13 | Paul Tracy (CDN) | 3 | Forsythe Racing Indeck Ford Cosworth/Lola B02/00 | BS | 109.370 | 1m 32.000s | 3 | 45 | Running | | |
| 14 | *Mario Haberfeld (BR) | 34 | Mi-Jack Conquest Racing Ford Cosworth/Reynard 02I | BS | 106.703 | 1m 34.299s | 16 | 43 | Running | | |
| 15 | Bruno Junqueira (BR) | 1 | Newman/Haas Racing PacifiCare Ford Cosworth/Lola B02/00 | BS | 109.377 | 1m 31.994s | 2 | 36 | Accident | | 2 |
| 16 | Roberto Moreno (BR) | 4 | Herdez Competition Ford Cosworth/Lola B03/00 | BS | 108.506 | 1m 32.732s | 7 | 23 | Accident | | |
| 17 | *Sébastien Bourdais (F) | 2 | Newman/Haas Racing Cialis/Lilly Ford Cosworth/Lola B2K/00 | BS | 109.706 | 1m 31.718s | 1 | 11 | Accident | | 1 |
| 18 | *Tiago Monteiro (P) | 7 | Fittipaldi-Dingman Racing Ford Cosworth/Reynard 02I | BS | 107.206 | 1m 33.857s | 13 | 3 | Gearbox | | |
| 19 | Oriol Servia (E) | 20 | Patrick Racing Visteon Ford Cosworth/Lola B02/00 | BS | 108.507 | 1m 32.731s | 6 | 1 | Accident | | |

*\* denotes rookie driver*

**Caution flags:** **Lap 1,** yellow start; **lap 2,** accident/Servia; **laps 11–13,** accident/Bourdais; **laps 14–15,** restart after red flag: **laps 16–17,** tow/Salo; **laps 19–20,** accident/Tracy, Tagliani, Manning, Salles & Moreno; **laps 31–34,** tows/Tagliani & Haberfeld; **laps 37–39,** accident/Junqueira & Haberfeld; **laps 41–42,** tow/Fernandez. Total: Nine for 20 laps.

**Lap leaders:** Bruno Junqueira, 1–29 (29 laps); Michel Jourdain Jr., 30–32 (3 laps); Ryan Hunter-Reay, 33–47 (15 laps). Totals: Junqueira, 29 laps; Hunter-Reay, 15 laps; Jourdain, 3 laps.

**Fastest race lap:** Roberto Moreno, 1m 35.561s, 105.294 mph on lap 10.

**Final championship positions:** 1 Tracy, 226; 2 Junqueira, 199; 3 Jourdain Jr., 195; 4 Bourdais, 159; 5 Carpentier, 146; 6 Dominguez, 118; 7 Servia, 108; 8 Fernandez, 105; 9 Manning, 103; 10 Tagliani, 97; 11 Vasser, 72; 12 Haberfeld, 71; 13 Moreno, 67; 14 Hunter-Reay, 64; 15 Monteiro, 29; 16 Salo, 26; 17 Papis, 25; 18 Lavin, 17; 19 Salles, 11; 20 Boss, 8; 21 Lemarie, 8; 22 Camathias, 6; 23 Yoong, 4; 24 Gonzalez, 3; 25 Herta, 2.

# SURFERS SNIPPETS

Gavin Lawrence/LAT

• Roberto Moreno (above) displayed a veteran's **CALM** in final qualifying after applying the power to his Herdez Ford Cosworth/Lola a little too audaciously and spinning at the final corner. Rather than risk trying to turn around within the narrow confines of the cement walls, and mindful that stalling the engine would risk the possibility of causing a red-flag stoppage, which would result in the loss of his fastest time, Moreno coolly selected reverse gear and drove backward all the way down the front straightaway and into the sanctuary of the pit lane. "That was a first for me," admitted the Brazilian with a broad smile.

• The 13th annual visit of the Champ Cars to Queensland's Gold Coast broke the **ATTENDANCE RECORD** for the second time in as many years, reaching above yet another major threshold of 306,184 over the four days. Sadly, however, as in 2002, atrocious weather conditions during the feature event saw many of the 108,110 fans heading for dry sanctuary long before the Lexmark Indy 300 was completed.

• Prior to the race weekend, several **DRIVERS** took the opportunity to spend some time vacationing in Australia, while others took part in the usual plethora of publicity stunts – such as swimming with dolphins or riding with the Royal Australian Air Force's Roulette aerobatic team. Jimmy Vasser, meanwhile, couldn't get enough of driving, so he gladly took up the offer of a couple of laps in the Stone Brothers Racing Ford Falcon AU sedan, which Mark Winterbottom had used shortly before to clinch the Konica V8 Supercar Series. "The car is fantastic and great fun to drive," said the 1996 CART Champion. "I am really impressed. I have to say, though, I feel bad because I think I was tough on the gearbox. That H-pattern with my left hand would definitely take some getting used to."

• Ryan Hunter-Reay became the fourth driver to score his maiden Champ Car **VICTORY** in Aus-

tralia, joining John Andretti (1991), Nigel Mansell ('93) and Mario Dominguez ('02). He also ensured that the event's remarkable record of never having a repeat winner remained intact.

• Mario Dominguez had **HIGH HOPES** of ending that streak when he moved into the top three prior to the red-flag stoppage, although the Mexican struggled when the track conditions were at their wettest and then encountered a rare miscue in the pits when the right rear wheel fell off his Herdez Lola following routine service on lap 32. Dominguez soon continued with a full complement of wheels and tires, although CART regulations demanded a one-lap penalty, dropping him from seventh at the finish to tenth. "Rules are rules, so we take our penalty," said the Mexican philosophically. "At least we finished and brought home a couple of points."

• The Reynard 1-2-3 **SWEEP** of the podium by Hunter-Reay, Darren Manning and Jimmy Vasser was the first time the Brackley, England, marque had achieved the feat since Vancouver in 2001, when Roberto Moreno, Gil de Ferran and Michael Andretti filled the top three places.

• At the age of just 17, Miami-based Frenchman Nelson Philippe became the **YOUNGEST** driver ever to test a Champ Car when he enjoyed an

outing at Sebring with Fittipaldi-Dingman Racing just before the team packed up its belongings and headed off to Australia. Philippe, an ex-kart racer who had showed great promise during his initial season of Barber Dodge Pro Series competition, made an excellent impression despite his run being blighted by rain showers.

• The scheduled final race of the season, due to have been held at Fontana's California Speedway (below) just one week after the annual visit Down Under, was **CANCELED** shortly after the teams arrived back in Southern California, due to severe wildfires just a few miles away from the racetrack. The championship already had been settled in favor of Paul Tracy, but the cancellation extinguished Michel Jourdain Jr.'s hopes of wresting second place from Bruno Junqueira.

Gavin Lawrence/LAT

# CLEAN SWEEP

Top: A winning team: Carl Russo is flanked by A.J. Allmendinger (left) and Aaron Justus.
Phil Abbott/LAT

Above: Allmendinger dominated the Atlantic season in much the same way as he had the previous year's Barber Dodge Pro Series.
Mike Levitt/LAT

Right: Justus was overshadowed, but did a very competent job and was a true team player.
Paul Mounce/LAT

Below: After switching engine builders early in the season, 2002 runner-up Michael Valiante was a relentless force to be reckoned with.

Below right: Luis Diaz was dogged by misfortune.
Photographs: Mike Levitt/LAT

by Jeremy Shaw

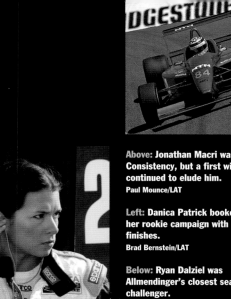

**Above:** Jonathan Macri was Mr. Consistency, but a first win continued to elude him.
Paul Mounce/LAT

**Left:** Danica Patrick bookended her rookie campaign with podium finishes.
Brad Bernstein/LAT

**Below:** Ryan Dalziel was Allmendinger's closest season-long challenger.
Phil Abbott/LAT

# 2003 CART TOYOTA ATLANTIC CHAMPIONSHIP
## Final point standings after 12 races

| Pos. | Driver (Nat.), Sponsor(s)-Team | Pts. |
|---|---|---|
| 1 | *A.J. Allmendinger (USA), RuSPORT | 201 |
| 2 | Ryan Dalziel (GB), Pro-Works/Discovery Lake/ Daily Record-Sierra Sierra Enterprises | 175 |
| 3 | Michael Valiante (CDN), Lynx Racing | 161 |
| 4 | Jonathan Macri (CDN), NTN Bearings-Polestar Atlantic LLC | 145 |
| 5 | *Aaron Justus (USA), RuSPORT | 123 |
| 6 | *Danica Patrick (USA), Argent Mortgage Company-Team Rahal | 109 |
| 7 | Joey Hand (USA), DSTP Motorsports | 108 |
| 8 | Luis Diaz (MEX), Telmex-Dorricott Racing | 88 |
| 9 | Alex Figge (USA), Wine Country Motorsports/Patrick Racing/ Trench Shoring-Pacific Coast Motorsports | 87 |
| 10 | Kyle Krisiloff (USA), US GP F1-Cameron M'sports/Dorricott/Sierra Sierra | 77 |
| 11 | Alex Garcia (YV), Dixien/Omnisource/LA Finess/Diestra-Transnet Racing | 60 |
| 12 | Eric Jensen (CDN), Westin Hotels-Starwood Team Jensen | 49 |
| 13 | Stephan C. Roy (CDN), PlayStation2/MGD/Mexxsport/Momo-P-1 Racing | 48 |
| 14 | *Bryan Sellers (USA), 3 Dimensional Services/Drive$USA-Lynx Racing | 30 |
| 15= | Jon Fogarty (USA), Norwalk Furniture-Team Rahal | 24 |
| 15= | *Philip Fayer (CDN), PaySystems-Starwood Team Jensen | 24 |
| 17 | *Marc Breuers (USA), Hamilton Lane-Brooks Associates Racing | 12 |
| 18 | *Louis-Philippe Dumoulin (CDN), Autovalue/Chevy Rock/Detente-Lynx Racing | 11 |
| 19 | *Marc DeVellis (CDN), Sierra Sierra Enterprises | 9 |
| 20 | *Romain Dumas (F), Scuadra Fortia | 7 |

All drove Swift 014.a chassis with Toyota 4A-GE motors and Yokohama tires.

* denotes rookie driver

## Performance Chart

| Driver | Wins | Poles | Fastest laps | Most laps led |
|---|---|---|---|---|
| A.J. Allmendinger | 7 | 9 | 7 | 7 |
| Michael Valiante | 3 | – | – | 3 |
| Ryan Dalziel | 2 | 2 | 2 | 2 |
| Luis Diaz | – | 1 | 1 | – |
| Jonathan Macri | – | – | 1 | – |
| Kyle Krisiloff | – | – | 1 | – |

THE most one-sided CART Toyota Atlantic Championship title chase in years saw A.J. Allmendinger cement his position as one of America's most promising young stars and Carl Russo's RuSPORT team emerge as a similarly potent force to be reckoned with in the future. The combination swept all before it during the 12-race campaign.

After making his fortune in the optical networking/telecommunications industry, Russo himself had contested the 2002 season as a driver, but had quickly realized where his skills would best be utilized. He ran a second car for underrated ex-Formula Ford 2000 Champion Aaron Justus in the final few races and formulated a plan to field two cars on a full-time basis for 2003, with an eye very much on the future. Russo put aside his own driving ambitions and resolved to hire the best people he could find, and not just on the driving strength.

Jeremy Dale, formerly managing director of the Barber Dodge Pro Series and no mean driver himself, before his career had been cut short by a terrifying sports car crash, came on board to oversee the fledgling RuSPORT team. He was joined by technical chief Gerald Tyler, who previously had guided both PPI Motorsports and Dorricott Racing to championship successes. Similarly accomplished crew chief Joe Korrigan also was there from the outset, while multiple-title-winning race engineer Burke Harrison joined in shortly after the start of the season.

Justus, 29, ensured valuable continuity. He had contested only three races in 2002, so retained his rookie status and thoroughly deserved his opportunity to take a shot at the title. Fellow Californian Allmendinger, 21, was selected from a short list of candidates for the second seat.

RuSPORT's debut in Monterrey was not particularly auspicious. Allmendinger, who had dominated the 2002 Barber Dodge Pro Series, winning six out of ten races, qualified a respectable third, but then left his braking too late for the very first corner and rudely assaulted the rear of polesitter Luis Diaz's car. Allmendinger rejoined at the back of the field, his nosecone in tatters, but had risen to eighth by the checkered flag. Justus, meanwhile, qualified tenth and drove a measured race to finish fifth.

Then came a remarkable turnaround. The pair blitzed the prestigious Toyota Grand Prix of Long Beach, Allmendinger winning as he pleased from the pole and Justus following him home in second, despite struggling with a broken nosecone in the closing stages. RuSPORT, and Allmendinger in particular, never looked back. The youngster moved into the overall points lead following a third-place finish at the Milwaukee Mile, the sole visit to an oval in 2003, then went on a tear, snaring the pole in all except one of the remaining nine races and winning six of them. He clinched the title, appropriately, in Denver, not far from the team's base in Loveland, Colorado, with one race remaining in the season, although he would have tied up the honors sooner had he not been punted off by Michael Valiante on the first lap at Mid-Ohio.

"It feels unbelievable," said Allmendinger. "I can't thank the team enough for all they've done for me – Carl Russo and everybody on the team that works their butts off during the week and at the weekend."

Justus couldn't quite match his younger teammate's speed or aggression, but still enjoyed a solid season to end up as the second highest-placed rookie. Unfortunately, if there was any bad luck going, he seemed to bear the brunt of it. He was involved in several incidents that led to a trio of non-finishes, although he still ended up fifth in the final points table with four podium appearances and eight top-five finishes to his credit.

Other than Allmendinger, only two drivers tasted the spoils of victory in 2003 – Ryan Dalziel and Michael Valiante. Each, on their day, was capable of dominating the proceedings, but neither of them could match Allmendinger's consistency. Aside from the opener in Monterrey, Scotsman Dalziel, in his sophomore

campaign, qualified among the top five in every race for the Sierra Sierra Enterprises team. He won convincingly from the pole at Milwaukee and Portland, but only in those two races – and in the Miami finale – did he start from the front row of the grid. Still, at only 21 years of age, Dalziel clearly marked himself as a potential future star.

Ditto Valiante, who began the year as a hot favorite for championship honors after narrowly losing out to Jon Fogarty in 2002. The 23-year-old British Columbian remained with Lynx Racing for his third year in the series and, after a poor provisional qualifying effort in the first race, rebounded to start fourth and then pounced into the lead after front-row starters Diaz and Joey Hand both hit trouble. The victory was to remain the sole success for engine supplier Comptech, which rarely was able to match the otherwise dominant units prepared by Paul Hasselgren. After struggling for ultimate pace at the next few races, and then being prevented from starting at Mazda Raceway Laguna Seca due to a stomach virus, Valiante took advantage of a switch to Hasselgren motors by starting and finishing among the top four in each of the last seven races. Wins at Mid-Ohio (where he came out on top of a clash with Allmendinger) and Miami (where he profited from a rare mechanical miscue for the champion) underlined his ability. Valiante, indeed, was due to make his Champ Car debut with Walker Racing at the Fontana finale before the wildfires took their toll.

Another Canadian, Jonathan Macri, claimed fourth overall for Paul Kiebler and Jim Griffith's new Polestar operation, which had taken over the assets of the former Sigma team. Macri, still only 21 but in his third full season of Toyota Atlantic, was Mr. Consistency, starting and finishing in the top ten of every race, although rarely showing the flair that took him to the 2000 Canadian Formula Ford Championship. He started only once among the first two rows and generally raced better than he qualified. A pair of second places, at Monterrey and his team's home event, Cleveland, represented his highlights.

Just two days before her 21st birthday, Danica Patrick made a stunning series debut for Team Rahal by finishing third at Monterrey and becoming the first female to score a podium finish in the 30-year history of Toyota Atlantic. She also rounded out a generally impressive rookie season by claiming second in Miami. Curiously, they remained her best two results, but she still did enough to claim a worthy sixth in the final points table, one marker clear of a desperately unlucky Joey Hand. Much was expected of the Californian, who had sat out most of the 2002 season following a horrific crash at Milwaukee, but for one reason or another the results rarely materialized. A second at Portland represented the lone podium finish for Hand and super-enthusiastic car owner Dede Rogers' DSTP Motorsports operation.

Mexican Luis Diaz also suffered all manner of misfortune, despite his own best efforts and those of Dorricott Racing, which lost a large proportion of its brains trust to the fledgling RuSPORT organization. For the second year running, the amiable Diaz qualified on the pole for his home race in Monterrey, only to be nudged off the road by Allmendinger. It was the first among a catalog of disasters that, as with Hand, prevented him from displaying his true worth.

Alex Figge showed some flashes of promise with Pacific Coast Motorsports, as did 17-year-old Kyle Krisiloff, who was superb at Milwaukee, but did himself no favors by switching between three teams as the season progressed. Sadly, defending champion Jon Fogarty was unable to find a ride in the Champ Cars for 2003, but he reminded everyone of his talent by scoring a pair of fourths when he was offered a couple of rides in a second Team Rahal Swift at season's end. Reigning FF2000 Zetec Champion Bryan Sellers also showed promise in sporadic outings aboard a second Lynx Racing entry during a year that, in general, was lacking in entrants – due to steadily increasing costs – but not in talent.

Right: **Leo Maia was the class of the field, and he wrapped up the title with two races to spare.**
Mike Levitt/LAT

Center right: **Maia gave a wet-weather masterclass at Mid-Ohio.**
Mike Weston/LAT

Below left: **Dan Di Leo took a fine victory at Laguna Seca.**
Phil Abbott/LAT

Below right: **David Martinez came up trumps at home in Mexico.**

Bottom left: **Fellow Mexican, Telmex-backed Memo Rojas won twice and emerged as series runner-up.**
Photographs: Mike Levitt/LAT

# JUST REWARD

## BARBER DODGE PRO SERIES REVIEW

by Jeremy Shaw

LEONARDO Maia clearly was paying attention during the 2002 Barber Dodge Pro Series. He had begun the season with high expectations after winning the coveted Skip Barber Racing "Big Scholarship" Award, but he and everyone else were soundly trounced by fellow rookie A.J. Allmendinger, who swept to the championship crown on the strength of six wins from ten races. Rather than becoming downhearted, however, after placing a disappointing sixth in the final points table, Maia realized he needed to work harder in his sophomore campaign.

So, over the winter, he put more effort into his fitness regimen. He vowed to learn more about the technical intricacies of the Barber Dodge/Reynards. He spent long hours with the driver coaches and engineers, figuring out how to maximize his opportunity. When the 2003 season kicked off at St. Petersburg, Florida, in February, Maia was ready. It showed. He qualified on the pole and led throughout the 40-minute race, holding off determined challenges from fellow series veterans Memo Rojas and Dan Di Leo.

The die was cast. Maia took the pole next time out in Monterrey, and although he was beaten in the race by local hero David Martinez, he bounced back to strengthen his grip on the title chase by winning the only oval race of the season at Milwaukee. More dominant wins followed at Portland and Cleveland, and yet another triumph at Vancouver – where he took advantage of the misfortunes of a couple of his rivals – enabled him to clinch the championship with two races remaining.

Maia had set himself the task of mimicking Allmendinger's 2002 campaign, and he delivered in style. He matched the latter's record tally of 188 points and six wins, and bettered his pole tally seven to four.

"It's so rewarding to dedicate yourself to something and then to achieve it," concluded Maia.

But don't be misled into believing he had meager competition. Far from it. The standard of driving once again reached new heights in 2003, and the average age of the top ten championship point scorers was a new record low of just 20.5 years.

While Maia left everyone in his dust, the battle for second place was an intense one. Rojas, Di Leo and Martinez proved to be very closely matched, and all three of them went into the final race in Montreal with their runner-up hopes alive; but it was Rojas who emerged on top by virtue of an accomplished victory, his second of the season. The win also assured Rojas of

## TOUGH FIGHT

**C**OMPETITION for the Formula Dodge National Championship Presented by RACER was tougher than ever in 2003. Six different drivers shared the victory spoils, although 22-year-old Rafael Matos emerged as a deserving champion after winning three times and adding five poles. Matos, from Belo Horizonte, Brazil, earned his ride by winning a Barber-Champ Car Scholarship and is hotly tipped to continue climbing the racing ladder toward his ultimate ambition of a drive in the Champ Car World Series. His tally of nine podium finishes from the 13 rounds was enough to head off determined challenges from a pair of teenagers, Mexican Salvador Duran and American Matt Jaskol.

Duran won twice and matched Matos' handful of poles, while Jaskol won three times and went on to claim one of the prestigious Red Bull Driver Search Scholarships following an end-of-season showdown in Estoril, Portugal.

Brian Frisselle, whose elder brother Burt had progressed into the Barber Dodge Pro Series, upheld family honor superbly and came on strong at the end of the season, winning each of the final three races to clinch fourth place in the standings ahead of American Ben Freudenberg and Canadian Philippe Gelinas, each of whom won once.

### 2003 FORMULA DODGE NATIONAL CHAMPIONSHIP
PRESENTED BY RACER
Final point standings after 13 races

| Pos. | Driver (Nat.), | Pts. |
|---|---|---|
| 1 | Rafael Matos (BR)* | 178 |
| 2 | Salvador Duran (MEX)* | 157 |
| 3 | Matt Jaskol (USA)* | 150 |
| 4 | Brian Frisselle (USA)* | 137 |
| 5 | Ben Freudenberg (USA)* | 128 |
| 6 | Philippe Gelinas (CDN)* | 122 |
| 7 | Gerardo Bonilla (USA) | 102 |
| 8 | Dominique Claessens (USA)* | 90 |
| 9 | Joe D'Agostino (USA)* | 87 |
| 10 | Zilvinas Oskutis (LIT)* | 77 |
| * denotes rookie driver | | |

top honors in the Dodge Trans-Canada Challenge, comprising the three North of the Border races at Toronto (where he also won) Vancouver and Montreal.

Second place in the overall standings for Rojas, who retained the support of Mexican telecommunications giant Telmex, was just reward for his unstinting effort.

Di Leo, meanwhile, had to accept the mantle of the season's unluckiest driver. He qualified among the top five in nine of the ten races (one shy of Maia's perfect score), but seemed to be afflicted by all manner of misfortunes. Otherwise he would surely have taken more than a solitary victory at Laguna Seca.

Martinez, too, emerged as a worthy challenger, and even though he never matched his magnificent performance in Monterrey, he did make three more visits to the podium and, like the others, marked himself as a man to watch in the future.

Martinez was ineligible for the Skip Barber Racing Rookie of the Year Award, which went instead to Colin Fleming as the top racing school graduate. The 19-year-old Californian narrowly bested fellow young Americans Burt Frisselle and Scott Poirier after a season-long battle. Fleming, though, was a deserved winner after making steady progress. His breakthrough came at Portland, where he took third. Then he added a second in Toronto and another podium place in the Montreal finale. Fleming, who had moved up from the CART "Stars of Tomorrow" Karting series and into the Formula Dodge National Championship, continued his march toward the top of the sport by claiming one of the Red Bull Driver Search Scholarships following an end-of-season shootout in Estoril, Portugal.

Frisselle, 20, from Kihei, Hawaii, displayed admirable consistency, gaining six top-six finishes and ending up a scant seven points shy of Fleming's tally, while Poirier, 20, from Deerfield Beach, Florida, built upon his second-place finish in the 2002 Formula Dodge National Championship Presented by RACER and recorded a best result of second in Vancouver.

German Quiroga made tremendous progress in his sophomore campaign. The amiable young Mexican garnered a maiden podium finish in Cleveland and thoroughly deserved his new-found support from Gigante, while 17-year-old Miami-based Frenchman Nelson Philippe also made great strides, culminating in three consecutive top-four results to round out a very impressive first season out of karts. Philippe also displayed a maturity beyond

his years when he was invited to test a Fittipaldi-Dingman Racing Reynard Champ Car at Sebring in October.

Puerto Rico's Victor Gonzalez used his wealth of experience to excellent effect on the Milwaukee Mile, where he finished second after snaring the pole. Several other drivers displayed great promise during another very exciting season of competition, including Mexican Luis Pelayo, Canadians Chris Green, Antoine Bessette and Ward Imrie, and Americans Ben Freudenberg, Al Unser and Ryan Millen.

## 2003 BARBER DODGE PRO SERIES
Final point standings after ten races

| Pos. | Driver (Nat.), Sponsor(s) | Pts. |
|---|---|---|
| 1 | Leonardo Maia (USA), Gatorz Eyewear/Pit Bull/Soy Tech/RDD Int'l | 188 |
| 2 | Memo Rojas (MEX), Telmex/Quaker State/Canel's/Ericsson/LNB | 128 |
| 3 | Dan Di Leo (CDN), Select Auto Collision/Autosports Media/FY2F2 Comms | 118 |
| 4 | *David Martinez (MEX), Herdez/Telcel/Aviacsa | 103 |
| 5 | *Colin Fleming (USA), Barber-CART Scholarship/Dodge/King Taco/Sparco | 83 |
| 6 | *Burt Frisselle (USA), Ventura Travel/Arkad Capital/Rapid 2 Way/FTQ | 76 |
| 7 | German Quiroga (MEX), Gigante/Mikels/Sante/Seman/Baker | 75 |
| 8 | *Scott Poirier (USA), Michelin/Team Autohaus Pompano | 70 |
| 9 | *Nelson Philippe (F), Lease Plan/FFSA | 66 |
| 10 | *Luis Pelayo (MEX), JF Crickets Prod./WTF Solutions/HFC | 46 |
| 11 | *Chris Green (CDN), DAC Aviation/Stelvio Inc./Oakley Canada/No Fear | 46 |
| 12 | *Antoine Bessette (CDN), Elan International/Groupe Bessette | 39 |
| 13 | *Al Unser (USA), 200+/Med Test/Simpson/Oakley | 38 |
| 14 | Chris Baker (USA), RABCO/Vector Energy/AutoCrze/RPM-Indoor Raceway | 26 |
| 15 | *Ben Freudenberg (USA), Biomet/South Coast Ear, Nose and Throat | 26 |

All drove Reynard 98E chassis with 3.5-liter Dodge V6 motors and Michelin tires.
* denotes rookie driver

### Performance Chart

| Driver | Wins | Poles | Fastest laps | Most laps led |
|---|---|---|---|---|
| Leonardo Maia | 6 | 7 | 6 | 4 |
| Memo Roja | 2 | 2 | – | 2 |
| David Martinez | 1 | – | 2 | 1 |
| Dan Di Leo | 1 | – | 1 | 2 |
| Victor Gonzalez | – | 1 | – | 1 |
| Chris Green | – | – | 1 | – |

**Below: As ever, the Barber Dodge paddock was abuzz with young hopefuls.**
**Phil Abbott/LAT**

# MOTOROCK TRANS-AM TOUR REVIEW
## MR. PERFECTION
### by Justin Anderson

**Above:** Pruett was the class of the field.
Mike Levitt/LAT

**Right:** Gentilozzi raced only sporadically, but finished on the podium in Cleveland.
Michael Kim/LAT

**Below right:** Boris Said scored the year's only non-Jaguar victory, at Long Beach.
Brad Bernstein/LAT

**Far right:** Diaz took a season-best second at Cleveland en route to top rookie honors.

**Below:** Randy Ruhlman battles to remain ahead of Max Lagod and John Baucom.

**Bottom right:** Johnny Miller enjoyed his most successful Trans-Am campaign yet.
**Photographs: Michael Kim/LAT**

**Below: Pruett added a third Trans-Am title to the ones he earned in 1987 and 1994.**
Mike Levitt/LAT

# 2003 MOTOROCK TRANS-AM TOUR

Final point standings after 11 races

| Pos. Driver (Nat.), Sponsor(s) Car | Pts. |
|---|---|
| Scott Pruett (USA), MotoRock/Jaguar R Performance Jaguar XKR | 340 |
| Johnny Miller (USA), Eaton Cutler-Hammer Jaguar XKR | 264 |
| Michael Lewis (USA), Westward Tools Available at Grainger Jaguar XKR | 228 |
| *Jorge Diaz Jr. (PR), DonQ Rum Jaguar XKR | 219 |
| *Bobby Sak (USA), Revolution/Trenton Forging Chevrolet Corvette | 209 |
| Randy Ruhlman (USA), Preformed Line Products/Coyote Closures Chevrolet Corvette | 186 |
| Stu Hayner (USA), Trenton Forging/GMAC Commercial Finance Chevrolet Corvette | 178 |
| John Baucom (USA), MAP Quality Engineering Jaguar XKR | 173 |
| Tomy Drissi (USA), Stuck on You, the Movie Jaguar XKR | 148 |
| Simon Gregg (USA), Derhaag Motorsports/Ultama Swimwear Chevrolet Corvette | 122 |
| Boris Said (USA), ACS/GE Access/Sun Microsystems Ford Mustang | 119 |
| *Joey Scarallo (USA), ROH Wheels Chevrolet Corvette | 108 |
| Paul Gentilozzi (USA), Rocketsports/Jaguar R Performance Jaguar XKR | 85 |
| Max Lagod (USA), Hypermax Engineering/Hypermax Diesel Turbo Systems Chevrolet Camaro | 78 |
| Bob Ruman (USA), McNichols/Cenweld Chevrolet Corvette | 69 |
| Greg Pickett (USA), Pickett Racing/Cytomax Exercise & Recovery Drink Jaguar XKR | 61 |
| *Marvin Jones (USA), Margraf Racing/M&L Jones Racing, LLC/BG Products Qvale Mangusta | 60 |
| *George Nolte (USA), Margraf Racing/www.Nolte.com/BG Products Ford Mustang | 60 |
| Glenn Andrew (USA), Tri-American Motorsports Chevrolet Camaro | 52 |
| Justin Bell (GB), Derhaag Motorsports/Ultama Swimwear Chevrolet Corvette | 44 |

* denotes rookie driver

## Performance Chart

| Driver | Wins | Poles | Fastest laps | Most laps led |
|---|---|---|---|---|
| Scott Pruett | 8 | 9 | 8 | 9 |
| Johnny Miller | 1 | 2 | 1 | 1 |
| Boris Said | 1 | - | - | 1 |
| Wally Castro | 1 | - | - | - |
| Paul Gentilozzi | - | - | 1 | - |
| Jorge Diaz Jr. | - | - | 1 | - |

ENSURING its 38th year would be one to remember, the 2003 MotoRock Trans-Am Tour marked a turning point for America's longest continuously running sports car series. A returning champion brought his career full circle, while a (relatively) young gun set his sights on the future, all under the watchful eyes of a new leader dedicated to creating a legacy of excellence. Meanwhile, the Trans-Am Tour heralded the future of sports car racing in the USA, both on and off the track.

Jaguar surged to the front at the beginning of the season and, like its namesake the big cat itself, never looked back. After placing its support behind veteran road racer Scott Pruett and his #7 MotoRock/Jaguar R Performance XKR, the British carmaker simply dominated. The opening round marked Pruett's return to Trans-Am competition after an eight-year hiatus, during which he competed in NASCAR and the Champ Car World Series. Pruett wasted no time starting his assault on the record books, as he won from the pole in the first round at St. Petersburg, Florida. With eight victories in 11 races, he surpassed former Jaguar racer Bob Tullius for fourth on the Trans-Am all-time win list with 22 career triumphs.

When Pruett clinched his third Trans-Am Tour Drivers' Championship in round ten at Miami, he joined the late Mark Donohue, Tommy Kendall and team owner Paul Gentilozzi as the only drivers to win three or more Trans-Am titles.

All told, Pruett had a nearly perfect season. He finished off the podium just twice, at Lime Rock and at the Puerto Rico Grand Prix season finale. Qualifying on the pole nine times, he passed Gentilozzi for second on the all-time fast-qualifier list with 29 pole positions. He ended his season by giving Jaguar's new four-valve, overhead-cam, fuel-injected, stock-block AJ-V8 its first pole in its race debut at Puerto Rico.

Pruett also gave Rocketsports its first Team Owners' Championship under the current format, which was adopted in 2002. For his efforts in helping Jaguar earn its third Trans-Am Manufacturers' Championship, he won a one-year lease on a Jaguar XK8 road car. In addition, Pruett was the only driver to claim the Flowmaster American Thunder Challenge Award, worth $2,000, for anyone who won the pole, led most laps, won the race and set fastest race lap. As a measure of his dominance, he secured the award on six occasions.

"It's just been a tremendous season," said Pruett. "But I couldn't have done this without my Rocketsports team. Every driver knows that it takes a good, determined and focused group of guys behind you. On the way to this championship, we had exactly zero mechanical failures. The only problems we had were when the driver parked it in the mud at Lime Rock, and a hub failure after we clinched the title. It was a nearly flawless season.

"I say this from the bottom of my heart: I really believe in Trans-Am. I'm here because I want to be here. I also believe in where Jaguar is taking this thing with its new engine. Hopefully, we can open that door for more manufacturers to get involved."

Johnny Miller, driving the #64 Eaton Cutler-Hammer Jaguar XKR, was one of three drivers able to keep Pruett in check. Miller, who finished second in the title chase, nailed down his second career victory in the rain at Lime Rock and scored eight podium finishes in ten starts. He capped his most competitive campaign to date by winning the season-ending Jaguar Pole Award, which gained him a one-year lease on a Jaguar XK8 road car.

"A lot of people refer to second place as the first loser, and second is certainly the hardest place to finish," said Miller of his best career effort in the championship. "However, I don't think we're losers. We had eight podiums, a win and two poles. We're going to take this and move forward. I came from the back of this field years ago, and I truly see this year as a stepping-stone for me to get the championship."

The only other winners were 2002 Trans-Am title holder Boris Said, who triumphed in a wild race at Long Beach, and newcomer Wally Castro, who was victorious in front of his hometown fans at the season finale in Puerto Rico. Castro, in just his second Tour start, used pit strategy to win what many considered to be one of Trans-Am's most competitive races in recent history.

Marking his best career championship effort, Michael Lewis and his #12 Westward Tools Available at Grainger Jaguar XKR finished third in the title chase. Driving one of two fuel-injected entries in the field, Lewis earned ten top-ten and four top-five finishes, including three podiums.

Finishing fourth was 27-year-old Puerto Rican driver Jorge Diaz Jr., who also earned Rookie of the Year honors. He secured the title following a season-long battle with Bobby Sak, 25, who was fifth in points with his Revolution/Trenton Forging Chevrolet Corvette and was the highest-placed non-Jaguar driver. Diaz, driver of the #8 DonQ Rum Jaguar XKR, set the standard for future rookies, finishing on the podium twice – at Lime Rock and at Cleveland – and earning nine top-ten and four top-five finishes in 11 starts.

Sak, too, had his own shot at greatness and finished strong. He earned two runner-up finishes, first at Lime Rock and later at Puerto Rico where he led several laps – a first for him in Trans-Am competition. In all, Sak finished on the podium three times and earned eight top-ten finishes.

Equally impressive was John Baucom, who received the BBS Wheels Most Improved Driver Award, as voted by his fellow drivers. The 2000 E- and G-Production National Champion and President's Cup winner in SCCA Club Racing competition, driving his family-owned #86 MAP Quality Engineering Jaguar XKR, prepared by an all-volunteer crew, finished a career-best eighth in points. He recorded six top-ten finishes and a fourth at Miami, his best placing ever.

Former ASA and Florida stock-car driver Jeff Emery claimed the GT-1 championship, newly created to recognize the top finishing GT-1 competitor on the Tour. He competed in the last two events of the year in the #15 TER Motorsports/Emery Scaffolding Chevrolet Corvette and scored one top-ten placing.

Trans-Am Tour veteran Bob Ruman earned the Westward Tools Tough Tools, Tough Guy Award for overcoming cancer diagnosed earlier in the year to post a best finish of fifth at Puerto Rico in the #23 McNichols/Cenweld Chevrolet Corvette. Tomy Drissi (#5 Stuck on You, the Movie Jaguar XKR) earned the Westward Tools Tough Tools, Tough Times Award for experiencing the worst luck in 2003. He at last brought his streak of misfortune to an end at Puerto Rico, where he finished a season-best third.

Jaguar North America was presented the Trans-Am Award of Excellence, given to the carmaker and Tour sponsor for its tremendous support of the MotoRock Trans-Am Tour.

As competitive as it was on the track, the action away from the races was just as scintillating. Gentilozzi had assumed the marketing and promotional rights to the Trans-Am Tour at the beginning of the season, taking the helm with one goal in mind: to make an already successful racing series even greater. His success was best exemplified by the welcoming of title sponsor MotoRock.

With its "Stars, Cars and Guitars" concept, MotoRock sought to bring concerts and other ambient programming to Trans-Am racing weekends. The MotoRock concept was about creating an integrated event, where all the facets worked together with one aim – to entertain the fans. MotoRock unveiled the concept at Miami, presenting concerts by Kid Rock and the Rocket Man himself, Elton John. Those events, combined with a successful unveiling of Club MotoRock, were just the start of what will certainly showcase the future of motorsports in the United States.

But 2003 was just the beginning of a new direction for the Trans-Am Tour, one that will return it to its former glory and, ultimately, deliver a new breed of speed.